RISING STARS
Mathematics

Year
5

Concept developed by
Caroline Clissold and Cherri Moseley

Year 5 Author Team
Caroline Clissold, Linda Glithro, Steph King

Homework Sheets written by
Jo Chambers

Practice Book written by
Paul Broadbent

Teacher's Guide

ISBN: 978 1 78339 532 3

Text, design and layout © Rising Stars UK Ltd 2015

First published in 2015 by
Rising Stars UK Ltd, part of Hodder Education,

An Hachette UK Company

Carmelite House
50 Victoria Embankment
London EC4Y 0DZ

www.risingstars-uk.com

Authors: Caroline Clissold, Linda Glithro, Steph King, Jo Chambers (Homework Sheets), Paul Broadbent (Practice Book)

Programme Consultants: Caroline Clissold, Cherri Moseley, Paul Broadbent

Publishers: Fiona Lazenby and Alexandra Riley

Editorial: Jane Carr, Sarah Chappelow, Lynette James, Shannon Keenlyside, Jackie Mace, Jane Morgan, Denise Moulton

Project manager: Sue Walton

Text design: Steve Evans and Mark Walker

Illustrations by Steve Evans

Cover design: Steve Evans and Words & Pictures

Printed by Ashford Colour Press Ltd, Gosport, Hants

A catalogue record for this title is available from the British Library.

Contents

Introduction

What is *Rising Stars Mathematics?*

Rising Stars Mathematics is a primary mathematics programme developed specifically for the 2014 National Curriculum Programmes of Study. The programme offers a complete solution to primary mathematics, adapting the best teaching and learning approaches from high-performing jurisdictions such as Shanghai and Singapore, but written bespoke to develop mathematics mastery in the context of UK classrooms.

Rising Stars Mathematics has been designed, developed and written by UK mathematics experts and educators to meet the Mathematics Textbook Guidance produced by the National Centre for Excellence in the Teaching of Mathematics (NCETM).

> 'A high-quality mathematics textbook is an educational resource that can be used by pupils in lessons and independently, and that also provides both subject knowledge and pedagogy support to teachers of mathematics. It is a comprehensive learning tool, providing support for the development of both procedural fluency and conceptual understanding in mathematics.'
>
> NCETM, January 2015
> (https://www.ncetm.org.uk/files/21383193NCETM+Textbook+Guidance.pdf)

Following these guidelines, *Rising Stars Mathematics*:

- provides the rigour teachers expect from quality schemes, without the prescription of scripted day-by-day lesson plans
- contains all the resources and CPD support teachers need to design outstanding mathematics lessons
- offers a wealth of opportunities for children to explore, practise, embed and extend learning
- follows the Concrete-Pictorial-Abstract approach to deepen children's understanding of mathematical concepts
- covers all the curriculum content with a wide variety of teaching ideas whilst respecting teachers' professionalism, to enable them to decide how best to teach their classes.

The pedagogy, approach and rationale

Rising Stars Mathematics is designed to develop fluency, build conceptual understanding and embed reasoning through an enquiry-based approach. It provides a 'light touch' comprehensive structure that allows teachers to retain the control, freedom and flexibility to adapt the timing and teaching activities to meet the needs of their own class. This means that they can focus their time and skills on teaching outstanding lessons in their own way. Carefully organised to provide a clear route through the yearly programmes of study, the curriculum concepts are revisited in a spiral way to reinforce and extend understanding and make links between content areas.

The programme has been developed based on the following key pedagogical beliefs:

1. Mathematical understanding is developed through using **concrete, pictorial** and **abstract** representations.

2. High-quality **textbooks used effectively as teaching tools** support teachers in explaining mathematical concepts clearly, encourage investigative thinking, questioning, discussion and application, all while encouraging children to engage with the wonder of mathematics (see page 6).

3. Children will only fully understand topics and **master concepts** through **step-by-step teaching** and **intelligent practice**. This means teaching concepts at a slower pace and dealing with each aspect of that concept in very small steps, in order to give children time to embed understanding. To achieve mastery, therefore, it is important to spend more time on teaching fewer topics in greater depth rather than moving on to a new topic or concept every few days (see page 6).

4. Mathematics is an interconnected subject in which children need to be able to **make connections** across mathematical ideas. This enables them to develop fluency, mathematical reasoning and problem-solving skills (see page 7).

5. Using **precise mathematical vocabulary** from the beginning is vital in ensuring children's understanding. **Rich talk and discussion** between teachers and children, and amongst peers, using mathematical terminology and constant probing questioning is an essential tool in the ongoing assessment of conceptual understanding for all children (see page 7).

Each of these key points of pedagogy is expanded on and explained in the following sections.

1. Concrete-Pictorial-Abstract (CPA) approach

Rising Stars Mathematics is based on the belief that mathematical understanding is developed through using **concrete, pictorial** and **abstract** (or symbolic) representations. Children will travel along this continuum again and again, often revisiting previous stages when a concept is extended.

Children use **concrete** objects to help them make sense of the concept or problem. This could be anything from real or plastic fruit, to straws, counters, cubes or something else meaningful. Whatever the objects are, they can be moved, grouped and rearranged to illustrate the problem. As the child's experience and confidence grows, they may no longer need physical objects to actually move around. Instead, they draw them. These simple **pictures** to represent the problem could be pictures of real objects they have used in the past, objects mentioned in the problem or something else meaningful. As understanding develops, children move on to use some form of **abstract** representation. This could be giving values to rectangular bars (bar model) to identify what is known and what is unknown, using a symbol to stand for a number, or something else.

It is important to realise that these are not stages gone through once, but a continuum. There will be occasions when a particular child will use concrete, pictorial and abstract representations all in one session. A child who uses abstract representations in one area may need concrete representations in another. On a different occasion, a child may need to revisit a concrete representation before moving on to a pictorial or abstract one.

Using the CPA approach encourages children to start by modelling a problem with concrete objects, before moving on to pictorial and abstract representations. It is important to ensure that a variety of manipulatives are available in all classrooms, not just for Key Stage 1 children. This will help children to develop their understanding more quickly and securely.

A variety of representations are used throughout *Rising Stars Mathematics*. These are both the teacher's and children's toolkit for illustrating and understanding a concept or a

Introduction

particular problem. Children will need to explore the various representations for themselves and be allowed the opportunity to choose which representations they use for a particular activity. (See pages 12–14 for examples and explanations of the main concrete resources and pictorial representations used throughout the *Rising Stars Mathematics* programme.)

2. Textbooks as teaching tools

Rising Stars Mathematics follows the Singapore and Shanghai approach to the use of textbooks. In these high-performing jurisdictions the textbook is a starting point for high-quality teaching. Teachers lead the usage of the textbook with the whole class as a starting point for high-quality teaching, rather than giving a textbook to children to work through on their own. This latter misuse of published resources unfortunately became common in England over a number of years and led to textbooks being seen as synonymous with poor-quality lessons. However, when used effectively as a teaching tool, evidence shows that this is not the case. Instead textbooks provide a framework for teachers to both introduce and develop new content, as well as providing a resource for children to refer back to as required.

The *Rising Stars Mathematics* Textbooks are designed specifically to be used as a teaching tool in conjunction with the teaching guidance and ideas provided in the corresponding Teacher's Guide pages. It is not intended that the Textbooks are given to children to work through in isolation. The Teacher's Notes tabs at the bottom of each Textbook page reference the relevant Teacher's Guide pages, so that the resources can be used in tandem.

The 'Let's learn' pages in the Textbooks should be used by the teacher as a starting point to introduce, teach, model and demonstrate new concepts. To support them in doing this, they can use the ideas in the Teacher's Guide or their own activities if preferred.

The 'Let's practise' pages in the Textbooks provide initial practice opportunities. They lead from basic practice and practice in context, to investigative, open-ended practice. These guided practice activities should be introduced by the teacher. The Teacher's Guide provides suggestions on questioning and how to give targeted support to children who may need additional help in order to move on with the group. The 'Let's practise' sections can be used to provide opportunities for independent working as appropriate for different children or as assessment opportunities to identify whether children have mastered the concept. This will then enable teachers to judge how much additional practice each child requires using the *Rising Stars Mathematics* Practice Books (or other practice materials that they choose to use).

3. The mastery approach

A mastery approach underpins the 2014 National Curriculum. This approach advocates spending longer on topics in order to embed understanding and developing rich connections across topics.

NCETM has identified further principles and features that characterise a mastery approach:

- Teachers reinforce an expectation that all pupils are capable of achieving high standards in mathematics.
- The large majority of pupils progress through the curriculum content at the same pace. Differentiation is achieved by emphasising deep knowledge and through individual support and intervention.
- Teaching is underpinned by methodical curriculum design and supported by carefully crafted lessons and resources to foster deep conceptual and procedural knowledge.
- Practice and consolidation play a central role. Carefully designed variation within this builds fluency and understanding of underlying mathematical concepts in tandem.
- Teachers use precise questioning in class to test conceptual and procedural knowledge, and assess pupils regularly to identify those requiring intervention so that all pupils keep up.

NCETM, October 2014
(https://www.ncetm.org.uk/public/files/19990433/Developing_mastery_in
mathematics_october_2014.pdf)

In December 2012, The Advisory Committee on Mathematics Education (ACME) published a report called 'Raising the bar: developing able young mathematicians'. The report identified that England needs to increase the number of young mathematicians with a robust grasp of the range of mathematical ways of thinking and working, through experiencing a deep, rich, rigorous and challenging mathematics education. Children should not be accelerated through the school curriculum: 'acceleration encourages only a shallow mastery of the subject, and so promotes procedural learning at the expense of deep understanding'. Not allowing children enough time to secure deep understanding can lead to feelings of insecurity and dislike of the subject.

Consequently, there is an expectation in the 2014 National Curriculum that most children should 'move through the programmes of study at broadly the same pace'. Children should not be accelerated into a future year group's work. Instead, it is expected that children who grasp concepts rapidly should be challenged through being offered rich and sophisticated problems before any acceleration through new content. There is also the expectation that those who are not sufficiently fluent with earlier material should consolidate their understanding, including through additional practice, before moving on. The aim is for mastery, which is the approach used by many of the high-performing jurisdictions in the international league tables.

With this in mind, there are some important questions for schools to consider when teaching for mastery, which should be discussed and agreed with the whole staff:

- To support the expectation that all children are capable of achieving high standards, what are the implications for whole-class teaching, class groupings or setting within the school?
- How will differentiation be managed to enable all children to access what is being taught? How and when will intervention be given to ensure misconceptions are dealt with immediately and shared with the whole class, so that no children fall behind?
- How will questioning and scaffolding be varied to provide support as needed? What different problems will be provided so that children who grasp the concept quickly are given complex problems which deepen their knowledge of the same content?
- Is there enough focus on the important ability to recall facts and manipulate them to work out other facts, so that children develop the fluency which comes from deep knowledge and practice?
- How will enough time be allowed for different types of intelligent practice (basic practice, variations such as practice within different contexts, extended practice which goes deeper and deeper), so that longer can be spent on key concepts? Will more than one mathematics session per day be required?
- How will practice and consolidation be provided within different contexts, e.g. time, money or length, to ensure connections are made across different areas of mathematics?
- How will teaching focus on the development of deep structural knowledge and the ability to make connections?
- Is the use of precise mathematical vocabulary consistent across the school? Is correct vocabulary introduced from the beginning of teaching? Are all teaching staff comfortable with mathematical terminology?

Practice and variation

Intelligent practice underpins the mastery approach. 'Intelligent practice' is a term used to describe practice that develops procedural fluency while at the same time exposing mathematical structures, patterns and relationships in order to deepen conceptual understanding.

Intelligent practice is clearly structured and incorporates carefully-designed variations. These variations may be conceptual or procedural:

• Procedural variation can be introduced by extending a problem (e.g. varying the number, the unknown or the context), varying the processes of solving a problem or varying the application of a method (e.g. applying the same method to a group of similar problems).

• Conceptual variation can be introduced by varying the representation of a problem.

The practice in *Rising Stars Mathematics* is based on the principles of intelligent practice.

• The 'Let's practise' pages in the Textbook are clearly structured. Steps 1 and 2 comprise bare (or, decontextualised) practice and include procedural variations. Step 3 provides practice within a variety of contexts (including time, money and statistics) and Step 4 offers open-ended, investigative practice. By working their way through the practice, children will build procedural fluency across a range of question types and in a range of contexts, while also developing their understanding of the concepts covered in the 'Let's learn' pages.

• The corresponding 'Let's practise' pages in the Teacher's Guide extend the opportunities for conceptual variation by suggesting a range of physical and pictorial representations that teachers may want to use to support children's practice.

• The Practice Book offers further carefully-crafted practice exercises. These exercises have been planned to include structured variation of a number or unknown (procedural variation), a range of representations (e.g. a question on length may use a variety of visuals such as ribbons, snakes and pencils) and open questions (e.g. 'What do you notice?') that encourage children to reason and spot patterns.

Teachers can use the carefully-designed questions and exercises as a starting point to introduce intelligent practice into their teaching. However, they retain the freedom to develop their own questions and activities, incorporating variation that best suits the needs of their children.

4. Making connections

The 2014 National Curriculum states that:

'Mathematics is an interconnected subject in which pupils need to be able to move fluently between representations of mathematical ideas. The programmes of study are, by necessity, organised into apparently distinct domains, but pupils should make rich connections across mathematical ideas to develop fluency, mathematical reasoning and competence in solving increasingly sophisticated problems. They should also apply their mathematical knowledge to science and other subjects.'

National Curriculum in England, Department for Education, 2013

In *Rising Stars Mathematics* there are a wide variety of opportunities to develop mathematics in other areas of the curriculum and in real life. E.g. the opening pages of each unit in the Textbook contain interesting photos and visuals to encourage children to identify instances of mathematics in the world around them, in order to make connections between what they are learning and how it might apply in real life. The programme is designed to provide opportunities to link together different areas of mathematics together. For example, when children practise a concept, such as addition, they will have the opportunity to do this through an area of measure, e.g. length, mass, temperature or time. This has the benefit of allowing more time to be spent on the big ideas of mathematics within its everyday applications.

The units in *Rising Stars Mathematics* are structured to focus on one of four key mathematical themes: Number Sense, Additive Reasoning, Multiplicative Reasoning or Geometric Reasoning (see page 9). These cover concepts from the related Programmes of Study areas, incorporating Measurement and Statistics where appropriate. This ensures that the end-of-year statements for these areas are covered through a multitude of practice opportunities across the units.

5. Mathematical vocabulary

The 2014 National Curriculum states that:

'The National Curriculum for mathematics reflects the importance of spoken language in pupils' development across the whole curriculum – cognitively, socially and linguistically. The quality and variety of language that pupils hear and speak are key factors in developing their mathematical vocabulary and presenting a mathematical justification, argument or proof. They must be assisted in making their thinking clear to themselves as well as others, and teachers should ensure that pupils build secure foundations by using discussion to probe and remedy their misconceptions.'

National Curriculum in England, Department for Education, 2013

Using correct mathematical language is crucial for thinking, learning and communicating mathematically. Children may build knowledge through remembering information that they hear, but it is only when they put these ideas into their own words that it becomes clear whether concepts have been learnt effectively. It is in listening to children talking about mathematics that teachers can best assess what they are actually learning and understanding, which in turn enables them to identify and address any misconceptions that might be developing.

Children should be encouraged to explain what they are doing and why they are doing it, through probing questioning from the teacher if necessary. Offering opportunities to use mathematical language frequently, e.g. by participating in paired activities, group discussions and games, will ensure that rich talk develops in the classroom. Spoken language in mathematics can be thought of as a rehearsal for recording, as well as an outcome in its own right. It allows children to extend and develop their reasoning skills as they explain and justify their thinking. It provides the opportunity to review existing knowledge, to explore new ideas and to extend their understanding.

The productive use of spoken language in mathematics allows children to evaluate their learning, support others' suggestions, challenge ideas, reason or justify and ask questions. Therefore, it is important to encourage children not just to learn and remember the correct vocabulary, but also to use these words regularly to communicate mathematically. Using mathematical vocabulary can help all children to make links across areas of mathematics, across the curriculum as a whole and also within real life situations. It can enable them to build confidence, communicate and problem-solve, so should be an integral part of every mathematics lesson.

Teachers need to plan the introduction of new words into lessons and provide opportunities for children to rehearse and use them on a regular basis. It is also essential that other adults working with children use mathematical vocabulary accurately and consistently. The 'Mathematical vocabulary' sections in the *Rising Stars Mathematics* Teacher's Guide identify key words that should be covered when teaching each concept. The glossary in the Textbook provides explanations for children and the glossary at the back of this Teacher's Guide offers detailed definitions on a wide variety of key mathematical terms.

Introduction
Getting started with
Rising Stars Mathematics

The components

Rising Stars Mathematics includes a wealth of resources for children and teachers. The pupil materials include full-colour Textbooks, single-colour write-in Practice Books and Homework Sheets (found at the back of the Teacher's Guides). The teacher materials comprise the Teacher's Guide and a variety of additional CPD, teaching resources, and digital teaching and learning resources be found on the My Rising Stars website. The contents for each of these components is summarised below.

Textbook

- Opportunities for children to develop problem-solving and reasoning skills.
- 14 units covering all the concepts to be learnt in Year 5.
- Glossary.

Practice Books

- 14 units providing further independent practice of all the concepts to be learnt in Year 5.
- Answers can be found on the My Rising Stars website.

Homework Sheets

- 84 expansion activities to enable children to explore mathematics further outside the classroom.
- Ideal for engaging parents/carers in children's learning.

Teacher's Guide

- CPD guidance on the pedagogy, approach and how to use the *Rising Stars Mathematics* resources.
- Scope and sequence chart and curriculum mapping grids to aid planning.
- Non-prescriptive teaching guidance for all 14 units in the Textbook.
- Photocopiable Homework Sheets and answers.
- Glossary.
- Bibliography for further reading.

Website and digital resources

- **CPD resources** including:
  1. Short, sharp **CPD videos** providing bite-sized insights into key areas of importance when teaching mathematics, as well as background subject knowledge videos for every theme.
  2. Ready-made **INSET Training PowerPoint presentation** to offer a time-saving way to introduce the principles and resources of *Rising Stars Mathematics* to staff.

- **Planning resources** including:
  1. **Scope and sequence charts** and **curriculum mapping grids** for each year group.
  2. The Rising Stars *Primary Maths Planning Framework* and **posters** for long-term planning support.
  3. Editable **medium-term planning grids** including references to other useful resources.
  4. Mathematical vocabulary **glossaries**.
  5. **Bibliography** of research papers and recommended further reading, including guidance documents from NCETM.

- **Teaching resources** including:
  1. **Teacher Toolkit** containing useful digital tools, which can be used to model concepts on the interactive whiteboard. Tools include:

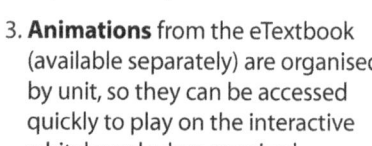

     - Counters
     - Numerals & Symbols
     - 100 Squares
     - Place Value & Abacus
     - Number Line
     - Clock & Timer
     - Calendar & Timezone
     - Money
     - Calculator
     - Dice, Coin & Number
     - 2D Shapes
     - Tangrams
     - 3D Shapes
     - Fraction Wall
     - Graphs & Charts
     - Geometry Instruments

  2. **eTextbook** – a digital version of the Textbook that can be displayed in the classroom on the interactive whiteboard or shared with parents/carers, so that children can access it from home. The eTextbook is enhanced with fun animations to help explain concepts.

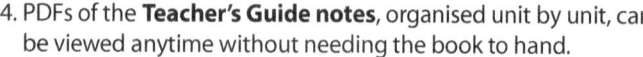

  3. **Animations** from the eTextbook (available separately) are organised by unit, so they can be accessed quickly to play on the interactive whiteboard when required.

  4. PDFs of the **Teacher's Guide notes**, organised unit by unit, can be viewed anytime without needing the book to hand.

  5. Editable versions of the **Homework Sheets**.

  6. Printable versions of the colour **gameboards** from the Textbooks.

  7. Editable versions of the **game instructions** from the Teacher's Guide.

  8. **Answers** to the Practice Books and Homework Sheets.

- **Pupil resources** including:
  1. **eTextbook** – see Teaching resources above.
  2. **Animations** – see Teaching resources above.
  3. **Printable gameboards** and **instruction sheets** organised unit by unit.
  5. Editable versions of the **Homework Sheets** organised unit by unit.
  6. **Answers** to the Practice Books and Homework Sheets.

Themes

Rising Stars Mathematics is built around four themes: Number Sense, Additive Reasoning, Multiplicative Reasoning and Geometric Reasoning. Each covers the concepts from the related Programme of Study areas. This approach ensures that clear connections are made between areas of mathematics.

1. **Number Sense** is about understanding our number system, with a focus on how our numbers work and fit together, and applying this understanding in different contexts. Units on Additive Reasoning and Multiplicative Reasoning are usually preceded by a unit on Number Sense, which explores the understanding needed for the subsequent unit.

2. **Additive Reasoning** is about understanding addition and subtraction together and the relationship between them, and using this understanding to solve problems.

3. **Multiplicative Reasoning** is about understanding multiplication and division together and the relationship between them, and using this understanding to solve problems.

4. **Geometric Reasoning** is about understanding the properties of shapes and the relationships between them, using this understanding to solve problems related to measure and movement within space.

Measures and statistics are included throughout as contexts for all four themes. These contexts are examples and teachers may wish to select different contexts to support each concept. **Algebra** (a new domain in Year 6) appears in all themes as part of generalisation of mathematical understanding.

The unit structure

Each year level of *Rising Stars Mathematics* contains 14 units. These units all follow the same structure as explained below. The Textbook and Teacher's Guide work alongside each other. Each double-page spread in the Teacher's Guide contains a reproduction of the corresponding Textbook page for ease of reference. The Textbook has teaching notes tabs at the bottom of each page to enable teachers to quickly find the corresponding Teacher's Guide page.

Textbook and Teacher's Guide: unit opener pages

In the Textbook, each unit begins with engaging photos of mathematics in real life. These unit opener pages give children the opportunity to discuss what they see and explore what could be going on, looking for mathematics in the world around them. 'I wonder…' questions encourage thinking around the topic. This sets the scene for exploring the underlying concepts in more depth throughout the unit. Such discussions give the teacher the opportunity to check current understanding before moving on to the concept explanation, modelling, exemplification, practice and application.

The corresponding Teacher's Guide pages highlight the main mathematical focus of the unit, expected prior learning and key new learning to be covered throughout the unit. It also provides: support for making connections across areas of mathematics or between concepts; a 'Talk about' section that focuses on the use of precise mathematical vocabulary; a variety of activities and questions about the visuals in the Textbook to engage and explore with children; a list of questions for teachers to think about regarding organisation and planning. Finally, there is brief guidance to support teachers in checking understanding as the unit progresses.

Textbook and Teacher's Guide: concept pages

Each has two pages: 'Let's learn' and 'Let's practise'. The 'Let's learn' page begins with a discussion between the year group character guides, illustrating a possible misconception. The key information about the new concept to be learnt is explained, supported by relevant pictorial representations.

The 'Let's practise' section develops children's reasoning incrementally through guided practice. In *Rising Stars Mathematics*, the first steps provide bare, decontextualised practice. The third step gives practice in a context (e.g. an area of measurement or statistics), while the fourth step is a more open-ended, investigative practice of the concept.

The corresponding Teachers' Guide pages for these sections provide: a list of key mathematical vocabulary, representations and resources; useful background knowledge; activities for warming up, modelling and teaching, digging deeper through practice and follow-up activity ideas. There is also a section on ensuring progress, with ideas for supporting and broadening understanding. These are ideas which can be adapted to the needs of the class – there is no specific script. There are also notes on how to identify when the key concepts have been mastered and answers to the 'Let's practise' activities in the Textbook.

Textbook and Teacher's Guide: gameboard pages

Each unit contains fun activities to encourage children to apply their knowledge and skills, whilst consolidating conceptual understanding. The attractive colour gameboards for these are contained in the Textbooks. Two versions of games that can be played using each gameboard are provided and children are also encouraged to invent their own game using the gameboard. The invented games are often a useful means of assessing understanding.

The corresponding Teachers' Guide pages provide further detail about playing each of the games, including the mathematics focus, resources needed, instructions for how to play and support for making the game activities easier or harder. A photocopiable sheet of 'How to play' instructions is also provided, should teachers wish to send the games home as an out-of-class activity. Printable versions of the gameboards are available to download from the website.

Textbook and Teacher's Guide: 'And finally …' review pages

The final part of each unit is a review section, which provides a variety of assessment tasks. The Textbook pages include three assessment tasks, followed by a colourful 'Did you know?' fun facts section to complete the unit. (For further information about assessment see page 11.)

The corresponding Teachers' Guide review pages provide further detail of any resources needed, instructions for how to run the tasks and guidance on what to look for in children's responses, in order to evidence mastery. There is also some background knowledge about the 'Did you know?' facts and a summary list of all the concepts children are expected to have mastered by the end of the unit.

Introduction

Practice Books

The Practice Books provide further opportunities for children to consolidate understanding and explore, explain and reason through different types of practice activities. These activities include conceptual and procedural variations, in order to develop fluency and conceptual understanding. There is practice for every concept in the Textbook. The write-in format ensures that children always have a record of their work that they can refer back to, so that they can learn from their mistakes and see the progress they are making.

The relevant Practice Book pages for each concept in the Textbook are referenced at the top of the corresponding Teacher's Guide page for each new concept.

Homework Sheets

The photocopiable Homework Sheets can be found at the back of the Teacher's Guide. Editable versions are also available on the My Rising Stars website. They provide expansion activities for children to continue to explore mathematics outside the classroom. Two activities are provided for each of the concept pages in a unit.

The relevant Homework Sheets for each concept in the Textbook are referenced at the top of the corresponding Teacher's Guide page for each new concept.

Teaching a unit

Teachers are advised to begin by looking at the Teacher's Guide to familiarise themselves with the content to be covered within a particular unit and reviewing the related CPD videos on the website if necessary.

1. Develop subject knowledge

- Watch the short online CPD videos to develop background subject knowledge before planning lessons.
- Refresh knowledge by reviewing the INSET training presentations as necessary.

2. Design lessons

- Plan and design lessons using the suggested activities in the Teacher's Guide.
- Choose how much time to spend on each activity to fit the needs of each class.
- Gather all the concrete resources and visual representations needed.
- Review the recommended Teacher Toolkit tools and any relevant concept animations on the My Rising Stars website.

3. Explore new concepts

- Introduce the unit using the Textbooks as a teaching tool. Remember to check the teaching notes tab at the bottom of each page and the corresponding Teacher's Guide pages before the lesson.
- Play any relevant animations (from the eTextbook or direct from the website) to the class and discuss them together.
- Explore, model and teach new concepts to children using a variety of representations and practical resources, following the 'Let's learn' page.
- Use tools from the Teacher Toolkit to model concepts on the interactive whiteboard where appropriate.
- Embed conceptual understanding and dig deeper into concepts through intelligent practice, using the 'Let's practise' page.

4. Embed and expand understanding

- Consolidate understanding using the fun games to provide extra practice and aid mastery. Print extra copies of the game boards and instructions from the website as necessary.
- Set expansion or out-of-class activities using the Homework Sheets or Practice Books. Answers can be found on the website.
- Encourage parents/carers to engage with children's learning by sharing the eTextbook to view the pages and animations at home.
- Provide further independent practice using the Practice Books to deepen understanding of the concepts taught using the Textbooks.

5. Assess progress and mastery

- Review the content covered throughout the unit using the assessment tasks to ensure children have mastered the concepts.
- Finish the unit by finding out some fun mathematical facts in the 'Did you know?' section.
- Use *Rising Stars Assessment Half-Termly Progress Tests* to measure progress independently, if desired.

Timing

As a guide, the expectation is that each unit will take two to three weeks to teach. The length of time spent on each unit will vary depending on the topic, the number of new concepts covered within it and how quickly children master the concepts. If teachers are confident that children have mastered a concept, then it is perfectly acceptable to move on more quickly, just as it is important to allow children to spend longer on a topic if necessary to ensure that they have fully mastered it before moving on. It is better to spend more time on fewer topics to ensure that they are fully understood and children have embedded what they have learnt, so that they can remember and apply it later on.

Mixed-age classes

For schools with mixed-age classes, the *Rising Stars Mathematics* resources can be used to teach the same topic to the whole class, as long as this is done age-appropriately. The pitch should be year-group based, regardless of the perceived ability of children within those year groups. It is important that however the classroom is managed, each year group sticks to what is expected for that year in order to meet the National Curriculum Programme of Study requirements. Children should therefore all be using the Textbooks and Practice Books appropriate for their year group. As teachers in this kind of setting will know all too well, this is like teaching two or more classes. This brings huge challenges in planning and organisation, especially in small schools where there are three to four year groups per class.

However, because the units in *Rising Stars Mathematics* all have a main focus on one of four themes (Number Sense, Additive Reasoning, Multiplicative Reasoning or Geometric Reasoning), similar topics are generally covered in the same unit in each year group. Therefore corresponding units from Year 1 and Year 2, Year 3 and Year 4, Year 5 and Year 6 will work together neatly as they focus on the same themes, e.g. Unit 1 in all year groups across the *Rising Stars Mathematics* resources is focused on Number Sense, so teachers are able to focus on similar topics at a different level within mixed-age classes.

On the website, there are Medium-term Planning Grid templates which break down the units into half-termly plans. These may be useful for teachers of mixed-age classes to compare the different year groups.

Assessment

Assessment opportunities

Each unit in *Rising Stars Mathematics* provides the opportunity for teachers to check existing understanding through the opener pages. Discussions around what children can see, how they interpret what they see and their response to the 'I wonder…' questions will reveal children's current level of understanding.

Likewise, the cartoon at the beginning of each concept, provides an opportunity to check understanding through class discussion of the misconception or error. Throughout each unit, there are continual opportunities for assessment. Teachers will probe conceptual and procedural understanding through questioning and observation as they model and teach. The way children respond to the modelling and teaching provides the teacher with valuable information on what to spend a little more time and what to move through quickly, as well as information on individual needs.

The Textbook activities provide further assessment opportunities, particularly the non-routine, open-ended types of activities offered in Step 4.

The final review activities are particularly useful assessment tasks, since they are designed to give children the opportunity to demonstrate what they know and the concepts they have mastered. In this way assessment is ongoing throughout the unit, with a summative assessment at the end of each unit.

End points to be tested in Key Stage 2 national tests

Some elements of the National Curriculum cannot be assessed in statutory tests although they will need to be assessed by teachers as part of their statutory assessment of the whole National Curriculum. Over time, all the end point requirements that can be tested in the 2014 National Curriculum will be tested at the end of Key Stage 2. It is therefore important to make a note of these, particularly for teachers in Years 5 and 6, and to make sure children are up to speed with these requirements, e.g. Roman numerals need to be taught from Years 3 to 5. There is no mention of them in Year 6. However, they could be tested in the end of Year 6 tests. *Rising Stars Mathematics* suggests times when these can be rehearsed and reinforced during the warm-up activities, practice or follow-up tasks.

Measuring progress

In a new world of assessment free from levels, it is now up to teachers to decide how best to assess the progress their children are making against the new Programmes of Study. For schools who wish to do this using regular half-termly or end-of-term tests using an independent resource outside of the *Rising Stars Mathematics* teaching materials, the *Rising Stars Assessment Half-termly Progress Tests* are an ideal resource to measure progress and inform future learning. They are organised to assess the content in the same order that it is covered in the scope and sequence of the Rising Stars Mathematics units, so that teachers can be sure that children are not being tested on content that they have yet to be taught. For more information, please visit www.risingstars-uk.com.

Ensuring progress for all children

If we consider any particular concept area as a pool, some children will paddle, others will swim with armbands and others will swim freely. They are all in the same pool, but accessing it at different levels and in different ways. This is a good metaphor for how differentiation should be managed when following a mastery approach. It will ensure that the broad majority of children all move on together into a new pool, as required by the National Curriculum.

Rising Stars Mathematics assumes that all children within the class will be taught the same content and given the same opportunities to understand the concepts. The 'Let's learn: Modelling and teaching' and 'Let's practise: Digging deeper' sections both include suggestions for a variety of representations, models and images that can be used to explain the concepts. The expectation is not that all children should be able to use all representations or methods, but rather that different representations will trigger understanding for different children. By using a wide variety of representations like this and multiple ways to explain concepts, teachers give each individual child the best possible chance of finding something that works for them. Some children may fully grasp the concept being introduced using the first or second representation, however that does not mean the rest of the lesson is irrelevant for them. Seeing the concept represented in different ways will give them the opportunity to deepen their understanding and make connections between the different methods.

Rising Stars Mathematics recognises that in every class it is likely that there will be some children who will need more support than others to achieve understanding of concepts. The Teacher's Guide includes a section on 'Supporting understanding' for children who need a little more reinforcement. The same section also offers ideas for 'Broadening understanding', for those children who have a good understanding of the concept.

In order to give all children the best possible chance to make progress in mathematics, the *Rising Stars Mathematics* approach to differentiation is that it should be managed through support and intervention, not through changing the content. Difficulties and misconceptions should be addressed as they occur and children should be challenged through more demanding problems, rather than being accelerated to future curriculum content.

Some schools are organising mathematics so that there are two shorter sessions each day. The first session is used for teaching the concept, the second is for practice. Using *Rising Stars Mathematics* for this approach, teachers would focus on the 'Let's learn' part of the unit in the first session and on the 'Let's practise' section in the second session. During the second session, the teacher could work with children who have struggled to understand as a guided group, whilst others work through the three or four steps in the Textbook more independently. A further 15-minute intervention session may be offered later the same day. Intervention must be carried out immediately to ensure that the majority of children move through the materials at the same pace. Some schools may wish to pre-teach a small group of children. This 10-minute session could be used to revise what children already know about today's concept and its vocabulary, before the concept is extended in the main session.

Children with significant special needs may require an individual programme of work. Although these children are unlikely to master concepts as deeply as others, they should still aim for mastery at a level appropriate for the individual.

Fast finishers can be challenged to deepen their understanding by generalising. Depending on the concept, they might be asked if what they have just explored will always, sometimes or never be true. They might be asked to give an example of the concept in money or measures. Alternatively, some of the other strategies to embed problem solving could be used. *Rising Stars Mathematics* provides some suggestions for broadening understanding in every unit.

Resources and representations

Representations are hugely important in helping children to develop a conceptual understanding of what they are learning. *Rising Stars Mathematics* aims to encourage all teachers to make use of these with all children from Year 1 through to Year 6. In the past, manipulatives and visual representations have often only been used in Key Stage 2 for children struggling to grasp certain concepts, but they are necessary for all. There are two main types of representations: visual (pictorial) and manipulative (concrete apparatus).

The key manipulatives included in this programme are:

- Straws (Years 1-3)
- Base 10 apparatus
- Place-value counters
- Place-value cards
- Number rods
- Double-sided counters
- Bead strings
- Plates
- Digit cards
- Coins
- Counting sticks
- Interlocking cubes
- Coloured counters
- 2-D shapes
- 3-D shapes
- Clock faces
- 1–6 dice
- 1–10 dice
- Percentage cards
- Modelling clay
- Number cards
- Tangrams

See below for further details.

The key visual representations included in this programme are:

- Number tracks
- Ten frames
- 100 squares
- Number lines
- The bar model
- Place-value grids
- Gattegno charts

See below for further details.

Concrete manipulatives
Straws

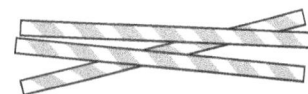

Straws are a great resource to enable children to see the cardinality of numbers. They could make bundles of ten and compare tens and ones. They could put ten bundles together to make 100 and compare these. Straws are particularly useful for younger children, when they still need to see and touch quantities.

Base 10 apparatus

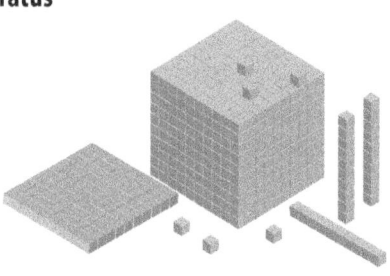

These are representations of numbers. In the first instance, the small cubes represent ones, the rods tens, the flats hundreds and the large cubes thousands. Children find these helpful because the size of the individual pieces helps to denote their value. Later, when children encounter decimals, the flats represent ones, the rods tenths and the small cubes hundredths. If children are familiar with using different manipulatives to represent numbers, it will be easy for them to make this transfer.

Place-value counters

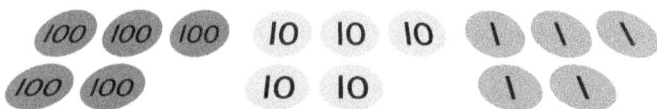

These also represent numbers. You can see clearly what each colour represents through the values written on each (often greens are hundreds, yellows are tens, and reds are ones). They are more abstract than Base 10 apparatus because the counters are all the same size and are therefore not proportional to their value. It is recommended that these are used in late Key Stage 1 and in Key Stage 2, when children are working with larger numbers. When children have used these, you may find that they can use any coloured counters and assign their own values to them.

Number rods

Coloured number rods are excellent for helping children to become flexible in their thinking about numbers. The rods represent any number that you would want them to represent. Assign a value to one and children can work out the values of the other rods. The rods are fractions of other rods, e.g. some are halves, quarters and eighths of others. This is a great resource to use when dealing with multiplication, division and fractions.

Coloured rods can also be used as bars to support thinking when using the bar model. Using a rod to represent a bar allows bars to be changed or manipulated to illustrate the problem under consideration. See the section on the bar model for further information on this.

Double-sided counters

These are great for helping children to develop reasoning and fluency. You could give children three counters each and ask them to show you 2, then 3, then 12. Children need to consider how they could represent 12 using three counters. The only rule is that one colour needs to represent the same number. So, two yellow sides could be 5 each and a red side could be 2. Or one yellow side could be 8 and one red side 4. There are numerous ways to represent 12 or other numbers using these counters.

Bead strings

Bead strings are helpful for early calculation. When children are familiar with them and know that each string of colour is 10, they can add, subtract, multiply and divide using them and develop the ability to do this without counting one at a time, e.g. for 10 + 6, they add 6 onto 10, without the need to count ten beads, six beads and then count them all. These can be used to represent other numbers, e.g. the whole string could represent 1, each coloured section would then be one tenth and one bead would be one hundredth. This flexibility makes the bead string a very useful manipulative for fractions, decimals and percentages.

Plates

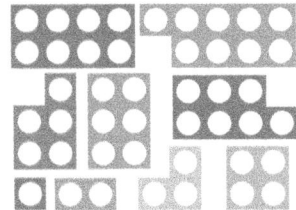

Plates like these are another manipulative which help children to move on from counting everything, e.g. if they add 5 and 9, they put the plates together. They match the result with 10 and 4 to give the answer 14. Paper 10 frames can be cut and used to represent a number in exactly the same way.

Visual representations

The bar model

The bar model is a very effective visual representation. It helps children to make sense of problems. Take missing number statements such as 35 − □ = 16. We know that 35 is the larger number, so it will be the larger bar. A smaller bar of 16 can be drawn below it. Drawing a bar from the end of the 16 bar to fill the space to the end of the 35 bar represents the missing number. We can then work out the missing number by counting back from 35 to 16 or counting on from 16 to 35.

35	
16	?

This can support children as they work out families of addition and subtraction facts.

$a = b + c$
$a = c + b$
$a - b = c$
$a - c = b$

a	
b	c

Addition and subtraction calculations can be represented using this model, e.g.

1) Samir scored 145 points on a computer game, Alex scored 76 more points. How many points did Alex score?

145	76
?	

(Alex scored 221 points.)

2) Jenny had a collection of shells. She gave her friend 123 of them. She was left with 146. How many shells did she have before giving some to her friend?

123	146
?	

(Jenny had 269 shells.)

3) Ben went for a run. He ran 12.5 km to the shop and 6.75 km back. Then he stopped to talk to a friend. How much further did he need to run to get home?

12.5 km	
?	6.75 km

(Ben has to run another 5.75 km.)

4) Ella has some cherries. She eats two. Then she eats half of what is left. She now has six. How many did she have to begin with?

?		
6	6	2

(Ella started off with 14 cherries.)

This model can be used very effectively for representing multiplication, division and fractions, as well as ratio and proportion problems. It is often helpful to use double-sided counters or coloured rods to set out the problems first and then move on to drawing them as bars, e.g.

1) There are 27 red flowers in the garden. There are three times as many red flowers as there are white flowers. How many white flowers are there?

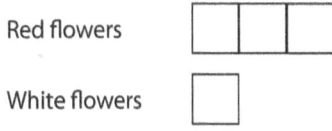

Red flowers

White flowers

If there are 27 red flowers, each part is worth 9. So there are 9 white flowers.

2) Sam had five times as many marbles as Tom. If Sam gives 26 marbles to Tom, the two friends will have exactly the same amount. How many marbles do they have altogether?

Tom's marbles | T |

Sam's marbles | S | S | S | S | S |

Sam gives 26 marbles to Tom.

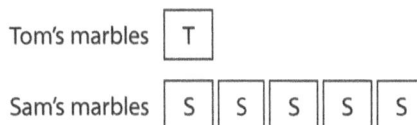

Tom's marbles

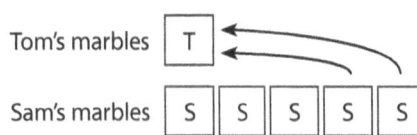

Sam's marbles

So, the model will look like this:

T	S	S
S	S	S

We now know that each part is worth 13. So they have 78 marbles altogether.

3) David spent $\frac{2}{5}$ of his money on a book. The book cost £10. How much money did he start off with?

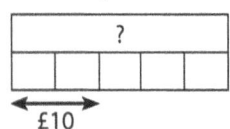

We know $\frac{2}{5}$ is equal to £10. Each part must be £5. So he started off with £25.

Introduction

4) In Class 4, 80% of children like crisps. 75% of children who like crisps also like chocolate. What percentage of Class 4 like both crisps and chocolate?

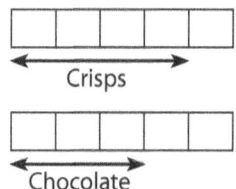

Each part in the model is worth 20%. So 60% of Class 4 like both crisps and chocolate.

5) A computer game was reduced in a sale by 20% and it now costs £48. What was the original price?

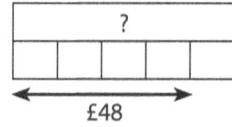

We know from this model that each part is worth £12. So, £12 is equivalent to the discount. Therefore the original cost was £60.

6) A gardener plants tulip bulbs in a flower bed. She plants 3 red bulbs for every 4 white bulbs. She plants 60 red bulbs. How many white bulbs does she plant?

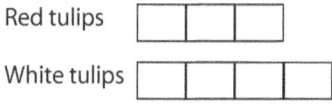

If she plants 60 red tulips, each part is worth 20. Therefore she must have planted 80 white bulbs.

Ten frames

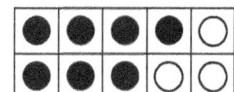

There are different types of ten frames. This is one example.

It draws out the odd and even properties of number. They are helpful for finding number bonds to 10, as well as for addition and subtraction.

These can also be used to represent fractions and decimals, e.g. if the whole frame is worth 1, what are the black counters worth? (0.7, $\frac{7}{10}$.)

Place-value grids

1000	100	10	1	.	10th	100th	1000th
				.			

Place-value grids are very useful for helping children to gain an understanding of the four main aspects of place value.

Gattegno charts

0.001	0.002	0.003	0.004	0.005	0.006	0.007	0.008	0.009
0.01	0.02	0.03	0.04	0.05	0.06	0.07	0.08	0.09
0.1	0.2	0.3	0.4	0.5	0.6	0.7	0.8	0.9
1	2	3	4	5	6	7	8	9
10	20	30	40	50	60	70	80	90
100	200	300	400	500	600	700	800	900
1000	2000	3000	4000	5000	6000	7000	8000	9000
10000	20000	30000	40000	50000	60000	70000	80000	90000

Gattegno charts are another useful resource that will help to secure children's conceptual understanding of place value.

Delivering the aims of the National Curriculum

Developing fluency

The first aim of the 2014 National Curriculum states that teachers must ensure that children: 'become fluent in the fundamentals of mathematics, including through varied and frequent practice with increasingly complex problems over time, so that pupils develop conceptual understanding and the ability to recall and apply knowledge rapidly and accurately'. Fluency includes:

- knowing number bonds for all numbers to 10, then 20 and 100.
- knowing multiplication facts up to 12 × 12.
- using these facts flexibly to create other facts, e.g. if you know that 6 × 7 = 42, you can work out that 6 × 70 = 420, 6 × 35 = 210 and so on.
- knowing efficient mental calculation strategies and written procedures for the four operations and using them efficiently.
- knowing when to use these methods appropriately. Children need to develop conceptual understanding, so that they know the facts and the procedures and how and why they work.

Developing reasoning skills

The second aim of the 2014 National Curriculum states that we should ensure that children: 'reason mathematically by following a line of enquiry, conjecturing relationships and generalisations, and developing an argument, justification or proof using mathematical language'.

Reasoning is about:

- making and testing predictions, conjectures or hypotheses
- searching for patterns and relationships
- making and investigating general statements by finding examples that satisfy them
- explaining and justifying solutions, results, conjectures, conclusions, generalisations and so on:
  - by testing
  - by reasoned argument
- disproving by finding counter-examples.

Many of the activities in *Rising Stars Mathematics* encourage reasoning. You can also provide extra activities to encourage reasoning. Only children can actually do the reasoning, but teachers can help them acquire and refine the necessary skills to do this. Teachers can also model reasoning by 'thinking out loud'.

The problem-solving strategies outlined in this introduction are useful ones to look at for developing reasoning. See also the introduction to the Textbooks, where there are some useful reminder prompts to help children think critically about reasoning and solving problems.

Strategies to embed problem solving

There are many strategies that will embed problem solving, which is the third aim of the 2014 National Curriculum. We need to ensure that children: 'can solve problems by applying their mathematics to a variety of routine and non-routine problems with increasing sophistication, including breaking down problems into a series of simpler steps and persevering in seeking solutions'.

Here are a few strategies that you might like to use, particularly when you work on activities that seek to deepen children's understanding of what you are teaching. Further guidance, detailed examples and activities using these strategies can be found in the Rising Stars *Problem Solving and Reasoning* programme developed by Tim Handley.

Always, sometimes, never

'Always, sometimes, never' is when you give children a statement and then ask whether it is always, sometimes or never true. This encourages the development of the skills of proof, generalisation and algebraic thinking. These are part of reasoning, which is the second aim of the National Curriculum. This strategy also encourages children to make connections between different areas of mathematics.

Another, another, another

'Another, another, another' is a strategy which involves giving children a statement and asking them to give you an example that matches it, and then another and another, e.g. say that $\frac{1}{2}$ and $\frac{2}{4}$ are equivalent fractions, then ask for another pair of equivalent fractions…and another…and another.

This strategy encourages children to give specific examples which meet a given general statement. It provides a good opportunity to assess children's conceptual understanding of an area of mathematics.

Convince me

'Convince me' activities are a useful way to encourage children to explore the structure of a mathematical concept. The teacher makes a statement to children and asks them to decide whether it is accurate or not, and then explain why. Their explanations to convince you allow them to develop their skills of reasoning in the context of mathematical proof, generalisation and algebraic thinking, which is the second aim of the National Curriculum.

Hard and easy

'Hard and easy' is an example of a strategy that encourages children to think closely about the structure of mathematics. It enables you to assess children's conceptual understanding of their mathematics. Ask them to give you an example of a 'hard' and 'easy' answer to a question and explain why one is 'hard' and the other is 'easy'. The choices children make when responding to this often provide valuable information about what they find difficult.

If this is the answer, what's the question?

'If this is the answer, what's the question?' activities encourage children to think creatively and explore the structure of mathematics. The strategy also allows children to develop their skills of generalisation. Give children an answer such as 25% and ask them to come up with as many questions as possible that could have that answer, e.g. 'What is $\frac{1}{4}$ of 100%?' or 'A jumper costs £15 in a sale and the original price was £20. What is the percentage discount?'

Mathematics stories

Giving children a number, geometric concept or measure and asking them to write its 'story', is a strategy that encourages children to explore everything they know about a mathematical concept. It is therefore particularly effective at developing children's subject knowledge, whilst also encouraging them to reason. Through telling a 'story', children are also likely to form and use their own generalisations and patterns, which can be a great starting point for further discussion.

Odd one out

'Odd one out' is a strategy which encourages conjecturing, making generalisations and reasoning about items in a set. All you need to do is give children a set of three or more numbers, shapes or statements and ask them to identify which is the odd one out and why. There will often be several potential responses involving each of the numbers, shapes or statements.

Peculiar, obvious, general

'Peculiar, obvious, general' is a strategy that encourages children to think about the structure of mathematics and to reason about it. Through focusing on what makes a peculiar, obvious or general example of a given statement, children have to think carefully about the statement given, the criteria needed to meet the statement, and what examples they could give.

Silly answers

'Silly answers' encourages children to make generalisations. In giving you a 'silly' answer to a question and explaining why it is such, they will have to reason about possible 'correct' answers. This will require them to consider the properties relating to the topic in the question, therefore deepening their conceptual understanding.

What do you notice?

The 'what do you notice?' strategy encourages children to look deeply at the structure of mathematics. By asking them 'What do you notice?' about a number, set of numbers, shape or mathematical statement, they will need to make their own generalisations and test them against specific examples.

What else do we know?

'What else do we know?' is a strategy that encourages children to see the links that exist in all areas of mathematics. It encourages them to reason and combine other known facts with a given statement, e.g. give children a statement such as 'If we know $8 \times 9 = 72$, what else do we know?' They could then create new statements by doubling, halving and multiplying or dividing by 10, such as $8 \times 90 = 720$, $8 \times 45 = 360$ and $4 \times 45 = 180$.

What's the same? What's different?

'What's the same? What's different?' is a strategy that encourages children to compare and contrast. Children will need to spot patterns and similarities, as well as making generalisations and connections between different aspects of mathematics.

Zooming in

'Zooming in' is a strategy that encourages children to reason about mathematical properties, e.g. give a criterion such as an odd number. Ask children to give an example that fits the criteria. Then 'zoom in' to give another criterion, e.g. an odd number which is also a multiple of 7. This strategy also encourages children to re-evaluate their decisions and helps them to try to make more reasoned choices for their initial 'answers'.

Effective questioning

Questioning is an important strategy which can help embed problem solving and reasoning into day-to-day mathematics teaching. It also allows you to assess children's conceptual understanding. Here are some examples of question structures and routines:

Can you give me an example of …?

- a prime number which is not odd
- an irregular quadrilateral
- a percentage fraction and decimal equivalence

What is the quickest or easiest way to …?

- find out if a number is prime
- find the area of a rectangle
- find out how many chairs will fit into our school hall

What are 7, 11 and 13 examples of …?

What about 36?

What about 72 cm²?

How can we be sure that …?

- all multiples of 6 are multiples of 3
- the area of a triangle = $\frac{1}{2}$ base × height
- $\frac{6}{8}$ is equal to $\frac{12}{16}$

What's the link between …?

- 12, 24 and 36
- $\frac{6}{8}$, 0.75 and 75%
- a rectangle and a square

Introduction

Developing mental and written calculation skills

Mental calculation strategies

Throughout the 2014 National Curriculum Programme of Study for Mathematics, children are expected to use mental calculation strategies as appropriate. Very often, after written methods have been introduced, children tend to use these as their default methods for answering calculations, whether they are appropriate or not. It is therefore important to provide opportunities where children are given calculations and have to decide which methods would be the most efficient to solve them. This encourages them to continue using mental arithmetic as much as possible.

If schools still have copies of the 1999 National Numeracy Strategy Framework, teachers may find the section on mental calculation strategies for addition, subtraction, multiplication and division a useful reference tool for identifying key mental calculation strategies to teach and practise regularly. The 1999 QCA booklet, Teaching mental calculation strategies: guidance for teachers at key stages 1 and 2, is another useful resource.

Key mental calculation strategies include:

- Partition and recombine: $36 + 24 = 30 + 20 + 6 + 4 = 50 + 10 = 60$
- Sequencing: $135 + 78 = 135 + 70 + 8 = 205 + 8 = 213$
- Doubles and near doubles: $154 + 153 = $ double $154 - 1 = 307$
- Using number pairs to 10 and 100: $462 + 138 = 460 + 130 + 10 = 400 + 100 + 100 = 600$
- Adding near multiples of 10 and adjusting: $1458 + 2998 = 1458 + 3000 - 2 = 4456$
- Using known number facts: if we know that $12 \times 7 = 84$ then $12 \times 14 = 168$, $1.2 \times 7 = 8.4$, $2.4 \times 7 = 16.8$
- Bridging though tens, hundreds, tenths: $36 + 8 = 36 + 4 + 4 = 40 + 4 = 44$
- Using relationships between operations: if $256 + 135 = 391$, then $135 + 256$ must also be 391, $391 - 256$ must be 135 and $391 - 135$ must be 256
- Counting on: $365 - 178$, $178 + 22 = 200$, $200 + 165 = 365$, so $365 - 178 = 22 + 165 = 187$
- ×4 by doubling and doubling again: 280×4, double $280 = 560$, double $560 = 1120$
- ×8 by doubling, doubling and doubling again: 56×8, double $56 = 112$, double $112 = 224$, double $224 = 448$
- ×5 by ×10 and halving: $364 \times 10 = 3640$, half $3640 = 1820 = 364 \times 5$
- ×9 by ×10 then subtracting: ×1 $17 \times 9 = (17 \times 10) - (17 \times 1) = 170 - 17 = 153$
- ×20 by ×10 and doubling: $470 \times 20 = 470 \times 10 \times 2 = 4700 \times 2 = 9400$
- ×25 by ×100 then halving and halving again: 37×25, $37 \times 100 = 3700$, half $3700 = 1850$, half $1850 = 925 = 37 \times 25$.

Rising Stars Mathematics encourages teachers to rehearse mental calculation strategies regularly with children during the 'Warming up' sections.

Mental strategies are often used in conjunction with written strategies, so the two do, in fact, go hand in hand. Children will use mental strategies to estimate the solution to a number statement. They will also use, e.g. their mental calculation skills in each column of a written calculation and when using an algorithm.

Approach to written algorithms

In the 2014 National Curriculum Programme of Study for Mathematics, formal written algorithms are introduced during Key Stage 2. It is not necessary to introduce any algorithms into Key Stage 1, these children should be focusing on mental calculation strategies. However, recording addition and subtraction in columns can be introduced if teachers wish to support understanding of place value and prepare for formal written methods later on.

When written algorithms are introduced, children need to develop a conceptual understanding of these and not just learn a method using a rote learning process. It is therefore very important that they use manipulatives, such as those outlined in the Resources and Representations section (see pages 12–14), when they learn a new method or use a method that they have previously learnt but are beginning to apply to larger numbers or decimals.

In Key Stage 2, Base 10 apparatus and place-value counters are very important for developing this conceptual understanding. It is useful for the teacher to model the procedure using this apparatus (which could be on the interactive whiteboard) and children follow their lead. The teacher should then model the written method and ask children to identify what is the same and what is different about the two methods. Some suggestions for how to model this for each operation are given below.

It is often a good idea, when beginning a series of lessons on one of the four operations, to write a selection of calculations on the whiteboard. Children can then discuss with a partner which methods would be the best to use. This highlights the fact that mental calculation strategies are often the most efficient methods to use.

Mental calculation uses the multiplicative property of place value and written methods use the positional property, e.g. if using the strategy of sequencing, one number needs to be partitioned, $246 + 132 = 246 + 100 + 30 + 2$. If subtracting 4567 and 1281, children will refer to the digits positioned in their columns. This is one reason that children need to have a deep conceptual knowledge of place value.

Addition

45 + 77

Encourage children to group the ones. They will have 12, 10 of which need to be changed to one ten. They then add the tens to give 12. 10 of these need changing to one hundred. Model the written method as children progress through each stage with the Base 10 apparatus.

$$\begin{array}{r} 4\ 5 \\ +\ 7\ 7 \\ \hline 1\ 2\ 2 \\ {\scriptstyle 1\ 1} \end{array}$$

How are these models different?
How are they the same?

Using the correct vocabulary is also important. With addition, the vocabulary is:

augend + addend = sum

Subtraction

182 – 147

In this example, children set out 182. When they need to subtract 7 from 2, they can see that there are not enough ones. They therefore need to exchange a ten for 10 ones. They can then take away the other numbers. Again, teachers should model the written method as children progress through the stages of the calculation using the Base 10 apparatus.

Using the correct vocabulary is also important. With subtraction, the correct vocabulary is:

minuend – subtrahend = difference

Multiplication

Arrays are a key visual representation for multiplication. They highlight the links with repeated addition and division. In this example, 38×3, 38 is made three times using manipulatives and then grouped. The model below shows how the physical array links to the grid method and then to the written method:

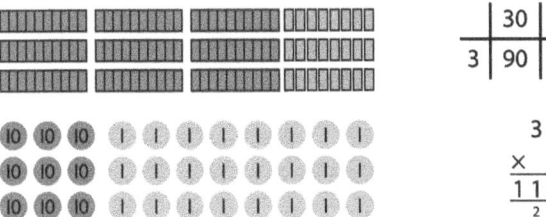

	30	8
3	90	24

$$\begin{array}{r} 38 \\ \times\ 3 \\ \hline 1\,1\,4 \\ {}_{2} \end{array}$$

What's different about all these models?
What's the same?

The correct vocabulary for multiplication is:

multiplicand × multiplier = product

Division

Division is basically grouping, i.e. how many groups of the divisor can be made out of the dividend? When children set out the number (the dividend) using manipulatives, they can clearly see how many groups of the divisor (the number they are dividing by) they can make out of the numbers of each particular value.

Step 1

135 ÷ 3

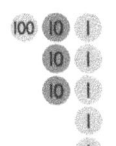

We can't make any groups of 3 hundred with the 1 hundred we have. Exchange the 1 hundred for 10 tens.

$$3\,\overline{)1\,3\,5}$$

What is different about these models?
What is the same

Step 2

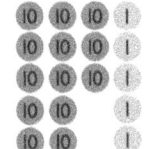

We now have 13 tens.

$$3\,\overline{)\!\!\;^{1}3\,5}$$

What is different about these models?
What is the same?

Step 3

We can make 4 groups of three 10s, leaving one 10

$$3\,\overline{)\!\!\;^{1}3\,5}\;\;\overset{4}{}$$

What is different about these models?
What is the same?

Step 4

We need to exchange the one 10 for ten 1s.

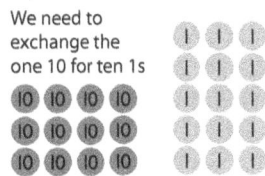

$$3\,\overline{)\!\!\;\mathcal{1}^{1}3^{1}5}\;\;\overset{4}{}$$

What is different about these models?
What is the same

Step 5

We can make 5 groups of three 1s, giving an answer of 45

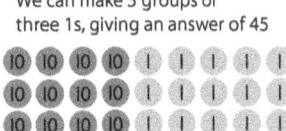

$$3\,\overline{)\!\!\;\mathcal{1}^{1}3^{1}5}\;\;\overset{4\,5}{}$$

What is different about these models?
What is the same

The correct vocabulary for division is:

dividend ÷ divisor = quotient

Use of calculators

The 2014 National Curriculum states that: 'Calculators should not be used as a substitute for good written and mental arithmetic. They should therefore only be introduced near the end of Key Stage 2 to support pupils' conceptual understanding and exploration of more complex number problems, if written and mental arithmetic are secure. In both primary and secondary schools, teachers should use their judgement about when ICT tools should be used'.

It is extremely important that children do not learn to rely on calculators instead of being able to use mental and written calculation methods securely. The calculations given to children as practice should be carefully chosen, so that they are able to perform them using appropriate mental or written methods. However, when working on a real life problem with a large amount of data, teachers may wish to allow children to perform calculations on a calculator, so that they focus more deeply on the problem-solving task at hand.

Calculators are also a very effective way to rehearse recognising numbers for Key Stage 1 and understanding place value in both Key Stage 1 and Key Stage 2, e.g. to rehearse place value, give children the following instructions. They must work out what operation to use at each stage:

- key in 3
- put 5 in front of the 3 (they must add 50)
- put a 2 in front of the 5 (they must add 200)
- change the 5 to a 2 (they must subtract 30)

and so on.

Mathematics outside the classroom

Homework

Rising Stars Mathematics provides a range of homework options:

1. The Textbook can be sent home for children to complete a particular step in the 'Let's practise' section. Within the Textbook, children will have access to the concept explanation, modelling, exemplification, practice and application that they have already explored in the 'Let's learn' section. This enables them to pick up where they left off in class. For schools that do not wish to send Textbooks home, eTextbook versions on the website can be shared with parents/carers, so that the content can be accessed online from home.

2. All the gameboards and game instructions can be downloaded and printed from the website and sent home for children to play with parents/carers/siblings/friends. Children can also be asked to design their own game using the game boards in the Textbook.

Introduction

3. There is a bank of Homework activities at the back of this Teacher's Guide, which can be used as expansion activities outside the classroom. There are two activities for each concept spread in the Textbook. These are also available as editable files on the website, enabling teachers to choose both the homework and its frequency.

4. The Practice Books provide a wide range of additional questions to consolidate and reinforce understanding of concepts taught using the Textbook in class. These extra practice activities can be set as homework or used as further practice within the classroom. Either way, they provide a good record for the child of their understanding and progress and will help teachers identify any misconceptions or gaps in understanding.

Engaging parents/carers

In order to engage parents/carers in their children's learning, it is important to share and explain the way in which mathematics is being taught in school and the key features and benefits of the *Rising Stars Mathematics* approach. An example of a letter to parents/carers is set out below:

Dear Parent/Carer,

As you know, mathematics is an integral part of your child's learning. We are using the innovative *Rising Stars Mathematics* programme to ensure mathematics is accessible for all children and that they achieve personal success in the subject.

Throughout the programme, there is a focus on the development of deep subject knowledge and the ability to make connections. The approach places importance on different types of practice, as well as the ability to recall facts and manipulate them to work out other facts.

The questioning in *Rising Stars Mathematics* is tailored to your child's needs, with a variety of different problems to solve. Any misconceptions are dealt with immediately. Children who grasp mathematical concepts quickly will be given complex problems which deepen their knowledge of the same content, rather than being accelerated into content from the next year level.

There is a focus on practice and spending longer on key concepts to embed understanding. This includes different types of practice, each of which requires a deeper level of understanding:

1. Basic practice, i.e. without any contexts

2. Variations or intelligent practice, this shows children patterns or helps them to make connections

3. Practice and consolidation within different contexts, e.g. time, money or length

4. Open-ended, investigative practice. This goes deeper and deeper, requiring greater reasoning.

Precise mathematical vocabulary will be taught from the start and used consistently throughout the school, including these terms:

Augend + addend = sum/total

Minuend – subtrahend = difference

Multiplicand × multiplier = product

Dividend ÷ divisor = quotient.

We are very excited to be using this unique programme and appreciate your continued support.

Yours faithfully,

The style of the *Rising Stars Mathematics* resources is clear and engaging, which will help to capture the interest of parents/carers. In the Textbook, explanations are supported by clear pictorial representations and followed by guided, step-by-step practice. This will enable parents/carers to quickly familiarise themselves with both what is being taught and how it is being approached. This is especially important if children are asked to complete activities from the Textbook as homework. Since the concepts are set out clearly in the 'Let's learn' section, children will be able to show and explain what they have been learning. Parents/carers will feel able to help without confusing their child by introducing a different method, particularly if they were taught mathematics in a different way themselves.

For schools that do not wish to send Textbooks home, online versions can be shared as eTextbooks and accessed online by parents/carers or children at home. These provide an enhanced version of the print Textbooks, with a number of pop-up animations throughout that help to explain key concepts. Parents/carers may wish to watch these with their child, to enable them to participate in their learning.

It may also be useful to share the school's Calculation Policy or the pages from this Teacher's Guide introduction on the *Rising Stars Mathematics* approach to mental arithmetic and written algorithms (see pages 16–17). This could help parents/carers understand how their child will be tackling calculations during practice or homework activities and explain how best they can support this.

Planning grids

Year 5 scope and sequence

The following grid shows the concepts and objectives that are covered within each *Rising Stars Mathematics* Year 5 unit and provides page references to each of the various components.

Unit	Concept	Objectives	Textbook	Teacher's Guide	Practice Book	Homework Sheets
1	1a Distances	• Read, write, order and compare numbers to at least 500 000 and determine the value of each digit. • Count forwards or backwards in steps of powers of 10 for any given number up to 1 000 000. • Round any number up to 500 000 to the nearest 10, 100, 10 000 and 100 000.	12-13	26-7	4-6	192
	1b Converting units of measure	• Multiply and divide whole numbers and those involving decimals by 10, 100 and 1000. • Convert between different units of metric measure, e.g. kilometre and metre; centimetre and metre; centimetre and millimetre. • Solve problems involving converting between units of time.	14-15	28-9	7-9	193
	1c Fractions and decimal equivalences	• Read and write decimal numbers as fractions, e.g. $0.71 = \frac{71}{100}$. • Recognise and use thousandths and relate them to tenths, hundredths and decimal equivalents. • Convert between different units of metric measure, e.g. grams and kilograms	16-17	30-1	10-12	194
	1d Reading, writing and ordering decimal numbers	• Round decimals with two decimal places to the nearest whole number and to one decimal place. • Read, write, order and compare numbers with up to three decimal places. • Solve problems involving number up to three decimal places.	18-19	32-3	13-15	195
2	2a Mental calculation strategies	• Add and subtract numbers mentally with increasingly large numbers. • Use rounding to check answers to calculations and determine, in the context of a problem, levels of accuracy. • Solve addition and subtraction multi-step problems in contexts, deciding which operations and methods to use and why.	26-7	40-1	16-18	196
	2b Written methods for addition and subtraction	• Add and subtract whole numbers with four digits, including using written methods (columnar addition and subtraction). • Solve addition and subtraction multi-step problems in contexts, deciding which operations and methods to use and why.	28-9	42-3	19-21	197
3	3a Exploring multiples, factors, squares and cubes	• Identify multiples and factors, including finding all factor pairs of a number, and common factors of two numbers. • Solve problems involving multiplication and division including using their knowledge of factors and multiples, squares and cubes.	36-7	50-1	22-4	198
	3b Mental calculation strategies for multiplication and division	• Multiply and divide numbers mentally drawing upon known facts. • Solve problems involving addition, subtraction, multiplication and division and a combination of these, including understanding the meaning of the equals sign.	38-9	52-3	25-7	199
	3c Written methods for multiplication and division	• Multiply numbers up to 4 digits long by a single- or 2-digit number using a formal written method, including long multiplication for 2-digit numbers. • Divide numbers up to 4 digits long by a single-digit number using the formal written method of short division and interpret remainders appropriately for the context.	40-1	54-5	28-31	200
4	4a Regular or irregular?	• Know angles are measured in degrees: estimate and compare acute and obtuse angles. • Distinguish between regular and irregular polygons based on reasoning about equal sides and angles. • Use the properties of rectangles to deduce related facts and find missing lengths and angles.	48-9	62-3	32-4	201

	4b Angles	• Know angles are measured in degrees: estimate and compare acute, obtuse and reflex angles.
		• Draw given angles, and measure them in degrees (°).
		• Identify:
		  • angles at a point and 1 whole turn (total 360°)
		  • angles at a point on a straight line and $\frac{1}{2}$ a turn (total 180°)
		  • other multiples of 90°.
		• Use the properties of rectangles to deduce related facts and find missing lengths and angles.
			50-1	64-5	35-6	202

	4c Drawing	• Know angles are measured in degrees: estimate and compare acute, obtuse and reflex angles. • Draw given angles, and measure them in degrees (°). • Distinguish between regular and irregular polygons based on reasoning about equal sides and angles. • Identify angles at a point and one whole turn (total 360°).	52-3	66-7	37-9	203
5	5a Place holders and comparing	• Read, write, order and compare numbers to at least 500 000 and determine the value of each digit. • Count forwards or backwards in steps of powers of 10 for any given number up to 1 000 000. • Round any number up to 500 000 to the nearest 10, 100, 1000, 10 000 and 100 000 • Solve number problems and practical problems that involve all of the above.	60-1	74-5	40-1	204
	5b Positive and negative numbers	• Interpret negative numbers in context. • Count forwards and backwards with positive and negative whole numbers, including through zero.	62-3	76-7	42-3	205
	5c Roman numerals	• Read Roman numerals to 1000 (M) and recognise years written in Roman numerals. • Solve problems involving units of time.	64-5	78-9	44-5	206

Introduction

Unit	Concept	Objectives	Textbook	Teacher's Guide	Practice Book	Homework Sheets
6	6a Mental or written methods?	• Add and subtract whole numbers with more than four digits, including using formal written methods (columnar addition and subtraction). • Add and subtract numbers mentally with increasingly large numbers. • Solve addition and subtraction multi-step problems in contexts, deciding which operations and methods to use and why. • Solve problems involving number up to three decimal places. • Use addition and subtraction to solve problems involving mass using decimal notation.	72-3	86-87	46-8	207
	6b Don't forget to check!	• Add and subtract whole numbers with more than four digits, including using formal written methods (columnar addition and subtraction). • Add and subtract numbers mentally with increasingly large numbers. • Solve addition and subtraction multi-step problems in contexts, deciding which operations and methods to use and why. • Solve comparison, sum and difference problems using information presented in a line graph and bar charts. • Use rounding to check answers to calculations and determine, in the context of a problem, levels of accuracy.	74-5	88-9	49-51	208
7	7a Comparing and ordering fractions	• Compare and order fractions whose denominators are all multiples of the same number. • Identify, name and write equivalent fractions of a given fraction, represented visually.	82-3	96-7	52-4	209
	7b Improper fractions and mixed numbers	• Recognise mixed numbers and improper fractions and convert from one form to the other and write mathematical statements > 1 as a mixed number (e.g. $\frac{2}{5} + \frac{4}{5} = \frac{6}{5} = 1\frac{1}{5}$). • Solve problems involving measures.	84-5	98-9	55-7	210
	7c Equivalences	• Read and write decimal numbers as fractions (e.g. $0.71 = \frac{71}{100}$). • Recognise and use thousandths and relate them to tenths, hundredths and decimal equivalents..	86-7	100-1	58-9	211
	7d Percentages	• Recognise the per cent symbol (%) and understand that per cent relates to 'number of parts per hundred', and write percentages as a fraction with denominator 100, and as a decimal.	88-9	102-3	60-3	212
8	8a Primes, squares and cubes	• Identify multiples and factors, including finding all factor pairs of a number, and common factors of two numbers. • Know and use the vocabulary of prime numbers, prime factors and composite (non-prime) numbers. • Recall primes up to 19. • Recognise and use square numbers and cube numbers, and the notation for squared (^{2}) and cubed (^{3}). • Solve problems involving multiplication and division including using their knowledge of factors and multiples, squares and cubes.	96-7	110-11	64-6	213
	8b Using fractions as operators for multiplication	• Solve problems that require knowing percentage and decimal equivalents of $\frac{1}{2}, \frac{1}{4}, \frac{1}{5}, \frac{2}{5}, \frac{4}{5}$ and those fractions with a denominator of a multiple of 10 or 25.	98-9	112-13	67-9	214
	8c Using scaling for multiplication and division	• Solve problems involving multiplication and division, including scaling by simple fractions and problems involving simple rates.	100-1	114-15	70-3	215
9	9a Reflecting and translating 2-D shapes	• Identify, describe and represent the position of a shape following a reflection or translation, using the appropriate language, and know that the shape has not changed.	108-9	122-3	74-8	216
	9b Identifying 3-D shapes	• Identify 3-D shapes, including cubes and other cuboids, from 2-D representations.	110-11	124-5	79-82	217

	9c Angles	• Know angles are measured in degrees: estimate and compare acute, obtuse and reflex angles.
		• Draw given angles, and measure them in degrees (°).
		• Distinguish between regular and irregular polygons based on reasoning about equal sides and angles.
		• Identify:
		  • angles at a point and 1 whole turn (total 360°)
		  • angles at a point on a straight line and half a turn (total 180°).
			112-13	126-7	83-5	218

10	10a Negative numbers and millions	• Read, write, order and compare numbers to at least 1 000 000 and determine the value of each digit. • Count forwards or backwards in steps of powers of 10 for any given number up to 1 000 000. • Interpret negative numbers in the context of temperature. • Count forwards and backwards with positive and negative whole numbers, including through zero. • Round any number up to 1 000 000 to the nearest 10, 100, 1000, 10 000 and 100 000. • Solve number problems and practical problems that involve all of the above.	120-1	134-5	86-8	219
	10b All about fractions	• Compare and order fractions whose denominators are all multiples of the same number. • Recognise mixed numbers and improper fractions and convert from one form to the other and write mathematical statements > 1 as a mixed number, e.g. $\frac{2}{5} + \frac{4}{5} = \frac{6}{5} = 1\frac{1}{5}$.	122-3	136-7	89-92	220
	10c All about decimal fractions	• Recognise and use thousandths and relate them to tenths, hundredths and decimal equivalents. • Round decimals with two decimal places to the nearest whole number and to one decimal place. • Read, write, order and compare numbers with up to three decimal places. • Solve problems involving numbers up to three decimal places.	124-5	138-9	93-5	221

Unit	Concept	Objectives	Textbook	Teacher's Guide	Practice Book	Homework Sheets
11	11a Mental and written calculations	• Add and subtract numbers mentally with increasingly large numbers. • Add and subtract whole numbers with more than four digits, including using formal written methods (columnar addition and subtraction). • Solve addition and subtraction multi-step problems in contexts, deciding which operations and methods to use and why. • Convert between different units of metric measure. • Use addition and subtraction to solve problems involving measurement using decimal notation. • Solve problems involving units of time.	132-3	146-7	96-9	222
	11b Adding and subtracting fractions	• Recognise mixed numbers and improper fractions and convert from one form to the other and write mathematical statements >1 as a mixed number. • Add and subtract fractions with the same denominator and denominators that are multiples of the same number. • Start to solve comparison, sum and difference problems using information presented in a line graph. • Start to solve problems involving units of time.	134-5	148-9	100-3	223
12	12a Exploring fractions	• Compare and order fractions whose denominators are all multiples of the same number. • Recognise mixed numbers and improper fractions and convert from one form to the other and write mathematical statements > 1 as a mixed number (e.g. $\frac{2}{5} + \frac{4}{5} = \frac{6}{5} = 1\frac{1}{5}$). • Multiply fractions by whole numbers.	142-3	156-7	104-7	224
	12b Working with decimals	• Multiply and divide whole numbers and those involving decimals by 10, 100 and 1000. • Read and write decimal numbers as fractions (e.g. $0.71 = \frac{71}{100}$). • Recognise and use thousandths and relate them to tenths, hundredths and decimal equivalents.	144-5	158-9	108-10	225
	12c Calculating and converting percentages	• Recognise and use thousandths and relate them to tenths, hundredths and decimal equivalents. • Recognise the per cent symbol (%) and understand that per cent relates to 'number of parts per hundred', and write percentages as a fraction with denominator 100, and as a decimal. • Identify, name and write equivalent fractions of tenths and hundredths.	146-7	160-1	111-13	226
13	13a All about factors	• Identify multiples and factors, including finding all factor pairs of a number, and common factors of two numbers. • Solve problems involving multiplication and division including using their knowledge of factors and multiples, squares and cubes.	154-5	168-9	114-17	227
	13b Mental calculation and scaling	• Multiply and divide numbers mentally drawing upon known facts. • Solve problems involving addition, subtraction, multiplication and division and a combination of these. • Solve problems involving multiplication and division, including scaling by simple fractions and problems involving simple rates.	156-7	170-1	118-20	228
	13c 4-digit and long multiplication	• Multiply numbers up to four digits by a single- or 2-digit number using a formal written method, including long multiplication for 2-digit numbers.	158-9	172-3	121-5	229
	13d Division with remainders	• Divide numbers up to four digits by a single-digit number using the formal written method of short division and interpret remainders appropriately for the context.	160-1	174-5	126-7	230
14	14a Finding perimeters	• Measure and calculate the perimeter of composite rectilinear shapes in centimetres and metres.	168-9	182-3	128-31	231
	14b Areas and perimeters	• Measure and calculate the perimeter of composite rectilinear shapes in centimetres and metres. • Use the properties of rectangles to deduce related facts and find missing lengths and angles. • Calculate and compare the area of rectangles (including squares), including using standard units, square centimetres (cm^2) and square metres (m^2), and estimate the area of irregular shapes. • Identify multiples and factors, including all factor pairs, and common factors of two numbers.	170-1	184-5	132-6	232
	14c Volume and capacity	• Estimate the volume of cuboids e.g. using cm cubes, and capacity, e.g. using water.	172-3	186-7	132-6	233

Introduction

Curriculum mapping grid

The following grid shows what children should be taught during Year 5, as laid out in the 2014 National Curriculum Programme of Study for Mathematics and how these are covered within the *Rising Stars Mathematics* Year 5 units.

Domain	Sub-domain	Statement	Unit 1	Unit 2	Unit 3	Unit 4	Unit 5	Unit 6	Unit 7	Unit 8	Unit 9	Unit 10	Unit 11	Unit 12	Unit 13	Unit 14
NUMBER	Number and place value	read, write, order and compare numbers to at least 1 000 000 and determine the value of each digit	a				a					a				
		count forwards or backwards in steps of powers of ten for any given number up to 1 000 000	a				a					a				
		interpret negative numbers in context, count forwards and backwards with positive and negative whole numbers, including through zero						b				a				
		round any number up to 1 000 000 to the nearest ten, 100, 1000, 10 000 and 100 000	a				a					a				
		solve number problems and practical problems that involve all of the above					a					a				
		read Roman numerals to 1000 (M) and recognise years written in Roman numerals						c								
	Addition and subtraction	add and subtract whole numbers with more than four digits, including using formal written methods (columnar addition and subtraction)		b			a, b						a			
		add and subtract numbers mentally with increasingly large numbers		a			a, b						a			
		use rounding to check answers to calculations and determine, in the context of a problem, levels of accuracy		a				b								
		solve addition and subtraction multi-step problems in contexts, deciding which operations and methods to use and why		a, b			a, b						a			
	Multiplication and division	identify multiples and factors, including finding all factor pairs of a number, and common factors of two numbers			a					a					a	b
		know and use the vocabulary of prime numbers, prime factors and composite (non-prime) numbers								a						
		establish whether a number up to 100 is prime and recall prime numbers up to 19								a						
		multiply numbers up to four digits by a single- or 2-digit number using a formal written method, including long multiplication for 2-digit numbers			c										c	
		multiply and divide numbers mentally drawing upon known facts			b										b	
		divide numbers up to four digits by a single-digit number using the formal written method of short division and interpret remainders appropriately for the context			c										d	
		multiply and divide whole numbers and those involving decimals by ten, 100 and 1000	b											b		
		recognise and use square numbers and cube numbers, and the notation for squared (^{2}) and cubed (^{3})								a						
		solve problems involving multiplication and division including using their knowledge of factors and multiples, squares and cubes			a					a					a	
		solve problems involving addition, subtraction, multiplication and division and a combination of these, including understanding the meaning of the equals sign			b										b	
		solve problems involving multiplication and division, including scaling by simple fractions and problems involving simple rates										c			b	
	Fractions (including decimals and percentages)	compare and order fractions whose denominators are all multiples of the same number							a				b		a	
		identify, name and write equivalent fractions of a given fraction, represented visually, including tenths and hundredths							a					c		
		recognise mixed numbers and improper fractions and convert from one form to the other and write mathematical statements > one as a mixed number [e.g. $\frac{2}{5} + \frac{4}{5} = \frac{6}{5} = 1\frac{1}{5}$]							b				b	b	a	
		add and subtract fractions with the same denominator and denominators that are multiples of the same number											b			

Domain	Sub-domain	Statement	Unit 1	Unit 2	Unit 3	Unit 4	Unit 5	Unit 6	Unit 7	Unit 8	Unit 9	Unit 10	Unit 11	Unit 12	Unit 13	Unit 14
NUMBER	Fractions (including decimals and percentages)	multiply proper fractions and mixed numbers by whole numbers, supported by materials and diagrams												a		
		read and write decimal numbers as fractions [e.g. $0.71 = \frac{71}{100}$]	c						c					b		
		recognise and use thousandths and relate them to tenths, hundredths and decimal equivalents	c						c			c		b, c		
		round decimals with two decimal places to the nearest whole number and to one decimal place	d									c				
		read, write, order and compare numbers with up to three decimal places	d									c				
		solve problems involving number up to three decimal places	d					a				c				
		recognise the per cent symbol (%) and understand that per cent relates to 'number of parts per hundred', and write percentages as a fraction with denominator 100, and as a decimal							d					c		
		solve problems which require knowing percentage and decimal equivalents of $\frac{1}{2}$, $\frac{1}{4}$, $\frac{1}{5}$, $\frac{2}{5}$, $\frac{4}{5}$ and those fractions with a denominator of a multiple of ten or 25								b						
MEASUREMENT	Measurement	convert between different units of metric measure (e.g. kilometre and metre; centimetre and metre; centimetre and millimetre; gram and kilogram; litre and millilitre)	b, c										a			
		understand and use approximate equivalences between metric units and common imperial units such as inches, pounds and pints														
		measure and calculate the perimeter of composite rectilinear shapes in centimetres and metres														a, b
		calculate and compare the area of rectangles (including squares), and including using standard units, square centimetres (cm^2) and square metres (m^2) and estimate the area of irregular shapes														b
		estimate volume [e.g. using 1 cm^3 blocks to build cuboids (including cubes)] and capacity [e.g. using water]														c
		solve problems involving converting between units of time	b				c						a, b			
		use all four operations to solve problems involving measure [e.g. length, mass, volume, money] using decimal notation, including scaling						a	b				a			
GEOMETRY	Properties of shapes	identify 3-D shapes, including cubes and other cuboids, from 2-D representations									b					
		know angles are measured in degrees: estimate and compare acute, obtuse and reflex angles				a, b, c					c					
		draw given angles, and measure them in degrees (°)				b, c					c					
		identify:														
		angles at a point and one whole turn (total 360°)				b, c					c					
		angles at a point on a straight line and $\frac{1}{2}$ a turn (total 180°)				b					c					
		other multiples of 90°														
		use the properties of rectangles to deduce related facts and find missing lengths and angles				a, b										a
		distinguish between regular and irregular polygons based on reasoning about equal sides and angles				a, c					c					
	Position and direction	identify, describe and represent the position of a shape following a reflection or translation, using the appropriate language, and know that the shape has not changed										a				
STATISTICS	Statistics	solve comparison, sum and difference problems using information presented in a line graph						b					b			
		complete, read and interpret information in tables, including timetables														

Numbers in real life

Mathematical focus

★ **Number: number and place value, multiplication and division, fractions**

★ **Measurement: length, mass, capacity, time**

Prior learning

Children should already be able to:

- recognise the place value of each digit in a 4-digit number (thousands, hundreds, tens, and ones)

- order and compare numbers beyond 1000

- round any number to the nearest 10, 100 or 1000

- solve number and practical problems that involve all of the above and with increasingly large positive numbers

- count up and down in hundredths; recognise that hundredths arise when dividing an object by 100 and dividing tenths by 10

- round decimals with one decimal place to the nearest whole number

- compare numbers with the same number of decimal places up to two decimal places

- convert between different units of measure, e.g. kilometres and metres, hours and minutes.

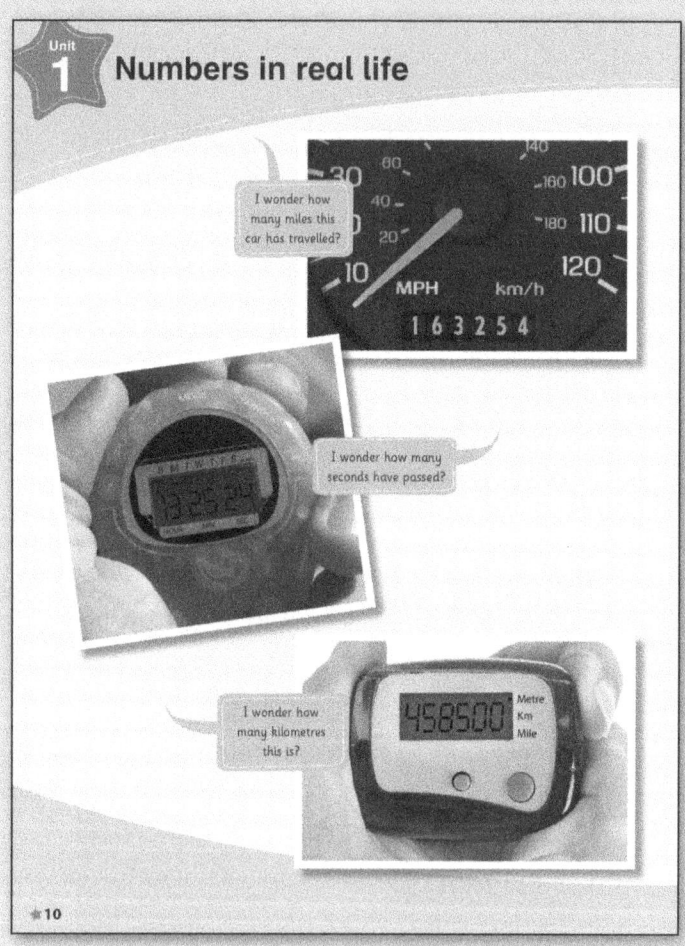

Unit

1

Numbers in real life

Key new learning

- Read, write, order and compare numbers to at least 500 000 and determine the value of each digit.

- Multiply and divide whole numbers and those involving decimals by 10, 100 and 1000.

- Read and write decimal numbers as fractions, e.g. $0.71 = \frac{71}{100}$.

- Round decimals with two decimal places to the nearest whole number and to one decimal place.

Making connections

- Make connections to real life in order to engage children. Explore time, distance and money using places, people and objects that are relevant to your children.

- Develop these real world connections by introducing conversions between different units of metric measure, e.g. kilometre and metre, centimetre and metre, centimetre and millimetre, kilogram and gram, litre and millilitre.

- Explore the numbers in this unit through practical activities in subjects across the curriculum, for example art, design, cookery, PE and geography.

 Talk about

It is important that children know about the positional, multiplicative, additional and Base 10 aspects of place value. Talk these through with them before beginning the unit opener. Use the terms explaining the first three clearly using a number such as 3592. Remind them that our number system is Base 10 and therefore increases and decreases in powers of 10.

Engaging and exploring

Ask children to look at the photo of the car milometer and to read the number aloud. Spend some time focusing on place value to review their understanding. Give children a set of digit cards each and a place-value grid. Ask them to make the mileage number in their grids. Discuss the place value of each digit: 1 is in the hundred thousands column, $1 \times 100\,000 = 100\,000$; 6 is in the ten thousands column, $6 \times 10\,000 = 60\,000$; 3 is in the thousands column, $3 \times 1000 = 3000$; 2 is in the hundreds position, $2 \times 100 = 200$; 5 is in the tens column, $5 \times 10 = 50$; and 4 is in the ones column, $4 \times 1 = 4$. These numbers are then added together to give $100\,000 + 60\,000 + 3000 + 200 + 50 + 4 = 163\,254$.

If you have place-value counters or Base 10 apparatus, ask children to make different 5- and 6-digit numbers using these, e.g. 124 567. As they do this, ask children to tell you what each digit represents.

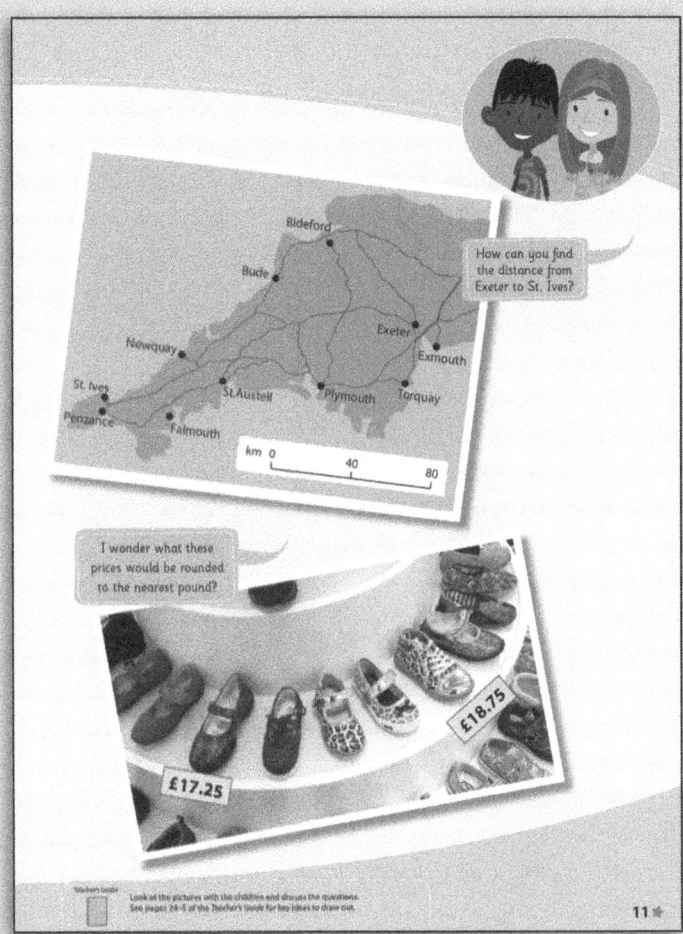

Things to think about

- The type of questions you will be asking, to encourage children to develop their reasoning skills.

- Ways of organising group work. Evidence suggests that mixed attainment groups are effective in raising the achievement of lower attainers and also help higher attainers to consolidate their understanding.

- How manipulatives can be used to help conceptual understanding with all children.

- Different strategies to use to draw out reasoning.

- How to ensure children experience practical opportunities to measure length, mass and capacity.

Look at the photo of the stop watch. Ask where children might have used or seen one in real life. What is one used for? Ask children to say the time reading aloud, i.e. 13 hours, 25 minutes and 24 seconds. Discuss how many seconds there are in a minute, minutes in an hour, hours in a day, etc. You may like to ask children what the seconds are as a fraction of a minute, e.g. $\frac{24}{60}, \frac{12}{30}, \frac{6}{15}$, or to convert total amount of time to minutes ($13 \times 60 = 13 \times 6 \times 10 = 780$, $780 + 25 = 805$ minutes 24 seconds), then to seconds ($805 \times 60 = 805 \times 6 \times 10 = 48\,300$, $48\,300 + 24 = 48\,324$ seconds). Discuss the place value of each number.

For the photo of the pedometer, find out if children know how many metres there are in a kilometre and then ask them to convert the reading into kilometres and metres (458 km 500 m). Establish that there are 1000 metres in a kilometre and 500 m in $\frac{1}{2}$ or 0.5 km. Ask children to tell you how many metres are in different fractions of a kilometre. Write some kilometre and metre distances on the board for children to convert to kilometres.

Find out if children know which part of England is shown on the map and ask them to identify the towns. Discuss what is meant by 'as the crow flies'. How could they find this distance? Encourage them to think about how they could find out the distance from Exeter to St. Ives along the roads. Agree that they could use string and follow one of the routes using this. They would then need to measure the string in centimetres and convert to kilometres using the scale on the map. Encourage them to use a mental calculation strategy for this.

Discuss that in the UK we usually use miles to measure distances, and that 0.6 miles ≈ 1 kilometre. Ask children to convert the kilometres to miles by multiplying the distance by 6 and then dividing by 10. Ask questions, e.g. If Fred was travelling at 60 miles per hour, how long would it take him to travel this distance? Repeat with other distances and speeds.

Look at the photo of the shoe shop. Ask children to read the prices in pounds and pence. Ask them to use digit cards to make the prices on a place-value grid and encourage them to identify the tenths and hundredths correctly. Discuss how there are 100 pennies in one pound, and how to approach rounding the prices to the nearest pound. You may like to use a place-value grid to explain how a decimal fraction of less than 0.5 would be rounded down, and one of 0.5 or greater would be rounded up, ensuring they understand that, e.g., £17.25 rounded down to £17 and £18.75 would be rounded up to £19.

Checking understanding

You will know children have mastered the concepts in this unit when they can:

- represent and explain the multiplicative nature of the number system, understanding how to multiply and divide by 10, 100 and 1000

- make appropriate decisions about when to use their understanding of counting, place value and rounding to solve problems

- explain and represent how, e.g. 71.7 m is greater than 17.57 m

- explain why it is easy to subtract, e.g. 0.7 m from 71.7 m and why rounding both numbers to the nearest metre gives the same result, suggesting other numbers that would round to, e.g. 72 m

- explain and represent the relationship between, e.g. 71.7 and 7.17.

1a Distances

- Read, write, order and compare numbers to at least 500 000 and determine the value of each digit.
- Count forwards or backwards in steps of powers of 10 for any given number up to 1 000 000.
- Round any number up to 500 000 to the nearest 10, 100, 1000, 10 000 and 100 000.

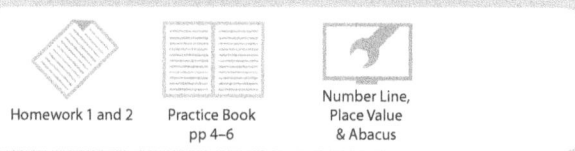

Homework 1 and 2   Practice Book pp 4–6   Number Line, Place Value & Abacus

Representations and resources

Pendulum (e.g. three interlocking cubes on a piece of string), sets of digit cards, place-value grids, rulers.

Mathematical vocabulary

Hundred thousands, ten thousands, thousands, hundreds, tens, ones, kilometre, greatest, least, round, estimate, approximate

Warming up

Swing the pendulum from side to side. As it swings children count in tens from different starting points, e.g. 140. They count forwards for 12 steps and then count back to the starting number. Repeat this for counting forwards and backwards in hundreds and thousands to 500 000 and back.

Background knowledge

Comparing, ordering and rounding numbers relies on a conceptual understanding of place value. If this is not achieved errors can be made later in a child's mathematical journey and cause problems.

Let's learn: Modelling and teaching
Ordering and comparing

- Before you begin it would be a good idea to find out if children know the cities mentioned in the Textbook and which countries they are the capitals of. They may like to find the countries on a map of the world.

- Ask children to write different pairs of numbers into a place-value grid. Ensure that some of the most significant digits are the same and ask them, firstly, to think about the place value of each and then discuss which is the largest or smallest number and why.

- They could work in pairs with two sets of digit cards to practise comparing larger numbers. They make up 6-digit numbers and then compare them using the 'greater than' and 'less than' symbols.

- In pairs, ask children to each draw a place-value grid. They pick a digit card and put it under a heading to make the largest number they can. They do this six times and then compare their numbers and explain to each other who made the largest number and how they know.

Rounding
- Discuss when rounding is useful in real life, e.g. when estimating the answer to a calculation.

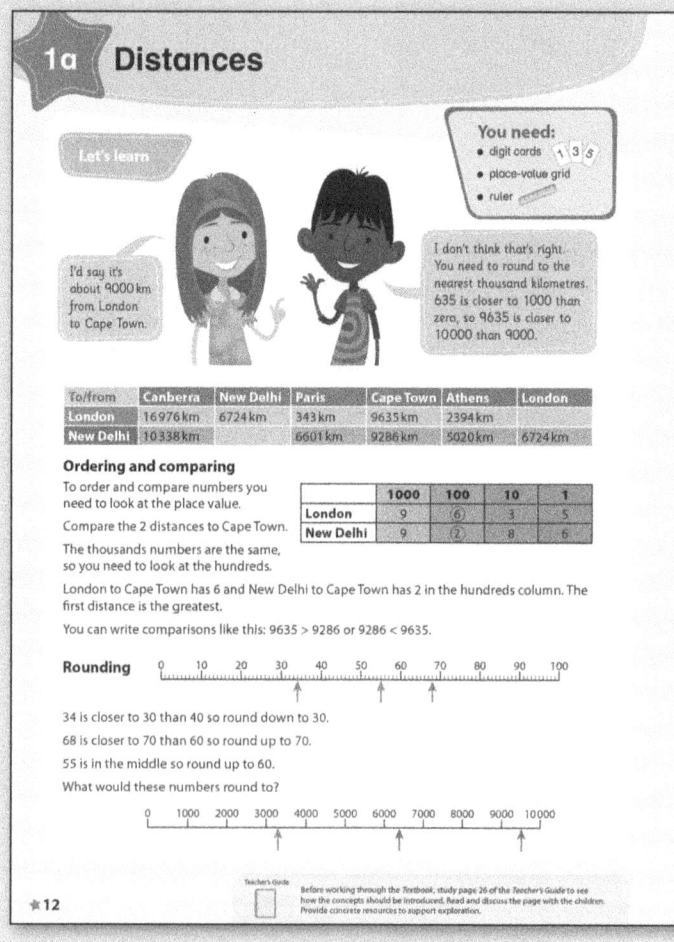

- Discuss what happens to numbers that end in, e.g. 5, 50, 500.

- Draw number lines on the board as in the Textbook and place arrows in different positions. Ask children to write down what these would be to, e.g. the nearest 1000. They could then draw their own number lines to a given value, plot arrows onto them and ask a friend to estimate what each number is and then to round it appropriately.

- Ask children to give you different digits to make a number and then to round each one to the nearest 10, 100, 1000, 10 000 and 100 000.

Let's practise: Digging deeper

Step 1

Children need to order the numbers given in each question. These numbers all have the same thousands numbers and some of the other numbers are the same as well. They need to use their reasoning skills so that they can order them successfully. Let them make notes to help them do this reasoning, e.g. they could identify those that have several digits that are the same and work out these first, making a note of their order, and then fit the others in around them.

Children then round the numbers to the nearest 100 before ordering. After they have ordered them, ask them to note if their orders are the same or different. Are there any numbers that are the same now?

Step 2

Children round the distances in the table to the nearest 10 km

and then order them. They can choose whether to order from smallest to greatest distance or vice versa. They then draw a number line and select a suitable scale so they can plot all the rounded distances on it.

Step 3

Children need to draw curvy lines as in the example. Encourage them to estimate the lengths of their lines. They could write their estimates and then compare them with the actual measurements by placing string along their lines and measuring with a ruler. They then write the length and then again rounded as an approximation.

Step 4

Children can use the Internet to find distances greater than that from London to Cape Town. They list and then compare these by writing number statements using the 'is greater than' and 'is less than' symbols. Use this opportunity to observe whether the children are recording their findings logically, for example in tables.

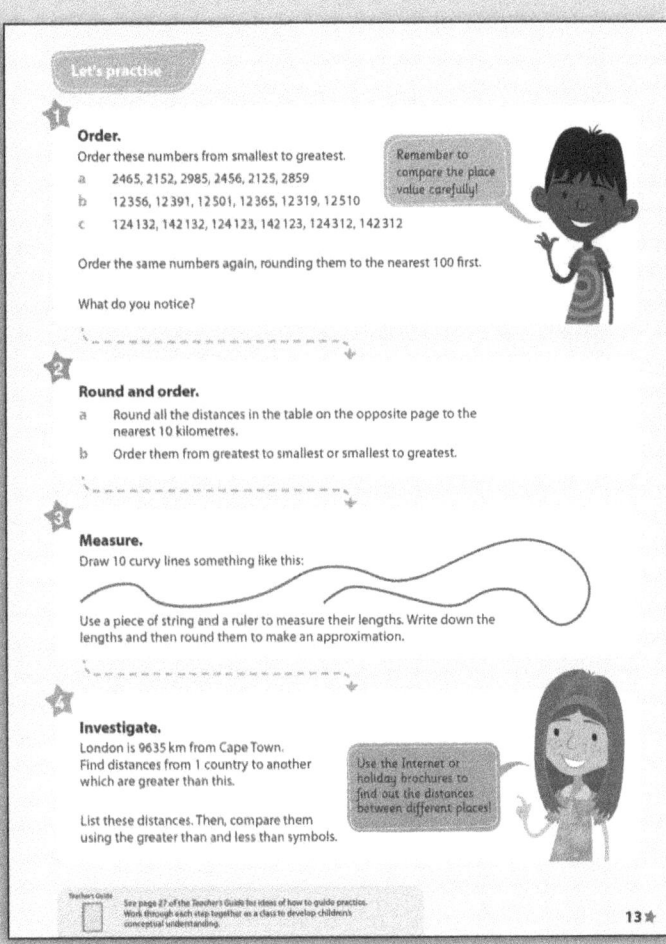

Ensuring progress

Supporting understanding

It is important that all children understand place value. It might be that you need to work with some children in a guided group to take them through this more thoroughly. This may require finding additional time to ensure they are developing their conceptual understanding. Provide them with place-value grids; the use of this visual representation will help them, with guidance from you.

Broadening understanding

Provide opportunities for children to consider place value in different contexts, e.g. money. Encourage them to make up problems for others to solve. This will help you to assess the true depth of their understanding.

✓ Concept mastered

Children can explain and demonstrate the positional, multiplicative and additive aspects of place value and explain and demonstrate how to round numbers to the nearest 10, 100, 1000, 10 000 and 100 000.

Follow-up ideas

- Ask children to research some distances from their nearest airport to favourite holiday destinations or countries that they are interested in. They could make up a distance table in miles and carry out similar activities to those suggested on the spread.

- Children could measure different items around the classroom in centimetres and millimetres and order these. They could also round them to the nearest centimetre.

- Write a distance or length on the board, e.g. 85 km or 72 m. Ask children to make a list of other kilometres or metres that would round to those numbers. Encourage them to include numbers with one decimal place.

Answers

Step 1

a   2125, 2152, 2456, 2465, 2859, 2985

b   12 319, 12 356, 12 365, 12 391, 12 501, 12 510

c   124 123, 124 132, 124 312, 142 123, 142 132, 142 312

2100, 2200, 2500, 2500, 2900, 3000

12 300, 12 400, 12 400, 12 500, 12 500

124 100, 124 100, 124 300, 142 100, 142 100, 142 300

The order is the same but now some of the numbers are the same.

Step 2

340 km, 2390 km, 5020 km, 6600 km, 6720 km, 9290 km, 9640 km, 10 340 km, 16 980 km (or vice versa if children choose to order from greatest to shortest distance)

Step 3

Answers will vary.

Step 4

Answers will depend on children's responses.

1b Converting units of measure

- Multiply and divide whole numbers and those involving decimals by 10, 100 and 1000.
- Convert between different units of metric measure, e.g. kilometre and metre; centimetre and metre; centimetre and millimetre.
- Solve problems involving converting between units of time.

Homework 3 and 4 Practice Book pp 7–9 Place Value & Abacus

Representations and resources
Counting stick, place-value grids, geared clocks.

Mathematical vocabulary
Kilometres, metres, centimetres, hours, seconds, minutes, place value, converting, Base 10, Base 60

Warming up
Practice the 6 times table using the counting stick. Explain that at one end there is zero and at the other 60. Point to each division in turn and children count in sixes from zero to 60 and back. Next, point at different divisions and ask them to tell you the number that would go there and also the multiplication and division statements, e.g. at the seventh division, children tell you that $6 \times 7 = 42$ and $42 \div 7 = 6$. Repeat this for the 60 times table. Ask them what they need to do to do this. Agree they simply multiply by 6 and then by 10.

Background knowledge
Multiplying and dividing numbers by 10, 100 and 1000 relies on an understanding of the Base 10 aspect of place value. They need to understand that our number system works within Base 10 and that when multiplying by 10 each digit in the original number gets 10 times bigger, i.e. the ones become tens, the tens become hundreds, and so on. We could say that the digits move one place to the left. When multiplying by 100 the digits move two places to the left and this is the same as multiplying by 10 twice. When multiplying by 1000, the digits move three places to the left and this is the same as multiplying by 10 three times. Dividing by 10, 100 and 1000 has the opposite effect.

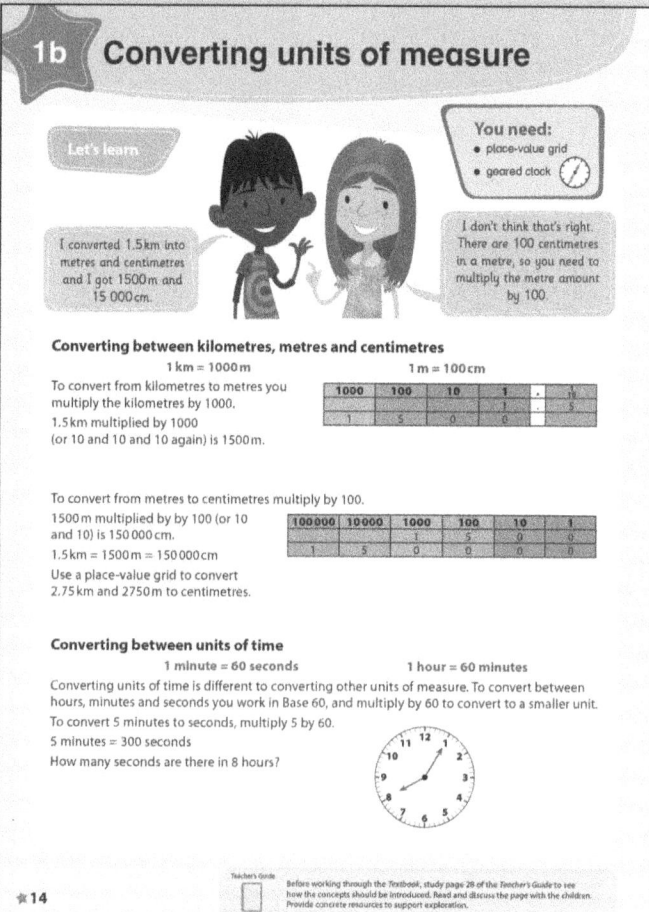

Let's learn: Modelling and teaching
Converting between kilometres, metres and centimetres

- Using place-value grids helps children develop a conceptual understanding of what happens when numbers are multiplied and divided by 10, 100 and 1000. They can place digit cards in the grids to make a number, e.g. 34. They then multiply it by 10, by moving each digit one place to the left so that each is 10 times bigger. Discuss how a place holder needs to go into the ones position to keep that place; otherwise the number will revert to the original one. Provide further examples.

- Ask children to convert various numbers of whole kilometres to metres and metres to centimetres. Extend this to converting centimetres to millimetres, finding out first if children know how many millimetres there are in a centimetre. You could then repeat using mixed units,

e.g. 3.7 km, 2.3 m, 1.2 cm.

Converting between units of time

- Discuss what the Base 60 number system is, i.e., the ones go up to 59 instead of 9 and then there are sixties instead of tens. You might like to share some of the history of the Babylonian number system or encourage children to do their own research on it.

- Explore multiplying by 60 by multiplying by 6 and then 10 (or vice versa). Write some single-, 2- and 3-digit hour numbers on the board for children to multiply in this way to find out the equivalent number of minutes..

- Discuss when it might be necessary to convert units of time into other units in real life. Use a geared clock to support this discussion.

Let's practise: Digging deeper

Step 1

Remind children of the conversions: 1 km = 1000 m, 1 m = 100 cm. Encourage them to use place-value grids and digit cards to work out the conversions, particularly those that involve decimals.

When converting kilometres to centimetres ensure that children understand that they have to multiply first by 1000 and then another 100, which is equivalent to multiplying by 100 000.

Step 2

Children need to multiply each number by 60 to achieve the solutions. Encourage them to multiply by 6 first and then 10. They should be able to do most of these mentally with jottings in their books. Remind them to add on any extra minutes or part minutes.

Step 3

This asks children to solve a problem by converting different units of time into the same unit so that they can be compared effectively. It might be helpful to discuss which unit of time they would find easiest to compare and why, and the calculations they need to do to convert, e.g. all of the times to minutes.

Once they have done this, children work with a partner and carry out an activity of their choice. You might need to discuss options first. They time themselves carrying out the activity and then write their times down and convert these to seconds. You will need to give children stop watches to use.

Step 4

Children need to find all the possible times when a 24-hour clock displays times as consecutive numbers. Encourage them to be systematic and begin with the first hour, e.g. 1:23 and then reverse it to show 3:21.

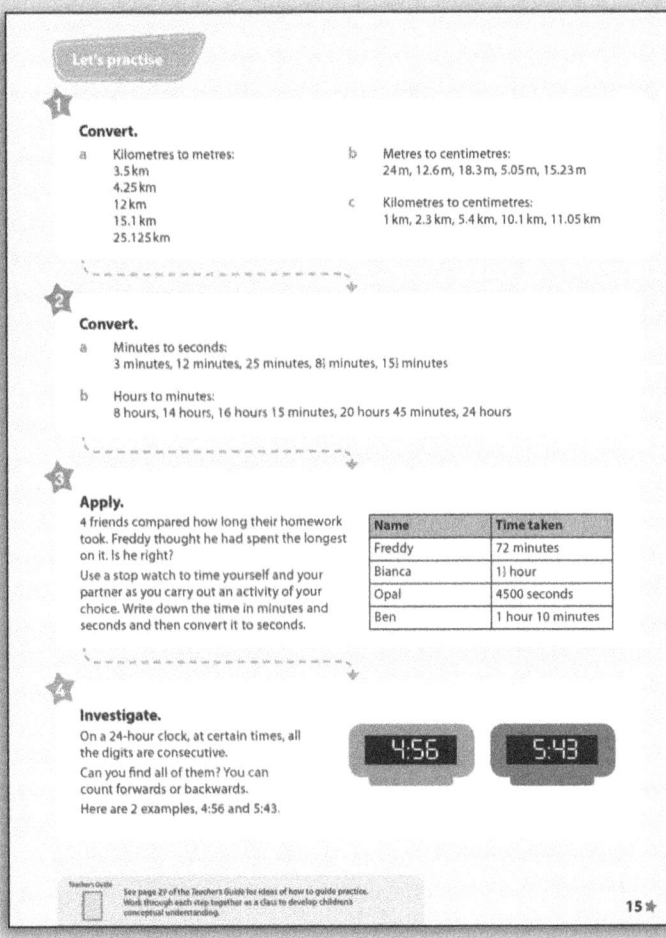

Ensuring progress

Supporting understanding

It is important that children have a good understanding of the Base 10 property of our number system. Some children may need to spend longer exploring multiplying and dividing by 10, 100 and 1000 using digit cards and place-value grids.

Time is a difficult concept for some children. It may be worth using geared clocks so that children can explore adding different numbers of minutes to different times to help them understand what happens when the minutes cross an hour.

Broadening understanding

Provide opportunities for children to multiply and divide by 10, 100 and 1000 in different contexts, e.g. money, mass and capacity.

 Concept mastered

Children can explain and demonstrate how to multiply and divide whole and decimal numbers by 10, 100 and 1000 and apply this within the context of measures.

Follow-up ideas

- Ask children to research the Babylonian number system and to work out how this relates to our system of telling the time.

- Explore converting between other units of measure, e.g. capacity and mass.

- Make up a board game which involves question cards containing time problems.

Answers

Step 1

a   3500 m, 4.25 m, 12 000 m, 15 100 km, 25 125 km

b   2400 cm, 1260 cm, 1830 cm, 505 cm, 1523 cm

c   100 000 cm, 230 000 cm, 540 000 cm, 1 010 000 cm, 1 105 000 cm

Step 2

a   180 seconds, 720 seconds, 1500 seconds, 510 seconds, 930 minutes

b   480 minutes, 840 minutes, 975 minutes, 1245 minutes, 1440 minutes

Step 3

Freddy: 72 minutes, Bianca: 90 minutes, Opal: 75 minutes, Ben: 70 minutes. Freddy is wrong, Bianca spent the longest on the homework.

Step 4

1:23, 2:34, 3:45, 4:56

3:21, 4:32, 5:43, 6:54

1c Fraction and decimal equivalences

- **Read and write decimal numbers as fractions,** e.g. $0.71 = \frac{71}{100}$.
- **Recognise and use thousandths and relate them to tenths, hundredths and decimal equivalents.**
- **Convert between different units of metric measure,** e.g. grams and kilograms.

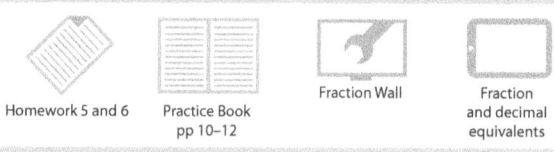

Homework 5 and 6 | Practice Book pp 10–12 | Fraction Wall | Fraction and decimal equivalents

Representations and resources

Place-value grids, digit cards, place-value (Gattegno) charts, weighing scales.

Mathematical vocabulary

Tenths, hundredths, fractions, decimal fractions, equivalent, denominator, numerator, powers

Warming up

Practice multiplying and dividing numbers by 10 and 100. Begin with multiples of 10 and 100 and then move on to other numbers that involve decimals when dividing, e.g. 235. Call out a selection of numbers and ask children to write their answers on their whiteboards to show you. Use this as an opportunity to assess their understanding of multiplying and dividing by powers of 10.

Background knowledge

It is really important that children have a good understanding of the Base 10 property of place value. This means that they understand what happens to a number when it is multiplied or divided by 10; this does not involve adding or taking away zeros! It can help children understand dividing by 100 by saying that the number is divided by 10 and 10 again. Similar statements help them understand dividing by 1000, i.e. dividing by 10, then 10 and 10 again.

Let's learn: Modelling and teaching

Writing decimal numbers as fractions

- Give each child a set of digit cards and ask them to make a whole number and then divide it by 10, using a place-value grid for support. Then ask them to divide it by 10 again, which is the same as dividing by 100. Talk about the decimal numbers and tenths and hundredths. Ask children to write some decimals on whiteboards as proper fractions. A place-value grid, such as the one in the Textbook, can help them to work out the equivalences.

- Ask children to weigh items from around the classroom. Once they have weighed them, they write down their masses as kilograms and convert any grams left to proper fractions. These may include tenths, hundredths or thousandths.

Comparing thousandths with hundredths and tenths

- Look at the place-value (Gattegno) chart in the Textbook and discuss what is happening across each row, e.g. how the numbers are increasing by 0.01, 0.1, 1, etc.

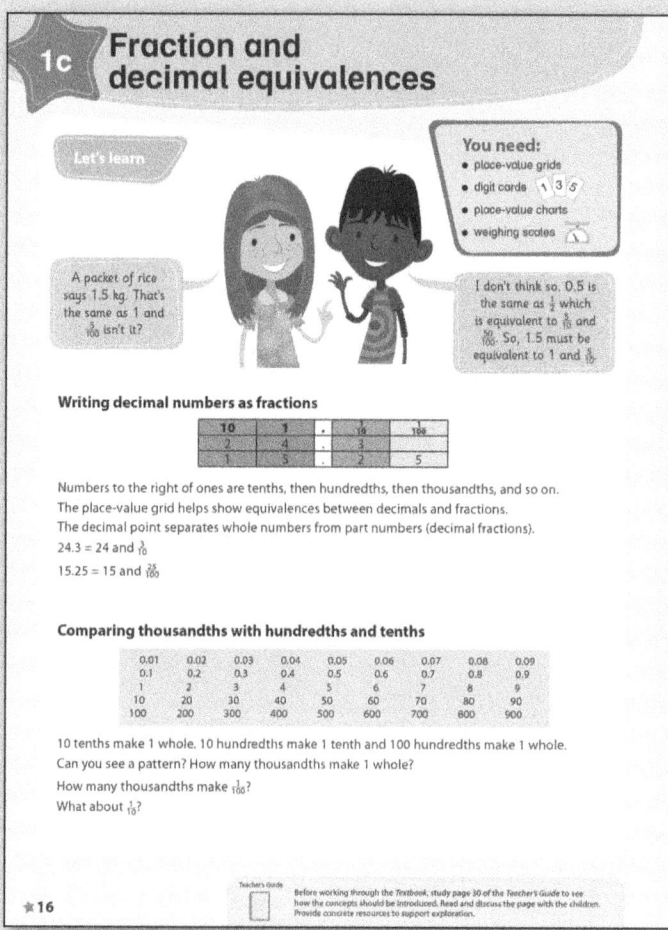

Ask children what is happening when they go vertically down a column, i.e. the number has been multiplied by 10. Next, ask them to put their fingers on a number then add some of the same type of digit, multiply by 10, 100 or 1000, add some more, then multiply or divide again. Repeat this a few times and check out where children's fingers are.

- Ask children to make a whole number with a set of digit cards. They then divide their number by 10, then 100 and 1000. Encourage them to discuss the new values of the digits in their numbers.

Let's practise: Digging deeper
Step 1

This activity encourages children to focus on tenths and hundredths as decimal numbers and convert these to fractions. It is not necessary for them to write down the whole number.

Step 2

In this activity children need to consider what they will do to the denominators and numerators to turn them into hundredths and then tenths. Encourage them to look at the 'Comparing thousandths with hundredths and tenths' paragraph in their Textbook if they need guidance. Encourage them to write an explanation of what they did to develop their reasoning skills.

Step 3

This activity brings fractions and decimals into the context of mass. Children collect 5 items from around the classroom

and find the mass of each in kilograms. Encourage them to convert the decimals to fractions.

Step 4

Children use the digits 3, 6 and 8 to make all the possible masses in kilograms to two decimal places. Use careful questioning to encourage children to work systematically to find all possible combinations of the digits. Then, they order the masses from lowest to highest. Extend this to asking children to make statements using the 'is less than' and 'is greater than' symbols.

Ensuring progress
Supporting understanding

Understanding the equivalences between fractions and decimal fractions is important. It may be that some children will need the support of place-value grids. It would be appropriate to ask them to focus on tenths until they completely understand and then move onto the hundredths.

Broadening understanding

Give children the opportunity to explain to other children what happens when changing fractions to decimals. You could ask them to make up different masses with fractions that are tenths, hundredths and thousandths and change these to decimals.

 Concept mastered

Children can explain and demonstrate how to change a decimal into a fraction and compare tenths, hundredths and thousandths.

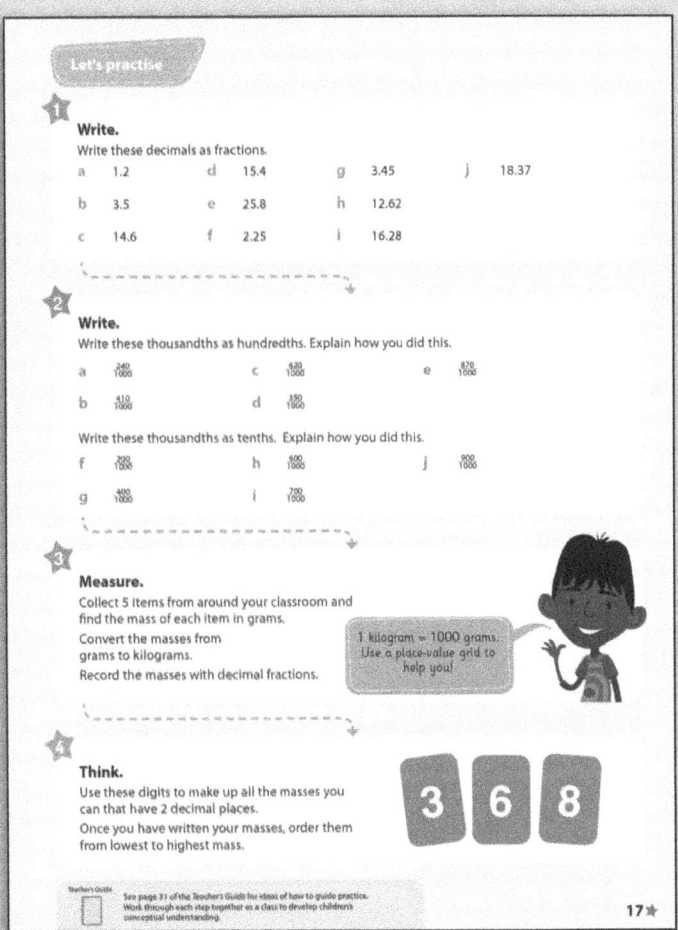

Answers

Step 1					
a	$1\frac{2}{10}$	i	$16\frac{28}{100}$	f	$\frac{2}{10}$
b	$3\frac{5}{10}$	j	$37\frac{37}{100}$	g	$\frac{4}{10}$
c	$14\frac{6}{10}$	**Step 2**		h	$\frac{6}{10}$
d	$15\frac{4}{10}$	a	$\frac{24}{100}$	i	$\frac{7}{10}$
e	$25\frac{8}{10}$	b	$\frac{41}{100}$	j	$\frac{9}{10}$
f	$2\frac{25}{100}$	c	$\frac{62}{100}$	**Step 4**	
g	$3\frac{45}{100}$	d	$\frac{35}{100}$	3.68 g/kg, 3.86 g/kg,	
h	$12\frac{62}{100}$	e	$\frac{87}{100}$	6.38 g/kg, 6.83 g/kg, 8.36 g/kg, 8.63 g/kg	

Follow-up ideas

- Give children activities that involve measuring liquid in litres, e.g. ask them to fill different containers with water, measure their capacities using measuring jugs and record. Children should record in litres with any millimetres as decimals and then fractions.

- Children could make up some distances in kilometres and metres. They then convert these to kilometres with one, two or three decimal places. They then order them from the shortest distance to the longest.

- Children could make a 'snap' card game. In small groups, they make two sets of 10 or 15 cards. One set with fractions in tenths, hundredths and thousandths. The other set with the equivalent decimal numbers. They then mix the cards and play a game according to the rules of 'snap'. Alternatively, they could make up and play a pairs game.

- Round decimals with two decimal places to the nearest whole number and to one decimal place.
- Read, write, order and compare numbers with up to three decimal places.
- Solve problems involving number up to three decimal places.

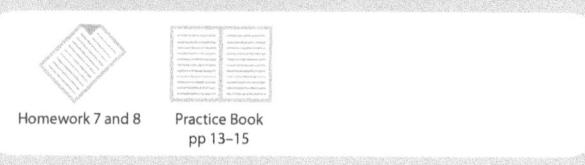

Homework 7 and 8   Practice Book pp 13–15

Representations and resources

Digit cards, differently-sized containers or bottles, measuring jugs.

Mathematical vocabulary

Decimal, decimal fraction, decimal place

Warming up

Write a selection of 4-digit numbers on the board. Give children a short time to order them from lowest to highest. Ask them to choose pairs of these numbers and to write number statements using the symbols > and <. Then ask them to round each one to the nearest ten and hundred. Repeat this for 5-digit and then 6-digit numbers.

Background knowledge

Children need to be able to round whole numbers to the nearest ten, hundred, etc. When they understand how to do this, and why, rounding decimals should be straightforward, as it is exactly the same procedure. This is also the case for ordering and comparing numbers with up to three decimal places. If children have a conceptual understanding of ordering and comparing whole numbers, decimals are simply an extension of this.

Let's learn: Modelling and teaching

Comparing and ordering decimal numbers

- Remind children of how they compared and ordered whole numbers in 1a – Distances. Let them know that ordering numbers with decimals is the same; they look at the digits from the most to the least significant. If any are the same, they look at the next digit and compare. The highest of these will give the highest number. Discuss what Amy and Theo are saying. Ask the class who they think is correct and why.

- Call out some numbers with one, two and three decimals places for children to write on their whiteboards and then order. You may wish to write three or four numbers with one decimal place on the board and ask children to order them, writing them from lowest to highest. Repeat this for two and three decimal places.

- Discuss what is meant by the symbols >, < and =. Write decimal numbers on the board, e.g. 2.5, 10.3, 12.8 and 15.3. Ask children to make number statements with the three symbols, e.g. 2.5 < 10.3, 15.3 > 10.3 and 2.5 + 10.3 = 12.8.

- You could set some problems that involve comparing capacities and volumes in litres with millilitres expressed as decimals, e.g. there was 2.6 l of juice in one jug and 2.7 l in another. Which jug held the most juice?

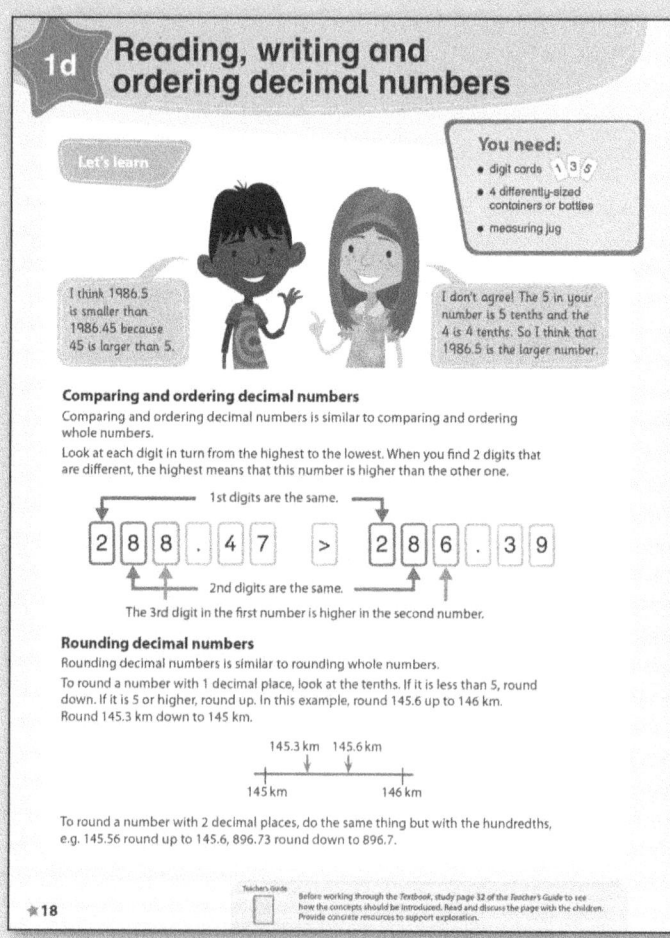

Rounding decimal numbers

- Remind children of how they rounded whole numbers in 1a – Distances. Let them know that rounding decimal numbers is the same; depending on what they are rounding to, they first look at the last digit. Any digit below five is rounded down and any digit of five or over is rounded up.

- Write some numbers on the board with one decimal place and ask children to round them to the nearest whole number. Repeat for numbers with two decimal places and ask children to round to the nearest tenth and then hundredth.

- Discuss how rounding is often used to find approximate totals. Set some problems that involve finding approximate totals of capacities and volumes.

Let's practise: Digging deeper
Step 1

The focus of this activity is comparing decimal numbers. Children do not actually have to add them. Encourage them to look carefully at the numbers. In most cases, one of each pair is the same and the other is either greater or less than in the first pair. For those that need the equals symbol, encourage children to see that the numbers can be adjusted so that each pair has the same number on each side, e.g. 14.4 +14.5 =14.2 + 14.7. They could take 0.2 from 0.4 and add it to 0.5 and then they will have 14.2 + 14.7 = 14.2 + 14.7.

Step 2

This task asks children to round tenths to the nearest whole number and then hundredths to the nearest tenth. Encourage them to look at the final digit of each number.

Step 3

Ask children to pour different amounts of water into different bottles or containers. They then measure the volumes, round them to the nearest litre and record them. They could then find out the capacities of the containers and record their findings in the same way.

Step 4

In this task, children need to work out possible volumes from the given clues. They must count in multiples of 75, so you may wish to rehearse counting in these steps before they begin.

Ensuring progress
Supporting understanding

Some children may need support when working with decimal numbers. Work with them in a guided group. Focus on tenths initially and use place value grids to secure their understanding. Ensure that they have developed a conceptual understanding of tenths before moving on to hundredths.

Broadening understanding

Provide opportunities for children to round, compare and order numbers with up to three decimal places within the contexts of mass, length (kilometres), as well as capacity and volume. Also provide opportunities for children to explain how to do this to children with less of an understanding.

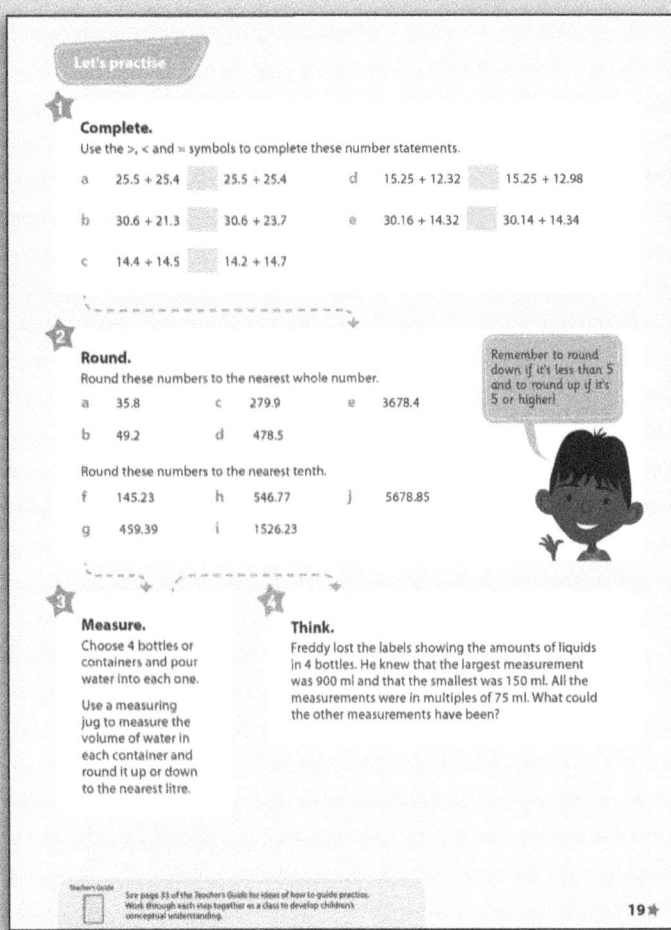

✓ Concept mastered

Children can explain and demonstrate how to read, write, order and round numbers with up to one decimal place.

Answers
Step 1

a   25.5 + 25.4 > 25.5 + 25.1

b   30.6 + 21.3 < 30.6 +23.7

c   14.4 + 14.5 = 14.2 + 14.7

d   15.25 + 12.32 < 15.25 + 12.98

e   30.16 + 14.32 = 30.14 + 14.34

Step 2

a	36	f	145.2
b	49	g	459.4
c	280	h	546.8
d	479	i	1526.2
e	3678	j	5678.9

Step 4

150 ml, 900 ml and any two of 225 ml, 300 ml, 375 ml, 450 ml, 525 ml, 600 ml, 675 ml, 750 ml, 825 ml

Follow-up ideas

- Ask children to look in catalogues and to find items with prices that involve pounds and pence. They make a list of them and order them from most to least expensive. They then round all the prices to the nearest pound.

- Give children the opportunity to weigh different items in the classroom and round their masses to the nearest kilogram.

- Children could make some cards with different decimal numbers on them. They take it in turns to pick a card and round it to the nearest whole number. They could then order all the numbers from smallest to greatest and vice versa.

Gridlock!

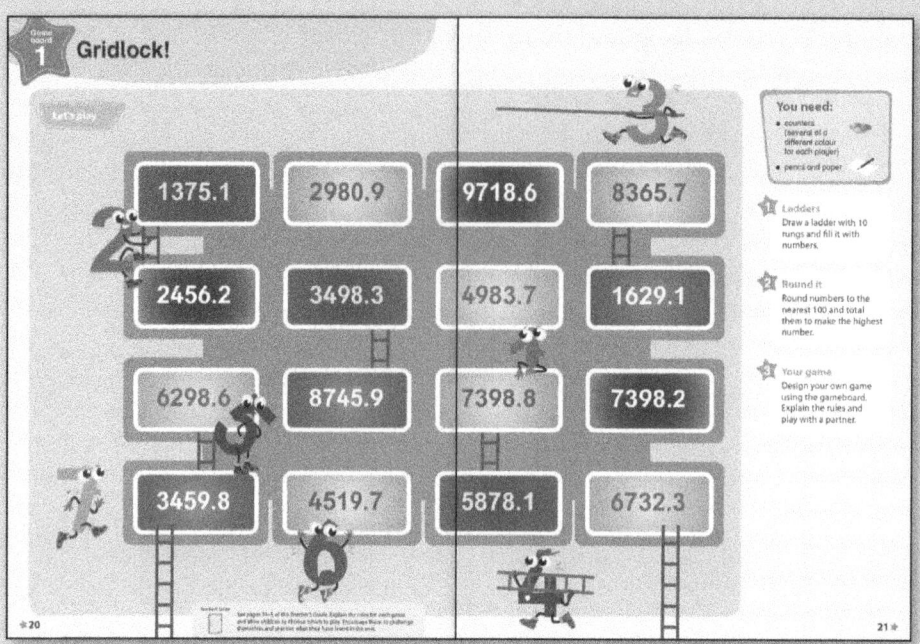

Game 1: Ladders

This game enables children to rehearse their place-value recognition. They will need to compare carefully the digits in the thousands, hundreds, tens, ones and tenths columns in order to make sure that each number they choose is greater than the one they chose before.

Maths focus

- Order decimal fractions

Resources

Counters (several of a different colour for each player), pencil and paper.

How to play

This game is best played in pairs, but small groups could also work. Children draw a ladder with 10 rungs. They then take it in turns to pick a number on the game board. As they do, they cover it with a counter. Numbers can only be used once. They write their number on a rung of their ladder. The idea is that the numbers go in ascending order. They keep doing this until their ladder is full. They need to consider carefully which numbers to pick and where to place them in order to complete the ladder.

Making it easier

Children draw a ladder with five rungs to complete.

Making it harder

Turn this into a game of strategy, where children have to stop the other players from completing their ladders, or children could start at the top of their ladders and play in descending order.

Game 2: Round it

This game gives children the opportunity to rehearse rounding to the nearest 100, paying careful attention to rounding decimal fractions up and down. They will also be able to practise adding 4-digit numbers.

Maths focus

- Round decimal numbers

Resources

Counters (several of a different colour for each player), pencil and paper.

How to play

This game can be played in pairs or small groups. Children take it in turns to pick a number and cover it with a counter. Numbers can only be used once. When they pick their number they round it to the nearest 100 and write it down. When all the numbers have been used, children total theirs. The winner is the player with the highest total.

Making it easier

Children could round to the nearest thousand. This will make the addition part simpler. Encourage children to look for thousands that total 10 when they add.

Making it harder

Children could round to the nearest whole number. This will increase the difficulty level of finding the total.

Game 3: Your game

Children should invent their own game, designing rules that use the concepts covered in the unit.

Challenge children to make their game easier or harder.

Gridlock!

Choose a game to play.

Game 1: Ladders

How to play

- Draw a ladder with 10 rungs.
- Take it in turns to pick a number from the grid.
- Cover that number with a counter (numbers cannot be used twice).
- Write your number on your ladder.
- Keep going until you have filled your ladder.
- The numbers must be in ascending order.
- The first player to fill their ladder is the winner.

You need

- counters (several of a different colour for each player)
- pencil and paper

Game 2: Round it

How to play

- Pick a number from the grid.
- Cover that number with a counter (numbers cannot be used twice).
- Round that number to the nearest 100 and write it down.
- Keep doing this until all the numbers have been used.
- Next find the total of your rounded numbers.
- The player with the highest total is the winner.

You need

- counters (several of a different colour for each player)
- pencil and paper

Game 3: Your game

- Make up your own game using the one word
- You could round numbers to the nearest 10.
- You could write numbers in a ladder in descending order.
- What are the rules for your game? Explain them to someone.

Please help your child by reading the instructions and playing the game together.

Assessment task 1

Resources

Digit cards, place-value grids (optional).

Running the task

Listen to groups of children discuss the statement and explain to each other why it is wrong. Encourage them to round each digit from the least significant digit to the thousands and assess their ability to do this.

Evidencing mastery

If children are able to do this easily and explain what they are doing, you can be assured that they have a conceptual understanding of rounding.

Assessment task 2

Resources

Digit cards, place-value cards.

Running the task

Children need to take pairs of numbers and make up number statements using the symbols '>', '<' and '='. They will also need '+' and '–' symbols to use.

Evidencing mastery

All children should be able to make up number statements using '>' and '<'. The statements for '=' are slightly more challenging, because children need to find two of the numbers to add or subtract to total a third, e.g. 22.7 – 7.6 = 15.1. Most children should be able to do this using mental calculation, and some children will be able to make up more complex statements, with two numbers on each side, e.g. 13.5 + 8.4 > 15.1 – 7.6.

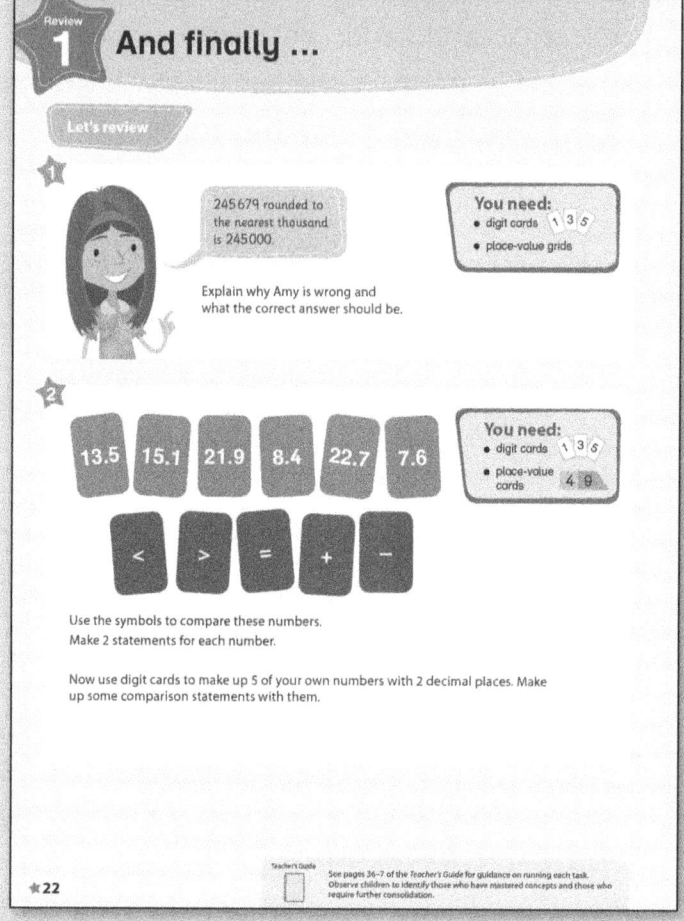

Concepts mastered

- ☑ Children can explain and demonstrate the positional, multiplicative and additive aspects of place value and explain and demonstrate how to round numbers to the nearest 10, 100, 1000, 10 000and 100 000.

- ☑ Children can explain and demonstrate how to multiply and divide whole and decimal numbers by 10, 100 and 1000 and apply this within the context of measures.

- ☑ Children can explain and demonstrate how to change a decimal into a fraction and compare tenths, hundredths and thousandths.

- ☑ Children can explain and demonstrate how to read, write, order and round numbers with up to one decimal place.

Assessment task 3

Resources

Place-value grids (optional).

Running the task

Encourage children to find as many similarities as possible, e.g. both are 5-digit numbers, both have two decimals places, they are both even, both have 4 in the tens position and 6 in the hundredths. Also, encourage them to find as many differences, e.g. the tenths digits are different. You could ask them to tell you the difference between the digits that are in the hundreds, ones and tenths positions.

Evidencing mastery

Some children may need support in doing this but most should be able to carry this activity out independently. If children can confidently carry out this task, they will have mastered this area of mathematics.

Did you know?

In some countries the decimal point is known as the separator which separates integers from part numbers. Sometimes the decimal point is a dot on the line or in the middle and in some countries it is a comma. The Babylonians had a Base 60 number system which was used in Europe up until the 1500s. Over time the Base 10 system which we use today became increasingly popular. The decimal point came into use by most people in England in 1619. It is interesting to note that some use of decimal fractions was made in ancient China, medieval Arabia and in Renaissance Europe. By about 1500, decimals were well accepted by professional mathematicians but not widely used.

To convert our numbers into Base 60, children would need to consider a place-value grid with the headings 360, 60 and 1. So 60 would be 10 and 360 would be 100.

Methods for addition and subtraction

Mathematical focus

★ **Number: addition and subtraction**

★ **Measurement: length, money**

Prior learning

Children should already be able to:

- add and subtract numbers with up to four digits using the formal written methods of columnar addition and subtraction where appropriate

- estimate and use inverse operations to check answers a calculation

- solve addition and subtraction two-step problems in contexts, deciding which operations and methods to use and why.

Key new learning

- Add and subtract numbers mentally with increasingly large numbers.

- Add and subtract whole numbers with four digits, including using formal written methods (columnar addition and subtraction).

- Use rounding to check answers to calculations and determine, in the context of a problem, levels of accuracy.

- Solve addition and subtraction multi-step problems in contexts, deciding which operations and methods to use and why.

Making connections

- It is straightforward to make use of addition and subtraction in a variety of other subjects, such as science. Make sure that you have a consistent whole-school approach to these calculation strategies.

- Throughout the unit, give children problems involving addition and subtraction in real-life contexts. By using familiar contexts you can show the relevance of mathematics.

- There are opportunities to use addition and subtraction to solve problems involving measure, such as mass, volume and money. This links to another area of number - decimal notation.

 Talk about

Discuss with children the importance of learning and using mental calculation strategies. Emphasise that these are often more efficient than written methods.

Engaging and exploring

For the picture with the wallpaper, you could:

- Ask children to talk to a partner about how they could add these amounts to find the total. Agree that they could use a written method but that it would be more efficient to round each number to the nearest pound, add these 2-digit numbers and then adjust by subtracting 4p.

- Tell children that the average length of a roll of wallpaper is 10.05 m and its width is 52 cm. Ask them to convert these measurements to centimetres and metres respectively. Give them some wall sizes, for e.g. a height of 2.29 m and width of 2.9 m.

For the picture of the wormery and worms you could:

- Ask children to discuss ways they could find the difference between the longest and shortest worms. Agree that,

because the lengths are close, counting on from the shortest to the longest, first in millimetres and then centimetres, would be an efficient strategy. Ask them to find differences between all the pairs of worms. How many can they find?

- Find totals of pairs of lengths. Practise the mental calculation strategy of finding pairs that make one, ten and one hundred.

- Rehearse other important strategies, such as, rounding and adjusting and sequencing.

- Give children some modelling material. Time them for 30 seconds as they roll their piece into the longest worm they can. Working in a group of four they can lay their worms on the table in order from shortest to longest. They then estimate the length of the shortest worm and measure to the nearest millimetre to check. They use this to estimate the length of the second worm, then measure it. They can do this for all the worms. They then find the difference between pairs of worms using a counting-on strategy. Following this they can find the total length of all the worms using a mental calculation strategy of their choice.

For the picture of the restaurant bill you could:

- Ask children to order the prices from least to most expensive.

- Ask them to take pairs of costs and work through how to use the short written method for addition. Give children pound and ten pence coins so that they can use real-life resources to show this method.

  It is important that children use the money as manipulatives. They add the five and six ten pence coins first, exchange ten of them for a pound. They write 1 in the ten pence position and 1 under the pounds. They repeat this process for the rest of the calculation. Observe them to assess their understanding.

For the picture of the petrol prices you could:

- Discuss with children the prices they can see. What do children think they are? Establish that they are petrol prices. Ask them what is strange about these prices. Agree that there are no pounds signs.

- Discuss how children could find the difference between the price of the diesel and unleaded petrol. Agree that the most efficient way would be to count on from the lowest amount to the highest. They can find this difference and work through other examples that you give them.

- Ask children to consider how they would add the amounts together. Take suggestions for the methods they might use. Agree that sequencing and the short written method would both be efficient. Ask them to add using sequencing and then check using the written method. Repeat this for other numbers with one decimal place.

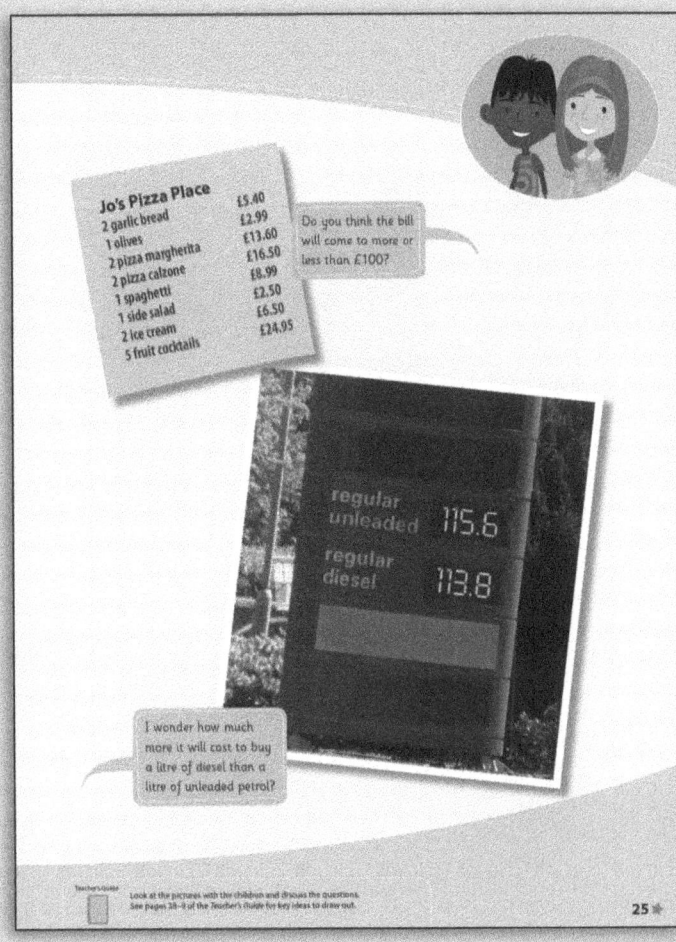

Things to think about

How will you:

- Organise groupings? Evidence suggests that mixed attainment groups are an effective way of raising the achievement of the lower attainers. It also helps higher attainers to consolidate their understanding when, e.g. they explain a particular concept to the rest of the group. Mixed attainment pairs are also effective.

- Use manipulatives to help develop conceptual understanding?

- Draw out reasoning? To do this ensure that you regularly ask children to explain their methods and talk about what they have done, how they have done it and why their particular method works.

Checking understanding

By the end of this unit children should be able to solve addition and subtraction problems in different contexts, appropriately choosing and using number facts, understanding place value and mental and written methods. They should be able to explain their decision-making and justify their solutions.

- Add and subtract numbers mentally with increasingly large numbers.
- Use rounding to check answers to calculations and determine, in the context of a problem, levels of accuracy.
- Solve addition and subtraction multi-step problems in contexts, deciding which operations and methods to use and why.

Homework 9 and 10   Practice Book pp 16–18   Numerals & Symbols

Representations and resources

Pendulum (three interlocking cubes on a piece of string or similar), sets of digit cards, number lines, money.

Mathematical vocabulary

Pounds, pence, kilometres, add, subtract, difference, partitioning, counting on, sequencing, rounding and adjusting, doubles, near doubles, number pairs to 100

Warming up

Swing the pendulum from side to side. As it swings one way call out a number and as it swings the other way children call out the number that goes with it to make 10. Repeat for pairs of numbers to 100, beginning with multiples of ten and five, then all numbers.

Background knowledge

It is very important that children frequently practise and develop their ability to use mental calculation strategies. Often, when children are taught written methods, these become the only methods that they use for calculations whether they are appropriate or not.

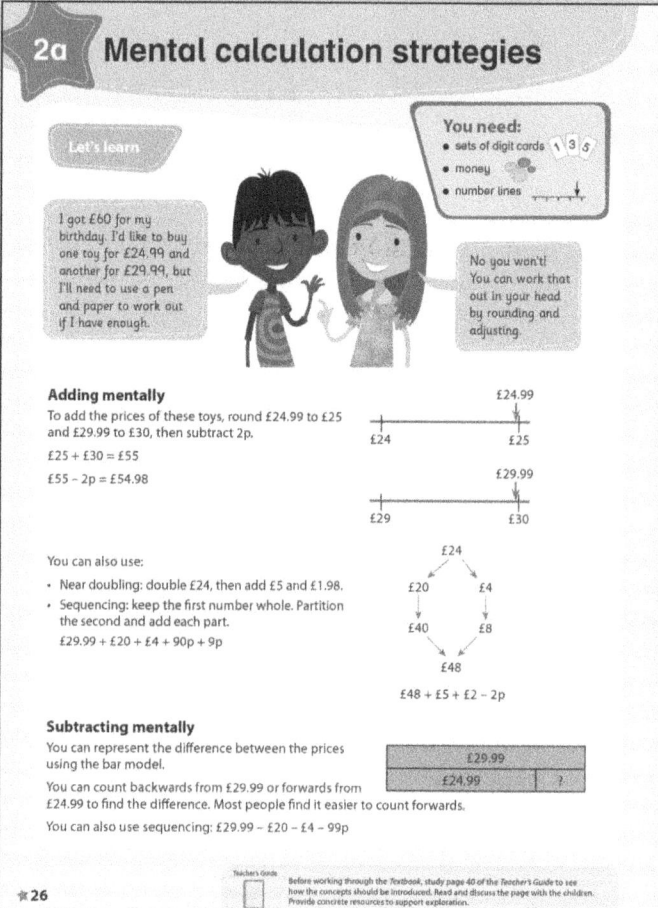

Let's learn: Modelling and teaching

- Over a period of three or four days, focus on each mental calculation strategy in the Textbook. Practise these with numbers, then move on to practise them within the context of measures (using coins as manipulatives where appropriate) and finally give children investigations and problem-solving tasks.

Adding mentally

- Discuss with children how Theo could make the addition in 'his head'. Use the example in the Textbook to model rounding and adjusting, e.g. £24.99 + £29.99. £24.99 rounds up to £25, £29.99 rounds up to £30, £25 + £30 = £55. Adjust, so £55 – 2p = £54.98. Plot the two prices on to a number line to show that they need rounding up.

- Use the bar model to represent these problems.

- Ask children to use digit cards and make 4- and 5-digit numbers. They can then add 199 to each of them using the rounding and adjusting strategy. Encourage them to draw the bar model to record their solutions.

- Give children some calculations to answer using the sequencing strategy where the first number is kept whole and the second is partitioned.

Subtracting mentally

- Some of the mental calculation strategies for addition can be used for subtraction. Practise rounding and adjusting for calculations such as 2345 – 1998 and sequencing for calculations such as 3875 – 2341.

- Ask children how they would find the difference in price between the two toys. Demonstrate, as shown in the Textbook, how to use the bar model. You could also demonstrate counting on along a number line or using sequencing.

Let's practise: Digging deeper

Step 1

For the first four questions children need to add the numbers using the rounding and adjusting strategy. They can use paper or whiteboards to make jottings as they work through the questions.

For the next four, they need to find differences between the numbers by counting on. Encourage them to do this using the bar model and check their answers using a number line.

Step 2

Children practise using the sequencing strategy to answer these addition and subtraction calculations which are in the context of measures. Again, allow children to make jottings to help them as necessary. You could remind them about the fact that in the UK miles are used to measure distance and inform

them that there are approximately 0.6 miles in a kilometre.

Step 3

This activity asks children to find totals and differences between the prices on the labels. Encourage them to pair up the amounts in all possible ways and to do this systematically, e.g. pick one price and find totals and differences with this and then other amounts. Provide money in form of notes and coins for the last part of the activity.

Step 4

Children need to work out possible questions to the answer of £75. Whatever questions they ask, they need to ensure that they can be answered using a mental calculation strategy. Give them the opportunity to explain their questions and the desired mental calculation strategy to a partner, small group or the class.

Ensuring progress

Supporting understanding

It is important that all children understand that mental calculation strategies can be more efficient than written methods. It may be necessary for some children to work on 2- and 3-digit numbers initially to rehearse strategies of rounding and adjusting and sequencing. They may benefit from using a 100 square and practise adding and subtracting 2-digit numbers that end with 1, 2, 8 and 9.

Broadening understanding

Provide opportunities for children to add and subtract using mental calculation strategies in different contexts, e.g. time, length, mass, volume and capacity. Give a mix of familiar and unfamiliar contexts, and observe how confidently children can apply their understanding to an unknown context.

✓ Concept mastered

You will know children have mastered this concept when they can make the decision to use a mental method to find the difference and totals because it is the most efficient method to use to answer the calculation.

Follow-up ideas

- You could ask children to look at toy catalogues on the Internet. They choose pairs of toys to find the total price and difference using a mental calculation strategy.

- Children could use take-away menus to plan a meal. They could choose four options and find the total cost using a mental calculation strategy. They could work within a budget and, using the counting-on strategy, find out how much of their budget is left.

- Children could make a board game that involves answering questions on cards. These questions should contain calculations that can be answered using a mental calculation strategy.

Answers

Step 1		Step 2	
a	3966	a	5579 km
b	8897	b	6699 km
c	14651	c	35 980 km
d	46 598	d	4454 km
e	216	e	4421 km
f	1317	f	12 431 km
g	66	**Step 3**	
h	252	Responses will vary.	

Step 4

Open-ended task.

- Add and subtract whole numbers with four digits, including using written methods (columnar addition and subtraction).
- Solve addition and subtraction multi-step problems in contexts, deciding which operations and methods to use and why.

Homework 11 and 12   Practice Book pp 19–21   Numerals & Symbols

Representations and resources

Counting stick, digit cards, place-value counters or coloured counters that children assign their own values to, Base 10 apparatus, dice.

Mathematical vocabulary

Subtraction, addition, tenth, hundredth, pounds, pence

Warming up

Show children the counting stick. Tell them that zero is at one end and 100 at the other. Ask children to tell you what steps they would count in to get from one end to the other. Agree steps of ten. Together, count from zero to 100 and back. Repeat this but jump around the counting stick. Next, say that zero is at one end and ten at the other. What are the step sizes this time? Next say that zero is at one end and one is at the other. What is the step size? Agree 0.1. Practise counting in steps of 0.1 as before. Do this again with one end being zero and the other 0.1. Discuss the pattern that is arising. Establish that each time they are counting in steps ten times smaller than previously.

Background knowledge

It is important that all children are taught written methods for the addition and subtraction of whole numbers and decimals. This should be in a way that helps them to develop their conceptual understanding and procedural fluency. It is important that when being introduced to the new elements of these methods, such as the addition of numbers with three decimal places, they use manipulatives such as Base 10 apparatus or place-value counters. When using Base 10 apparatus, change their value: the small cubes can represent thousandths, the ten sticks, hundredths, the 100 flats, tenths and the thousands cubes, ones.

Let's learn: Modelling and teaching
Written method for addition

- Write this calculation on the board: 256.9 + 167.8. Explain that when a mental calculation strategy can't be used efficiently to add numbers together, the written method should be used. Ask children to make the two numbers using counters. They assign values to different colours. Once they have made the numbers you set the calculation out vertically on the board and, as they work, model each step of the calculation. Children add the tenths to make 17 tenths. They exchange 10 of them for a one. You write the 7 in the tenths position and 1 in the ones, and so on.

- Give children more 3-digit numbers with one decimal place to practise adding together. After doing it practically, they can show how it will look as a written method.

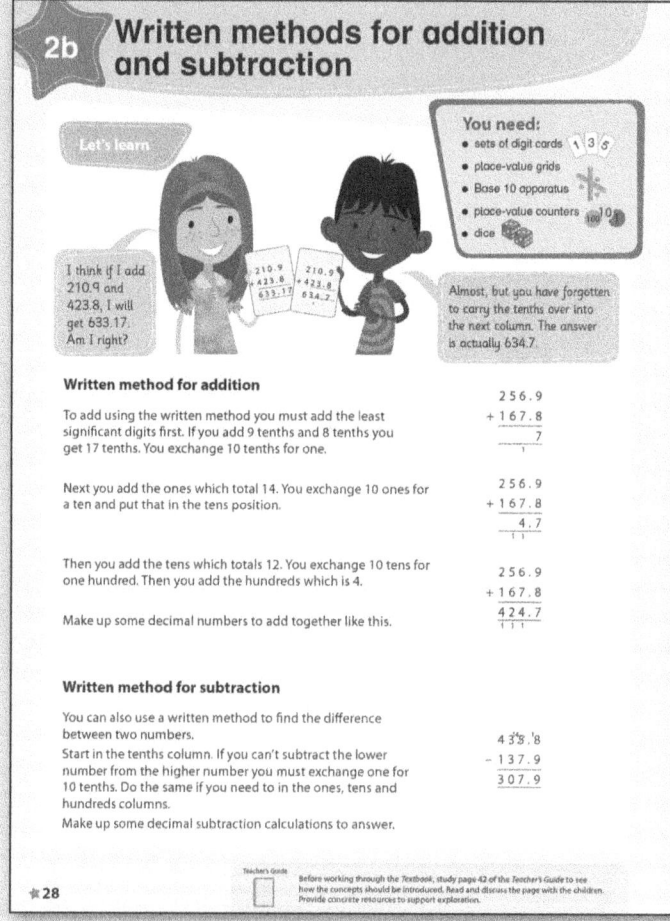

- Give children digit cards to create their own decimal numbers to add using the written method.

- **Written method for subtraction**

- Ask children to make 4345.8 using place-value or coloured counters. They don't need to make the lower number as this is the one to be taken away. As they work through the calculation model the written method on the board. Children need to take 9 tenths away from 8 tenths. This is not possible, so a one must be exchanged for tenths. Children exchange one counter for ten tenths and you cross out the ones and put a 4 then 1 beside the 8. There are now 18 tenths and 9 tenths can be taken away. Children do this and you write the answer to the tenths column in the appropriate place. This is repeated for the ones. Finally the tens and hundreds columns can be completed.

Let's practise: Digging deeper

Step 1

This step is basic practice without decimals. Children need to set these calculations out so that they can answer them using the formal written method they have discussed. Encourage them to round the numbers to get an approximate answer to check their work. Allow children to use counters to which they assign their own values if they wish. They can then model each calculation first.

Step 2

These problems involve both addition and subtraction within the context of money. With these problems, children are starting to use decimals. Again, children can use counters if they are helpful to them. They should also use rounding for an approximate answer as a check.

Step 3

These questions require children to find the missing numbers. Some of them might need several attempts, using a trial and error method. It would be a good idea to let them practise on paper. Other children will be able to use their understanding of the written methods to solve these.

Step 4

Children draw a 3 × 2 grid on paper or in their books. They throw a dice six times. They put the digits in the grid and make an addition. Their aim is to get a total as close to 1000 as they can. They need to reason about where to place the digits as they work through this problem.

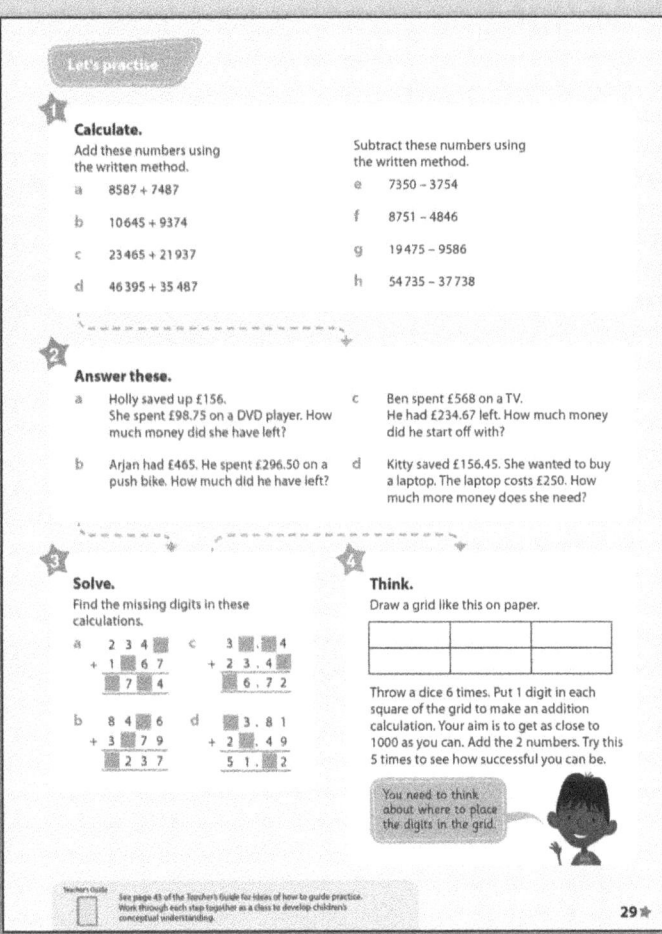

Ensuring progress

Supporting understanding

It is important that all children develop a conceptual understanding of the written methods and don't simply learn rules. Some children might need to use manipulatives for longer than other children. If this is the case they should use place-value counters or similar for as long as is necessary.

Broadening understanding

You could provide opportunities for children to make up and solve word problems and missing number problems within different contexts such as length, mass, capacity and volume.

 Concept mastered

You will know children have mastered this concept when they can make the decision to use a written method to find differences and totals because it is the most efficient method to use to answer the calculation.

Follow-up ideas

- Children could make a board game with cards that have calculations to answer using written methods. They could also make cards that are word problems.

- You could try asking children to measure the length of different items in the classroom using centimetres and millimetres. They can find out the differences between the lengths and also the totals.

- Children could measure masses of objects in the classroom using kilograms and grams. Again, they find totals and differences.

Answers

Step 1

a   16074

b   20019

c   45402

d   81882

e   3596

f   3905

g   9889

h   16997

Step 2

a   £57.25

b   £168.50

c   £802.67

d   £93.55

Step 3

a
```
   2 3 4 7
 + 1 3 6 7
   3 7 1 4
```

b
```
   8 4 1 6
 - 3 1 7 9
   5 2 3 7
```

c
```
   3 3.2 4
 + 2 3.4 8
   5 6.7 2
```

d
```
   7 3.8 1
 - 2 2.4 9
   5 1.3 2
```

Step 4

Open-ended task.

Follow the instructions!

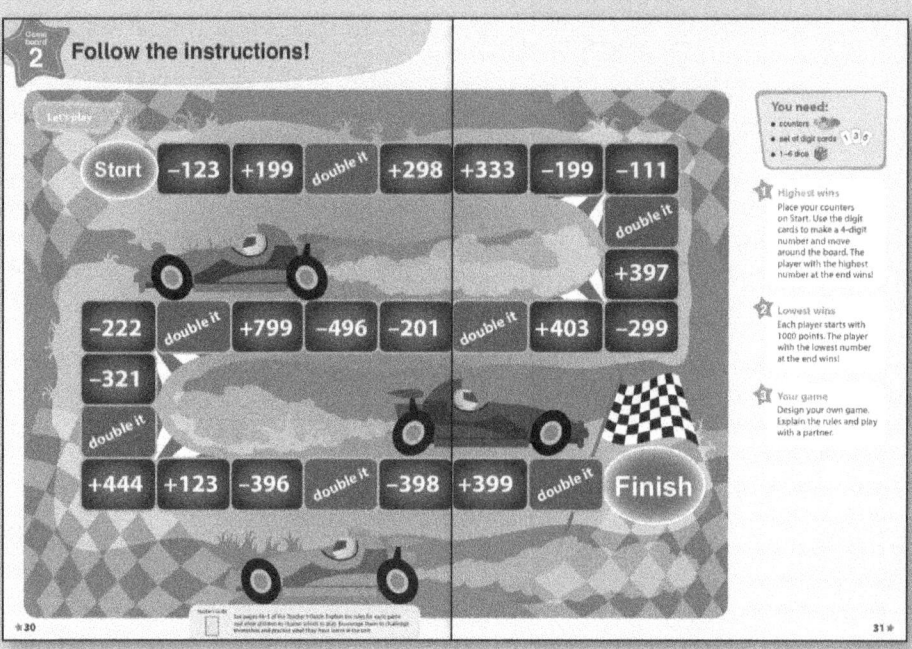

Game 1: Highest wins

In this game children have to select appropriate mental calculation strategies to complete calculations as they move around the board.

Maths focus

- Mental calculation strategies for addition and subtraction

Resources

1 counter per player, digit cards.

How to play

Children place their counters on Start. They take it in turns to pick four digit cards and make a 4-digit number. They then take it in turns to move around the board. On each place they must do what it says to their number, however, they must use a mental calculation strategy, e.g. if they make 3567 as their starting number, they will need to firstly take away 123 when they move to the first place. They could use sequencing for this. When they move to the next place they then add 199 to their answer. This time they could use rounding and adjusting. They keep doing this until they get to Finish. The player with the highest number at the end is the winner.

Making it easier

Children could throw a dice to determine how many places they move around the board for each go. They will therefore carry out fewer calculations.

Making it harder

Children could answer each calculation using two different mental calculation strategies, one as a check.

Game 2: Lowest wins

In this game children start with 1000 points and move around the board, completing calculations using appropriate mental addition or subtraction strategies.

Maths focus

- Mental calculation strategies for addition and subtraction

Resources

1 counter per player, 1–6 dice (1).

How to play

Each player starts with 1000 points. They take it in turns to throw the dice and move that number of places on the gameboard. They do what it says on the place they land to 1000, using a mental calculation strategy. On their next throw, they do what it says to the answer they got before. They must keep going until everyone has finished. The player with the lowest number at the end is the winner.

Making it easier

Children could be given a starting number of 500 points.

Making it harder

Children could be given a more complicated starting number of points, such as 9999.

Game 3: Your game

Children should invent their own game, designing rules that use the concepts covered in the unit.

Challenge children to make their game easier or harder.

Follow the instructions!

Choose a game to play.

Game 1: Highest wins

How to play

- Place your counters on Start.
- Pick 4 digit cards and make a 4-digit number.
- Take it in turns to move around the board, landing on every place. Do what it says to your number, using a mental calculation, e.g. if you make 3567, you first need to take away 123 (you could use sequencing for this). On the next place you add 199 to your answer (you could use rounding and adjusting).
- The player with the highest number at the end is the winner!

You need:

- 1 counter per player (1 colour per player)
- set of 0–9 digit cards

Game 2: Lowest wins

How to play

- Each player starts with 1000 points.
- Take it in turns to throw the dice and move that number of places. Do what it says on the place to 1000 using a mental calculation. On your next throw, do what it says to the answer you got before.
- Keep going until everyone has finished.
- The player with the lowest number at the end is the winner!

You need:

- 1 counter per player (1 colour per player)
- 1–6 dice

Game 3: Your game

- Make up your own game using the gameboard.
- Will you use the dice, counters and digit cards?
- Will the winner of your game have a high or a low score?
- What are the rules for your game? Explain them to someone.

Please help your child by reading the instructions and playing the game together.

Assessment task 1

Running the task

Listen to groups of children discuss the statement and explain to each other why it is correct. Encourage them to consider all the different strategies that would be efficient to use to find the difference between two numbers.

Expect them to be able to talk about:

- sequencing (2465 – 1832 = 2465 – 1000 – 800 – 30 – 2)

- rounding and adjusting (2354 – 1998 = 2354 – 2000 + 2)

- counting on (7465 – 3982: + 18 + 3000 + 465, which makes a difference of 3483).

You could ask them why these methods are more efficient than the formal written method. Establish that they can be carried out more efficiently and accurately than a written method. Agree that sometimes children will need to make brief jottings or draw a number line so that they don't lose track of what they are doing, which is a good strategy.

Agree that Amy is correct, she can use a mental calculation for 5876 – 4999. One she might use for these numbers is rounding and adjusting: 5876 – 5000 + 1. She could also use counting on from 4999 which gives an answer of 877.

Evidencing mastery

If children are able to do this easily and can explain and demonstrate what they are doing, you can be assured that they have a good understanding of mental calculation strategies and when to use them. They are flexible thinkers.

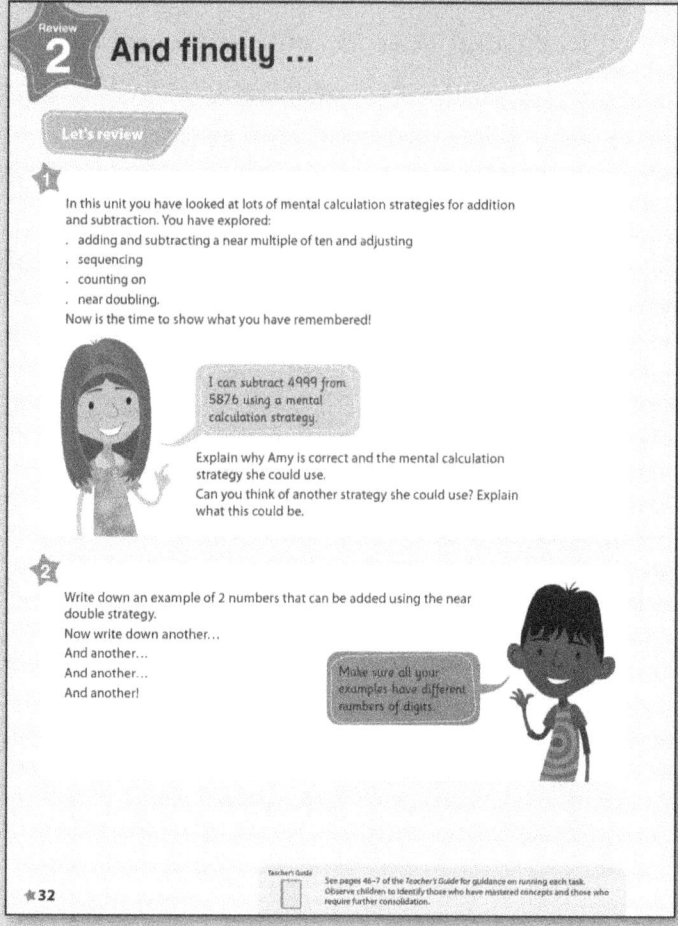

Assessment task 2

Running the task

Before children work on this task, ask them what is meant by the near doubling strategy. Agree that it is when two numbers are close together. One of them can be doubled and then adjusted. Ask them to give you some examples of these and write them on the board, e.g. 35 + 36, 121 + 120, 3600 + 3700. For each, discuss how both numbers can be doubled and for each what they need to do to adjust:

- For 35 + 36, they could double 35 and add one or double 36 and subtract one. Each time the answer will be 71.

- For 121 + 120, they could double 121 and subtract one or double 120 and add one. Each time the answer will be 241.

- For 3600 + 3700, they could use their knowledge that double 36 is 72, so double 3600 is 7200. They then add 100 to this. They could use their knowledge that double 37 is 74 so double 3700 is 7400. They then subtract 100. Each time the answer will be 7300.

For the task, children need to think of two numbers that can be added using near doubles. Once they have found one they can think of others, each time increasing the number of digits by one, e.g. 25 + 26, 154 + 152, 2234 + 2236.

Evidencing mastery

All children should be able to make up some near doubles statements. If they show fluency in doing this it is evidence of mastery.

Concepts mastered

☑ Children can make the decision to use a mental method to find the difference and totals because it is the most efficient method to use to answer the calculation.

☑ Children can make the decision to use a written method to find differences and totals because it is the most efficient method to use to answer the calculation.

Assessment task 3

Resources

Place-value counters or similar.

Running the task

The task asks children to answer an addition and a subtraction calculation in four different ways. Before they begin the task, write some 3- and 4-digit examples on the board, so that they can practise. For their strategies they should consider: sequencing, rounding and adjusting, near doubles and the written method. If they have other strategies that they can think of they should demonstrate these. Once they have practised these, they can work on the task.

Let them use visual representations such as drawing number lines if they wish and also to use manipulatives such as place-value counters or coloured counters that they assign their own values to. It would be worth asking them to explain how they are using their visual representations and manipulatives as this will give you an assessment opportunity that will show how deep their understanding is.

They should also demonstrate that they can perform the written method, so this must be one of their methods. Encourage them to discuss with you or a partner which they think is the most efficient method and why. Stress that for these examples, the written method certainly isn't the most efficient, for example:

- For 2387 + 1996, the most efficient mental calculation strategy would be rounding and adjusting. They would round 1996 to 2000, add to 2387 and then subtract 4 because in rounding up they added 4 too many. The answer is 4383.

- For 5245 − 4999, the most efficient mental calculation strategy would be either rounding and adjusting or counting on. For rounding, they round 4999 to 5000, take that away and because they have taken away 1 too many, they add 1. For counting on they add 1 to 4999 to give 5000 and then add 245.

Evidencing mastery

If children can confidently demonstrate a variety of methods for adding and subtracting the numbers using mental calculation strategies and the written method, they will be showing mastery.

Did you know?

The 'Did you know' section in the Textbook explains the basics of what an algorithm actually is – a set of rules to follow to get to the end of a procedure, which could be something really simple like getting dressed or making a cup of coffee. Rules are really important in many aspects of life. In primary mathematics an algorithm usually refers to a set of rules involved in finding the answer to a calculation that can't be answered using a mental calculation strategy. We often call these formal written methods.

Methods for multiplication and division

Mathematical focus

★ **Number: multiplication and division**

★ **Measurement: length, volume, capacity**

Prior learning

Children should already be able to:

- recall multiplication and division facts for multiplication tables up to 12×12
- use place value, known and derived facts to multiply and divide mentally
- multiply 2- and 3-digit numbers by a single-digit number using a formal written layout.

Key new learning

- Identify multiples and factors, including finding all factor pairs of a number, and common factors of two numbers.
- Solve problems involving multiplication and division including using their knowledge of factors and multiples, squares and cubes.
- Solve problems involving addition, subtraction, multiplication and division and a combination of these, including understanding the meaning of the equals sign.
- Multiply and divide numbers mentally drawing upon known facts.
- Multiply numbers with up to four digits by a single- or 2-digit number using a formal written method, including long multiplication for 2-digit numbers.
- Divide numbers with up to four digits by a single-digit number using the formal written method of short division and interpret remainders appropriately for the context.

Making connections

- There are opportunities to make connections with geometry when children explore square and cube numbers.
- Children can use calculations to solve problems involving length, volume and capacity using decimal notation.

Unit 3 Methods for multiplication and division

How can I find out how many cups there are without counting every one?

60p per 250 ml

I wonder how much juice was in the jug?

★34

 Talk about

Refresh the vocabulary that children will need to use during this unit. Ask them to tell each other what the words multiplicand, multiplier, product, dividend, divisor and quotient mean. Encourage them to say statements such as: Multiplicand multiplied by multiplier equals product. Repeat this for other relevant words such as factor, commutative and square number.

Engaging and exploring

You could ask children to look at each picture and the question that goes with it and discuss with a partner.

For the picture with the cups, you could discuss what the arrangement of cups is similar to. Establish that it is an array. Provide pairs with counters and ask children to make different arrays and to describe these using a written multiplication and division statement.

Ask children to estimate how many cups there are in the photograph. Discuss why it is impossible to give an exact amount. Give them different numbers of rows and columns. Ask them to make arrays of these using counters and then to work out how many there are and heights to multiply together, e.g. a row of 12 and 5 rows. You could then give them a height, e.g. 6. Ask them how they could find out how many cups there would be altogether.

For the picture of the jug and glasses you could give children containers, measuring jugs and water. Ask them to estimate 250 ml into a container, measure it and compare their estimates with the actual amounts.

Discuss capacity and volume. Do children know the difference? What are they looking at in the picture? Establish that this is the volume. The capacity would be the amount that the jug and the glasses would hold.

Focus on the speech bubble. The jug is now empty, but it was used to fill the glasses. Discuss methods for finding how many millimetres of juice the jug must have started off with. Agree that they would need to multiply 250 ml by 5. How could they do this? If they don't suggest these two methods, share them with children: use their knowledge that there are four lots of 250 in 1000, so the total would be 1250 ml. Alternatively, because 5 is half of 10, they could multiply 250 ml by 10 and halve it. Practice these two methods for multiplying using mental calculation strategies, e.g. 250×9, 365×5.

For the picture with the bag of oats you could provide children with sand, scales, sticky labels and plastic bags. Ask them to weigh out different amounts of sand into the bags and label them with their masses. They then choose the bags that total 1.5 kg. They need to consider what masses the bags could be first, e.g. 50 g, 100 g 150 g, 300 g, 400 g and 500 g.

Ask them to consider how they would work out how many batches of flapjacks they could make. Discuss that they have 1.5 kg of oats and the recipe for one batch needs 250 g. Encourage children to recall how many grams are in a kilogram and to convert one of the masses before scaling up or down appropriately to find that they could make 6 batches.

For the picture with the pizza you could discuss what area is. Establish that it is the amount of space inside a given perimeter. What shape is the pizza? Agree that it is a square and so all the sides must be the same length. Agree that they would need to find a number that when it is multiplied by itself it would give a product of 144. Establish that when a number is multiplied by itself it is squared. The inverse of this is a square root. The square root of 144 is 12.

Discuss how they can prove the area of the pizza is 144 cm²: they would measure the sides to see if they were all 12 cm. Ask children to draw squares, measure one side and square it to find their areas.

Encourage them to practise squaring all the numbers to 12×12.

My flapjack recipe needs 250g of oats. How many batches could I make?

1.5 kg

Apparently, this pizza has an area of 144 cm². I wonder how I could prove that it was true?

Look at the pictures with the children and discuss the questions. See pages 48–9 of the Teacher's Guide for key ideas to draw out.

35

Things to think about

- How will you organise mixed attainment groupings?
- Will there be opportunities for you to work with children who need extra reinforcement of the concepts taught?
- Are manipulatives being used to help develop conceptual understanding for multiplication and division?
- How can you draw out reasoning through your questioning?
- Are you providing opportunities for children to work practically with different aspects of measure?

Checking understanding

Children can solve problems involving multiplication and division in different contexts, appropriately choosing and using number facts, understanding place value and mental and written methods. They can explain their decision making and justify their solutions.

You will know children have mastered the concepts if they can explain and represent different ways of solving the calculation, give reasons for which is the most efficient and suggest contexts where these contexts might be needed, and if they can explain and show why the solution to a calculation is different in two different contexts.

- Identify multiples and factors, including finding all factor pairs of a number, and common factors of two numbers.
- Solve problems involving multiplication and division including using their knowledge of factors and multiples, squares and cubes.

Homework 13 and 14   Practice Book pp 22–24

100 Squares

Representations and resources

Counting stick or similar, sets of digit cards, squared and plain paper, rulers, interlocking cubes.

Mathematical vocabulary

Multiply, divide, multiplication, division, factor, factor pair, product, multiple, square number, cube number

Warming up

Use a counting stick to count in steps of whatever multiplication tables you want children to rehearse. Ask them what steps they need to count in to get from one end to the other and count them together. Stop at various intervals and ask children to tell you the associated multiplication and division statements.

Background knowledge

Square numbers are numbers that are multiplied by themselves. These link well to work on finding the area of squares. Cube numbers are numbers that are multiplied by themselves twice. These link well to work on finding the volume of 3-D shapes. Provide opportunities to work on these different concepts at the same time.

Multiples are found in the answers to multiplication tables and can be divided by another number without a remainder. A factor is a number that will divide exactly into another. When working on multiples and factors it is helpful to use this: factor × factor = multiple. Multiples and factors work together and are inverses.

Children will be introduced to the term 'factor pair'. A factor pair is two numbers that are factors of another number. If these numbers are multiplied together the result will be the other number.

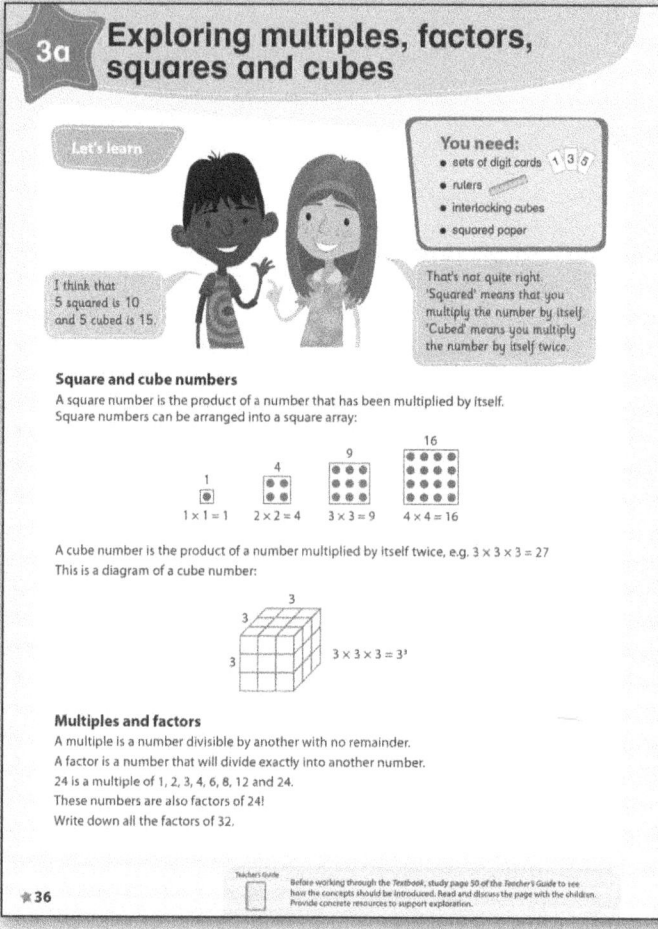

Let's learn: Modelling and teaching

Square and cube numbers

- Discuss the comments made by Theo and Amy. What has Theo done to get his answers? What should he have done? Ask children to work out what the answers should have been.

- Explore square numbers by linking to area. Ask children to draw squares of different sizes on squared paper and work out the areas. Some may count squares. If they do, encourage them to repeatedly add rows.

- Give children interlocking cubes. Ask them to make a cube and write down the dimensions of it. They could then count how many cubes there are. What calculation can they write to describe this? Can they see the link between this and cube numbers?

- You could then explore areas of cuboids. Can they develop a formula for working out the volume of a cuboid?

Multiples and factors

- Rehearse counting in steps of different multiples to the 12th multiple and link to multiplication and corresponding division facts.

- Discuss that you multiply a factor of a number by another factor and the product will be the common multiple of the two factors. Display 'factor × factor = multiple' in the classroom for reference. Explain that these are known as a factor pair.

- Give children a number, e.g. 64, and ask them to write down the factor pairs and then put them in two multiplication statements to show that they understand the commutativity of multiplication.

Let's practise: Digging deeper

Step 1

This task asks children to work out which of the numbers are square numbers and then cube numbers. Once they have, encourage them to write number statements, e.g. $6^2 = 36$ and $3^3 = 27$. You could give them calculators to check that their decisions are correct.

Before they begin the next part of the task recap what a common multiple is. Agree that it is a multiple of more than one factor, e.g. 12 is a common multiple of 1, 2, 3, 4, 6 and 12. Children write their list of multiples to the 10th multiple for 6 and 8 and then identify the common multiples.

Step 2

Before children carry out the task recap what is meant by multiples and factors. Call out some numbers and ask children to write four or five of their multiples. The task asks children to

write five multiples of six different numbers. Encourage them to be creative and also to record the factors that make each multiple in a number statement, e.g. multiples of 4 include 80 (20×4), 112 $(20 \times 4 + 8 \times 4)$.

Once they have done this, they find all the factors of the given numbers. Encourage them to record these by writing division statements.

Step 3

This task asks children to draw squares of given sizes. They should do this accurately with a ruler. Some children may benefit from using centimetre-squared paper. However, most children should be able to attempt this on plain paper. Remind them that they need to write the unit of measure as cm^2. Ask children what they notice about the areas of the squares.

Step 4

Children should carry out this investigation without any discussion beforehand. They should find that square numbers always have an odd number of factors because one of those factors is multiplied by itself to get the product, e.g. 9 has 1, 3 and 9 as factors: 1×9, 3×3 and 9×1.
Other numbers will have an even number of factors, e.g. 12 has 1, 2, 3, 4, 6 and 12 as factors: 1×12, 2×6, 3×4, 4×3, 6×2 and 12×1. Encourage children to express what they notice in both written form and verbally. You could ask children to write down the multiplication facts for all their numbers as a check to make sure that they have found them all.

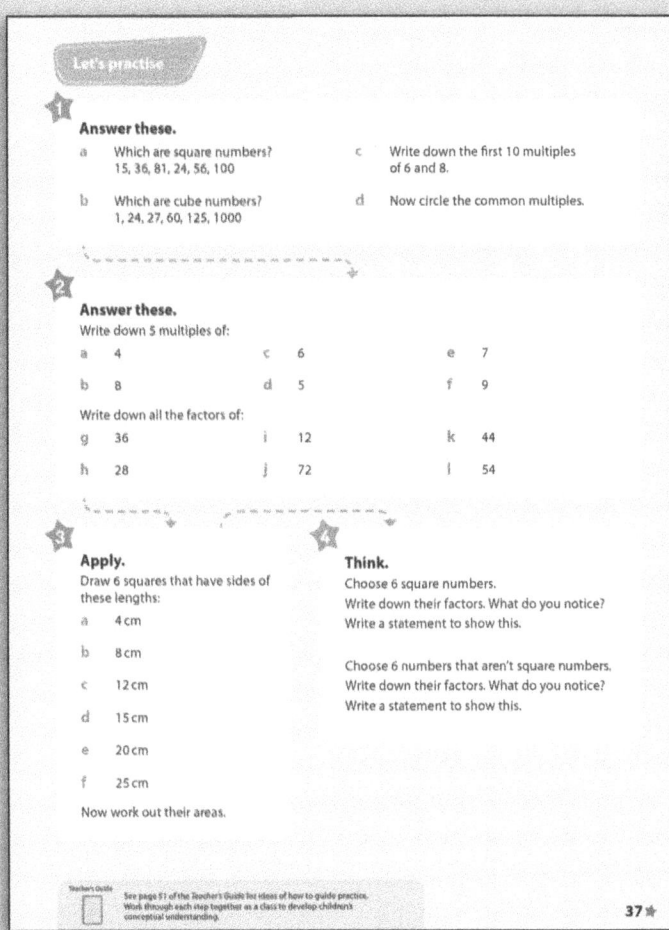

Ensuring progress

Supporting understanding

Some children may not be confident with recalling multiplication and division facts. They would benefit from using a multiplication grid for the activities that involve finding multiples and factors. Additionally, in Step 1 some children could benefit from drawing square numbers on squared paper and making cube numbers using interlocking cubes.

Broadening understanding

Provide opportunities for children to explore these properties on the Internet to find out more about them and when they are used in real life or other parts of mathematics. They could then make an information poster to display in the classroom.

✓ Concept mastered

Children can explain and demonstrate what square and cube numbers are as well as factors, factor pairs, multiples and common multiples.

Follow-up ideas

- Children make up a pairs game for square numbers. The object of the game is to match the card with the square number on it to the other card with the number it is a square of.

- They could play a 'What's my number?' type activity. One child thinks of a multiple and the other has to guess what it is. They say numbers and the child says 'yes' or 'no' depending if it is a multiple or not.

- Children make a list of numbers that they see regularly, e.g. house or bus numbers, minutes past the hour. They then explore whether these are square or cube numbers and their factors. They could also work out some of their multiples.

Answers

Step 1

a 36 ($6^2 = 36$), 81 ($9^2 = 81$), 100 ($10^2 = 100$)

b 1 ($1^3 = 1$), 27 ($3^3 = 27$), 125 ($5^3 = 125$), 1000 ($10^3 = 1000$)

c 6, 12, 18, 24, 30, 36, 42, 48, 54, 60 and 8, 16, 24, 32, 40, 48, 56, 64, 72, 80

d Common multiples are 24 and 48

Step 2

Open ended task.

Step 3

a $16\,cm^2$

b $64\,cm^2$

c $144\,cm^2$

d $225\,cm^2$

e $400\,cm^2$

f $625\,cm^2$

Step 4

Square numbers have an odd number of factors. All other numbers have an even number..

- **Multiply and divide numbers mentally drawing upon known facts.**
- **Solve problems involving addition, subtraction, multiplication and division and a combination of these, including understanding the meaning of the equals sign.**

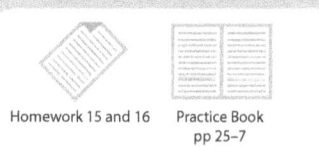

Homework 15 and 16   Practice Book pp 25–7

Representations and resources

Sets of digit cards, place-value grids (thousands, hundredths).

Mathematical vocabulary

Multiply, divide, multiplication, division, multiple, factor, product, dividend, divisor, quotient

Warming up

Draw a clock face on the board.

Write the multiplication table you wish to rehearse in the middle of the clock face. Point to the 'hour' numbers around the clock. Children call out the answer when the number is multiplied by the multiplication table you are rehearsing. Move around from 1 to 12 initially and then jump around the clock, revisiting frequently any facts that children don't remember or are slower at recalling. Repeat this for other tables. You could then write the answers around the clock face and point to these. This time children tell you the answer when the number is divided by the multiplication table you are practising.

Background knowledge

You may have noticed that when children are taught written methods that these become the only methods that they use for calculations. However, mental calculation strategies are often more efficient than written ones. Ensure that children become confident in the following mental calculation strategies:

- multiplying by 5 by multiplying by 10 and halving
- multiply by 20 by multiplying by 10 and doubling
- using known multiplication facts, e.g. $6 \times 7 = 42$, $6 \times 70 = 420$, $6 \times 35 = 210$.

This will prepare them to make sensible decisions about when to use mental and written methods.

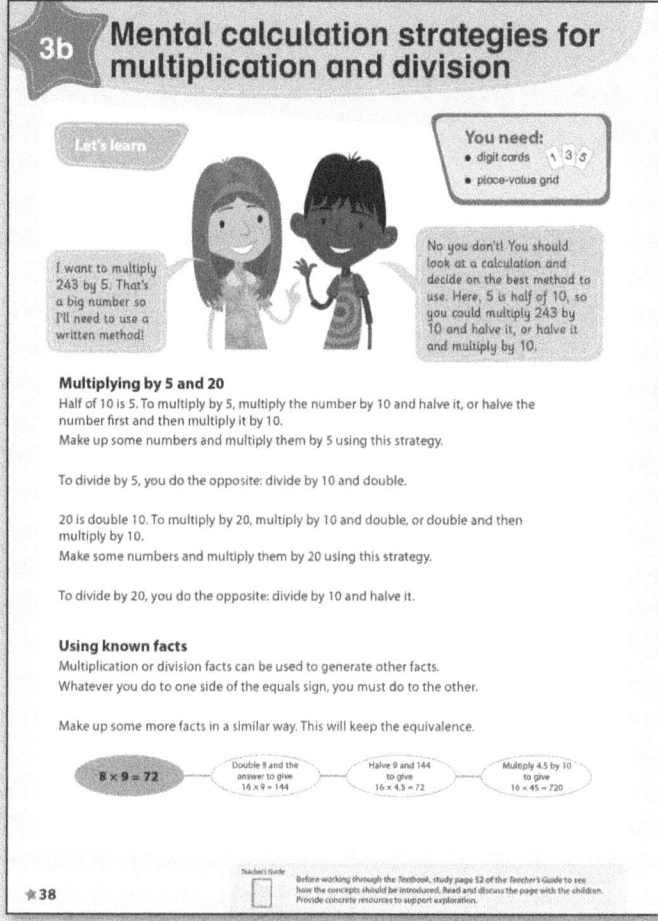

Let's learn: Modelling and teaching

Multiplying by 5 and 20

- Discuss how the mental calculation strategy for multiplying by 5 by multiplying by 10 and halving (or vice versa) works.

- Discuss why, when dividing by 5, they would divide by 10 and then double. Agree that when dividing by 10 they find one tenth of a number. They need one fifth which is two tenths, so they need twice the amount which is double.

- Discuss the relationship between 10 and 20. Agree that 20 is double 10, so when multiplying/dividing they can multiply/divide by 10 and double/halve. Call out some numbers for children to multiply/divide by 20.

Using known facts

- Recap the meaning of the equals sign. Establish that it is a sign

of equivalence and that what is on one side needs to be the same as the other. You could make up some missing number statements to do with multiplication and division, e.g.:

- $n \times 10 = 25 \times 6$
- $56 \div 7 = 72 \div n$
- $24 \div n = 2 \times 4$

- Ask them to write down a multiplication fact and generate other facts from it, e.g. $9 \times 8 = 72$, $90 \times 8 = 720$, $45 \times 8 = 360$. Agree that what happens to one factor must also happen to the product.

- This is an opportunity to link to line graphs. Show children how to construct one. Make the vertical axis go up in divisions of a multiplication table you would like them to practise.

Let's practise: Digging deeper

Step 1

Before children begin the task, rehearse multiplying by 5 by multiplying by 10 and halving. Write some 2- and 3-digit numbers on the board for them to multiply by 5. Repeat for multiplying by 20. When children embark on the task, ensure that they use the mental calculation strategies of multiplying by 10 and halving or doubling for this. Remind them that they can perform the two operations in either order. Some children may be tempted to use a grid or written method but discourage this. If they need to, allow them to make jottings.

Step 2

Before children begin the task, rehearse dividing by 5 by dividing by 10 and doubling. Ask them to explain why this works. Write some 2- and 3-digit numbers on the board for them to divide by 5. Repeat for dividing by 20. When children embark on the task, ensure that they use these mental calculation strategies with jottings if required.

Step 3

Children should begin by carrying out the multiplication calculations. Encourage them to do this as quickly and fluently as possible. Once they have completed the calculations, they should draw their lines and order them from longest to shortest. Encourage children to talk about what they are doing at each step.

For the second part of the task, they do the same but for division.

Step 4

Ask children to discuss in pairs how they could work out possible questions for the original multiplication fact. Draw out that they should work from what they know: the new statement. They could work backwards from this. If both numbers were doubled, they could begin by halving both factors: 60×4.5. If one was multiplied by 10 and the other halved, they could then divide one by 10 and double the other. Encourage them to find different possibilities for the fact. They could then make up similar problems for a partner to solve.

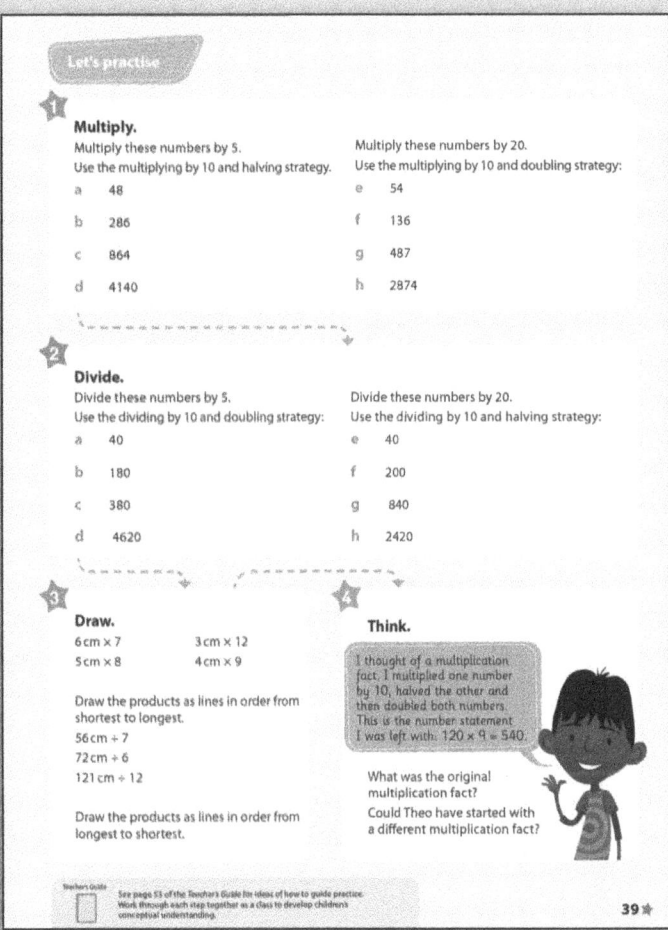

Follow-up ideas

- Children could make a board game that involves answering questions on cards. These questions should contain calculations that can be answered using the mental calculation strategies from this concept spread.

- Use digit cards to generate 3-, 4-, 5- or 6-digit numbers to multiply by 5 and 20. Children could work with a partner and see who can do both operations first. If they are correct they could score a point. They could do this 10 times and see who the winner is.

- Children could work with a partner. Together they make up a multiplication or division fact and time themselves for 2 minutes. Who can generate the most other facts from their original fact?

Ensuring progress

Supporting understanding

It is important that all children understand that mental calculation strategies and can be more efficient than written methods. It may be necessary for some children to have extra practice with the strategies covered in this spread. They may benefit from working with smaller numbers and also digit cards and place-value grids.

Broadening understanding

Provide opportunities for children to multiply and divide using mental calculation strategies in different contexts, e.g. time, length, mass, volume and capacity. Encourage them to make up problems for others to solve using these methods. This will help you to assess their true understanding.

 Concept mastered

Children can explain and demonstrate the mental calculation strategies for multiplying and dividing by 5 and 20.

Answers

Step 1		h	57 480	g	42
a	240	**Step 2**		h	121
b	1430	a	8	**Step 3**	
c	4320	b	36	Open ended.	
d	20 700	c	76	**Step 4**	
e	1080	d	924	The original multiplication fact could have been: $6 \times 9 = 54$, $9 \times 6 = 54$, or $120 \times 0.45 = 54$	
f	2720	e	2		
g	9740	f	10		

- Multiply numbers up to 4 digits long by a single- or 2-digit number using a formal written method, including long multiplication for 2-digit numbers.
- Divide numbers up to 4 digits long by a single-digit number using the formal written method of short division and interpret remainders appropriately for the context.

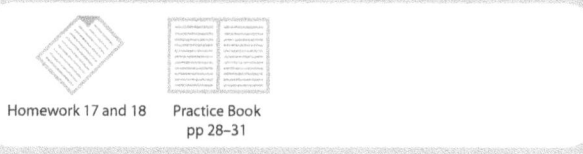

Homework 17 and 18   Practice Book pp 28–31

Representations and resources

Pendulum, sets of digit cards, counters (three colours).

Mathematical vocabulary

Multiplication, division, factor, product, dividend, divisor, quotient

Warming up

Tell children that they will rehearse multiplication facts. Swing a pendulum from side to side. As it swings one way, call out a number. As it swings the other way, get children to call out the product when the number you called out is multiplied by a multiplication table you wish to practice. Repeat this a few times. You could then call out the products and they call out the missing factor for each one.

Background knowledge

The 2014 National Curriculum requires all children to be taught written methods for multiplication and division. They should be taught these in a way that helps them to develop their conceptual understanding and procedural fluency. When being introduced to these methods, it is important that children use manipulatives, such as Base 10 apparatus or place-value counters. Revisit the mathematical vocabulary for multiplication and division and ensure that all adults in the classroom are using it consistently.

Let's learn: Modelling and teaching

Multiplication

- Inform children that the array and grid methods of multiplication rely on an understanding of the multiplicative property of place value and the column method relies on the positional property.

- Give children three colours of counters. Write some 3-digit by single-digit multiplication calculations on the board. Ensure they follow the three steps demonstrated in the Textbook and have the experience of making the array, writing the grid and then the column method, discussing what is happening each time.

- Set some word problems that involve multiplying different measures.

- Work through the mistake that Theo has made. Can children spot his error? Recap these three properties of place value: positional, multiplicative and additive.

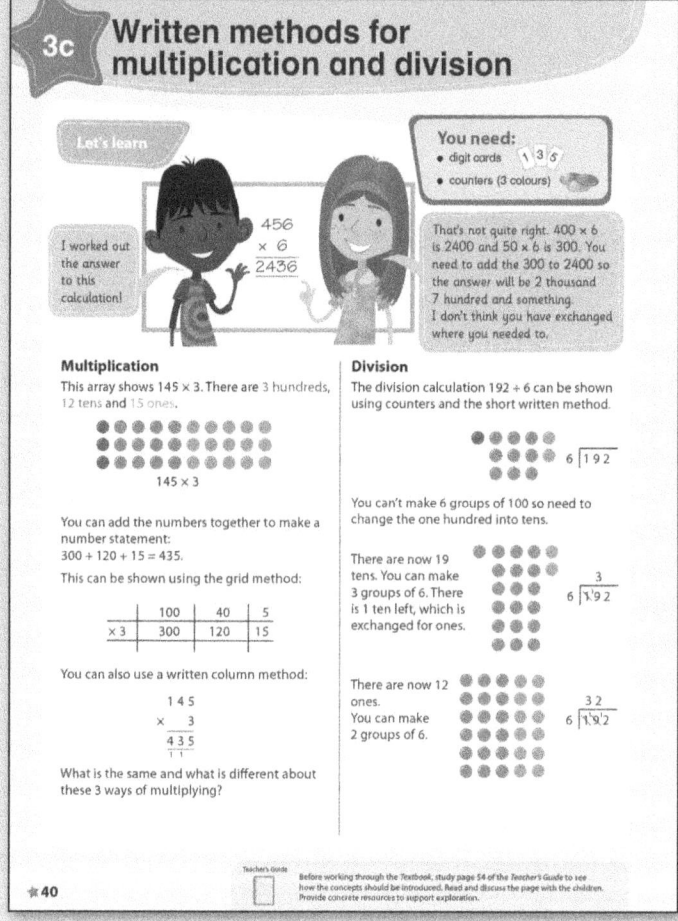

Division

- Discuss what aspect of place value children think that they need to consider for this method of division. Establish that it is positional. Children need to consider the number of hundreds, tens and ones and work out if they can make groups of these.

- Write some calculations on the board. Work through these with children using counters and you modelling the written method. Select your examples carefully so that children don't have to exchange too many counters. Do this slowly and clearly, e.g.:

$$3 \overline{)4^16^12}$$
$$\ \ 1\ 5$$

> You can make 5 groups of 3 tens. There is 1 left, which needs to be exchanged into ones.

- Set some problems that involve measures.

Let's practise: Digging deeper

Step 1

The task asks children to make a set of calculations using counters. They can assign their own value to their counters, e.g. red counters for hundreds, blue for tens and green for ones. They set them out as arrays. Once they have set them out, they draw the grid method and find the answers. They then write the column method to check their answers.

Step 2

Before the task, recap how to show division calculations using counters and ask children to describe to a partner how these relate to the written method. The task asks children to answer some division calculations using manipulatives and then the short written method. As before, they use counters to set up the calculation and manipulate these exchanging and grouping as required. As they do this they record what they have done using the short written method.

Step 3

The first part of this task requires children to multiply different measurements. They could begin by setting the calculations out in arrays using counters that they assign their own values to. When they complete the calculations, encourage them to change the units to, e.g. kilometres and metres, kilograms and grams and litres and millilitres. Ask them to carefully consider which units would be appropriate. The second part requires them to find the quotient. Again, ask them to set out the calculation using counters. They should record any remainders. If any children can, encourage them to write these as fractions.

The third part of this task asks them to draw five lengths in millimetres and then multiply them each by 9. They then need to divide their lengths by 10. They record any remainders as tenths. Finally they find the difference between the two new measurements for each line.

Step 4

This is an excellent opportunity for problem solving. Some of them might need several attempts, using a trial and error method. It would be a good idea to let them practise on paper. Some children might benefit from the use of manipulatives. After completing the task, discuss the methods children used. Draw out the most successful. Give them time to make up some missing number division calculations for the class to solve.

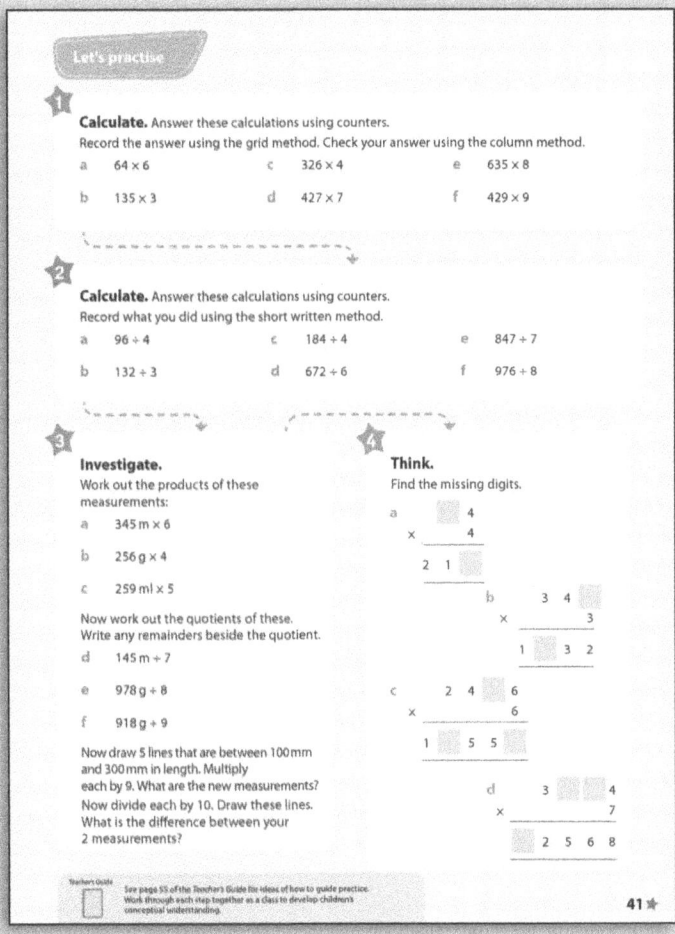

Ensuring progress

Supporting understanding

It is important that all children develop a conceptual understanding of the written methods and don't simply learn rules. Some children may not be ready to use counters to which they need to assign their own values. If this is the case, use Base 10 apparatus or counters that have the values on them. If you do not have the latter, you could write them on.

Broadening understanding

Provide opportunities for children to make up and solve word problems and missing number problems within different contexts such as length, mass and money.

Follow-up ideas

- Children could make a board game with cards that have calculations to answer using written methods. They could also make cards that are word problems.
- Children could measure a length of string in centimetres and, if appropriate, millimetres. They then work out the total length of 2, 4, 8 lengths. These could be scaled up by doubling. They could then use this information to find other lengths by addition and/or subtraction.
- Children could do the above activity this time measuring the mass of an object.

Answers

Step 1

a	384	d	2989
b	405	e	5080
c	1304	f	3861

Step 2

a	24	d	112
b	44	e	121
c	46	f	122

Step 3

a	2070 m or 2 km 70 m
b	1024 g or 1 kg 24 g
c	1295 ml or 1 l 295 ml
d	20 m remainder 7 m

e	122 g remainder 2 g
f	102 g

Some example of values children may choose:
100 mm × 9 = 900 mm
300 mm × 9 = 2700 mm
900 ÷ 10 = 90 mm
2700 ÷ 10 = 270 mm
270 − 90 = 180 mm

Step 4

a	54 × 4 = 216
b	344 × 3 = 1032
c	2426 × 6 = 14 556
d	3224 × 7 = 22 568

 Concept mastered

Children can explain and demonstrate how the written methods for multiplication and division work.

Game 1: Winning stars

This is a simple game where children need to win stars using their knowledge of multiplication and division strategies, square and cube numbers and factors and multiples.

Maths focus

- Identify multiples, factors and common factors
- Solve problems involving factors and multiples, squares and cubes

Resources

Several counters per player (1 colour per player), digit cards, 1–6 dice (1)

How to play

Children both place a counter on the same star, then follow the instructions. The winner keeps their counter on the star. The aim is to win as many stars as possible. For multiplication stars, encourage children to use efficient strategies. The highest answer wins.

For square number stars, the child who makes the most wins. If no one can make any, no one wins the star.

For cube number stars, the highest cube number wins.

For factor stars, the child who finds the most factors wins the star.

Making it easier

Children can use manipulatives or visual representations to help them.

Making it harder

Increase the number of digit cards that they use by 1.

Game 2: Going down!

Maths focus

- Identify multiples, factors and common factors.
- Solve problems involving factors and multiples, squares and cubes

Resources

1 counter per player (1 colour per player), digit cards, 1–6 dice (1), calculator, pencil and paper

How to play

Children place their counters outside the gameboard. They take it in turns to throw the dice and move that number of stars around the board in numerical order. They follow the instructions on the star they land on. The number that results from what they do is their score. They go around the board twice, recording their scores as they go. When they have finished they total their scores. The player with the highest total is the winner.

Making it easier

Give children manipulatives, e.g. Base 10 apparatus or place-value counters, and visual resources such as multiplication grids to help them. They could use a calculator to find the total points.

Making it harder

They move around the board three or four times to accumulate more points. Expect them to find the total number of points using a variety of methods for addition, e.g. mental calculation for single- and 2-digit points, and written methods for larger numbers.

Game 3: Your stars

Children should invent their own game designing rules that use the concepts covered in the unit. Challenge children to make their game easier or harder.

Choose a game to play.

Game 1: Winning stars

How to play

- Each place 1 of your counters on the same star.
- Follow the instructions. If you win, your counter stays on the star. If you don't win, remove your counter.
- Rules for winning a star:
  - For multiplication stars: *Do the calculation using the method you prefer. The highest answer wins.*
  - For square number stars: *The player that makes the most square numbers wins the star. You can use single digits, make a 2-digit number or both. If no one can make a square number, no one wins the star.*
  - For cube number stars: *The highest cube number wins the star.*
  - For division stars: *Divide your number in the best way possible. The lowest answer wins the star.*
  - For the factor stars: *Whoever finds the most factors wins the star.*

You need:

- several counters per player (1 colour per player)
- digit cards
- 1–6 dice

Game 2: Going down!

How to play

- Place your counters outside the gameboard.
- Take it in turns to throw the dice and move that number of stars around the board in order.
- Follow the instructions on the star you land on.
- The number you get from that is your score. Write it down.
- Go around the board twice.
- When you have finished, add up your scores to get your total. The highest total wins.

You need:

- 1 counter per player (1 colour per player)
- digit cards
- 1–6 dice
- pencil and paper

Game 3: Your stars

- Design your own game using the gameboard.
- Explain the rules and play with someone else.
- Try and find ways to make your game easier or harder.

Please help your child by reading the instructions and playing the game together.

Assessment task 1

Resources

Counters, 12 × 12 multiplication square (optional).

Running the task

Before they begin the task, ask children what is meant by factors and multiples. Ask those who you particularly wish to assess to explain. If they can tell you that two factors multiplied gives a product and a product divided by a factor gives another factor they have understood this part of multiplication and division.

When children begin the task, listen to groups discuss the statement and explain to each other why it is correct. Encourage them to explain clearly what they think a factor is. You could ask them to use the word to describe a multiplication statement: factor × factor = multiple. Encourage them to find all the missing factors of 60. They should write these in factor pairs with the appropriate calculation, e.g. 1 and 60, 1 × 60 = 60. You could give less confident children a multiplication square to help them.

Evidencing mastery

Look for children who can explain what a factor is clearly and can give examples. If they can do this they are evidencing mastery.

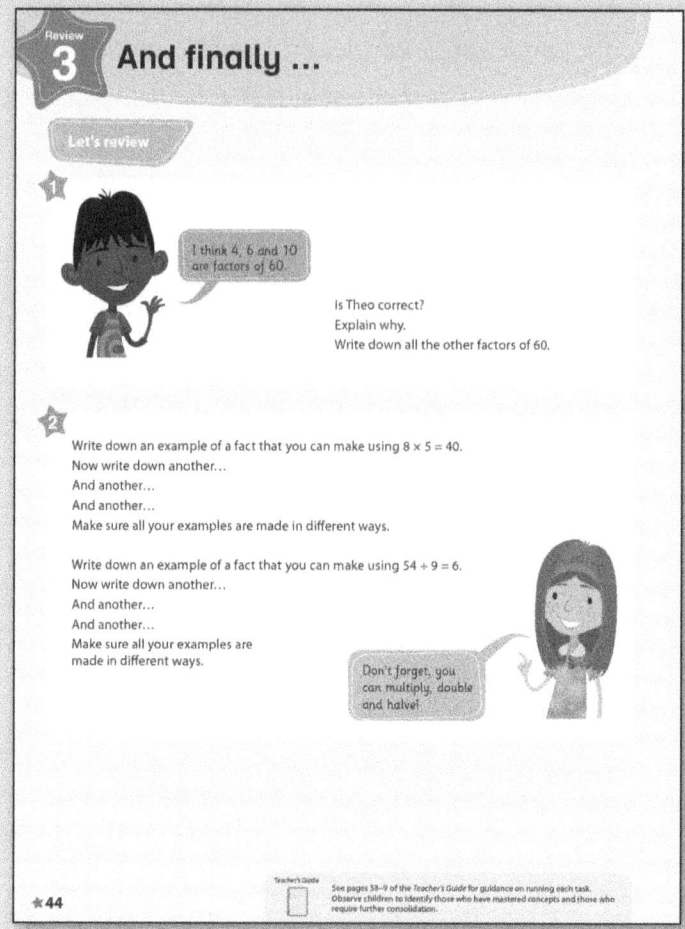

Assessment task 2

Running the task

Before children begin the task, recap using known facts to generate others. Write a multiplication or division statement on the board, e.g. 7 × 9 = 63, 32 ÷ 8 = 4 and ask them to make up other facts from these.

For the task children need to use 8 × 5 = 40 to generate other facts. Encourage them to do this in different ways, e.g. multiplying by 10 (80 × 5 = 400), halving (80 × 2.5 = 200) and doubling (160 × 2.5 = 400). Encourage them to generate their new facts from the ones they create. Some children may need to use 8 × 5 = 40 each time as opposed to generating facts from the new ones they create.

Children then need to use 54 ÷ 9 = 6 to generate other facts, using a similar approach to the multiplication facts they found in the first part of the task, e.g. multiplying by 10 (540 ÷ 9 = 60), halving (540 ÷ 4.5 = 120) and doubling (108 ÷ 9 = 12).

Evidencing mastery

Listen to children explaining the way they generate their new facts. If they can use a variety of strategies for this, including multiplying by 10, doubling and halving, they are evidencing mastery.

Concepts mastered

✓ Children can explain and demonstrate what square and cube numbers are as well as factors, factor pairs and multiples and common multiples.

✓ Children can explain and demonstrate the mental calculation strategies for multiplying and dividing by 5 and 20.

✓ Children can explain and demonstrate how the written methods for multiplication and division work.

Assessment task 3

Resources

Counters

Running the task

Before beginning the task, ask children to tell you the different mental calculation strategies that they can use to multiply and divide, e.g. multiplying by 4 by doubling and doubling again, dividing by 5 by dividing by 10 and doubling. Ask them to write down examples of these and to share them with the class. Reinforce the idea that using a mental calculation is preferable when possible and that written methods should be used when these are more efficient. Ask them to make up some calculations that would be best answered using a written method. They share these with the class and the other children decide if they agree or not.

When children carry out the task, encourage them to use the mental calculation strategies and written methods that they have learnt about in this spread and any others that they can think of. Encourage them to discuss with you or a partner which they think is the most efficient method and why. Some children may need manipulatives to help them access the task, so have them available in case they choose to use them. For multiplying 468 × 4, one key mental strategy would be doubling and doubling again. Encourage all children to do this. Other strategies could include partitioning (400 × 4, 60 × 4, 8 × 4, 1600 + 240 + 32 = 1872). Written methods could include the grid and the written methods.

A key mental strategy for 675 ÷ 5 would be to divide by 10 and double. Encourage them to demonstrate how they would use the written method and also grouping.

Evidencing mastery

If children can confidently demonstrate a variety of methods for multiplying and dividing the numbers using mental calculation strategies and the written method and justify which they think are the most efficient, they will be showing mastery.

Did you know?

The Ancient Egyptians used to multiply and divide by doubling. They would double the multiplicand up to eight times and then add the number of multiples until they obtained the multiplier, e.g. 36 × 6.

| **1** 36 | **2** 72 | **4** 144 | **8** 288 |

2 + 4 = 6   72 + 144 = 216   so 6 × 36 = 216

The way they did division was similar to their multiplication.
156 ÷ 12.

| **1** 12 | **2** 24 | **4** 48 | **8** 96 |

12 + 48 + 96 = 156   1 + 4 + 8 = 13   so 156 ÷ 12 = 13

This links with scaling up and down. You could practise some of these with your class as they are relevant to what is taught in the National Curriculum.

Triangles – and other polygons

Mathematical focus

★ **Geometry: properties of shapes**

Prior learning

Children should already be able to:

- compare and classify geometric shapes, including quadrilaterals and triangles, based on their properties and sizes

- identify acute and obtuse angles and compare and order angles up to two right angles by size.

Key new learning

- Identify regular and irregular polygons based on reasoning about equal sides and angles; know that angles are a measure of turn and are measured in degrees.

- Use a protractor to draw angles accurately and calculate angles in triangles using knowledge of properties of triangles and appropriate understanding and language of angles.

- Estimate and draw angles and identify the information required to construct triangles accurately.

Making connections

- Understanding the properties of 2-D shapes is intrinsic to the study of 3-D shapes, which have faces that are polygons.

- An awareness and appreciation of polygons in the world may be useful in art and design topics.

- This topic includes many precise mathematical words to describe shapes. These enrich children's vocabulary and they may recognise Greek prefixes from their literacy work.

- Using a protractor and learning to estimate angles with reasonable accuracy is a useful practical skill. Many sports involve accurate use of angles, e.g. football and snooker. Children may have used a clinometer in their science lessons.

Unit 4 Triangles – and other polygons

I wonder if there are other buildings that are regular polygons?

What measurements do I need to make to calculate the height of the tree?

I wonder what polygons I can find in the pylon structure?

★46

Talk about

Ensure that you always use the terms regular and irregular to describe polygons precisely. Define these terms with an example. While there are countless irregular shaped pentagons, there is only one regular pentagon, where all the angles and sides are equal. The same is true for all polygons.

Engaging and exploring

Ask children to work with a partner to name as many polygons as they can. How can they sort them? There are specific names for each type of triangle and quadrilateral while polygons with more sides are usually only described as either regular or irregular. Children may only identify a polygon when it is regular. This unit emphasises that each polygon has only one regular shape but many irregular ones.

The photos show polygons in a variety of different contexts to engage children. Give them some time to look at the photos in the Textbook and discuss what they notice with their partner before sharing ideas with the class. Extend this further by asking them to discuss polygons that they can see around the classroom. Challenge them to talk about where else they have seen polygons in their daily lives.

Discuss with children which photo they find most appealing/beautiful/impressive. Ask them to say what polygons they

can find in the pictures. This will help to revise the names of polygons. Ask them whether they are regular or irregular. Only a few children may be familiar with the Pentagon but all children will have experience of pylons. Encourage children to contrast man-made and naturally occurring polygons. In the photo of giraffes, ask them if all the patterns are polygons. (Polygons are closed shapes made from straight lines). Children may point out that the sides look quite curved so they are not strictly polygons. You could contrast these naturally occurring 'polygons' with the mathematical precision of man-made polygons. Other polygons in nature include honeycomb, snakeskin, tortoise shell and pineapple.

Look at the photo of the tree and ask children what metric unit you would use to measure its height and how it could be measured. Explain that one way is to use a clinometer. This instrument measures the angle from the ground in a right-angled triangle. When the distance is measured from the base of the tree, this length and the two angles gives sufficient information to calculate the height of the tree or other tall object. You may like to return to this photo when children have learnt about drawing triangles.

Despite their visual complexity, Islamic patterns are simply drawn using a pair of compasses and a ruler. You can see videos of them being constructed on the Internet. Ask children to identify what polygons they can see in the patterns. Look at the colours, repetition and reflection of shapes.

The aerial photo of the Pentagon may stimulate discussion about other buildings that are in the shape of different polygons. These include the Tower of the Winds in Athens (octagonal), the Flatiron building in New York (triangular) and octagonal cathedral chapter houses.

Encourage children to find examples of polygons in their everyday life, e.g. the UK 50p and 20p coins are regular heptagons!

What shapes can you see? How are they used to make patterns like this?

Are the patterns on giraffes polygons? Where else do you find polygons in the natural world?

Look at the pictures with the children and discuss the questions. See pages 60–1 of the Teacher's Guide for key ideas to draw out.

47

Things to think about

- Are both the classroom and outside areas of the school shape-rich environments?

- How will you organise groupings for discussions and activities?

- How will you check conceptual understanding?

- What support will you provide for left-handed children or those with a degree of dyspraxia who find using a protractor and construction activities very challenging?

- What opportunities will you provide to build fluency?

- Which problem-solving strategies are most appropriate in Year 5, e.g.:
  - ▶ What is the same? What is different?
  - ▶ Always, sometimes, never
  - ▶ Convince me
  - ▶ What do you notice?

Checking understanding

You will know children have mastered these concepts when they can identify regular and irregular polygons and describe polygons accurately using appropriate vocabulary. They can explain an angle as a measure of turn, and draw, measure and compare angles.

- **Know angles are measured in degrees: estimate and compare acute and obtuse angles.**
- **Distinguish between regular and irregular polygons based on reasoning about equal sides and angles.**
- **Use the properties of rectangles to deduce related facts and find missing lengths and angles.**

Homework 19 and 20   Practice Book pp 32–4   2D Shapes   Polygons; Properties of triangles

Representations and resources

Ruler, 2-D shapes, 2 geo-strips with paper fastener (per child).

Mathematical vocabulary

Regular, irregular, perpendicular, parallel, opposite, adjacent, (also see vocabulary in Background knowledge, below)

Warming up

Ask children to show you an acute (obtuse, reflex and right) angle, using two geo-strips with a paper fastener and define the types of angle. Discuss how angles are a measure of a turn and are measured accurately using degrees. Ask them to show you 90°, 30°, 150°, etc. Using 2-D shapes revise the names of polygons and quadrilaterals.

Background knowledge

In Year 4, children learnt to compare and classify geometric shapes, including quadrilaterals and triangles, based on their properties and sizes. There is a wealth of specific mathematical vocabulary in this topic and children will need to refresh their memory of these words and definitions:

Equilateral triangle: three equal sides, three equal angles, each 60°.
Isosceles triangle: two equal sides, two equal angles.
Scalene triangle: no equal sides, no equal angles.
Parallelogram: opposite sides are parallel, all opposite angles are equal.
Rectangle: all opposite sides are of equal length, four right angles.
Rhombus: all sides have equal length, all opposite sides are parallel, opposite angles are equal.
Square: all sides are equal, all angles are right angles.
Trapezium: one pair of opposite sides are parallel.
Kite: each pair of sides is equal in length.

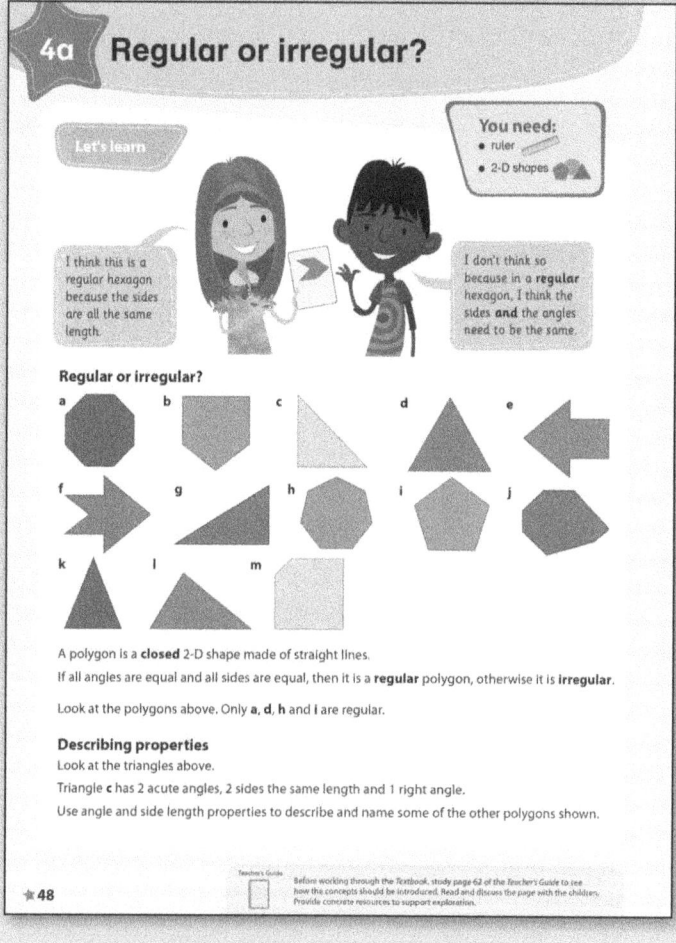

Let's learn: Modelling and teaching

Regular or irregular?

- Discuss with children the definition of a polygon. A polygon is a closed 2-D shape made of straight lines. A closed shape with a curve is not a polygon. Move on to the definition of a regular polygon. If all angles are equal and all sides are equal, then it is a regular polygon, otherwise it is irregular. Provide 2-D shapes for children to describe.

- Refer to the misconception and ask them to explain what is wrong with the shape. The sides are the same length but there are acute, obtuse and even a reflex angle in the shape. The shape does have symmetry and this is where the misconception arises.

- Ask children to visualise specific regular polygons and then draw them in the air.

Describing properties

- Explain that to describe a polygon accurately, we need to think about the angles and sides. We can describe the angles as acute, obtuse, reflex or right. We can state the number of sides and describe them as equal in length, perpendicular (two lines which meet at a right angle) or parallel. Other important words are opposite and adjacent. Work together to describe some other polygons.

- Challenge children to describe a polygon orally for the class to identify.

Let's practise: Digging deeper

Step 1

This step consolidates children's understanding of regular and irregular shapes. Keep encouraging children to describe the properties to practise using the vocabulary.

Step 2

In this section, children are using a diagram to sort quadrilaterals. It requires them to reason carefully about the properties of the shapes. They should sketch the quadrilaterals first and then decide where each one fits in the table. You may like to provide children who are less confident with the concept with an empty pro-forma so that they do not waste time copying the table.

Step 3

Children use their knowledge of polygons alongside multiplication and division skills. They could begin by listing regular polygons and seeing which ones have a number of sides that is a factor of 60.

Step 4

Children may benefit from working in pairs on this investigation to discuss the shapes that they find and to describe as many properties as possible. Guide children to test common 2-D shapes, e.g. using triangles gives quadrilaterals and pentagons. They will be able to use a wide variety of vocabulary in context. They should consider the size of angles, the length and position of lines.

Ensuring progress

Supporting understanding

Children differ in their ability with space topics and some arithmetically-able children may find visualising shapes challenging. Use careful questioning to support them, e.g. *Imagine an equilateral triangle, cut the corners off. What shape have you made?* (Hexagon.) *Is it regular or irregular? Depending on where you cut can you see both a regular and irregular shapes?* You may also have children in the class whose physical dexterity is less mature. Ensure that they have good-quality equipment and try to spend some time practising drawing shapes with them.

To help children internalise the vocabulary, you could play card-matching games.

Broadening understanding

Children who have grasped the concepts easily may enjoy investigating polygons with large numbers of sides using the Internet. Ask them to explain what happens to the size of the internal angles as the number of sides increases.

In Step 4, you may like to challenge children with specific tasks, e.g. can they find particular shapes in the overlap, the shape that has the maximum number of sides or justify why a particular shape cannot be made?

 Concept mastered

Children can recognise and describe regular and irregular polygons, using the correct mathematical vocabulary.

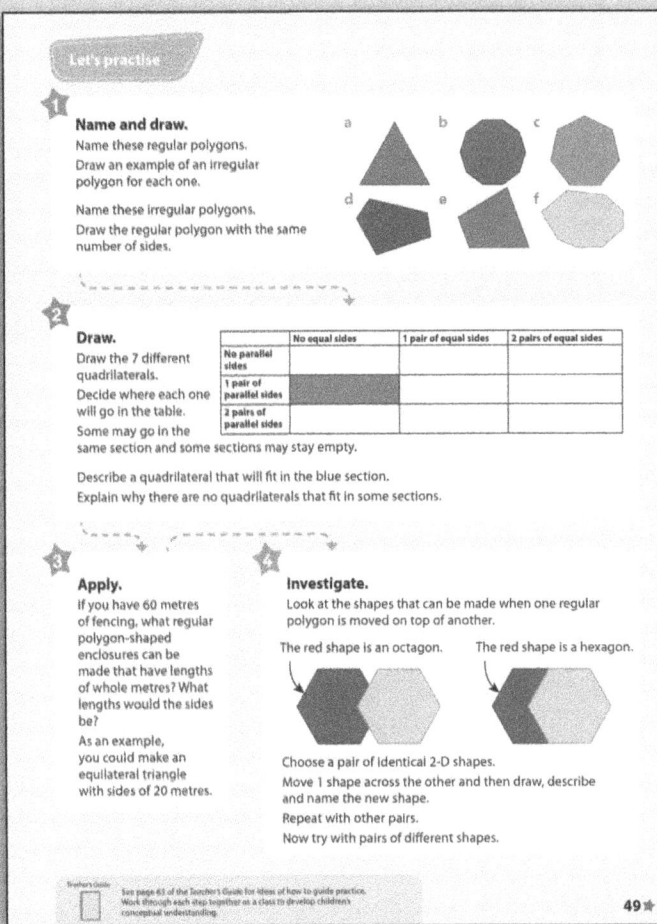

Follow-up ideas

- Leave a wide range of 2-D shapes for children to handle freely. Ask them to sort them in various ways. Challenge each child to write a card describing a particular polygon. Other children can use this set of cards to find the matching polygon.

- Use bamboo canes, dowelling or rope to make large regular (and irregular) polygon shapes outside the classroom.

- Ask children to look for pictures of polygons in the everyday world and make a display.

Answers

Step 1

a   Equilateral triangle.
b   Regular decagon.
c   Regular heptagon.
d   Irregular pentagon.
e   Irregular quadrilateral.
f   Irregular octagon.

Step 2

	No equal sides	One pair of equal sides	Two pairs of equal sides
No parallel sides	irregular quadrilateral	quadrilateral with a pair of adjacent sides equal	kite
One pair of parallel sides		trapezium with non-parallel sides equal in length	
Two pairs of parallel sides			square, oblong, rhombus, parallelogram

Blue section:

Trapezium with all sides of different lengths.

Accept any appropriate explanations, e.g. if there are two pairs of parallel sides, the opposite sides have to be equal so you cannot have two pairs of parallel sides and no equal sides.

Step 3

square – 15 m; pentagon – 12 m; hexagon – 10 m; also, decagon – 6 m; 12 sides (dodecagon) – 5 m, 15 sides – 4 m; 20 sides – 3 m; 30 sides – 2 m; 60 sides – 1 m.

4b Angles

- Know angles are measured in degrees: estimate and compare acute, obtuse and reflex angles.
- Draw given angles, and measure them in degrees (°).
- Identify:
  - angles at a point and 1 whole turn (total 360°) - angles at a point on a straight line and $\frac{1}{2}$ a turn (total 180°)
  - other multiples of 90°
- Use the properties of rectangles to deduce related facts and find missing lengths and angles

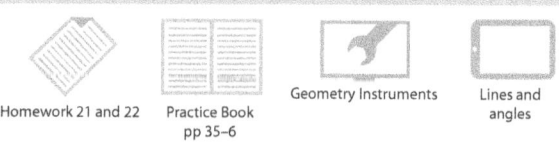

Homework 21 and 22   Practice Book pp 35–6   Geometry Instruments   Lines and angles

Representations and resources

30 cm ruler, protractor, 2-D shapes.

Mathematical vocabulary

Protractor, internal angle, vertex

Warming up

Elicit from children that two right angles, i.e. 180°, make a straight line and four right angles, i.e. 360°, make a complete turn.

Next you might like to draw a straight line on the board and make an acute and obtuse angle. Ask children to calculate the missing angle given one angle, e.g. 25°. Repeat with different angles. This is a good opportunity for children to rehearse their mental calculation strategies.

Background knowledge

The fact that the angles in a triangle total 180° is used in many angle problems. To calculate an unknown angle in a triangle where two angles are known, add the two known angles and subtract the sum from 180°. Recap mental strategies for adding 2-digit numbers and subtracting 2-digit numbers from a 3-digit number, here 180.

Let's learn: Modelling and teaching
Measuring angles with a protractor

- It is worth spending some time ensuring that children know how to use a protractor proficiently. Use simple transparent protractors with no parts cut out. To measure an angle, you place the protractor exactly at the vertex where the two lines meet. Ask them to draw a triangle, measure the angles and find the total of the three angles. Encourage them to estimate the angle before they begin to measure; this helps them to avoid using the wrong scale. There are two scales on the protractor, use the scale that starts at zero for that angle. Explain to children that they are allowed a margin of error of one or two degrees in their measurement but they should take care that the protractor is very carefully positioned before they make the reading.

- Check the children's totals so that you can pick up user error at this stage. Their calculations should total 180° +/– a few degrees. If they are wildly out they are probably still reading the wrong scale. If they are out by more than

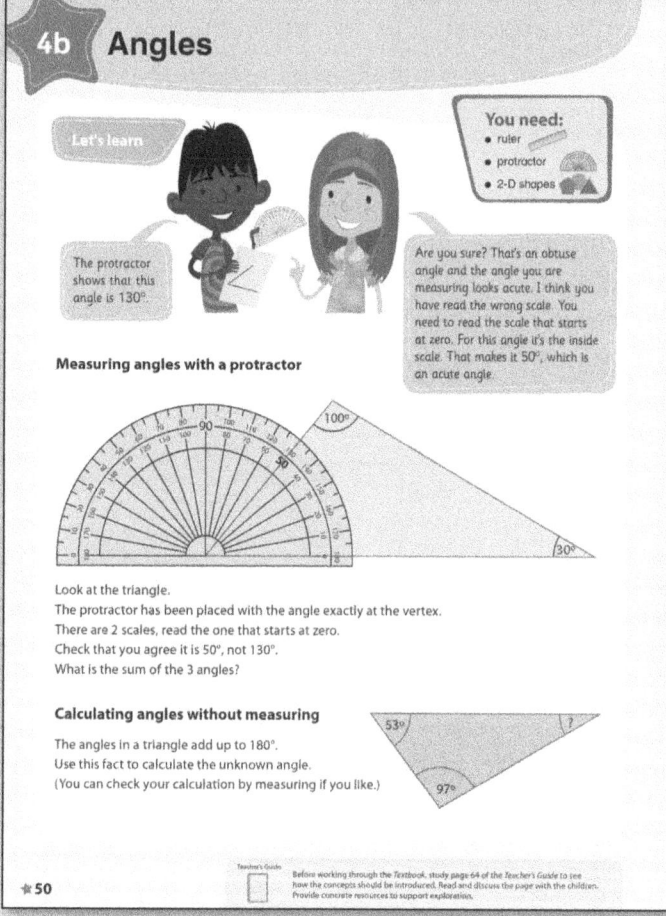

about 5°, they need to try to measure more carefully and you will need to watch them using the protractor and correct them.

Calculating angles without measuring

- Once children have calculated the missing angle in the first triangle, you could provide further examples on the board for them to complete.

- Children will discover by measuring that the angles in triangles add up to 180°. This happens for every triangle not just the ones they measured!

- Ask children if they can express this as an algebraic expression, $180° - a - b$.

Let's practise: Digging deeper

Step 1

Children are using their knowledge of triangles, symbols and angle marks and deducing the size of the missing angles.

When children are expected to calculate the size of angles, the geometric sketches are often deliberately not drawn to scale so children cannot simply measure an angle, they must calculate it.

Step 2

This section explores children's knowledge of isosceles triangles and the sum of the internal angles in a triangle. The angles in children's diagrams are not measured, just estimated. Encourage them to draw the triangles as precisely as possible so that an obtuse angle looks obtuse.

Step 3

This section allows children a degree of creativity while providing

practise in the new skill of using a protractor. Asking children to check the angles in each other's boats enables them to self-correct, which reinforces their learning.

Step 4

Children may need different levels of support to complete this challenge. One way to complete this investigation is to mark the centre of the polygon and draw lines from the centre to each vertex. Each of the triangles is isosceles and so the size of the angles can be calculated.

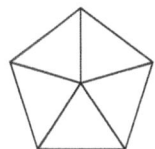

The five angles around the centre are equal and are $360° ÷ 5 = 72°$. This can be marked on the diagram. The triangles are isosceles so the angle equals $(180° − 72°) ÷ 2$. Therefore each internal angle is 108° and the sum of the internal angles is $108° × 5 = 540°$. Other polygons can be calculated in a similar way.

The internal angles of a triangle are 180°; a square is 360°; a pentagon is 540°. The pattern is that the sum of the angles increases by 180° each as another side is added. Children who have grasped the concept well may be able to deduce a formula so that they can predict the sum of the internal angles for any polygon. Encourage them to articulate the pattern using precise mathematical vocabulary.

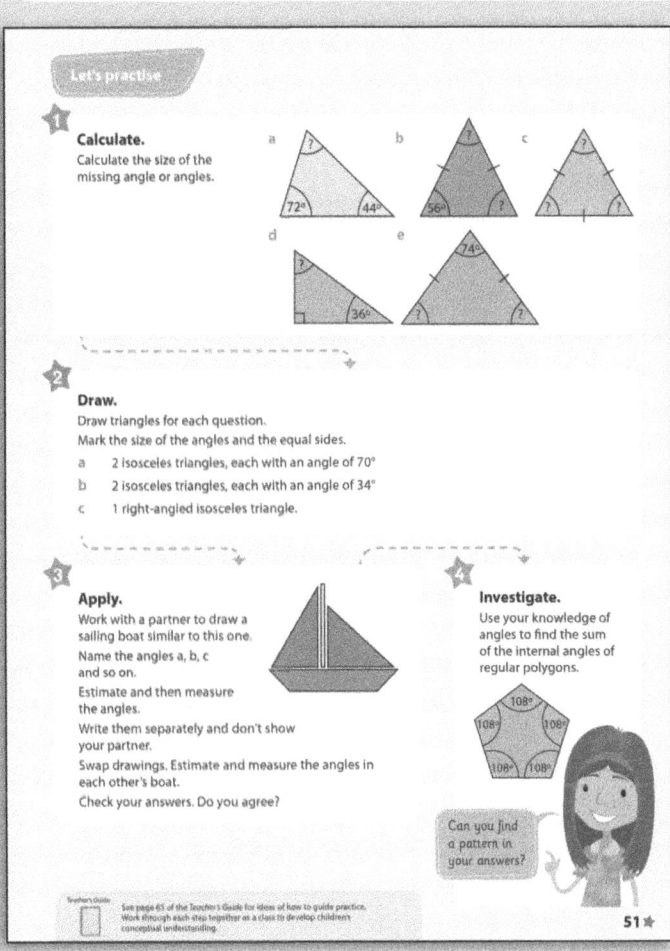

Ensuring progress

Supporting understanding

Using a protractor to measure angles is a task that requires a high level of hand-eye coordination. This may be particularly challenging for some children and you might like to work with them one-on-one to help them use it accurately.

Broadening understanding

Children have now mastered important angle facts. Confident application of this knowledge will allow them to try a range of geometry puzzles, that can be widely found on the Internet.

✓ Concept mastered

Children can estimate, measure and compare angles. They can use the angle fact that the internal angles in a triangle total 180° to solve problems.

Follow-up ideas

- Include a wide range of 2-D shapes in the classroom for children to handle freely. Pick two shapes at random and ask children to tell you one similarity and one difference between them.

- Older children still enjoy making tessellated patterns. Semi-regular tessellations can be constructed using two or more regular polygons. The pattern at each vertex must be the same.

- Children may like to investigate polygons with large numbers of sides. A polygon with 100 sides is called a hectagon and one with a million sides is a megagon. There are rules that allow you to name every possible polygon using Greek prefixes, e.g. a polygon with 34 sides is called a tricontatetragon. However, it is also acceptable (and much easier) to write 34-gon!

Answers

Step 1		Step 2	
a	64°	a	Triangle with angles 70°, 70°, 40°; triangle with 70°, 55°, 55°.
b	56° and 68°		
c	60°	b	Triangle with angles 34°, 34°, 112°; triangle with 34°, 73°, 73°.
d	54°		
e	53°	c	Triangle with angles 90°, 45°, 45°.

- **Know angles are measured in degrees: estimate and compare acute, obtuse and reflex angles.**
- **Draw given angles, and measure them in degrees (°).**
- **Distinguish between regular and irregular polygons based on reasoning about equal sides and angles.**
- **Identify angles at a point and one whole turn (total 360°).**

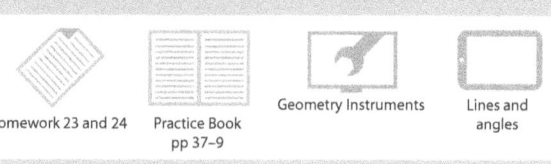

Homework 23 and 24   Practice Book pp 37–9   Geometry Instruments   Lines and angles

Representations and resources

ruler (transparent), protractor, isometric grid paper, 2-D shapes.

Mathematical vocabulary

Protractor, vertex

Warming up

You could start by showing children a regular octagon and asking them to describe its properties, including identifying lines of symmetry and estimating the size of the internal angle. You might try asking a child to measure the angle and discuss how close their estimate was.

Repeat the exercise as time permits with other polygons, e.g. an obtuse isosceles triangle, a regular heptagon, a reflex-angled kite and so on.

Background knowledge

It is important to teach children to visualise angles before drawing them. This will help to eliminate the error of using the incorrect scale on the protractor.

Let's learn: Modelling and teaching

Drawing angles

- In the previous lesson, children learnt how to use a protractor to measure angles. In this lesson, they use a protractor to draw angles. They also need to draw lines accurately to the nearest millimetre. Show children the method outlined in the Textbook carefully and give them time to practise. Provide them with a sharp pencil, a simple protractor (with no cut outs) and a transparent ruler to help make the results more accurate. You can use a digital protractor to demonstrate how to measure angles on an interactive whiteboard.

Drawing triangles

- In this exercise children are using a ruler and protractor to draw triangles. You can explain to them that there is another method using compasses which is used to construct accurate polygons. They will learn this later.

- You might like to elicit from children that the size of each angle in an equilateral triangle is 60°. Demonstrate how to draw the triangle on the board. Use a small dot to show

the size of each angle and tell children that they should draw each line longer than is needed so that the lines of the triangle clearly intersect. These construction lines should not be rubbed out. Explain that they can measure the lengths of the two sides of the equilateral triangle that they have drawn to check their accuracy!

- Ask children to draw an isosceles triangle with base 6 cm and 2 angles of 65°. The third angle should measure 50°. Check their accuracy.

Let's practise: Digging deeper

Step 1

It is important that children practise drawing angles with the vertex on both the right and the left so that they experience choosing the correct scale on the protractor. When the vertex is on the left of the page, they need to use the inside scale. Children will almost certainly make mistakes. Make sure that you reassure them that this is quite normal until they gain experience in handling a protractor.

Step 2

This step moves children on to drawing a polygon rather than simply an angle. Children have now learnt to use the protractor with the vertex on either side so they can achieve this. They can also try drawing some accurate quadrilaterals.

Step 3

This question requires children to think deeply about what

information is sufficient to draw an accurate triangle. Talk through the question before they begin. The answer is that you need to know either:

the size of two angles and the length of the side between them
or
the length of two sides and the size of the angle between them.

The misconception at the beginning of the lesson shows one combination that will not work and explains why not. The way that children express their ideas will demonstrate the depth of their understanding.

Step 4

This investigation uses isometric grid paper. The task is readily accessible to all children but some polygons are much easier to find than others, e.g. hexagons. Children who are less confident about the concept will simply find further examples of different irregular hexagons. This will develop their fluency but you may need to support them to find the more challenging polygons.

Children who have grasped the concept well will be able to recall the polygons that they are searching for and will approach the task in an organised and methodical manner. They have determination and persistence to complete the task and can see how to adapt one polygon to form another.

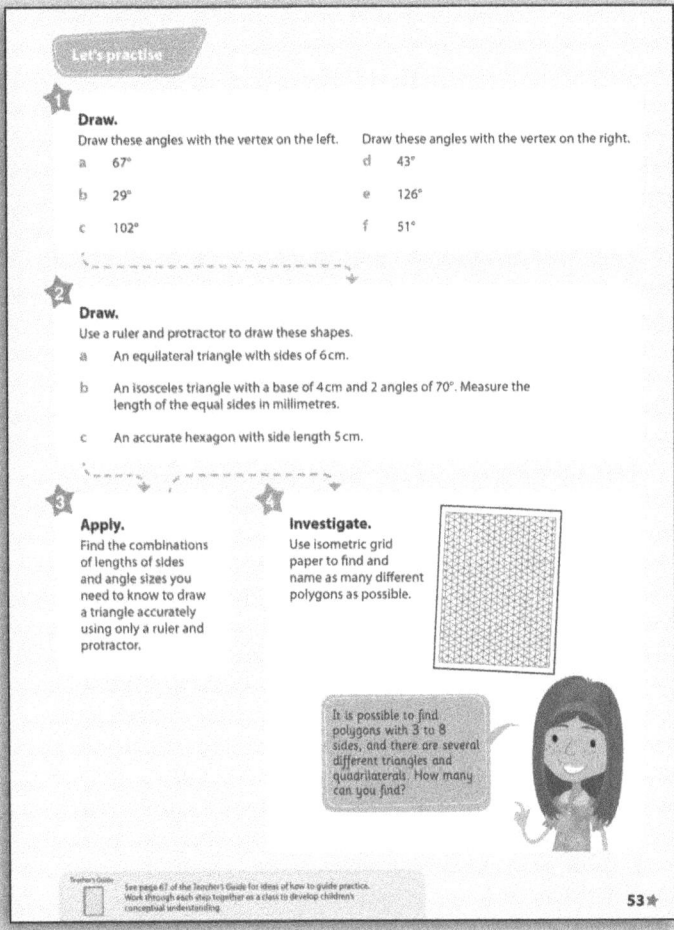

Ensuring progress

Supporting understanding

Using a protractor will be challenging for some children. It is a good idea to acknowledge that you understand they are trying as hard as they can (if you think they are) and explain that they will become more skilled with practice. In the meantime they can focus on understanding the process itself and in calculating angles, which is not a dexterity test.

Broadening understanding

Many children who are working at a high level will relish solving angle problems and these can provide a natural and visual introduction into formulating algebraic expressions for an unknown. Encourage children to explore this. Consider, e.g. an isosceles triangle with angles a, a and b. All of these equations are true.

- $2a + b = 180$
- $2a = 180 - b$
- $b = 180 - 2a$

 ## Concept mastered

Children can draw angles using a protractor. They can use angle facts about internal angles, angles on a straight line and at a point to solve problems.

Follow-up ideas

- Use a board protractor, chalk and a length of dowelling (as a ruler) to draw large polygons outside in the playground.

- Ask children to design a poster illustrating the main angle facts – angles at a point total 360°, angles on a straight line total 180°, internal angles in a triangle total 180°, internal angles in a quadrilateral total 360°.

- Angles and turns are very important in many sports. Collect newspaper or magazine pictures that illustrate this.

Answers

Step 2

a   Equilateral triangle with sides 6cm.

b   The equal sides measure 59 mm +/– 1 mm.

c   Regular hexagon with side length 5 cm and internal angles of 120°.

Step 3

Using only a ruler and protractor you can construct a triangle accurately if you know either: the size of two angles and the length of the side between them or the length of two sides and the size of the angle between them.

Making polygons!

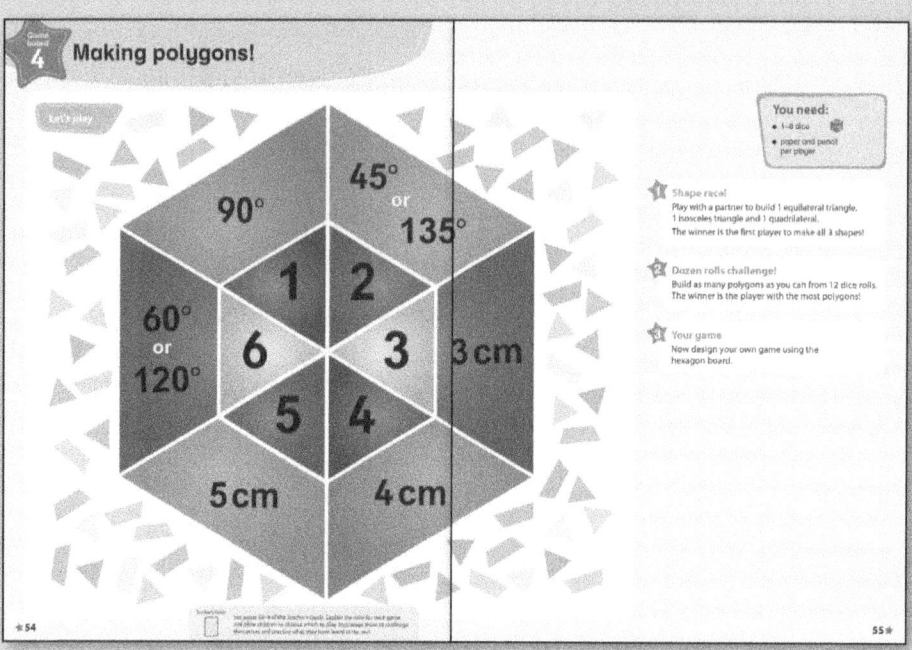

Game 1: Shape race!

This game allows children to build a variety of different-sized triangles and quadrilaterals. To play, they need to understand what combinations of sides and angles make actual polygons, so the game combines luck and skill.

Maths focus

- Know the angle and length properties of triangles and quadrilaterals to make polygons

Resources

1–6 dice (1), paper and pencil per player.

How to play

Each child plays with a partner and the aim is to build one equilateral triangle, one isosceles triangle and one quadrilateral. They need to try to be the first to complete the challenge. To play children take turns to roll the dice, find the number they rolled on the inner hexagon of the game board and record the value (angle or side length) it corresponds to on the outer hexagon of the gameboard. When each player has enough values to make a shape, they draw the polygon and those values cannot be used again. Once a shape is made it cannot be taken apart and the values used in a different way. The winner is the first person to make all three shapes.

Making it easier

Discuss the dimensions of possible polygons with children before they play.

Making it harder

Ask children if it is possible to make a scalene triangle with the given values. (There are two ways using 3 cm, 4 cm, 5 cm or 3 cm, 4 cm and 90°.) Change the target to building one equilateral triangle, one isosceles triangle, one scalene triangle and one quadrilateral.

Game 2: Dozen rolls challenge!

In this variation children can decide how to maximise their score because they have not used any of their values before making polygons. It is often possible to use all eight values.

Maths focus

- Know the angle and length properties of triangles and quadrilaterals to make polygons

Resources

1–6 dice (1), paper and pencil per player.

How to play

The aim of the game is for children to build as many polygons as possible from 12 dice rolls. They need to decide the best combinations of angles or lengths to make the most polygons. They work in a pair, taking turns to roll the dice 12 times, writing down the angles and lengths. They then make as many triangles and quadrilaterals as possible using each value only once. Children check each other's answers. The winner is the child with the most polygons.

Making it easier

Reduce the number of rolls of the dice to ten.

Making it harder

Change the rules to allow polygons to be joined so that a side can be used in two polygons.

Game 3: Your game

Children should invent their own game, designing rules that use the concepts covered in the unit. Challenge children to make their game easier or harder.

Making polygons!

Choose a game to play.

Game 1: Shape race!

You need:
- 1–6 dice
- paper and pencil per player

How to play
- You each have to build 1 equilateral triangle, 1 isosceles triangle and 1 quadrilateral.
- Take turns to roll the dice and record the value.
- When you have enough values to make a shape use them to draw a polygon. The values cannot be used again.
- Once a shape is made it cannot be taken apart and the values used in a different way.
- The winner is the first player to make all 3 shapes!

Game 2: Dozen rolls challenge!

You need:
- 1–6 dice
- paper and pencil per player

How to play
- You have to to build as many shapes as possible from 12 dice rolls. Decide the best combinations to make the most polygons.
- Take turns to roll the dice 12 times, writing down the angles and lengths.
- Make as many triangles and quadrilaterals as possible using each value only once.
- Check each other's answers.
- The winner is the player with the most polygons.

Game 3: Your game

- Make up your own game using the hexagon gameboard.
- You could use more than one dice or introduce new polygons.
- You could give polygons different scores.
- Explain the rules and play with a partner.

Please help your child by reading the instructions and playing the game together.

Rising Stars Mathematics Year 5 © Rising Stars UK 2015   **69**

Assessment task 1

Resources

Blank or cm² paper, ruler, triangle shapes.

Running the task

It is a good idea to check that children understand the task and give them time to explore. They need to be able to list the range of quadrilaterals and to work logically through the task. The easiest way to approach the task is to draw the quadrilaterals and then divide them into triangles with a diagonal.

Here is the solution.

Square	2 congruent right-angled isosceles triangles
Rectangle	2 congruent right-angled scalene triangles
Rhombus	2 congruent isosceles triangles
Parallelogram	2 congruent scalene triangles
Trapezium	2 scalene triangles
Kite	2 different isosceles triangles
Irregular quadrilateral	2 scalene triangles

Evidencing mastery

Evidence of mastery is clear when children are able to break the task down into separate steps and record their results in a clear, well-organised table showing precise diagrams with appropriate mathematical vocabulary and/or correct geometric symbols.

While some children will be able to visualise the effect of putting two specific triangles together others may benefit from the support of experimenting with actual triangles.

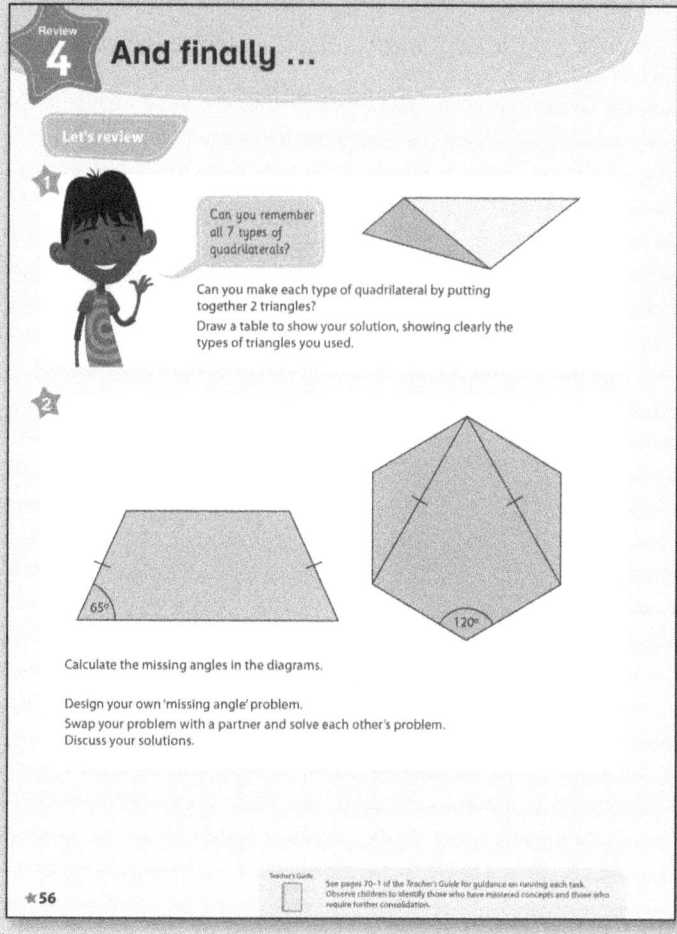

Assessment task 2

Running the task

This task relies on children being able to recall their knowledge of angle facts and geometric symbols and then apply this knowledge to solve the problem. Calculating the angles in the trapezium is relatively simple. A trapezium has one pair of parallel sides, shown in the Textbook at the base and top. The small line on the two sloping sides indicates that theses lines are equal in length, making the shape symmetrical. Therefore the other acute angle must be 65°. The obtuse angles must also be equal and are 180°– 65°.

The hexagon is a more challenging exercise, involving a greater number of steps and some children may require hints to move them along. You can suggest that they redraw the shape and add in missing lines so that they make triangles. The next hint might be reminding them that the hexagon is regular and therefore the shape is symmetrical. They should then be able to

deduce that the angles in the triangles to the left and right have angles of 120°, 30° and 30°. The central triangle that they have drawn is an equilateral triangle with angles of 60°. This gives the missing angles in the kite as 60°, 90° and 90°.

When children have designed their own problem you may like to pair them up appropriately to test their questions on each other.

Evidencing mastery

Designing their own missing angle problem will help you to assess children's depth of understanding and their ability to extrapolate the examples to new situations e.g. children who have fully mastered the concepts may be able to draw a similar problem involving an octagon or a kite. Children who are less secure are more likely to design a simple missing angle problem involving a single triangle.

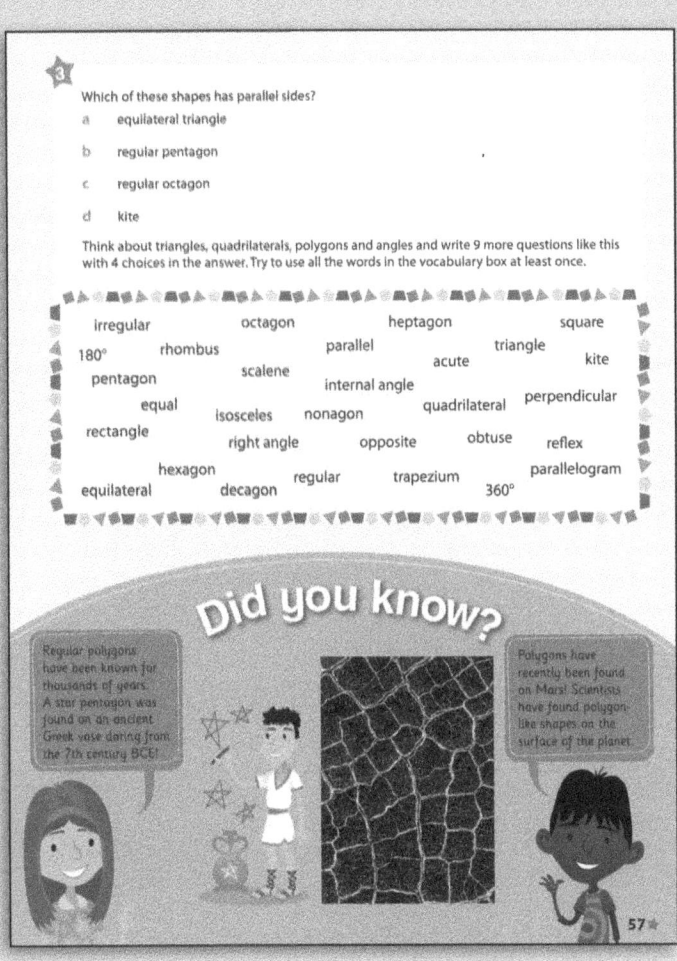

Concepts mastered

- ☑ Children can recognise and describe regular and irregular polygons, using the correct mathematical vocabulary.

- ☑ Children can estimate, measure and compare angles. They can use the angle fact that the internal angles in a triangle total 180° to solve problems.

- ☑ Children can draw angles using a protractor. They can use angle facts about internal angles, angles on a straight line and at a point to solve problems.

Assessment task 3

Resources
Isometric grid paper, ruler.

Running the task
This is a low threshold task that is readily accessible to all children. It is also an enjoyable activity that is probably best done in pairs to stimulate discussion on the questions and choices. Each question is constructed with four multiple choice options. Children may be familiar with this format from television quiz shows. As children proceed they may need support to find areas that they have not covered or ideas to turn into questions.

Here are some types of questions that you could give to children to develop.

- Which of these statements about a _____ is not true?

- How many sides does a _____ have ?

- Which one of these polygons could have a reflex angle?

- Which of these polygons is not a quadrilateral?

Evidencing mastery
The quality and coverage of children's questions will demonstrate their mastery of the subject. Their answer choices will be sensible. The ability to teach a topic is a good way to give evidence of secure understanding. They will be able to ensure that all aspects of the unit have been covered.

Did you know?

The word polygon comes from the Greek meaning 'many angled'. There are names for polygons with every possible number of sides, based on Greek prefixes and ending in 'gon'. Children who are fascinated by this can research the naming of polygons on the Internet. The Greeks were passionate about geometry and considered it the crown jewel of sciences!

Scientists think that the massive polygons that have been observed on Mars may be evidence of the existence an ancient Martian sea.

Polygons also occur in rock formations on Earth. Regular hexagons can occur when lava cools to form columns of basalt. The most famous example is the Giant's Causeway in Northern Ireland.

Mathematical focus

★ **Number: number and place value, multiplication and division**

★ **Measurement: time, mass**

Prior learning

Children should already be able to:

- count backwards through zero to include negative numbers

- recognise the place value of each digit in a 4-digit number (thousands, hundreds, tens, and ones)

- order and compare numbers beyond 1000

- round any number to the nearest 10, 100 or 1000

- solve number and practical problems that involve all of the above and with increasingly large positive numbers

- read Roman numerals to 100 (I to C) and know that, over time, the numeral system changed to include the concept of zero and place value.

Key new learning

- Read, write, order and compare numbers to at least 500 000 and determine the value of each digit.

- Count forwards or backwards in steps of powers of 10 for any given number up to 1 000 000.

- Round any number up to 500 000 to the nearest 10, 100, 1000, 10 000 and 100 000.

- Solve number problems and practical problems that involve all of the above.

- Interpret negative numbers in context, count forwards and backwards with positive and negative whole numbers, including through zero.

- Read Roman numerals to 1000 (M) and recognise years written in Roman numerals.

5 Different types of number

I wonder how many thousands of people were at the match?

STADIUM

Today's Attendance

27 306

Hottest recorded temperature: 56.7 °C

Could you work out the difference between these 2 temperatures?

Coldest recorded temperature: −94.7 °C

★58

Making connections

- Comparing numbers relies on children's understanding of place value and has many real-life applications, including in the context of metric measures.

- The ability to read a scale accurately, including negative numbers, will be essential when children are required to read information presented in a line graph to solve comparison, sum and difference problems.

- Using Roman numerals also relies on an understanding of our own place value system, and their presentation here gives children practice in interpreting tables. Work with Roman numeral clocks will reinforce their understanding of the units of time.

Talk about

Place value is key to children's conceptual understanding. Recap the properties of place value regularly, using the terms 'positional', 'multiplicative', and 'additive' to describe its properties. Use digit cards, the place-value grid and place-value cards to support the discussion. In the course of your discussion, encourage children to make numbers using these resources. The grid highlights the positional property and the place-value cards highlight the multiplicative property.

Engaging and exploring

Focus on each picture in turn. For the picture with the match attendance table, you could:

Ask children to tell you how many people attended the match. Focus on the ones, hundreds and thousands numbers in turn, beginning with the least significant and discuss the positional multiplicative and additive properties of the number.

To rehearse and reinforce children's understanding of place value, you could go on to ask questions such as:

• What if there were 10 000 more? 30 000 more? 3000 more? 900 more? Five more?

• What if there were 10 000 less? 100 less? 600 less? 200 less? 400 less? 10 less? 50 less?

Ask children to round the attendance number to the nearest 10, 100, 1000 and 10 000.

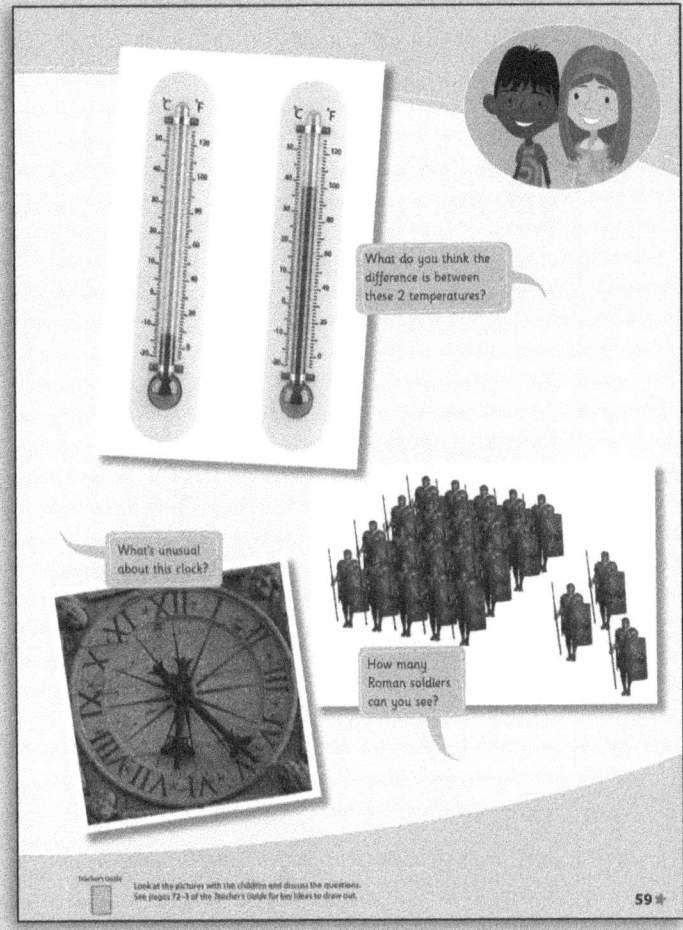

Write some other 5-digit numbers on the board for children to round in this way.

Put some imaginary attendance figures on the board for ten football matches and ask children to make a bar graph to show all attendances.

Ask children to create a line graph of people coming to the match over a period of time during the afternoon and then leaving after the match finishes.

For the desert and Antarctic photos you could:

• Ask children where they think these photos were taken. (Sahara Desert and Antarctica) Do they know where these places are? Discuss why these are the hottest and coldest regions in the world, focusing on their positions related to the Sun.

• Ask children to round the two temperatures to the nearest whole number. They can draw a number line, plot these onto it and find the difference by counting on.

For the picture with the thermometers you could:

• Ask children to describe what a thermometer does and to describe those in the picture to a partner.

• Establish that the intervals on the thermometers go up in ones. Ask them to read the temperatures. Ask questions, e.g.: *If the temperatures fell by 10 degrees, what would they be? If the temperatures rose by 17 degrees what would they be?*

• Ask children to find the difference between the two temperatures using a counting-on strategy. You could also ask them to find the differences between different negative numbers and between negative and positive numbers.

For the picture with the Roman soldiers you could:

• Find out what children know about the Romans.

• Ask them to tell you an efficient way to count how many soldiers there are. Can they see an array? Encourage them to multiply for the group of soldiers and then add three.

• Ask them to tell you the Roman numerals that they can remember from work in Year 4. Call out some numbers to 100 and ask children to convert these to Roman numerals.

For the picture of the clock face you could:

• Agree that the clock has Roman numerals to represent the hours. On most Roman numeral clocks the four is represented as four ones (IIII), however, on this one it is written IV.

• Give children a piece of card and a paper fastener and ask them to make a Roman numeral clock face with hands. Ask them to find different times. They can write them down as digital times in both 12-hour and 24-hour time.

Things to think about

How will you:

• Plan focus group work?

• Ensure that all children are able to access their learning?

• Help those who haven't understood to catch up? There are times when you might need to give extra help outside the mathematics lessons to certain children. This would involve repeating the teaching points made during the lesson.

• Use visual representations to help conceptual understanding with all children? You could encourage them to use place-value grids and digit cards to reinforce or develop their understanding of place value.

Checking understanding

By the end of this unit children should be able to make appropriate decisions about when to use their understanding of counting (including counting below zero), place value and rounding for solving problems including adding and subtracting. They should be able to explain the representation of 3-digit positive numbers as Roman numerals.

- Read, write, order and compare numbers to at least 500 000 and determine the value of each digit.
- Count forwards or backwards in steps of powers of 10 for any given number up to 1 000 000.
- Round any number up to 500 000 to the nearest 10, 100, 1000, 10 000 and 100 000.
- Solve number problems and practical problems that involve all of the above.

Homework 25 and 26

Practice Book pp 40–1

100 Squares; Place Value & Abacus

Representations and resources

Sets of digit cards with extra zeros, place-value grids to 100 000, place-value cards, sand, small plastic bags, scales.

Mathematical vocabulary

Hundred thousands, ten thousands, thousands, hundreds, tens, ones, kilometre, greatest, least, round, place holder, digit

Warming up

Start a clapping rhythm with children. As you all clap, count in tens from different starting points, e.g. 70. They should count forwards for 12 steps and then count back to the starting number. Ask them to tell you what multiplication table they need to know to be able to do this. Repeat for counting from 700, 7000 and 70 000. Choose other multiples of 10 to 120 and repeat the process.

Background knowledge

Comparing, ordering and rounding numbers relies on a conceptual understanding of place value. It is important to know about the positional, multiplicative, additive and Base 10 properties of place value, and to identify numbers that are more and less than others using the symbols > and <. Other important ideas to highlight are that the equals sign is a sign of equivalence and what is on one side must be the same as what is on the other, and the role of the place holder.

Let's learn: Modelling and teaching

Place holders

- Give children a set of digit cards with some extra zeros and a laminated place-value grid. Ask them to make a number, e.g. 234 067. Do they do this correctly with the place holder? Can they explain what each digit represents? Repeat for other numbers with an increasing number of place holders. Ask them to read the number out loud. They could then make other numbers with zeros in them for a partner to read.

- Repeat the above but ask children to write the numbers in words.

- Encourage children to round the numbers they make to the nearest 10, 100, 1000, 10 000 and 100 000.

- Focus on the Base 10 property of place value. Ask children to make a number in their place-value grid. They then multiply their number by ten and then by ten again.

Comparing numbers

- Ask children to explain what each symbol is used to mean: <, >, =. Ensure that children understand that the equals symbols signifies equivalence. Ask children to make pairs of 4-, 5- or 6-digit numbers. They then use them to make number statements using >, < and =.

- Ask children to weigh items, write their masses down and make up number statements using the appropriate symbols. Repeat for capacity in millilitres.

Let's practise: Digging deeper

Step 1

Children need to make as many different numbers as they can from the four digits given. Encourage them to be systematic as they do this, e.g. find all the possibilities for numbers with 6 in the thousands position. You could ask them to predict how many there will be, once they have done this for the six possible numbers for six thousand. Once they have all their numbers they should order them from largest to smallest. Remind them that they will need to compare in order to do this. You could ask children to identify the place holder and tell you which position it is in.

Step 2

Children identify the position that the place holder takes and write this down. They then write the number in words. Ask them to say the number out loud first so that they can

identify if and where the 'and' will go. 'And' is often said when there is a place holder, e.g. 1065, one thousand and sixty five.

Step 3

Children need to weigh three different amounts of sand into plastic bags. They then use the masses to create all possible greater and less than and equals number statements. Encourage them to say their statements aloud to ensure that they understand the symbols they are using.

Step 4

Children need to write an explanation of what the equals symbol means. They should demonstrate that they understand that the symbol is one of equality and that what is on one side is equivalent to what is on the other. This is an excellent opportunity to encourage children to explain in their own words an idea that they often take for granted.

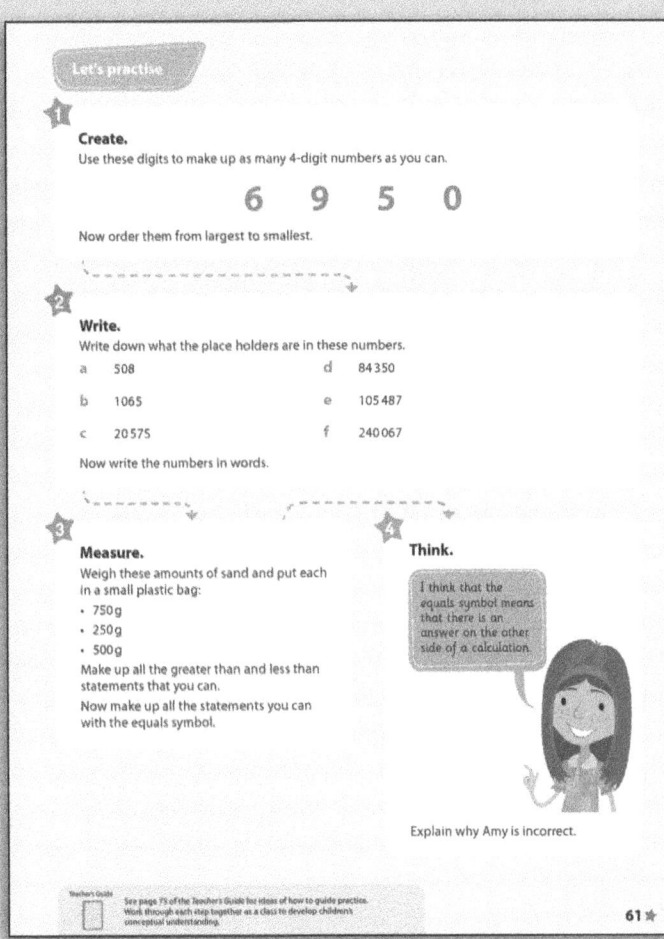

Let's practise

1 Create.
Use these digits to make up as many 4-digit numbers as you can.

6   9   5   0

Now order them from largest to smallest.

2 Write.
Write down what the place holders are in these numbers.
a   508
b   1065
c   20575
d   84350
e   105487
f   240067

Now write the numbers in words.

3 Measure.
Weigh these amounts of sand and put each in a small plastic bag:
• 750g
• 250g
• 500g
Make up all the greater than and less than statements that you can.
Now make up all the statements you can with the equals symbol.

4 Think.

I think that the equals symbol means that there is an answer on the other side of a calculation.

Explain why Amy is incorrect.

See page 75 of the Teacher's Guide for ideas of how to guide practice. Work through each step together as a class to develop children's conceptual understanding.

61

Follow-up ideas

• Children could make up cards with different 4-, 5- or 6-digit numbers written on to them. They could then place the cards in a pile face down on the table and take it in turns to pick one. The player with the highest card keeps it. They keep playing until all are taken. The player with the most cards wins.

• Children could make up some word problems that involve identifying highest and lowest numbers.

• You could write a mass on the board, e.g. 24 kg 250 g. Ask children to write some number sentences with this and other masses that are equal.

Ensuring progress

Supporting understanding

It is important that all children understand the purpose of the place holder. It might be that you need to work with some children in a guided group to take them through this more thoroughly. You could ask them to make up numbers using place-value cards and then partition these to make equivalent numbers, e.g. 4507 = 4000 + 507 or 4500 + 7.

They also need to master ordering and comparing numbers. It may be that you need to work with them in a focused group or to plan a specific task for an additional adult in your class to work on with them.

Broadening understanding

Provide opportunities for children to order and compare numbers in different contexts, e.g. money and time. Encourage them to make up problems for others to solve within the theme of this spread. This will help you to assess their true understanding.

✓ Concept mastered

Children can tell you the value of each digit in a number and explain how each gets its value. They can explain the role of zero and use >, < and = to compare numbers.

Answers

Step 1

Largest possible number 9650; smallest possible number 5069.

Step 2

a   tens (five hundred and eight)

b   hundreds (one thousand and sixty five)

c   ones of thousands (twenty thousand five hundred and seventy five)

d   ones (eighty four thousand three hundred and fifty)

e   tens of thousands (one hundred and five thousand four hundred and eighty seven)

f   ones of thousands and hundreds (two hundred and forty thousand and sixty seven)

Step 4

Any statement that alludes to the fact that the equals symbol shows equivalence, that what is on one side is the same as what is on the other.

5b Positive and negative numbers

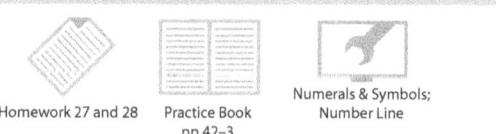

Homework 27 and 28   Practice Book pp 42–3   Numerals & Symbols; Number Line

- Interpret negative numbers in context.
- Count forwards and backwards with positive and negative whole numbers, including through zero.

Mathematical vocabulary

Negative number, positive number, temperature, thermometer, degrees

Representations and resources

Counting stick, number lines, thermometers, picture of a thermometer for each child.

Warming up

Use the counting stick to practise counting in negative number steps. Begin by placing your finger on the fifth division and tell children that this is zero. Ask them to tell you what numbers would go at either end if counting in ones. Move your finger up and down the stick counting in ones. Next have zero at the end and ask children to count backwards and then forwards in steps of one, two, five and any others you want to practise. What do children notice? Agree it is similar to counting in positive numbers.

Background knowledge

Negative numbers should be taught in context to begin with as these numbers are very abstract. They are positional numbers and not cardinal because you can't count them. In secondary school children will work more in depth calculating with negative numbers. It is important that they understand why, e.g. when two signs are the same you add, e.g. $5 + (+) 3 = 5 + 3 = 8$ and $5 - (-3) = 5 + 3 = 8$ and when two signs are different you subtract, e.g. $9 + (-4) = 9 - 4 = 5$ and $8 - (+3) = 8 - 3 = 5$).

Let's learn: Modelling and teaching

Negative numbers

- Discuss when negative numbers are found in real life. Ask children when they would find negative temperatures (usually in winter), negative floor numbers (floors that are underground) and negative bank balances (when people are overdrawn at the bank). Tell children that negative numbers mirror positive numbers below zero.

- Ask children to take their fingers for a walk on the number line in the Textbook, or individual –30 to 30 number lines. Ask them to begin on zero, add five, take away seven, take away another seven, add ten. Every so often ask them what number they are on so that everyone can keep together.

- Establish that a negative number always has a – sign in front of it so that people can tell the difference between the two.

- Inform children that a negative number is always positional and that you can place its position on a number line. It is different from a positive number because you can't hold, see and count a negative number of things.

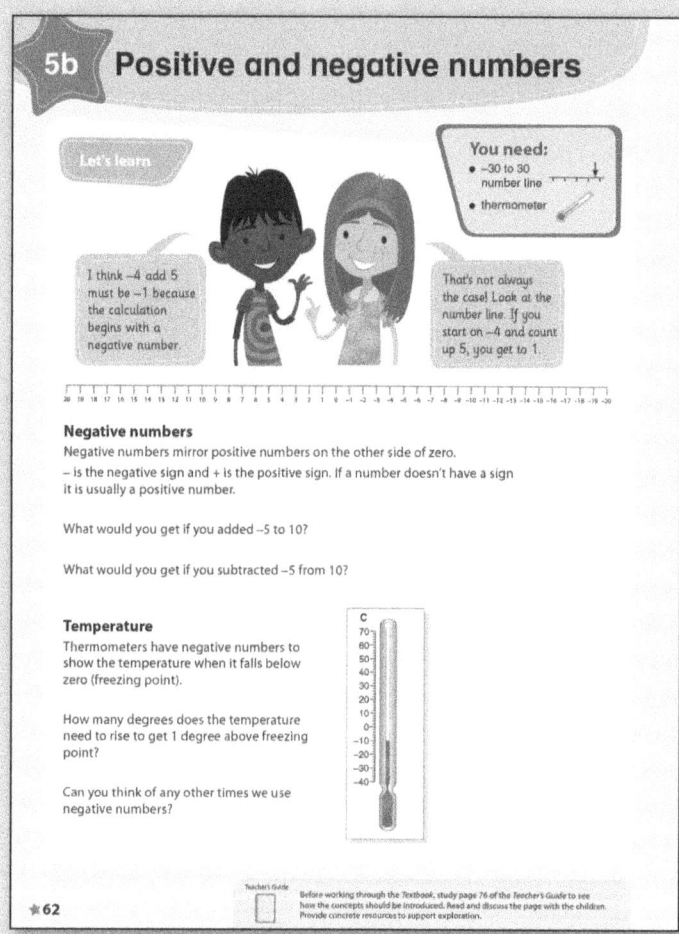

Temperature

- Give pairs or small groups a thermometer to look at. Ask them to describe it to each other and then to the class. They should include the intervals that the marks go up in.

- Ask children to give examples of temperatures that might be found during different seasons. You could tell them that the coldest recorded temperature in the UK was on 10th January 1982 and 30th December 1995 in Scotland when it fell to –27.2°C. Ask children to work out the differences between these and the current temperature outside using a counting-on strategy. Provide a number line to help them.

- Find or make up a line graph that shows temperatures that are both positive and negative. Ask children to make up questions from it to ask each other.

Let's practise: Digging deeper

Step 1

Children need to add and subtract positive and negative numbers. Remind them to look at the diagram of the number line in the Textbook to help them answer these. Demonstrate that when two signs are the same they add and when they are different they subtract.

Step 2

You could give children pre-drawn thermometers so that they can focus on plotting the temperatures rather than drawing the thermometers. Encourage them to use the −30 to 30 number lines to find the difference between the lowest and highest temperatures.

Step 3

In this step children need to solve word problems that involve finding the difference between negative and positive numbers within the context of temperature. Let them use number lines to help - they might use a ready-made number line or draw their own. After using the number lines, ensure that they jot down each step that they have taken. Part e) asks them to write their own questions.

Step 4

Children are aiming to cross out all the numbers on their number line. This will involve working out how to make negative numbers, for example, if they throw 5 and 3 they can make -2 by subtracting 5 from 3. Children may roll the same numbers on their dice more than once. Encourage them to persevere in throwing different numbers.

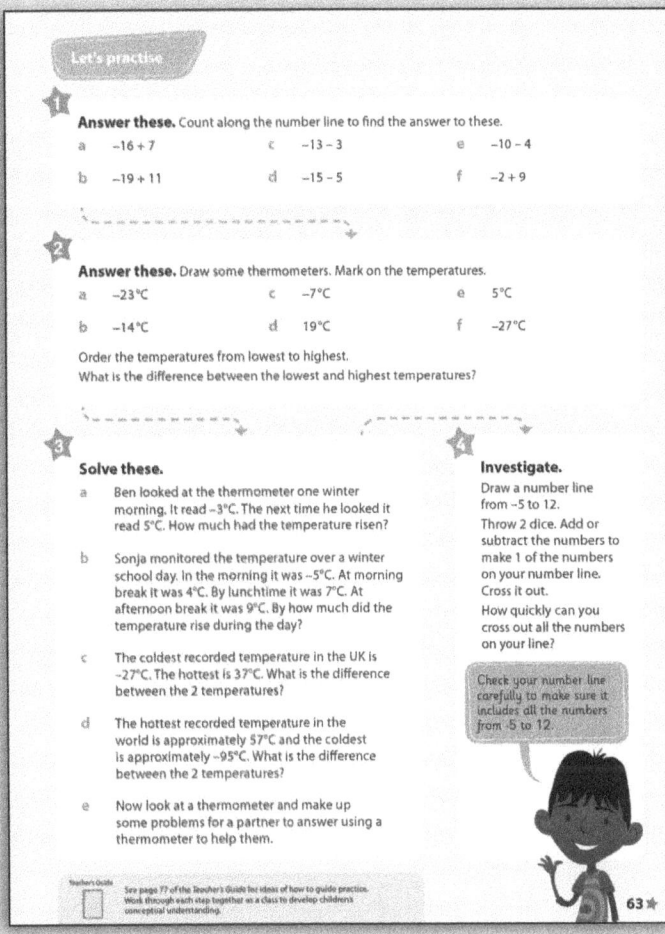

Ensuring progress

Supporting understanding

Because negative numbers can't be counted, this concept can be quite tricky for some children. They will benefit from using a number line and marking those numbers given on to it. Provide larger format number lines for them to use.

You could work through the scenario of a hot air balloon basket rising and falling:

- If you add a balloon to the basket, it will go up. You are adding a positive value, so $3 + 1 = 4$.

- If you take away a balloon, it will go down. You are subtracting a positive value, so $3 - 1 = 2$.

- If you add weights to the basket, it will go down. You are adding a negative value, so $3 + (-1) = 2$.

- If you take away a weigh, it will go up. You are subtracting a negative number, so $3 - (-1) = 4$.

Subtracting a negative number is the same as adding!

Broadening understanding

Provide opportunities for children to add and subtract larger positive and negative numbers. Once they have finished Step 2, they could find the differences between all pairs of numbers.

✓ Concept mastered

Children can explain and represent how they know that 206 is greater than −206 and explain why it is easier to subtract 6 from 206 than −206 and also explain and represent the difference between negative and positive temperatures.

Follow-up ideas

- You could ask children to research when negative numbers were first used. This is documented on at least one well-known mathematical website.

- Play a game using a −30 to 30 number line. Children write positive and negative numbers on cards. They each put a counter on zero. They take it in turns to pick a card and move in the direction of the number on the card. The winner is the player who remains on the number line after the other counters have come off.

- Find bank statements where someone has negative amounts in their account and ask children to investigate them.

Answers

Step 1		Step 2	Step 3	
a	−9	Order: −27 °C, −23 °C, −14 °C, −7 °C, 5 °C, 19 °C.	a	8 °C
b	−8		b	14 °C
c	−16	Difference is 46 °C.	c	64 °C
d	−20		d	152 °C
e	−14			
f	7			

5c Roman numerals

- **Read Roman numerals to 1000 (M) and recognise years written in Roman numerals.**
- **Solve problems involving units of time.**

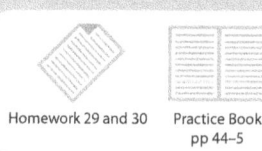

Homework 29 and 30   Practice Book
pp 44–5

Mathematical vocabulary

Roman numerals, thousands, hundreds, tens, ones, place value, hours, minutes, seconds

Warming up

Rehearse the mental calculation strategy of making ten, e.g. 68 + 34 = 70 + 32 = 102, 134 + 87 = 140 + 81 = 221. Write up some 2- and 3-digit calculations for children to answer in their books or on whiteboards.

Background knowledge

Roman numerals can be useful in helping some children to develop a conceptual understanding of place value. The Romans counted in powers of ten as we do. X is ten, C is 100 (10 × 10) and M is 1000 (10 × 10 × 10). They recorded groupings by repeating symbols which were letters instead of numerals. The symbols were placed in descending order as with our numbers.

The use of Roman numerals declined in the 14th century but we still use them sometimes today, e.g. names of monarchs and Popes (Queen Elizabeth II, Pope Benedict XVI) the year of production of films and television shows; page numbering of prefaces and introductions of books; hour marks on timepieces. In this final context 4 is usually written as IIII, however, the clock tower of Big Ben is an example where 4 is written IV.

Let's learn: Modelling and teaching
Roman numerals

- Give children some information about the Roman number system, e.g.:

  ▶ It seems that Roman numerals first appeared as notches on tally sticks. I was a notch on the stick to represent one of something, II was two, III was three and early IIII was four. Λ or V stood for a hand and five because of the number of fingers. The X stands for two hands (one inverted) and ten for ten fingers. The first Roman numerals would have looked something like this: IIIIΛIIIIXIIIIΛIIIIXII.

  ▶ The Romans made abbreviations and introduced symbols for specific numbers. V represented five and X ten. Later L represented 50, C 100 and M 1000.

- Ask children to look at the patterns of symbols in the table of Roman numerals in the Textbook. Can they see how they are made up?

- Write some Roman numerals on the board and ask children to write on their whiteboards what they are in our numbers.

Representations and resources

Roman numeral and our number cards, blank 100 squares, pictures of clocks showing Roman numerals, clock with Roman numerals, clock faces.

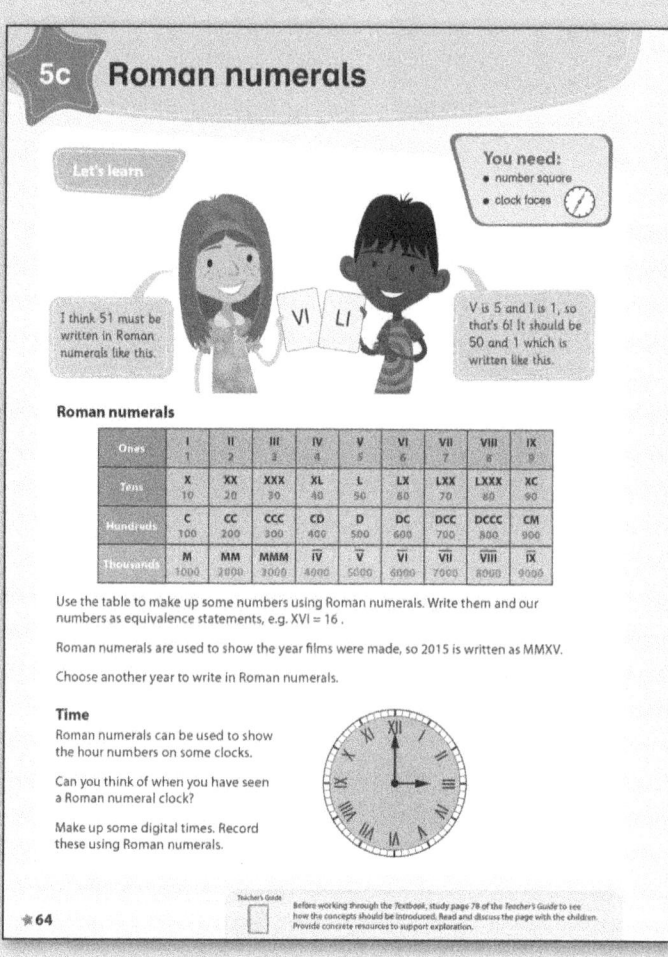

They could refer to their Textbooks for these. Ask children to write some of our numbers in Roman numerals.

- Ask children to make a Roman numeral 100 square.

Time

- If possible, use a clock with Roman numerals, or ask children to each make one. Show times and ask children to write them down as analogue and digital times.

- Show different starting times and ask children to tell you what the time would be, e.g. 45/50/75/90 minutes or 2 hours 5 minutes later.

- Show different finishing times and ask children to tell you what the time would be, e.g. 45/90/180 minutes or 3 hours 55 minutes before.

Let's practise: Digging deeper

Step 1

Children need to convert our numbers to Roman numerals. Encourage them to partition the numbers and convert each type and then recombine them. They should either write a statement or tell you how they worked out their answers. If any children find this straightforward, you could give them thousands numbers to convert.

Step 2

In this activity children convert Roman numerals to our numbers. Encourage them to partition these into the symbols that represent hundreds, tens and ones as appropriate and convert each group and then recombine. Again, use written statements or discussion to allow children to explain what they have done and why.

Step 3

Provide children with clocks so that they can find the times before they draw them. Once they have drawn them, they label them with 12-hour digital times. They could then pretend that they are all afternoon and evening times and write these down as 24-hour times. You could them ask them to work out the differences between pairs of times.

Step 4

Explain that the Ancient Romans used to play games with dice. Provide children with a cube so that they can visualise what the net would look like. They then use this to create a cube of their own. They label each face with the Roman numerals from I to VI. Encourage children to keep score as they play and then find their total. They should do this writing in Roman numerals.

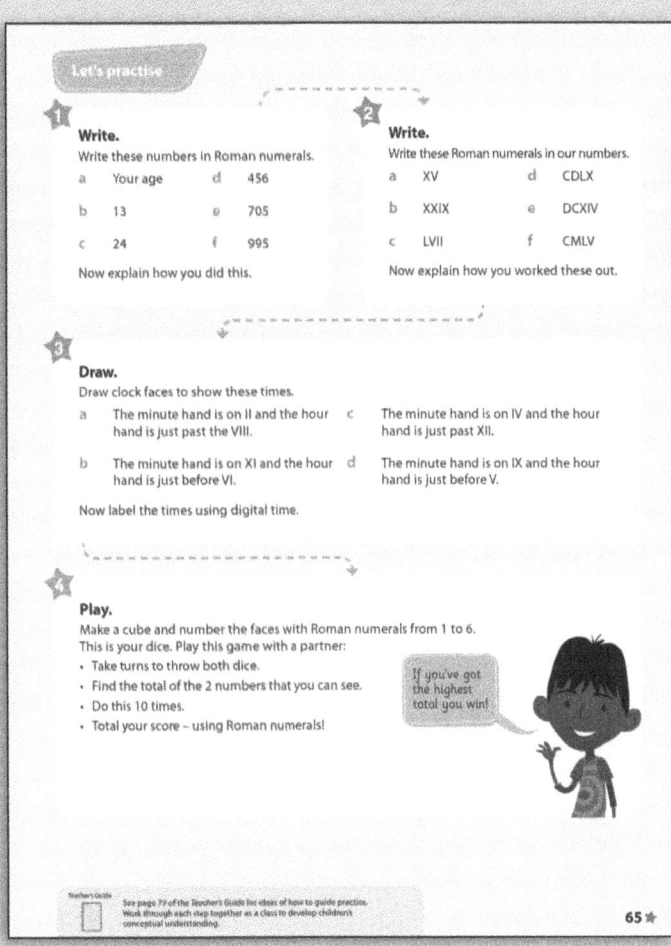

Ensuring progress

Supporting understanding

- Explain to children that to translate any Roman numeral they should partition it into separate groups and these are found where a lower value follows a higher one. Each group can then be dealt with separately, and then recombined to give the whole number, e.g.:

  ▶ CCCXLVI = CCC + XL + V + I = 300 + 40 (10 before 50) + 5 + 1 = 346

  ▶ MCDLXIV = M + CD + L + X + IV = 1000 + 400 (100 before 500) + 50 + 10 + 4 = 1464

- Observe children as they work through the activities. If any struggle they should focus on converting 2-digit numbers. Encourage them to use the information in the Textbook to help them. You might provide them with a net of a cube to make their dice.

Broadening understanding

- Children could add and subtract Roman numerals using a partitioning strategy and then using a column method. Invite them to share with the class what they did and how hard/easy they found this.

- You could ask children to make up an imaginary bus or train timetable using Roman numerals. Make up departure and arrival times for four or five different stops. They could then make up some problems to go with their timetables for a partner, group or the whole class to solve.

Follow-up ideas

- In pairs children could make up a Roman numeral game. They write a normal number on a sheet of paper and then their partner can write the corresponding Roman numeral. They could take turns creating numbers. When they have 12 of each, they could play a pairs game.

- Children might like to make up a class birthday chart or book. In this they could convert their birthdays to Roman numerals, e.g. August 20, 2007, would become XX August MMVII.

- Children could spell out Roman numerals using their bodies. Divide them into groups. Groups take it in turns to decide on a number. They then use their bodies to spell out the number on the floor while other children try to guess what it is.

✓ Concept mastered

Children can explain how to represent numbers in Roman numerals.

Answers

Step 1	Step 2		Step 3	
a IX or X	a	15	a	8:10, 20:10
b XIII	b	29	b	5:55, 17:55
c XXIV	c	57	c	12:20, 00:20
d CDLVI	d	460	d	4:45, 16:45
e DCCV	e	614		
f CMXCV	f	955		

A mixture of numbers

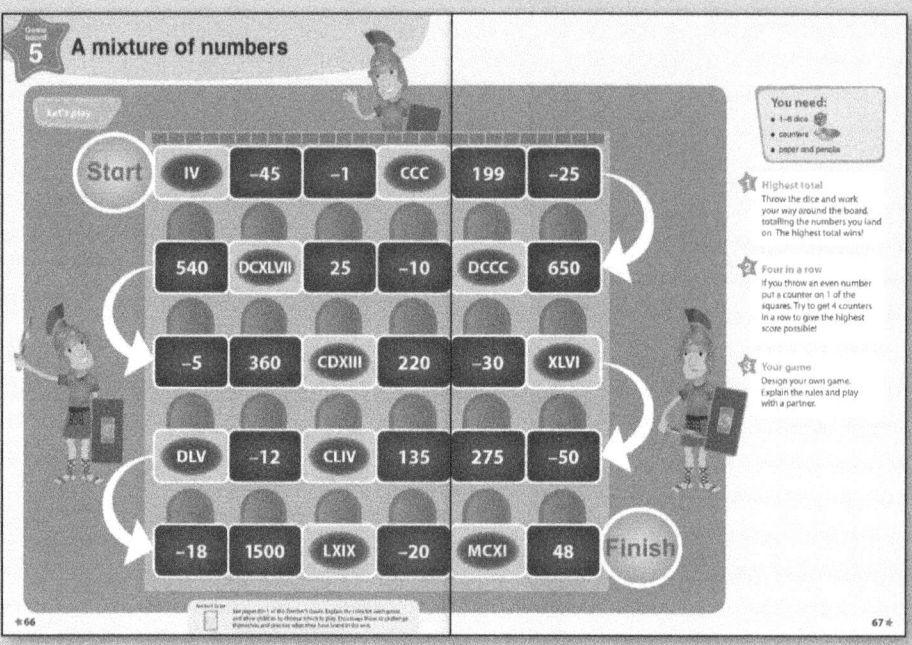

Game 1: Highest total

In this game children have to convert Roman numerals to our numbers as they work their way around the board. They collect numbers as they go, then have to total all their numbers (including negative numbers) at the end. Who can get the highest total?

Maths focus

- Negative numbers
- Roman numerals

Resources

1–6 dice (1), 1 counter per player (1 colour per player), paper and pencils.

How to play

Each player puts their counter on the Start box. They throw the dice and work their way around the board, each using a counter. Each time they land on a square, they write the number on a piece of paper. If it is a Roman numeral they convert it to our numbers. They continue until they reach the end of the board. At the end they then find the total of their numbers. They need to remember to subtract the negative numbers that they landed on. If they prefer, they could make a running total as they move around. The highest total wins. They could play this game again with the lowest total winning.

Making it easier

You could provide children with a Roman numeral converter for the numbers on the gameboard and also a number line to help them subtract the negative numbers.

Making it harder

You could ask children to double the numbers they land on. Ask them to explain why they need to subtract the negative numbers.

Game 2: Four in a row

In this game children have to try to make a row of four numbers with their counters, while at the same time preventing their partner from doing the same!

Maths focus

- Negative numbers
- Roman numerals

Resources

1–6 dice (1), counters (15 of one colour per player).

How to play

Children take it in turns to throw the dice. If they throw an even number they put a counter on one of the squares. Their aim is to get four counters in a row to give the highest score possible. Of course, each player, as well as aiming to get a line of four, needs to prevent the other player from getting a row of four first. The counters making the rows can be vertical or horizontal. When one player has a row of four they both find their totals. The one making the row earns a bonus of 20. The winner is the player with the highest score.

Making it easier

Children could play three in a row with the same rules as above.

Making it harder

You could ask children to consider making a diagonal row of four as well as horizontal and vertical rows. Encourage them to look at the grid and predict which row will give the highest score. Again, you could ask them to double or even halve the numbers they land on.

Game 3: Your game

Children should invent their own game, designing rules that use the concepts covered in the unit. Challenge children to make their game easier or harder.

A mixture of numbers

Choose a game to play.

Game 1: Highest total

How to play

- Each place your counter on Start.
- Throw the dice and work your way around the board.
- Each time you land on a square, write down the number. If it's a Roman numeral, convert it to our numbers.
- At the end, find the total of your numbers. Remember to subtract the negative numbers!
- The player with the highest total wins.

You need:

- 1 counter per player (1 colour per player)
- 1–6 dice
- paper and pencils

Game 2: Four in a row

How to play

- Take turns to throw the dice.
- If you get an even number put a counter on 1 of the squares.
- Try to get 4 counters in a row to give the highest score possible. Rows can be vertical or horizontal. Try to stop your partner getting a row of 4 first!
- When one player has a row of 4, both players find their totals. The player making the row gets a bonus of 20.
- The winner is the player with the highest score.

You need:

- 15 counters per player (1 colour per player)
- 1–6 dice

Game 3: Your game

- Make up your own game using the gameboard.
- Your game could include converting our numbers to Roman numerals!
- Perhaps it could include adding or subtracting negative numbers.
- What are the rules for your game? Explain them to someone.

Please help your child by reading the instructions and playing the game together.

Assessment task 1

Running the task

Discuss the picture and establish that it is a view of the Sun and the planet Mercury. Make sure children know that Mercury is the planet that is closest to the Sun. Ask them to tell you what is meant by atmosphere. Agree that it is the gases that surround the Earth and some other planets. The atmosphere acts like a blanket and helps to keep heat around the planet it surrounds. It also acts as protection against the Sun's strong rays.

Discuss the fact that there is no atmosphere around Mercury and therefore the planet is only heated when it faces the Sun. Ask them to imagine how hot it must be when the planet faces the Sun and how cold when it is away from the Sun. Ask them to read the two temperatures. The task asks them to find the difference in temperature between the two.

Encourage children to draw a number line from –120° to 160° to help them to find the difference between the two temperatures. They should mark the divisions of the number line in 10s. Encourage them to count on from –115° to 158°. Listen to children that you particularly wish to assess as they explain how they worked out the answer.

Take the opportunity to question children about what happens when you add a negative number to a negative number and what happens when you subtract a negative number from a negative number to find out how much they really understand about this area of mathematics. Encourage them to give you examples to demonstrate their explanations.

Evidencing mastery

If children are able to explain how to find the difference between negative and positive numbers by counting on they have mastered one part of the National Curriculum requirement. Encourage them to explain why adding a negative number to a negative number gives an answer that is lower than the original number, and subtracting a negative number from a negative number gives an answer that is higher. Once they can do this they have mastered this area of mathematics for Year 5.

Assessment task 2

Resources

Vocabulary words for numbers.

Running the task

The first part of this task asks children to write each number in words. You could provide vocabulary words to help them with the spelling. Check that they write 'and' in the correct place, i.e. where the place holder is and between the hundreds and tens, e.g. 207549 should be written as *two hundred and seven thousand five hundred and forty nine*. Once they have done this, or as they write each number, ask them to explain what each digit represents and what its true value is. Ask them what value the place holder represents. Focus your attention on children who you specifically wish to assess.

Evidencing mastery

After the work that you have carried out in this unit, all children should be able to identify what the place holder represents in 3-digit numbers. They should all be able to identify the position of these numbers and the real values. Those that are able to identify the place holders for all the numbers to 900000 and identify each digit's position and value are showing mastery of this concept at this stage in Year 5.

Concepts mastered

☑ Children can tell you the value of each digit in a number and explain how each gets its value. They can explain the role of zero and use >, < and = to compare numbers.

☑ Children can explain and represent how they know that 206 is greater than −206 and explain why it is easier to subtract 6 from 206 than −206 and also explain and represent the difference between negative and positive temperatures.

☑ Children can explain how to represent numbers in Roman numerals.

Assessment task 3
Running the task

The main idea for this task is to find out how proficient children are at converting our numbers to Roman numerals and vice versa. The first part asks children to convert our numbers to Roman numerals. Remind them to partition the numbers into tens and ones, or hundreds, tens and ones, and to convert each part.

The second part of the task asks them to convert Roman numerals to our number system. Encourage them, again, to partition. They should find the ones number and then the tens and hundreds as appropriate and then write the numbers as we do. You could suggest that they look back at the table on Roman numerals in the Textbook for this unit if they need extra support.

Evidencing mastery

Most children should be able to convert some of these numbers to Roman numerals. They should also be able to convert some of the Roman numerals to those of our number system. For more complex numbers they may need some support from the table in the Textbook. If children are able to convert these numbers without any assistance or reminder from the Textbook, they have mastered this area of mathematics.

Did you know?

From the 14th century, Roman numerals began to be replaced by the Hindu-Arabic number system, which is what we use today. This process was gradual and we still have Roman numerals in some instances now, e.g. dates on films, hour numbers on some clocks, preliminary pages in a book, sporting events and numbering of monarchs with the same name.

The Romans didn't have a symbol to represent zero. The Latin word 'nulla' was used to describe nothing or none. Various number systems used zero but it is believed that we have the Italian mathematician Leonardo Fibonacci to thank for first promoting the use of zero in Europe in the 13th century.

Mathematical focus

★ Number: addition and subtraction

★ Measurement: mass and time

★ Statistics: solving problems, interpreting information

Prior learning

Children should be able to:

- add and subtract numbers with up to four digits using the formal written methods of columnar addition and subtraction where appropriate

- estimate and use inverse operations to check answers to a calculation

- solve addition and subtraction two-step problems in contexts, deciding which operations and methods to use and why.

Key new learning

- Add and subtract numbers mentally with increasingly large numbers.

- Solve addition and subtraction multi-step problems in contexts, deciding which operations and methods to use and why.

- Solve problems involving number up to three decimal places.

- Use addition and subtraction to solve problems involving mass using decimal notation.

- Add and subtract whole numbers with four digits, including using formal written methods (columnar addition and subtraction).

- Use rounding to check answers to calculations and determine, in the context of a problem, levels of accuracy.

- Solve comparison, sum and difference problems using information presented in a line graph and bar charts.

Making connections

- Providing problems involving length, mass, volume and money enables children to apply their understanding of addition and subtraction to real-life contexts.

- Understanding how to use decimal notation will enable children to convert between different units of measures and solve real-life problems involving decimal numbers.

- This unit includes opportunities to read and interpret information presented in line graphs, bar charts and tables. This will help children to understand why information is presented in different ways, and support their work in science and geography.

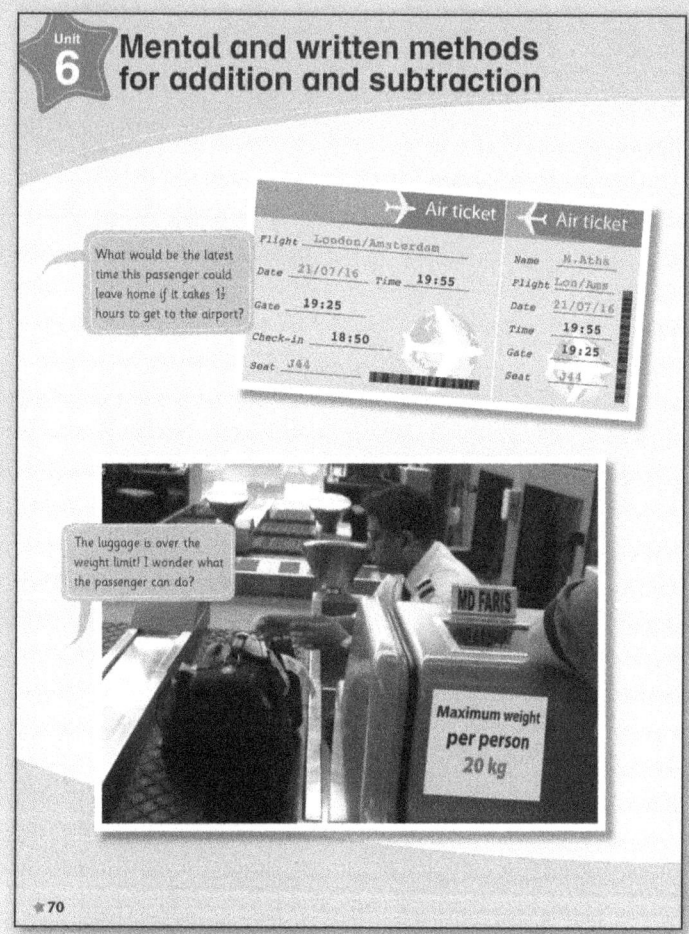

Unit 6
Mental and written methods for addition and subtraction

Talk about

It is important to use precise mathematical vocabulary from the beginning so that children use the correct vocabulary to refer to place value when using mental or written methods. The language ensures that the size of the numbers is still explicit.

Engaging and exploring

Ask children to look at each picture and to discuss the questions with a partner. Focus on each picture in turn.

For the picture of an airline ticket, encourage children to read the times using the different language of time, e.g. the flight departs at five to eight in the evening. Compare with the language used for an analogue clock. Compare the 12-hour and 24-hour digital clock. What is the same and what is different? Discuss the importance of using the 24-hour clock for timetables and other information related to travel. What could be the problem if the 12-hour clock was used?

Encourage children to make up questions using the information shown on the ticket, e.g. *How long have they got to wait between the time the gate closes and the departure time?* Consider different strategies to solve the problems, e.g. model the use of a number line or use an analogue clock.

Decide what information is important to answer the given question, i.e. the departure time is not important but check-in times are. Check children's fluency when counting on or back in steps of one hour or half an hour, etc.

For the luggage picture, discuss the use of kilograms to measure mass rather than grams. Revisit kilogram to gram conversions and ask children to give the weight of the bag in grams. Ask them to think about two bags that would have the same total mass as the bag being weighed.

Discuss the problem the passengers have and reason about how it could be resolved. Encourage the use of the language 'heavier than' and 'lighter than' to compare the weight to the required 20 kg, e.g. the 22.45 kg bag is 2.45 kg heavier than 20 kg. Suggest that using a mental method is better here. Children could explain why they think you have made this decision, i.e. spotted number bonds to 100.

For the cinema bar chart, ask children to discuss what they notice about the chart. Encourage them to use mathematical language, e.g. *We noticed that the scale is labelled every 500 but the intervals are 250.* Discuss why the maximum seating capacity at each cinema has been given rather than the reader having to use the scale to work them out. Include discussions about approximate values and accurate values. Ask: *Why can an accurate value not be established on this bar chart?*

For the phone calls line graph, revisit the difference between discrete and continuous data. Why is this graph showing continuous data? How would the information need to be adapted so that it represented discrete data, e.g. total number of calls per hour, or per day over a period of a week? Discuss the use of accurate and approximate values. Why is it sensible to use approximate values here? Look at the strategy of rounding to the nearest hundred or thousand. Ask children to find the missing values on the y-axis scale and find some positions on the line graph where there were approximately this number of calls received.

Challenge children to find the approximate number of calls at 09:30 or 11:00, i.e. a time that is not labelled on the x-axis. Encourage them to reason about the higher and lower points in the graph. Why may this have been the case? Model the subtraction of $11\,500 - 6000$ as a formal written method and encourage children to challenge the method you have used and the better use of a mental method.

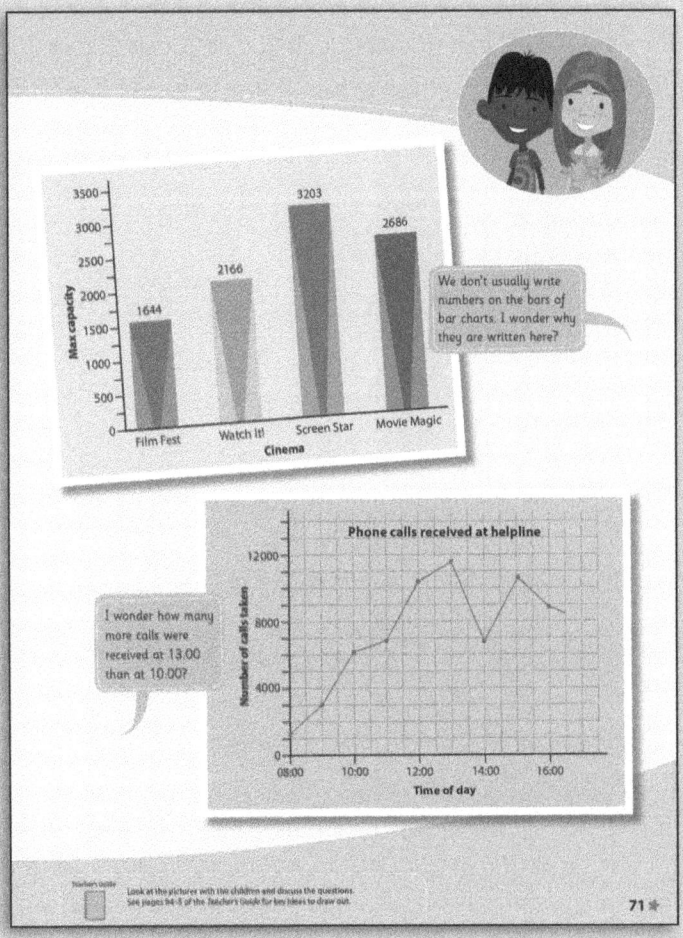

Things to think about

- How will you raise the profile of mental calculation?

- How will you organise groupings? Mixed ability groupings can raise the achievement of those who find mathematics difficult, while providing those who have grasped concepts well with opportunities to deepen their learning by explaining it.

- How might you use manipulatives to secure conceptual understanding and provide practical tasks to develop additive reasoning through measurement and statistics?

- What opportunities will you provide to draw out reasoning, encouraging children to explain their thinking?

- How will you provide opportunities to develop problem-solving strategies?

Checking understanding

You will know children have mastered the concepts when they can solve addition and subtraction problems in different contexts, appropriately choosing between mental and written methods. They use number facts and their understanding of place value and can explain their decision making and justify their solutions.

6a Mental or written methods?

- **Add and subtract whole numbers with more than four digits, including using formal written methods (columnar addition and subtraction).**
- **Add and subtract numbers mentally with increasingly large numbers.**
- **Solve addition and subtraction multi-step problems in contexts, deciding which operations and methods to use and why.**
- **Solve problems involving number up to three decimal places.**
- **Use addition and subtraction to solve problems involving mass using decimal notation.**

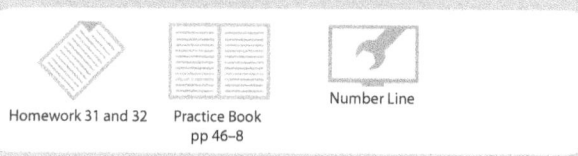

Homework 31 and 32   Practice Book pp 46–8   Number Line

Representations and resources

Place-value chart, number lines, calculators, bead strings.

Mathematical vocabulary

Gram, kilogram, add, subtract, total, sum, difference, partitioning, counting on, sequencing

Warming up

Use a place-value chart, including decimals, so children can make up some numbers with up to two decimal places, e.g. the child chooses 3, 0.2 and 0.05 to make 3.25. Use the relationship between rows to help multiply numbers. All parts of the number will need to be multiplied. Explore different ways of multiplying by 1000, i.e. by ten, by ten again and by ten again or by 100 and by ten again, etc. Establish that the result is the same each time. You could practise multiplying other numbers in the same way. Link this to converting between units of measurement.

Background knowledge

Children should frequently practise and develop their ability to use mental calculation strategies. The curriculum sets out the type of calculations that children are expected to do mentally. Remember to refer to previous year groups, e.g. add and subtract pairs of 2-digit numbers in Year 2; add and subtract multiples of 10 and 100 to any 3-digit number in Year 3.

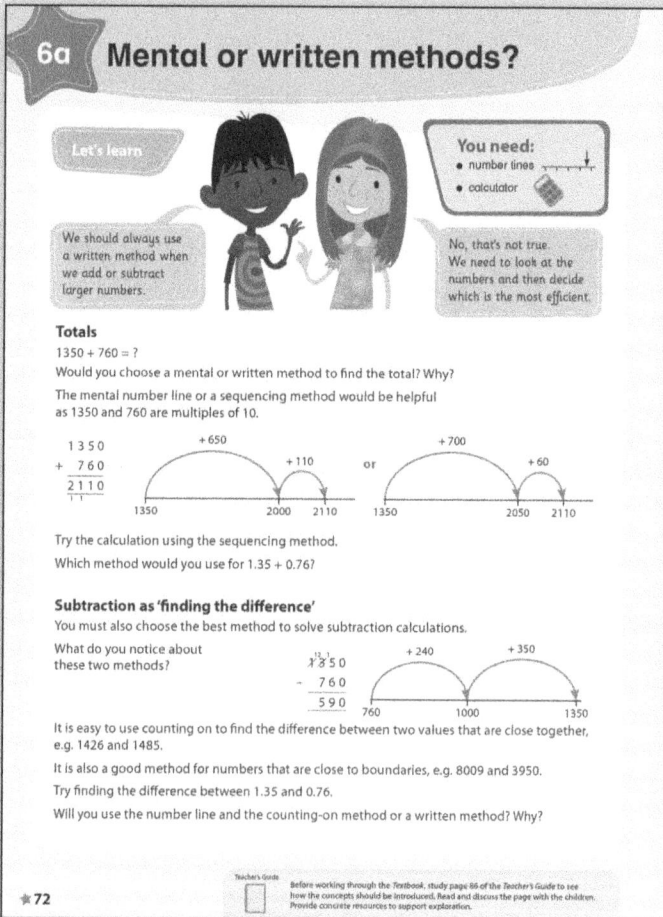

Let's learn: Modelling and teaching
Totals

- Ask children to suggest some examples where they would definitely use the written method or mental method. Create a list of children's given criteria for choices.
- Return to 1350 + 760 and use the criteria to help decide whether to use a mental or written method. Discuss the different types of mental methods.
- Model the use of the number line, sequencing, e.g. 1350 g + 700 g + 60 g, and the written method. Practise other calculations using the sequencing method, e.g. 2370 + 860 or 2375 + 875. Ask children to consider whether the calculation with decimals is trickier or can a mental method such as sequencing be used?

Subtraction as 'finding the difference'

- Ask children how they would find the difference between 1350 and 760 and what would be a good estimate. Consider using the bar model to represent this calculation.
- Demonstrate how to use a number line and the written method. Discuss the two methods. The written method could result in errors due to the exchanging, whereas the number line requires fewer and easier steps for the numbers involved. Focus on the use of number bonds to count on to the next boundary. Write a range of other calculations for children to solve using these methods.
- Discuss the use of mental and written methods to find the difference between decimals. Again, focus on the use of number bonds when counting on to the next whole number.
- Discuss why it is easier to use the finding the difference method when two values are close together.

Let's practise: Digging deeper

Step 1

Children are asked to choose two calculations to solve using a mental method and two using a written method. They should be encouraged to reason about the numbers involved and make a decision about all calculations rather than choosing as they go along. E.g. b) would require rounding and adjusting; d) would involve using number bonds. The next four questions require them to make a decision about using the mental counting-on method or a written method of subtraction. In the same way, all questions should be considered before they start working.

Step 2

Children practise using the sequencing strategy to answer these addition calculations. They must first use rounding to help them make an estimate for each before calculating.

Allow children to make jottings to help them as necessary.

Step 3

Children add and subtract using whichever calculation strategy they wish. They must also check that the units of measurement are the same each time and, if not, convert one value accordingly before calculating. They are encouraged to use a calculator to check their calculations and so identify any place-value errors relating to converting between units of measurement.

Step 4

There will have been plenty of opportunities to identify calculations where a mental method of finding the difference will be more efficient. Children should apply this understanding to calculations involving mass and suggest other examples where the mental method is the better choice.

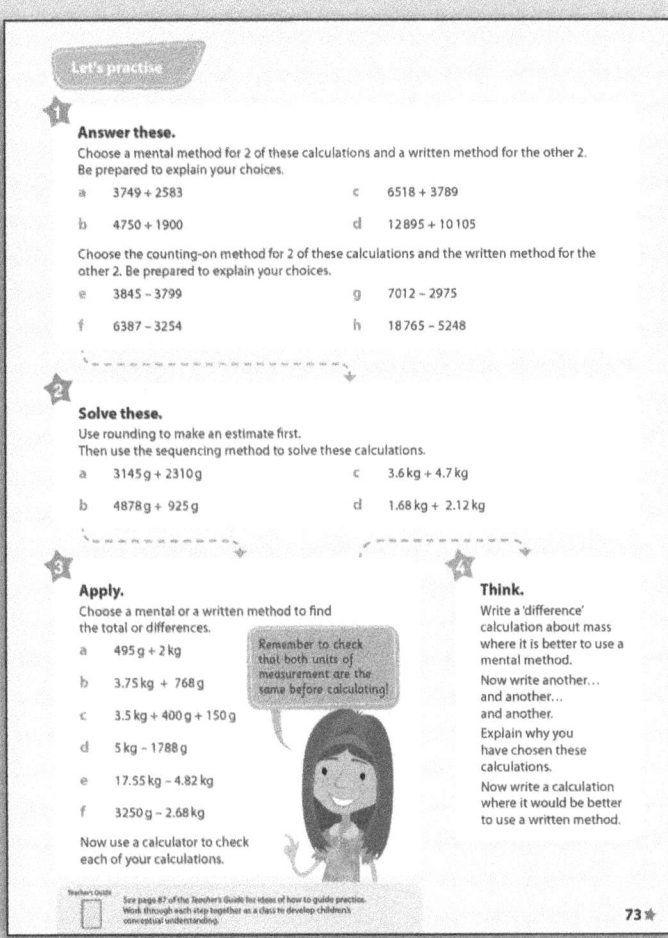

Ensuring progress

Supporting understanding

It may be useful to return to 2- or 3-digit whole numbers initially to particularly focus on the criteria for finding the difference. Bead strings could be used to support conceptual understanding of finding the difference between 2-digit numbers. Use word problems and puzzles that encourage this decision making both within and without a familiar context.

Broadening understanding

Refer back to previous work on additive reasoning and provide opportunities for children to add and subtract using mental calculation strategies in the context of money or length. Again, units of measurements can be mixed so that they have to convert before calculating. Use puzzles and two-step or multi-step word problems that encourage children to make decisions about methods to use.

✓ Concept mastered

Children can choose to use an appropriate mental or written method of addition and subtraction depending on the numbers involved. They explain their decisions giving reasons for which would be the most efficient and why. They can apply these skills to a range of contexts and can explain how the mental and written methods will help them.

Follow-up ideas

- Children could use recipes to look at the weight of ingredients needed and look at options of weights sold on the Internet of, e.g. flour, and how much would be left in the bag.

- The amount of flour in different cake recipes could be compared and children could decide to use mental or written methods to find the difference. They could reason about whether there is enough flour in one bag or how much they need of a second bag to make all the different cakes.

- Children could make up games that involve adding and subtracting amounts. They should include questions that can be more efficiently answered using a mental calculation strategy.

Answers

Step 1

a	6332
b	6650
c	10307
d	23000
e	46
f	3133
g	4037
h	13517

Step 2

a	5455 g
b	5803 g
c	8.3 kg
d	3.8 kg

Step 3

a	2.495 kg or 2495 g
b	4.518 kg or 4518 g
c	4.05 kg or 4050 g
d	3.212 kg or 3212 g
e	12.73 kg
f	0.57 kg or 570 g

- Add and subtract whole numbers with more than four digits, including using formal written methods (columnar addition and subtraction).
- Add and subtract numbers mentally with increasingly large numbers.
- Solve addition and subtraction multi-step problems in contexts, deciding which operations and methods to use and why.
- Solve comparison, sum and difference problems using information presented in a line graph and bar charts.
- Use rounding to check answers to calculations and determine, in the context of a problem, levels of accuracy.
- Complete, read and interpret information in tables, including timetables

Homework 33 and 34   Practice Book pp 49–51

Representations and resources

Place-value counters, number lines, clocks, Base 10 apparatus, number rods.

Mathematical vocabulary

Minute, hour, analogue and digital clocks, 24-hour clock, time graphs, bar charts, add, subtract, total, sum, difference, counting on, sequencing, approximate, accurate, estimate

Warming up

Re-visit the importance of using the 24-hour clock for timetables by asking children what they notice about the times shown in a bus timetable.

Bus garage	School	Park	Station	Town Hall	Cinema
14:10	14:25	14:52	15:00	15:09	15:26

Children can practise converting these 24-hour times to a.m. and p.m. times by partitioning the hours into 12 hours and a bit. Encourage them to check the conversion by adding 12 hours to any p.m. times.

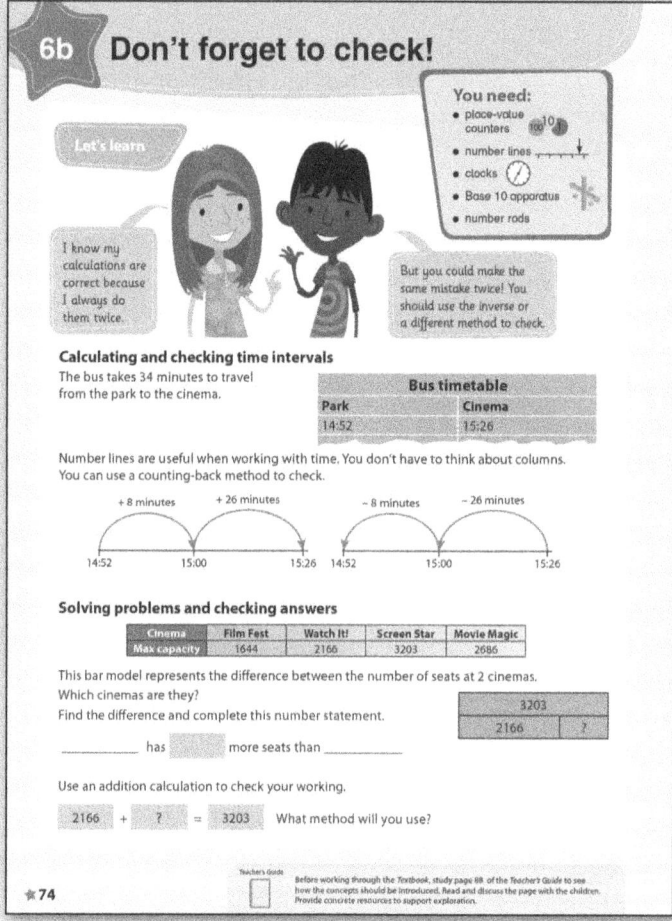

Background knowledge

Children are often reluctant to make estimates and even more so to check their answers. They will tend to check by re-doing the same method but this may simply repeat an error. Throughout, encourage children to use a different calculation or the inverse to check their answers.

Let's learn: Modelling and teaching
Calculating and checking time intervals

- Model the number line in the Textbook showing the journey time from the park to the cinema. What's the same and what's different about this and number lines they have used previously to find the difference?

- Discuss why a number line is a useful way to calculate time intervals rather than a written method. Model an inappropriate use of the column method.

- Focus on why it is important to check working and think about whether an answer is possible. Model counting back from 15:26 to 14:52 on a number line to check the calculation.

- Children choose two stops on the bus route from the

Warming up activity and calculate the time interval. Partners check using the counting-back method.

Solving problems and checking answers

- Children discuss what the bar model in the Textbook represents and how to find the value of the question mark using the strategies from the previous concept..

- Discuss different strategies to support finding the difference, e.g. using a number line and counting on from the smaller number, focusing on the use of number bonds when counting on to the next multiple of 10, 100 or 1000.

- Explore the use of the inverse or re-writing the number statement to check calculations. Ask children to explain which methods they find the most effective and why.

Let's practise: Digging deeper

Step 1

Children must find the intervals between pairs of given times. The times are presented in different ways, i.e. using a.m. and p.m., 24-hour clock notation or the language of noon and midnight. They should practise using the number line to find the difference. They could check using a geared clock.

Step 2

Children must find totals using the cinema seating capacities, reasoning about what they already know and how this can aid calculation. They should practise using a written method as this will also be more efficient when adding three or more amounts. Encourage children to make estimates and use place-value counters or Base 10 apparatus when needed. They must also find an inverse calculation to check their workings.

Step 3

This is a word problem that builds on the context of the cinema but relates to money. Ensure that children begin by drawing a bar model to represent the problem. They must then select the correct calculation and apply a written method to carry out a subtraction with 5-digit numbers. They convince their partner that the steps in their calculation are correct and model how an inverse calculation can be used to check.

Step 4

This is a more open problem that requires children to apply their knowledge of rounding and reason about possible pairs of numbers that meet the criteria.

They must find at least three different solutions but this could be extended to finding possible ranges of numbers that would suit the criteria, e.g. range of the sum is 2250 to 2349 and the range of the difference is 450 to 549. Children must reason about how one variable affects the other. Is it still possible to achieve the difference when the sum is at its highest possible value?

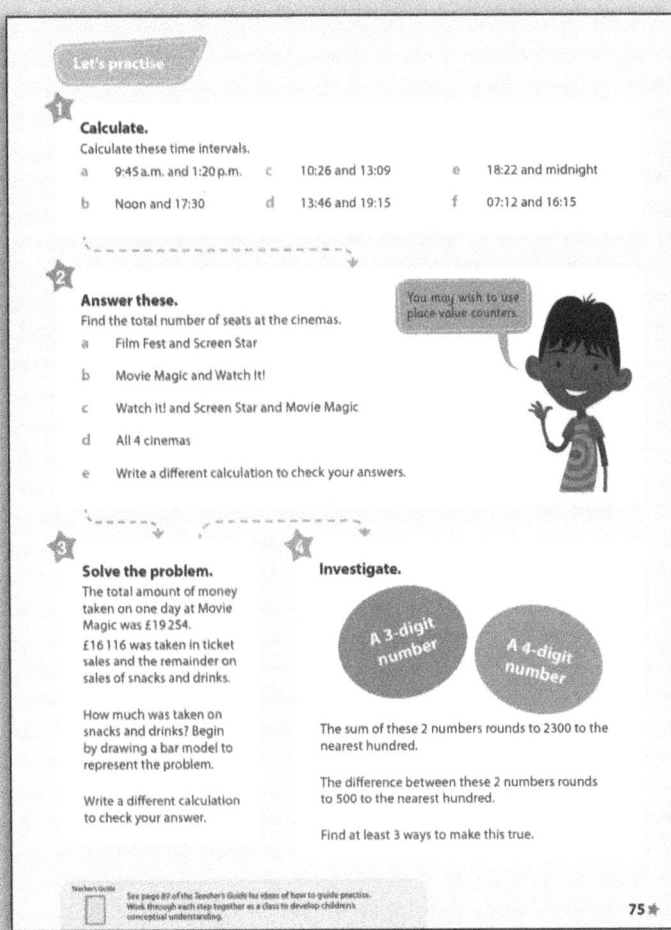

Ensuring progress

Supporting understanding

Use the number rods with smaller numbers to secure children's understanding of how related facts are found and can be used for checking. Throughout the lesson, model written methods using manipulatives such as Base 10 apparatus or place value counters.

Broadening understanding

Extend the work on time intervals by exploring durations that cross midnight or involve a period that is longer than 24 hours, e.g. an overnight train journey or ferry crossing. Children should present their findings as days, hours and minutes.

✓ Concept mastered

Children can confidently select mental and written methods when working within the contexts of measurement and statistics. They can explain why a mental method should be used for calculating time intervals rather than a columnar method.

Follow-up ideas

- Children could use timetables to plan a journey, looking at the time needed to make connections. This may be related to a school trip. They could compare town and country bus routes and timetables, reasoning about the start and end of a service, time taken between stops, etc. The routes could be mapped out and compared in terms of distance (km). Similarly, local and national train services could be compared.

- Seating capacities at the local cinemas (or for each screen of one cinema) can be compared and shown as a bar chart. They can also apply multiplicative reasoning looking at arrays to represent rows of seats, e.g. if there are 480 seats in Screen 1, how could the seats be arranged if all rows are the same length?

Answers

Step 1

a	3 h 35 min
b	5 h 30 min
c	2 h 43 min
d	5 h 29 min
e	5 h 38 min
f	9 h 3 min

Step 2

a	4847
b	4852
c	8055
d	9699
e	4847 − 1644 = 3203 or 4847 − 3203 = 1644
	4852 − 2166 = 2686 or 4852 − 2686 = 2166
	8055 − 4852 = 3203
	9699 − 4847 = 4852 or 9699 − 4852 = 4847

Step 3

£3138
and £16 116 + £3 138 = £19 254
or £3 138 + £16 116 = £19 254

Step 4

Answers will vary, e.g. 1350 and 900, 1375 and 920, 1420 and 876.

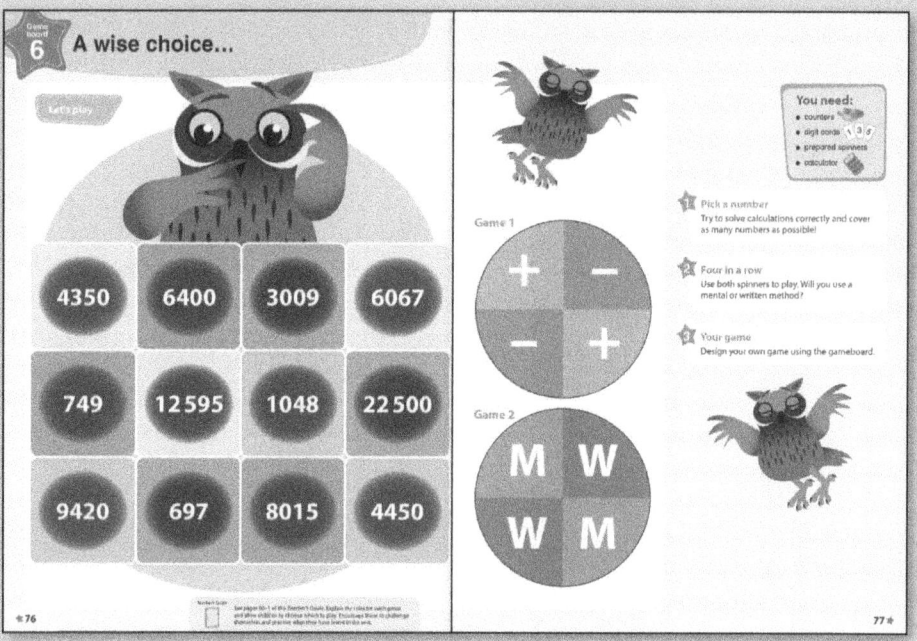

Game 1: Pick a number

In this game players need to think carefully about numbers to select from the grid to make up calculations.

Maths focus

- Written methods and mental calculation strategies for addition and subtraction.

Resources

Counters (1 colour per player), set of digit cards, calculator. (card, pencil and paper clip to make the spinner)

How to play

This game can be played in pairs so children can discuss strategies. Make card spinners as shown in the Textbook. They take turns to pick digit cards to make a 4-digit number, then spin the spinner to find out if they need to add or subtract. They should think carefully about the number they will select from the grid to make up a calculation with their own 4-digit number. To avoid negatives, children will need to decide which number to use first.

Both players should solve their calculations simultaneously. They must check their partner's answer using a calculator. When a player's answer is correct, they can cover the number with a counter. The game continues until the whole grid is covered. Children should choose a new 4-digit number each time. The winner is the player with the most counters on the board at the end.

Making it easier

Children can play the game in small groups so each player has a partner to work with. The game could also be adapted so that the 4-digit number does not have to be changed each time or that children simply choose two numbers from the grid each time and do not make up a 4-digit number at all.

Making it harder

You could turn this into a game of strategy, where children have to try to get three counters in a row, column or a diagonal and score points.

Game 2: Which method?

In this game children need to think about which numbers are appropriate for mental or written calculations.

Maths focus

- Written methods and mental calculation strategies for addition and subtraction.

Resources

Counters (1 colour per player), set of digit cards, calculator. (card, pencil and paper clip to make the spinners)

How to play

In this game children must spin both spinners. This means that they must use a written or mental method depending on the result on the second spinner. They will need to think carefully as they will not want to run out of numbers that are better saved for mental methods.

Making it easier

Children could work with a partner to discuss strategies or the game could be adapted so that they are only working with addition or subtraction, but not both.

Making it harder

The aim of scoring points by covering three in a row (as with the extension to Game 1) would also increase the level of decision making as they may not always be able to go with an easier calculation.

Game 3: Your game

Children should invent their own game, designing rules that use the concepts covered in the unit.

Challenge children to make their game easier or harder.

A wise choice...

Choose a game to play.

Game 1: Pick a number

How to play

- Play with a partner. Take turns to make a 4-digit number with the digit cards.
- Spin the spinner to see if you need to add or subtract. Both choose a number from the grid to make up a calculation using your number, e.g. you could make the number 2386, spin to subtract then make up a calculation 2386 – 697. Solve your calculation using any method you choose. Check your partner's answer using a different checking calculation on the calculator.
- If your answer is correct, cover the number on the grid with a counter.
- Make a new 4-digit number each time and play until the grid is covered.
- The winner is the player with the most counters on the gameboard at the end.

You need:

- counters (1 colour per player)
- set of 0-9 digit cards
- prepared spinners
- calculator

Game 2: Which method?

How to play

- Play the same way as for Game 1, but this time use both spinners. For 'M' you must use a mental method and for 'W' a written method.
- Choose your numbers carefully from the grid – you do not want to use a number in a written method that would have been better for a mental method.

You need:

- counters (1 colour per player)
- set of 0-9 digit cards
- card
- calculator

Game 3: Your game

- Make up your own game using the gameboard and spinners.
- You could use 1 or both spinners.
- You could create a new spinner of your own.
- Explain the rules and play with a partner.

Please help your child by reading the instructions and playing the game together.

Assessment task 1

Running the task

You could ask children to suggest what Theo could have done to check his work, e.g. make an estimate or use the inverse. Observe how they use knowledge of the written method to either check Theo's method or to do the calculation themselves.

They also will need to check the number line calculation by looking carefully at each step. Children could be encourage to think about the inverse calculations that Theo could have used to check his working.

Evidencing mastery

Children who can fluently apply the written methods of addition and subtraction that involve exchanging are showing mastery of this approach, particularly when the number of digits in each number is different, e.g. 5-digit number + 4-digit number. You may also wish to include some calculations of this type to gather further evidence.

Children who clearly explain that Theo has reversed parts of the subtraction calculation rather than exchanging or suggest that an estimate would have helped Theo realise his error, are showing a good level of understanding.

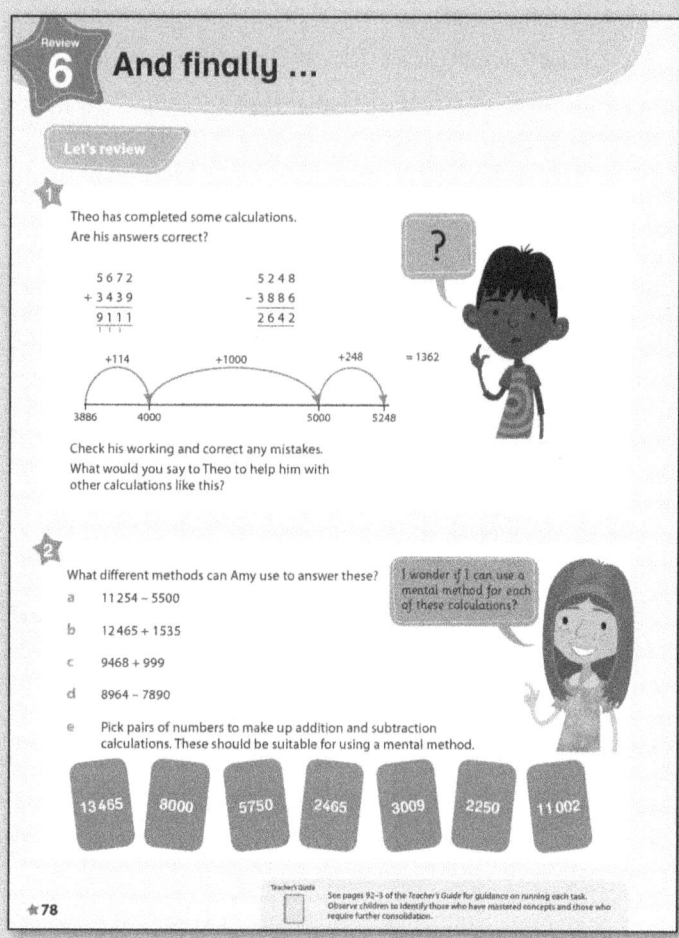

Assessment task 2

Running the task

Listen to groups of children discuss the statement and suggest different mental strategies that can be used. Encourage them to consider all the different strategies that would be efficient here and look for those who recognise a good opportunity to round and adjust, which is a strategy that has been used in previous units. Ask them to explain why these methods are more efficient than the formal written method for the numbers involved and suggest some examples where the written method would be better.

Part e) requires children to reason about pairs of numbers to use for mental addition and subtraction calculations. Look for children who make use of number bonds and who recognise when numbers are close to a hundred or a thousands boundary.

Evidencing mastery

If children are able to do this easily and explain what they are doing, they have a good understanding of different mental calculation strategies and when to use them. Look for those who can refer to the proximity of numbers when making a decision about a finding the difference method.

Concepts mastered

☑ Children can choose to use an appropriate mental or written method of addition and subtraction depending on the numbers involved. They explain their decisions giving reasons for which would be the most efficient and why.

☑ They can apply these skills to a range of contexts and can explain how the mental and written methods will help them.

☑ Children can confidently select mental and written methods when working within the contexts of measurement and statistics. They can explain why a mental method should be used for calculating time intervals rather than a columnar method.

Assessment task 3

Resources

- Number lines

Running the task

This is an open-ended task where children are asked to suggest an easy and a hard solution to the problem. They are working with an approximate difference rather than an actual or accurate difference. You could ask children to discuss some masses that it could not be based on as this is an approximation, e.g. it cannot be 2 kg and 5.5 kg because this would be an actual difference of 3.5 kg.

Encourage children to convince you or the rest of the class of their solutions.

The second part of the problem requires them to reason about Theo's solution and present proof that shows that this is not possible as the difference is approximately 3 kg and not 3.5 kg as stated. The masses given are in kilograms and grams and so children are required to use conversions before making decisions.

Evidencing mastery

Look for children who make use of a number line or bar model to represent the difference. This would show a secure understanding of the concept. They will also need to apply knowledge of rounding. Look for those who recognise that rounding to the nearest 100 g is going to be useful and rounding to the nearest kilogram will not. This will show evidence of mastery.

Did you know?

The symbols that we use for the operations addition (+) and subtraction (−) did not always exist as the symbols we use today. Symbols developed over time and were often quite varied, e.g. the ancient Egyptians used a pair of legs walking forwards to signify addition, and a pair of legs walking backwards for subtraction.

The first time that the symbols + and − were seen in English was in a book on algebra in 1551 called *The Whetstone of Witte*. It was written by a Welsh mathematician called Robert Recorde. He was also responsible for inventing the equal sign (=) in 1557 because he was fed up with writing 'is equal to' in his equations. He chose the two lines because 'no two things can be more equal'.

Fractions, decimals and percentages

Mathematical focus

★ **Number:** number and place value, fractions

★ **Measurement:** length, mass, capacity

Prior learning

Children should already be able to:

- recognise and show, using diagrams, families of common equivalent fractions

- recognise that hundredths arise when dividing an object by one hundred and dividing tenths by ten

- solve problems involving increasingly harder fractions to calculate quantities, and fractions to divide quantities, including non-unit fractions where the answer is a whole number

- add and subtract fractions with the same denominator

- recognise and write decimal equivalents of any number of tenths or hundredths

- recognise and write decimal equivalents to $\frac{1}{4}$, $\frac{1}{2}$, and $\frac{3}{4}$.

Key new learning

- Compare and order fractions whose denominators are all multiples of the same number.

- Identify, name and write equivalent fractions of a given fraction, represented visually.

- Recognise mixed numbers and improper fractions and convert from one form to the other and write mathematical statements > 1 as a mixed number (e.g. $\frac{2}{5} + \frac{4}{5} = \frac{6}{5} = 1\frac{1}{5}$).

- Read and write decimal numbers as fractions (e.g. $0.71 = \frac{70}{100}$).

- Recognise the per cent symbol (%) and understand that per cent relates to 'number of parts per hundred', and write percentages as a fraction with denominator 100, and as a decimal.

Making connections

- The ability to compare, order and convert fractions and decimals has many real-life applications, particularly in the context of length, mass and volume.

- Working with percentages builds on children's understanding of fractions and decimals. Percentages are seen frequently in everyday life, and in other subjects, such as science and geography.

- A solid understanding of fractions, decimals and percentages will help children solve word problems involving all four operations later on.

Talk about

Discuss the fact that fractions are shapes and quantities that are shared into equal groups and that the denominator is the operator. Demonstrate how to write a fraction, using this as an opportunity to reinforce the correct mathematical language. Draw the line (the vinculum) to indicate that a number has been broken into parts, then the denominator to show how many parts and finally the numerator to show how many of those parts there are. Ensure that children understand that 'reducing' a fraction means the same as 'simplifying' a fraction. Both terms mean that you're making the numbers in the fraction smaller, without changing the size of the fraction.

Engaging and exploring

Ask children to look at each picture and the comments or questions that go with it and to discuss with a partner what each might be about.

For the picture with the pies, you could:

Ask children to identify what fraction each pie has been cut into and what fraction of each pie is on the plate. Encourage them to explain how they know. They should write this fraction. Encourage them to draw the line first to show that the pies have been divided into parts, then the denominator to show how many parts and finally the numerator to indicate how many of those parts there are.

Discuss which fraction is the largest and then the smallest slice. Ask them to write the fractions of pie on the plates in order from smallest to largest. Encourage them to explain why $\frac{1}{16}$ is

smaller than $\frac{1}{2}$. Establish that the larger the denominator, the more parts and therefore the smaller the fraction.

Look at pairs of pies, beginning with the half and quarter. Discuss what fraction could be common to both these. Establish quarters. Discuss how many quarters there would be in total and write this as an improper fraction: $\frac{9}{4}$. If they take away the amount on the plates, what fraction would be left? Can they change the result of $\frac{5}{4}$ into a proper fraction? Discuss the fact that $\frac{4}{4}$ is equivalent to one whole so $\frac{5}{4}$ would be $1\frac{1}{4}$.

For the photo of the chocolate you could:

Focus on the plate showing the whole bar. Discuss that there are seven sticks of chocolate on the plate, and one being eaten by the boy. Ask children to write down what fraction one of the sticks would be, then two and three. Consider using cubes to model this. Can children tell you the equivalent fraction for $\frac{4}{8}$? Ask them to write down as many other equivalent fractions for $\frac{1}{2}$ as they can. Then ask them to make up equivalences for $\frac{1}{4}$ and $\frac{3}{4}$. Can they see any patterns? Encourage them to notice what is happening to both the numerator and the denominator.

Ask them to the find equivalences for other simple fractions, such as thirds, fifths and tenths.

If the boy is eating one of the chocolate sticks, discuss what fraction of the whole amount he is eating and what fraction is left, e.g. he is eating $\frac{1}{8}$ and $\frac{7}{8}$ is left.

For the picture with the food packaging you could:

Ask children to identify the foods. Discuss what children's favourite vegetables and fruit are. Take a vote and make a tally for each and then ask children to put the information into a table. They could then represent this as a bar chart.

Ask them to identify the different masses of the foods. Can they convert these to gram and kilogram equivalences?

Ask them to focus on the decimal element of each. What is 0.75 as a fraction? Establish that 0.75 is the same as $\frac{75}{100}$ or $\frac{3}{4}$, 0.5 is $\frac{50}{100}$ or $\frac{5}{10}$ and 0.25 is $\frac{25}{100}$ or $\frac{1}{4}$. Ask them to read and then write the masses on the food packages as whole numbers and fractions.

Ask children to order the decimal parts of the masses from least to greatest.

For the picture of the food label you could:

Give children a variety of food packaging and ask them to sort the different numbers that they can see, e.g. into weights, capacities, decimals.

Discuss what 6.9 g of carbohydrate means. Agree that this is the amount of carbohydrates in 100 g of the food. Discuss how many carbohydrates there would be in different amounts.

Discuss the percentages on the label. Do children know what a percentage is? Can they tell you where they might see these in other areas of real life, e.g. shops at sale times. Explain that a percentage is a special fraction and each part is always out of 100.

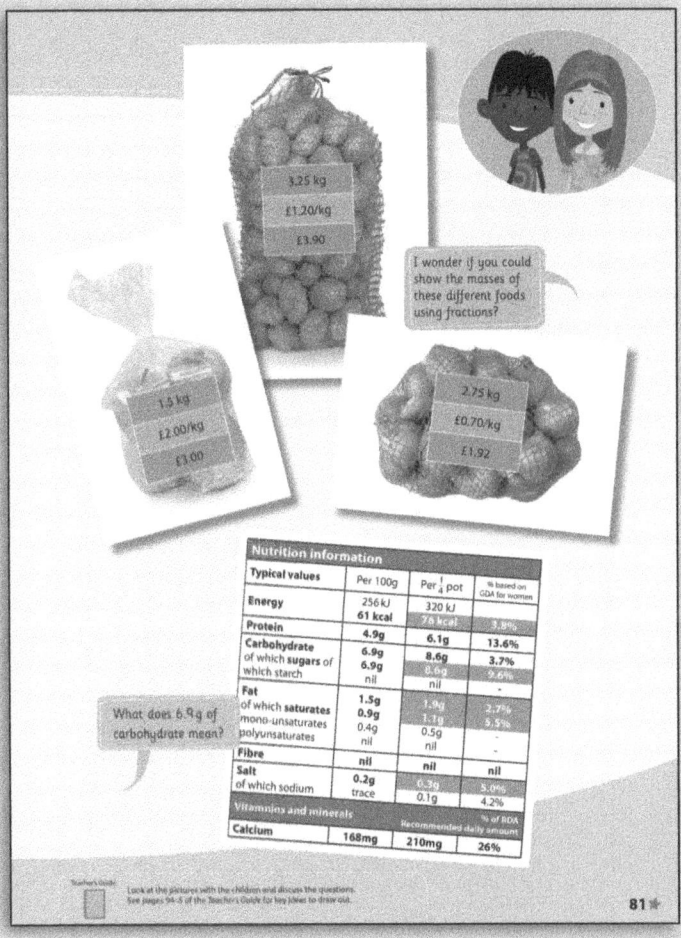

Things to think about

How will you:

- Share the big picture of the sequence of lessons with children?

- Organise your class into mixed attainment groups of four and also give opportunities for children of similar attainment levels to work together?

- Plan focus group work?

- Ensure that all children are able to access their learning?

- Develop reasoning through questioning?

- Use visual representations to help conceptual understanding with all children?

Checking understanding

You will know children have mastered these concepts when they can represent and explain the relationship between decimals, fractions and percentages. They use this understanding to solve problems.

- Compare and order fractions whose denominators are all multiples of the same number.
- Identify, name and write equivalent fractions of a given fraction, represented visually.

 Homework 35 and 36  Practice Book pp 52–4 Fraction Wall Common multiples

Mathematical vocabulary

Fraction, numerator, denominator, vinculum, equivalent, order, compare

Representations and resources

Digit cards, strips of paper, dice, scales, measuring jugs, 2-litre bottles, plastic bags, sand, water, calculators.

Warming up

It is important to rehearse place value fairly regularly. Give each child a calculator. Ask them to key in 4. Next ask them to add a 1 in front of the 4 (+10) and then 3 in front of the 1 (+300). Keep doing this until they have a 6-digit number. When they have this ask them to change different digits to other digits, e.g. change the 4 to a 3 (–10).

Background knowledge

Comparing and ordering fractions requires a conceptual understanding of what a fraction is. We can help children develop their understanding of fractions in the way we teach them to write them. The word fraction comes from the Latin 'fractio' which means to break up. If we draw the line separating the numerator and denominator first to indicate breaking an amount, then write the denominator to show how many parts it is broken up into and finally the numerator to show how many parts are needed, children will get a clearer idea of what a fraction is.

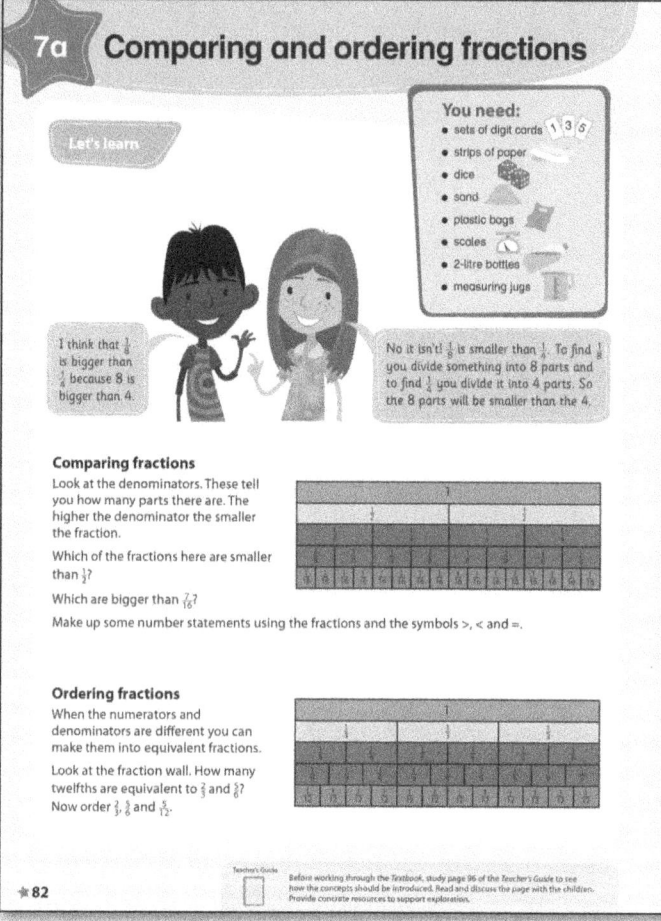

Let's learn: Modelling and teaching

Comparing fractions

- Give children four strips of 2-cm-wide A4 paper each. Ask them to keep the first whole and write 1 in the middle. They fold a second strip in half, open it up and mark each half with $\frac{1}{2}$. They repeat for quarters and eighths. Ask questions such as: *How many eighths are equivalent to one quarter? What are one half and one quarter equivalent to?*

- Repeat for one whole, thirds, sixths and ninths and ask children to order with half, quarter and eighth.

- Discuss equivalent fractions. Establish that these are the same fraction with a different appearance. Point out the equivalences in the Textbook. Ask them to write these equivalences on paper and to work out what has happened to the denominators and numerators. Agree that to make an equivalent fraction to, e.g. $\frac{1}{4}$, the denominator must be a multiple of four and that whatever it is multiplied by, the same must happen to the numerator. Write some fractions on the board for children to convert to other equivalent fractions.

- Refer to the images in the Textbook and ask children to tell you what each part would be if the whole represented 1 m, 1 kg and/or 1 l.

Ordering fractions

- Explain to children that to order fractions we need to look at their denominators as when comparing. This is easy for fractions where the numerator is 1. When both the numerators and denominators are different we can make them into equivalent fractions.

- Ask children to focus on the size of each fraction in the Textbook and order them. It is important to mention that these are fractions of the same amount. Answers might vary if they are fractions of different quantities.

- Ask them to find fractions of different amounts of money, e.g. $\frac{1}{3}$ of £3.60, $\frac{1}{9}$ of £81 and to explain why some of the smaller fractions result in higher answers.

Let's practise: Digging deeper

Step 1

The task asks children to compare pairs of fractions and write them as statements using >, < or =. Explain that they are comparing fractions with denominators that are multiples and factors of each other. Encourage those who might need support to use the visual representations in the Textbook. Once they have completed the task, they can make up some fraction statements of their own. You might give them digit cards to create their fractions.

Step 2

The task asks children to throw dice to generate fractions. Once they have made up five they order them from largest to smallest. Some children may need to order unit fractions. If so, they throw a dice to make the denominator only.

Step 3

Children need to measure the masses given in sand and put these in plastic bags. They need to work out how many grams each fraction is worth. Once they have done this, they order the masses from smallest to largest and write down the results.

They then measure amounts of water into two or more two-litre bottles. Again they work out the number of millilitres each fraction is worth. Discuss the fact that their results will be volumes, because these are the amounts in a bottle with a capacity of two litres. You could also discuss that the volumes in the full bottles will equal the capacity. Once they have completed the practical task, they order these from greatest to least volume and write down the results.

Apart from the last one, children order unit fractions. In the last one, there are two non-unit fractions with which children are familiar and this familiarity should enable them to be successful.

Step 4

Children need to write an explanation as to why the larger the denominator the smaller the fraction. Expect some children to explain why this is always the case for the same amount but sometimes the case for differing amounts, e.g. $\frac{1}{5}$ of 20 is smaller than $\frac{1}{10}$ of 100. Ensure that all children use mathematical vocabulary accurately in justifying their answer.

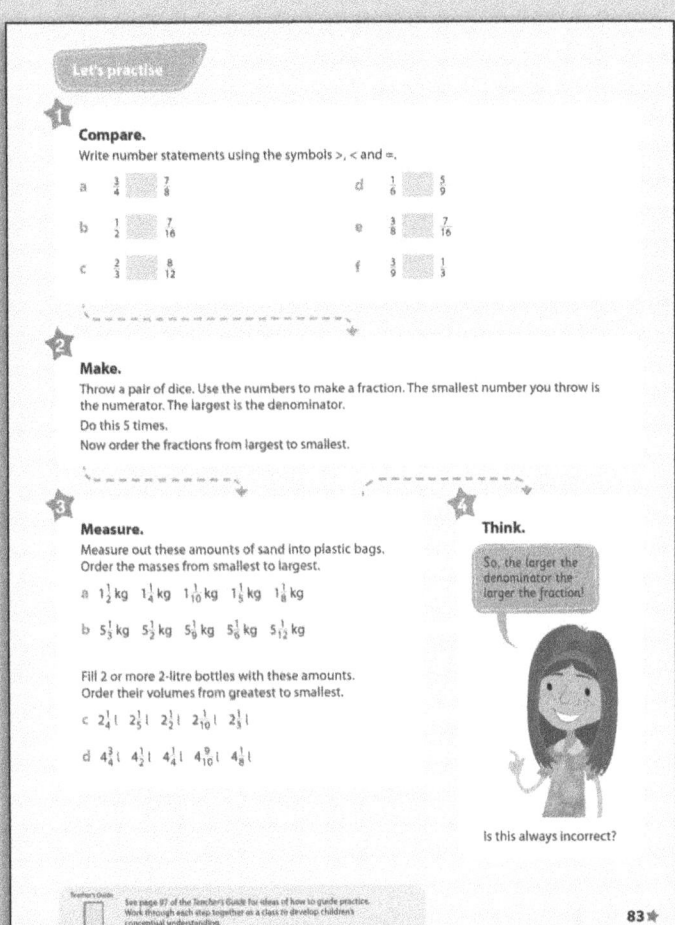

Ensuring progress

Supporting understanding

Some children may need to focus on comparing and ordering unit fractions initially. Adapt the tasks suggested in order that they can master this and work with children in a focus group to explore fractions with denominators that are the same. Use cubes to support understanding during the focus groups..

Broadening understanding

Ask children to make up a 'hard' problem and an 'easy' problem related to ordering and comparing fractions. Ask them to explain why one is hard and one is easy.

✓ Concept mastered

Children can confidently and accurately explain and demonstrate how to compare and order fractions whose denominators are multiples of the same number.

Follow-up ideas

- Children could make up cards with different unit and non-unit fractions written on to them. They could then place them in a pile face down on the table and take it in turns to pick a card. They should set out their cards in order from lowest to highest.

- Children could make up some Would you rather ...? word problems as described above.

- You could write a length statement on the board, e.g. 5 m 40 cm ≈ 1. Ask children to find different amounts from this, e.g. $\frac{1}{2}$, $\frac{1}{4}$, $\frac{1}{3}$, $\frac{1}{6}$.

Answers

Step 1

a $\frac{3}{4} < \frac{7}{8}$

b $\frac{1}{2} > \frac{7}{16}$

c $\frac{2}{3} = \frac{8}{12}$

d $\frac{1}{6} < \frac{5}{9}$

e $\frac{3}{8} < \frac{7}{16}$

f $\frac{3}{9} = \frac{1}{3}$

Step 3

a $1\frac{1}{10}$ kg, $1\frac{1}{8}$ kg, $1\frac{1}{5}$ kg, $1\frac{1}{4}$ kg, $1\frac{1}{2}$ kg

b $5\frac{1}{12}$, $5\frac{1}{9}$ kg, $5\frac{1}{6}$ kg, $5\frac{1}{3}$ kg, $5\frac{1}{2}$ kg

c $2\frac{1}{4}$ l, $2\frac{1}{3}$ l, $2\frac{1}{4}$ l, $2\frac{1}{3}$ l, $2\frac{1}{10}$ l

d $4\frac{9}{10}$ l, $4\frac{3}{4}$ l, $4\frac{1}{2}$ l, $4\frac{1}{4}$ l, $4\frac{1}{8}$ l

Step 4

Explanations need to show that children understand that if the amount is the same, the larger denominator will divide that amount into more parts.These will therefore be smaller than the number of parts for a fraction with a smaller denominator.

- Recognise mixed numbers and improper fractions and convert from one form to the other and write mathematical statements > 1 as a mixed number (e.g. $\frac{2}{5} + \frac{4}{5} = \frac{6}{5} = 1\frac{1}{5}$).
- Solve problems involving measures.

Homework 37 and 38   Practice Book pp 55–7   Place Value & Abacus

Representations and resources

Place-value grids (from thousands to hundredths), digit cards, cubes, counters, strips of paper.

Mathematical vocabulary

Fractions, unit fractions, non-unit fractions, improper fractions, mixed numbers, denominator, numerator

Warming up

Ask children to make a 3-digit number, e.g. 276, and place it in their place-value grid. Invite individuals to explain the positional aspect of place value (the digit 2 is in the hundreds position, the digit 7 is in the tens position and the digit 6 is in the ones). Invite others to explain the multiplicative aspect (2 is in the hundreds so it must be multiplied by 100 to give its true value of 200, etc.). Invite others to explain the additive aspect (200 + 70 + 6 = 276). Once they have done this, ask them to multiply the number by ten and explain the effect, including placing the place holder zero in the ones. Then ask them to divide the number by 100 explaining the effect. Repeat this a few times.

Background knowledge

Some children may have difficulty understanding that a fraction can be more than one whole. It is worth demonstrating this using, e.g. a picture of two pizzas cut into quarters with one slice taken away. They should be able to see that there are seven quarters ($\frac{7}{4}$) which is the same as $1\frac{3}{4}$. The fraction representing one whole has the same numerator and denominator. A numerator that is higher than the denominator results in an improper fraction.

Let's learn: Modelling and teaching

Improper fractions

- Ask children to make improper fractions using cubes. They use one colour as the numerator and another as the denominator. Work through the examples of improper fractions in the Textbook. Can children work out how to change an improper fraction to a mixed number?

- Ask children to make improper fractions using digit cards. They could make single- or 2-digit numerators and denominators. They then work out what these are as mixed numbers. Encourage them to work out a rule for how to change an improper fraction into a mixed number.

- Link to measures, e.g. write $\frac{22}{10}$ on the board. Explain that these are millimetres. Ask children to work out how many centimetres and millimetres this is. Repeat for kilograms and grams and litres and millilitres.

Mixed numbers

- Give pairs of children digit cards. They can use these to

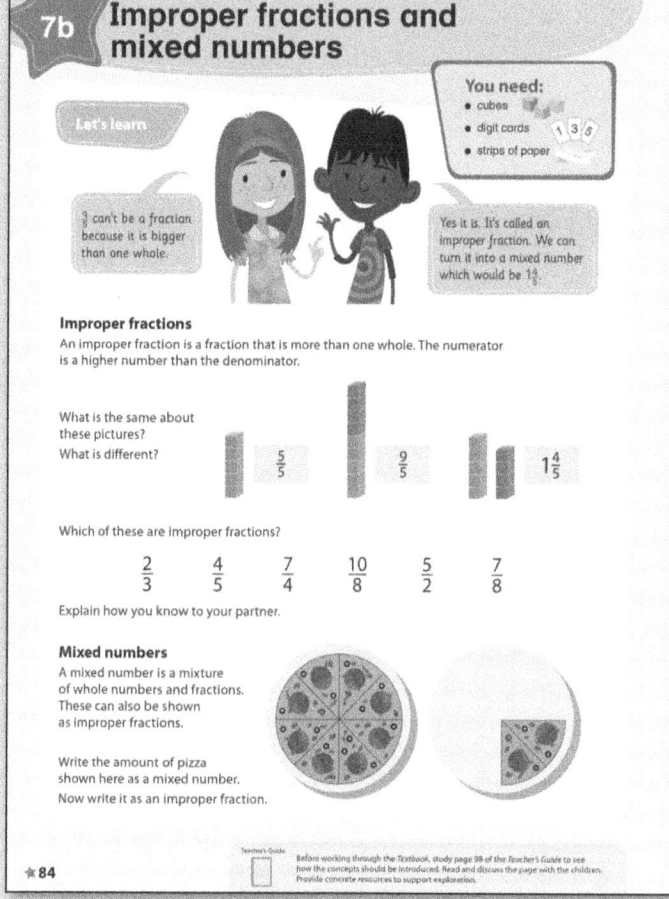

make a mixed number. Once they have done this, they can change the mixed number to an improper fraction. Ask them to consider what they did to change the mixed number and to work out a rule for doing this.

- Ask children to make up their own mixed numbers and use the rule they made up in the previous activity to change these to improper fractions. Does their rule work?

- Give children a selection of measures to convert to improper fractions of the smallest unit, e.g. 1 kg 500 g = $\frac{1500}{1000}$, 5 l 245 ml = $\frac{5245}{1000}$, 7 m 50 cm = $\frac{750}{100}$.

- You could ask problems such as

Mark had $1\frac{1}{2}$ pizzas and he gave his friend $\frac{3}{4}$ of one. What fraction was left?

Let's practise: Digging deeper

Step 1

Before the task, write some improper fractions on the board. Revise what they need to do to turn them into mixed numbers. Some children may benefit from using two different-coloured counters or cubes to set these out first.

Step 2

Before the task, discuss how to turn a mixed number into an improper fraction. Agree that children first need to know how many of the numerator are needed to make one whole. They could multiply the whole number by the denominator and then add the numerator to give the improper fraction.

The task asks children to convert mixed numbers to improper fractions, using counters or cubes to help them if needed. It may be that you need to work with a group who are less confident. If so, ask questions that lead them to finding the solutions.

Step 3

This task follows on from Steps 1 and 2 in that it applies the work children have covered to a practical context. In the first part of the task, children need to write down the lengths in their books and then identify those that show improper fractions by circling them. Once they have done this they measure out the lengths using strips of paper.

In the second part of the task, they change the improper fractions to mixed numbers. Encourage them to simplify $\frac{5}{10}$ to $\frac{1}{2}$ and $\frac{5}{20}$ to $\frac{1}{4}$ if you think they can. They then measure these out using strips of paper as described above.

Step 4

This task asks children to make up thousandths fractions using the four given digits. Some children might need to use real digit cards; others will be comfortable using the visual representation in the Textbook. Encourage them to be systematic in their approach and to record each fraction carefully. Once they have made the fractions, ask them to reduce them to their lowest form. Ask children to make number stories from their fractions. This is a good opportunity to observe the depth of their understanding.

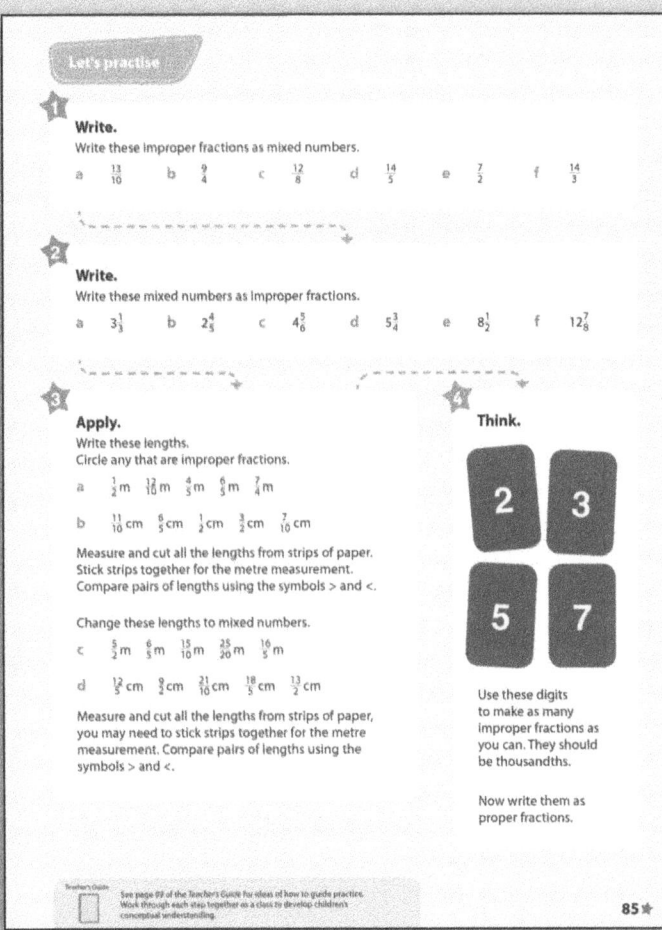

Ensuring progress

Supporting understanding

Provide practical opportunities for children to explore this concept. Some children may need longer exploring this concept with cubes and or counters. This will help them to 'see' how many of a particular fraction makes a whole number. Once they understand this, they should be able to develop an understanding of improper fractions.

Broadening understanding

Provide opportunities for children to find where mixed numbers and improper fractions are found in real life. You can give children higher fractions to work with during the tasks.

✓ Concept mastered

Children can confidently explain and demonstrate what improper fractions and mixed numbers are and can convert from one to the other.

Follow-up ideas

- You could give children some cards and ask them to make up a pairs game. On half of the cards they write improper fractions. On the other half they write the equivalent mixed numbers. They then place the cards face down on the table and take it in turns to pick two at a time. If they match the child keeps the pair, if they don't they return them to the table.

- You could give children five digit cards and ask them to make up as many improper fractions as they can using three cards at a time. They record their fractions and convert these to mixed numbers.

- Ask children to make up a board game which involves question cards that ask them to convert improper fractions to mixed numbers and vice versa.

Answers

Step 1

a $1\frac{3}{10}$

b $2\frac{1}{4}$

c $1\frac{4}{8}$

d $2\frac{4}{5}$

e $3\frac{1}{2}$

f $4\frac{2}{3}$

Step 2

a $\frac{10}{3}$

b $\frac{14}{5}$

c $\frac{29}{6}$

d $\frac{23}{4}$

e $\frac{17}{2}$

f $\frac{103}{8}$

Step 3

a $\frac{12}{10}$ m, $\frac{6}{5}$ m, $\frac{7}{4}$ m

b $\frac{11}{10}$ cm, $\frac{6}{5}$ cm, $\frac{3}{2}$ cm

c $2\frac{1}{2}$ m, $1\frac{1}{5}$ m, $1\frac{5}{10}$ or $1\frac{1}{2}$ m, $1\frac{5}{20}$ or $1\frac{1}{4}$ m, $3\frac{1}{5}$ m

d $2\frac{2}{5}$ cm, $4\frac{1}{2}$ cm, $2\frac{1}{10}$ cm, $3\frac{3}{5}$ cm, $6\frac{1}{2}$ cm

Step 4

There are 18 possible answers; for example $\frac{1250}{1000} = \frac{5}{4}$, $\frac{2015}{1000} = \frac{403}{200}$ and $\frac{5210}{1000} = \frac{521}{100}$

- Read and write decimal numbers as fractions (e.g. $0.71 = \frac{71}{100}$).
- Recognise and use thousandths and relate them to tenths, hundredths and decimal equivalences.

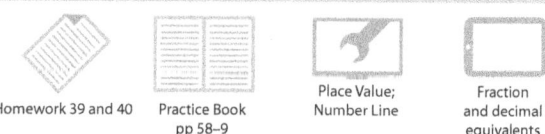

Homework 39 and 40   Practice Book pp 58–9   Place Value; Number Line   Fraction and decimal equivalents

Mathematical vocabulary

Fractions, proper fractions, decimal fractions, equivalence

Representations and resources

Whiteboards, place-value grids (thousands to hundredths), digit cards, coloured counters, Base 10 apparatus, scales.

Warming up

Call out some 2-digit numbers and ask children to multiply them by 10, 100 and 1000 and to write their answers on their whiteboards. Next call out multiples of 1000 and ask children to divide these by 10, 100 and 1000. Ask children to explain what happens to the digits each time. Expect them to tell you that they become 10/100/1000 times smaller and so the hundreds digit becomes a 10/1/10th, the tens become 1/10th/100th and the ones become 10th/100th/1000th. Repeat for other numbers.

Background knowledge

Children need to understand that proper fractions can be written as decimals. They therefore need to know about tenths and hundredths and how these link to decimals. A decimal that has one place is a tenth, one that has two places is a hundredth and one that has three places is a thousandth. It is important to put decimals into context initially. Measures are an ideal way of doing this: kilometres and metres, kilograms and grams and litres and millilitres. Once children develop a conceptual understanding of these, they will be ready to deal with decimals without a context. Place value plays an important role in developing a conceptual understanding of decimals so provide plenty of opportunities to rehearse multiplying and dividing by 10, 100 and 1000 using place-value grids.

Let's learn: Modelling and teaching
Decimal fraction equivalences

- Give children a place-value grid and digit cards. Ask them to make 458 on the grid. Ask them to explain to a partner the positional, multiplicative and additive aspects of place value. Next, ask them to divide the number by ten and to explain what has happened. Repeat this for dividing by 100.

- Ask children to make decimal numbers using digit cards, with a rubber to represent the decimal point. They can write each number as a decimal and its equivalent fraction.

- Recap reducing fractions by finding a multiple that is common to both the numerator and denominator.

- Give children three differently-coloured counters to make numbers with two decimal places. Each colour should represent different number values, e.g. red for ones, blue tenths and yellow hundredths.

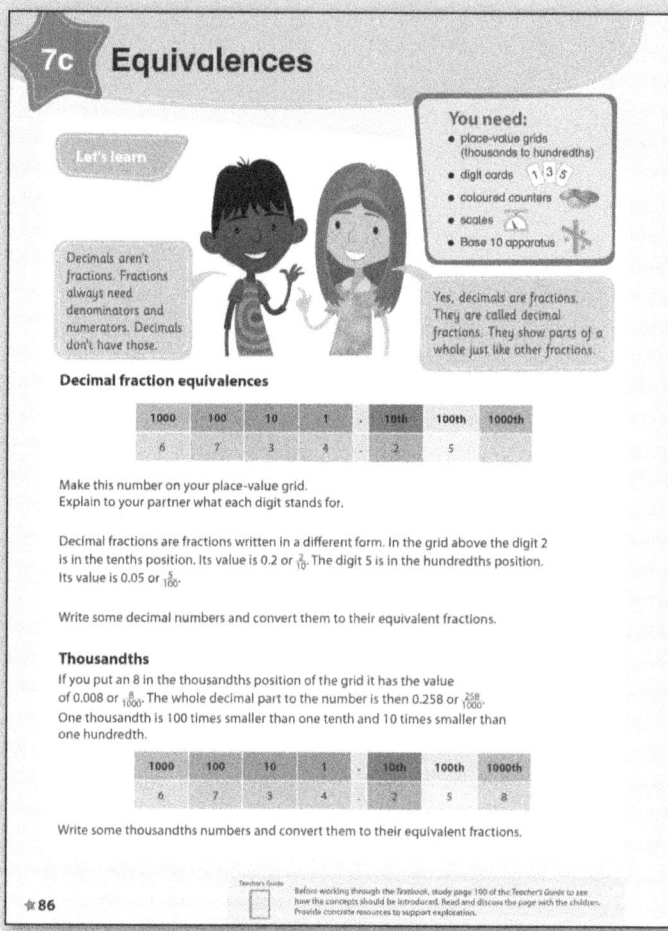

Thousandths

- Give children a place-value grid and set of digit cards. Ask them to make 2458 and place the digits in the correct positions on the grid. Ask them to explain to a partner the positional, multiplicative and additive aspects of place value. Next, ask them to divide the number by ten and to explain what has happened. Repeat this for dividing by 100 and then 1000. Discuss what happens to turn tenths into hundredths and hundredths into thousandths.

- Give children four differently-coloured counters to make numbers with three decimal places, e.g. 4.139, 5.364. You could then ask them to write the decimals as fractions.

- Ask children to weigh different items from around the classroom and record these accurately with decimal amounts.

Let's practise: Digging deeper

Step 1

Children need to convert decimal numbers to equivalent fractions. Encourage those that can to reduce these fractions by dividing by multiples common to both the numerator and denominator. Some children may wish to use Base 10 apparatus to support them in completing some or all of these questions. For each question, they need to write a brief explanation to show what they did. Once they have finished their task ask them to make up some more, different whole numbers with one, two and three decimal places to convert to fractions.

Step 2

Before they work on the task, you may need to remind children that fractions and decimals are the same type of number but appear differently. In the same way that they could turn 0.2 into $\frac{2}{10}$, they can turn $\frac{2}{10}$ into 0.2. The process is simply reversed. Encourage those children who need support to make the numbers in their place-value grids so that they can see what the decimals would look like. For each, they need to write a brief explanation to show what they did. Once they have finished their task ask them to make up some more, different whole numbers with fractions to convert to decimals.

Step 3

Children must apply their understanding of mixed numbers and improper fractions to a problem in context. Begin by modelling a similar example on the whiteboard. Children should then work through the problem step-by-step. Some children might choose to sketch the problem as they work through it. Ask them whether they find the problem easy or hard. Note down their responses as this gives valuable feedback as to the depth of their understanding.

Step 4

Encourage children to discuss the question with a partner first. They could make the amount in their place-value grids to help them with their thinking. You may need to remind them that there are 1000 grams in a kilogram. Doing this may help any children who are unsure to realise that 75 g is $\frac{75}{1000}$ g which means that there needs to be a place holder in the tenths position. Ensure that children generalise as part of their explanation.

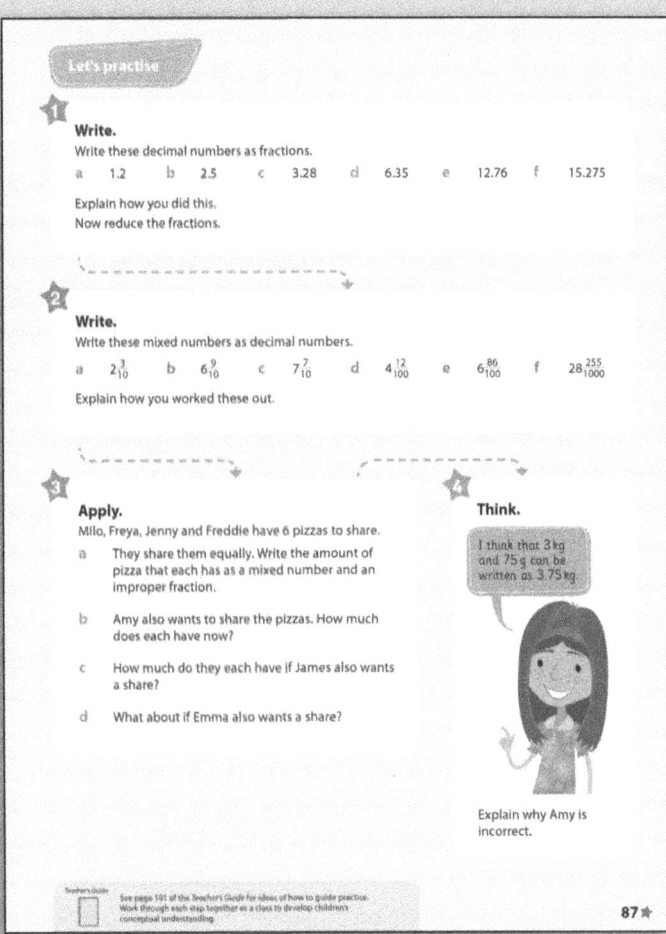

Ensuring progress

Supporting understanding

Observe children as they work through the activities. If any struggle they should focus on converting tenths initially and master this first. Encourage them to use place-value grids and digit cards to make all the numbers that they need to convert.

Broadening understanding

Assess children as they work through the activities. If they have mastered tenths, hundredths and thousandths, ask them to write the numbers in words. They could also make up problems within the context of measures for a partner to solve.

✓ Concept mastered

Children can confidently and accurately explain and demonstrate how to convert fractions to decimals.

Follow-up ideas

- Children could examine food packaging of different types and make a list of the decimal fractions that they find. They could then write the decimals as fractions.

- Children could write down ten decimal fractions to tenths, hundredths and thousandths. They then draw a ladder on paper with ten rungs. With a partner, they take it in turns to place the numbers they made on the rungs of the ladder as fractions. The numbers need to go up in order from smallest to largest. The winner is the player who puts the most numbers on their ladder.

Answers

Step 1	Step 2	Step 4
a $1\frac{2}{10}$ reduces to $1\frac{1}{5}$	a 2.3	3 kg 75 g should be written as 3.075 kg. There are no hundredths and so a place holder needs to be put in the position.
b $2\frac{5}{10}$ reduces to $2\frac{1}{2}$	b 7.7	
c $3\frac{28}{100}$ reduces to $3\frac{7}{25}$	c 6.9	
d $6\frac{35}{100}$ reduces to $6\frac{7}{20}$	d 4.12	
e $12\frac{76}{100}$ reduces to $12\frac{19}{25}$	**Step 3**	
f $15\frac{275}{1000}$ reduces to $15\frac{11}{40}$	a $\frac{6}{4} = \frac{3}{2} = 1\frac{1}{2}$	
	b $\frac{6}{5} = 1\frac{1}{5}$	
	c $\frac{6}{6} = 1$	
	d $\frac{6}{7}$	

7d Percentages

- Recognise the per cent symbol (%) and understand that per cent relates to 'number of parts per hundred', and write percentages as a fraction with denominator 100, and as a decimal.

Homework 41 and 42   Practice Book pp 60–3

Mathematical vocabulary

Fractions, proper fractions, decimal fractions, percentages, equivalence

Warming up

Ask children to multiply and divide a selection of numbers that you write on the board by 10, 100 and 1000. Expect them to write their new numbers down and to explain what has happened each time. Each digit has increased or decreased by 10/100/1000.

Background knowledge

Percentages are a type of fraction. Per cent means one part out of 100. Percentages can be converted into equivalent hundredths as proper or decimal fractions. If they are multiples of ten the fraction can be reduced to tenths. The curriculum requires Year 5 children to understand equivalences between fractions, decimals and percentages. This concept provides an opportunity for additional challenge by exploring how to find simple percentages. Most children can confidently use calculation strategies learned previously to do this.

Let's learn: Modelling and teaching

Percentages

- Discuss when children might have seen percentages in real life. Make a list of their ideas and what the percentage might indicate.

- Provide holiday and food shopping brochures, toy catalogues and food packaging for children to look at. Ask them to find percentages in these. What do they signify?

- Ask children to take their finger for a walk on the percentage grid in their Textbook. Ask them to put their finger on 8% then add 9%, add 29%, take away 8%. Encourage them to use the strategy of rounding to the nearest multiple of ten and adjusting.

- Ask children to find percentages of different amounts of money. Reassure them that this only involves using strategies that they are familiar with. They should find 10% first and use doubling, halving, addition and subtraction to find them, e.g. 15% of £35. They find 10% (£3.50), then halve it for 5% (£1.75) and add the two amounts together (£5.25). Repeat this for other measures.

Percentage equivalences

- Ask children to cover 50% on their grid with five strips of paper. Ask them to tell you what fraction this is. Establish

Representations and resources

Strips of paper, money (coins and notes), measuring jugs and containers of different sizes, scales, holiday brochures, catalogues and a selection of food packaging, multiplication charts.

that because half the grid is covered, this is $\frac{50}{100}$ or $\frac{5}{10}$ or $\frac{1}{2}$. So, 50% is equivalent to $\frac{1}{2}$. Repeat this for 10% ($\frac{1}{10}$), 20% ($\frac{2}{10}$ or $\frac{1}{5}$), 25% ($\frac{25}{100}$ or $\frac{1}{4}$), 30%, 40%, 60%, 70%, 75%, 80% and 90%. Next work these amounts out as decimals.

- Ask children to weigh different items from around the classroom or bags of sand. They can record these accurately and then find 10% more and 10% less than that mass.

- Repeat this for volume. Ask children to fill a container with 250 ml, to work out how much would be 20% more and then to top up their container to that amount.

- Ask children to measure lines to whole centimetres and then work out the measurement that is 50% more and then less and draw the new lines.

Let's practise: Digging deeper

Step 1

Before giving children this task, ask them to explain what a percentage is. Ask them to write different percentages that you put on the board as hundredths. Remind them that some fractions can be simplified. Discuss how this is done and ask children to reduce any that they can.

The task asks children to change the percentages to hundredths. They explain to a partner what they did. For those that are able to, they then reduce each fraction to its lowest form.

Step 2

Before children carry out the task ask them to describe to each other how they would change the percentages to fractions and decimals. Ask them to practise converting percentages to fractions, changing them to their lowest form straight away. Write examples on the board for them to convert. Write some

more for them to convert to decimals. Encourage them to write them to one decimal place if this is possible and two if it is not. Ask children to answer the questions in the Textbook and observe their fluency and confidence.

Step 3

Before the task give pairs of children a pile of coins and notes. Give them the opportunity to find percentages of £1 and then to make this amount and the amount left from £1 using the fewest possible coins. Repeat this for £10.

Children can then approach the task, using their experience with the physical coins as a foundation for pictorial and abstract representations of the problems. The task challenges children to find simple percentages of different amounts of money. They then need to draw the fewest number of coins and notes that make this value.

Step 4

Discuss the question with the class. Allow children to choose the resources and representations that they would like to support them in finding the percentages. Ultimately they need to justify their choice using mathematical ideas and vocabulary. Allow them to choose how they would like to record their justification. You might like to extend the task by asking children to find the decimal equivalent. Encourage children to be creative as they make up two of their own 'would you rather' questions.

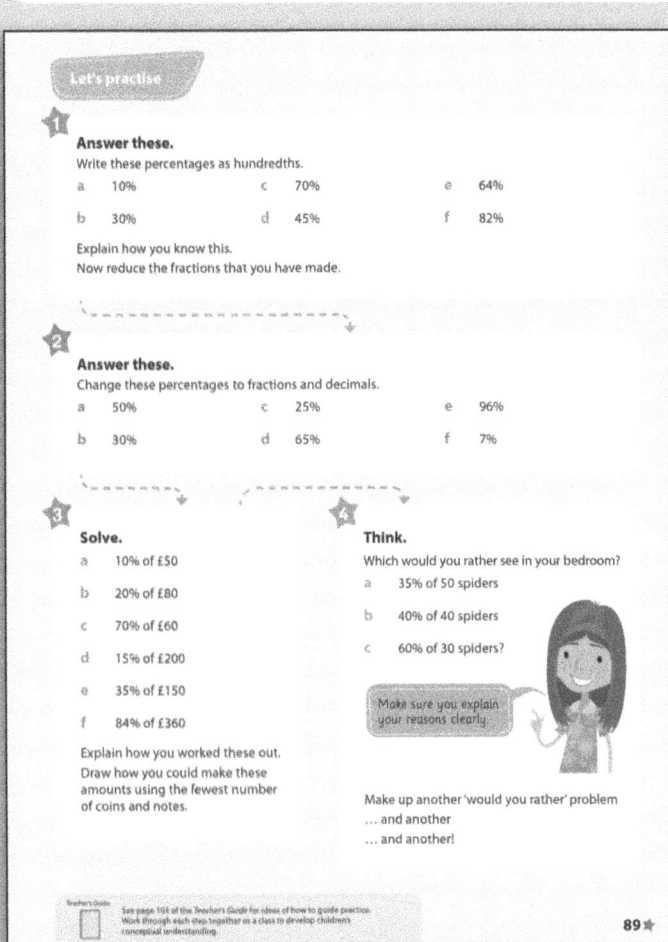

Ensuring progress

Supporting understanding

Some children may struggle to find simple percentages. They should focus on percentages that are multiples of ten initially and master this. You could give them multiplication charts if they need support with the divisions and multiplications that they encounter.

Broadening understanding

Assess children as they work through the activities. If they appear to have mastered this area of maths, they should practise finding more complicated percentages, rather than multiples of ten.

✓ Concept mastered

Children can confidently and accurately explain and demonstrate how to find simple fraction, decimal and percentage equivalences.

Follow-up ideas

- Children could examine food packaging of different types and make a list of the percentages that they find. They could order these from smallest to largest and then convert them to fractions and decimals. They could also convert other amounts, e.g. those listed in decimals, to percentages. You could lead a discussion on what 1.5 g would look like as a percentage. Is it possible to have more than 100%?

- Children could write down ten percentages. They then draw a ladder on paper with ten rungs. With a partner, they take it in turns to place the numbers they made on the rungs of the ladder. The numbers need to go up in order from smallest to largest. The winner is the player who puts the most numbers on their ladder.

Answers

Step 1

a $\frac{10}{100}$ $\left(\frac{1}{10}\right)$

b $\frac{20}{100}$ $\left(\frac{3}{10}\right)$

c $\frac{70}{100}$ $\left(\frac{7}{10}\right)$

d $\frac{45}{100}$ $\left(\frac{9}{20}\right)$

e $\frac{64}{100}$ $\left(\frac{16}{25}\right)$

f $\frac{82}{100}$ $\left(\frac{41}{50}\right)$

Step 2

a $50\% = \frac{1}{2} = 0.5$

b $30\% = \frac{3}{10} = 0.3$

c $25\% = \frac{1}{4} = 0.25$

d $65\% = \frac{13}{20} = 0.65$

e $96\% = \frac{24}{25} = 0.96$

f $7\% = \frac{7}{100} = 0.07$

Step 3

a £5

b £16

c £42

d £30

e £52.50

f £302.40

Step 4

a 17.5

b 16

c 8

40% of 40 is best (unless you want spiders in your room)

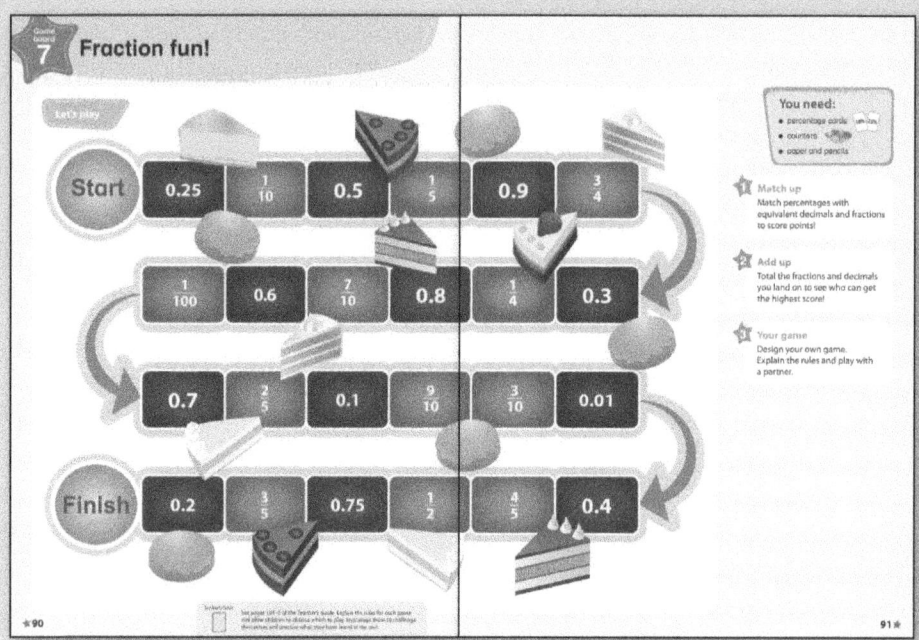

Game 1: Match up

This game is to rehearse, reinforce and consolidate children's understanding of the connections between fractions, decimals and percentages. As children play, they need to use their understanding of equivalence and how these numbers are connected by matching pairs.

Maths focus

• Percentage equivalences

Resources

2 sets of cards, 2 sets of counters (1 colour per player).

How to play

You can ask children to make their own set of percentage cards with the following percentages on them: 1%, 10%, 20%, 25%, 30%, 40%, 50%, 60%, 70%, 75%, 80%, 90%. When they have done this they shuffle the cards together and place them face down on the table. Each player needs a pile of the same-coloured counters. They then take it in turns to pick a percentage card and match the percentage to a number on the game board, either a fraction or decimal. They place a counter onto it. Play continues until the board is covered with counters. They then look at where there counters are placed and if they have theirs on the equivalent fraction and decimal they score two points. The winner is the player with the most points.

Making it easier

Children could just focus on matching the percentage with the appropriate decimal. They score a point for each match they make. If they play with two sets of percentage cards this will allow for more chance of someone winning.

Making it harder

You could extend the game board on paper adding different fractions and decimals for 7%, 68%, 34%. Ensure the fractions are in their lowest forms.

Game 2: Add up

This game aims to reinforce, rehearse and consolidate children's understanding of the equivalences between fractions and decimals and how to convert from one to the other.

Maths focus

• Fractions, decimals

Resources

1–6 dice (1), one counter per player (1 colour per player).

How to play

Children take it in turns to throw the dice. They move around the board according to their dice throw. They write down the numbers that they land on. When they reach the Finish circle they find their total score by adding the fractions and decimals. This means that they will need to change the fractions to decimals or vice versa to do this. The highest score wins.

Making it easier

Children could focus on decimals. When they throw the dice they move that number of squares. If they land on a decimal, they write it on their paper. If they land on a fraction they don't. At the end of the game they find the total of all the decimals.

Making it harder

You could ask children to also pick a percentage card (from Game 1) when it is their turn. At the end they find the total of all the fractions, decimals and percentages.

Game 3: Your game

Children should invent their own game, designing rules that use the concepts covered in the unit. Challenge children to make their game easier or harder.

Fraction fun!

Choose a game to play.

Game 1: Match up

You need:
- card and pens
- 2 sets of counters (1 colour per player)

How to play

- Make 2 sets of cards with these percentages written on them: 1%, 10%, 20%, 25%, 30%, 40%, 50%, 60%, 70%, 75%, 80%, 90%. Shuffle the cards together and place them face down on the table.
- Each player has a pile of the same-coloured counters.
- Take it in turns to pick a percentage card and match the percentage to a number on the gameboard, either a fraction or decimal. Place one of your counters on the number.
- Continue until the board is covered with counters. Look at where the counters are placed. If yours are on the equivalent fraction and decimal you score 2 points.
- The winner is the player with the most points.

Game 2: Add up

You need:
- 1–6 dice
- 1 counter per player (1 colour per player)

How to play

- Take it in turns to throw the dice and move around the board according to your dice throw.
- Write down the numbers that you land on.
- When you reach the Finish, you need to find your total score by adding the fractions and decimals.
- You will need to change the fractions to decimals or decimals to fractions to do this.
- The player with the highest score wins.

Game 3: Your game

- Make up your own game using the gameboard.
- Perhaps you could continue the game back to the Start with a different rule?
- Will you need to add anything to your gameboard – maybe some percentages?
- What are the rules for your game?

Please help your child by reading the instructions and playing the game together.

Assessment task 1

Running the task

Before giving the assessment task, write some single-digit numbers with one decimal place on the board and ask children to order them from smallest to greatest. These numbers need to have the same ones numbers. Ask individuals to explain how they know that their order is correct.

Next write single-digit numbers with two decimal places on the board. Keep the whole numbers the same and some of the tenths. You could then ask children to order them from largest to smallest. Invite individuals to explain how they know their orders are the same.

Finally write a mixture of single-digit numbers with one and two decimal places on the board. You can ask children to order these and explain what they have done and why. You might like to choose one number with a single decimal place and one with two decimal places and ask children to discuss with a partner which is the largest number and why. Establish that just because there are more digits the number isn't always the largest.

Now that children have practised they can carry on with the assessment task. Listen to groups of children discuss the statement and explain to each other why it is incorrect. They should be able to tell you that 1.1 is 1 and $\frac{1}{10}$ or $\frac{10}{100}$ and 1.01 is 1 and $\frac{1}{100}$ so 1.01 is smaller than 1.1. Ask children why Amy might have thought that 1.01 is the larger number. Encourage them to think about the fact that there are two decimal places in the number and not one. She might have assumed that because of this the number must be larger.

Evidencing mastery

If children are able to explain why 1.1 is a higher number than 1.01 by linking to tenths and hundredths, they have mastered this area of mathematics.

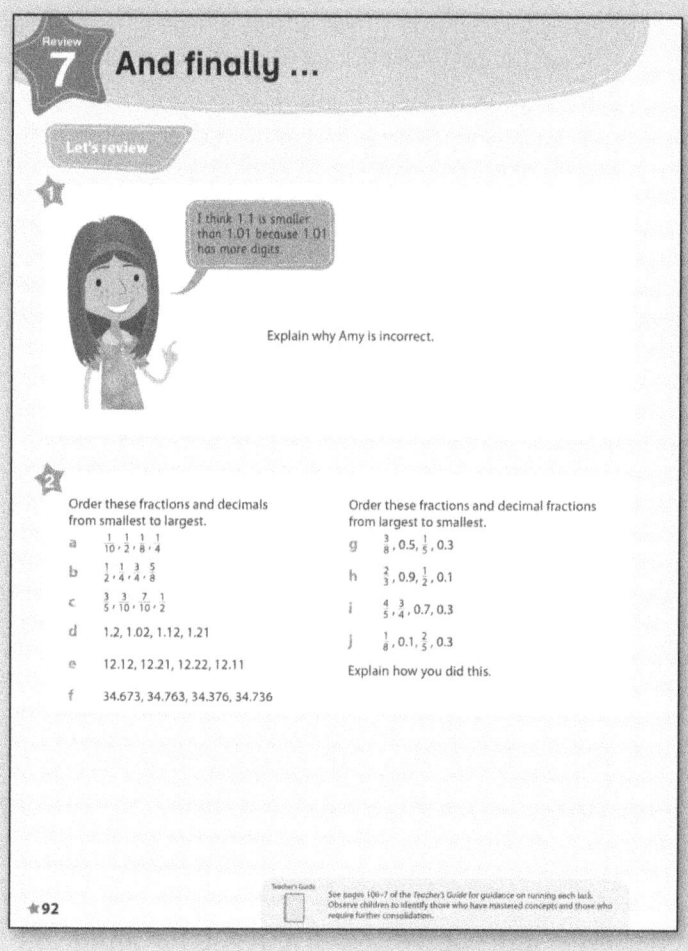

Assessment task 2

Running the task

Before setting children this task, briefly revisit equivalent fractions for halves, quarters and eighths and also fifths and tenths. Write the larger fractions on the board and ask children to find the equivalences of the others. Write some non-unit fractions on the board and ask children to order these and to explain how they know they are correct.

For this task children need to order a mixture of fractions and then decimals. The lists of fractions contain a variety of denominators. The first list a) shows unit fractions, the second b) two non-unit fractions. In order to complete lists a), b) and c) of this activity successfully children need to visualise the equivalences between halves, quarters and eighths and fifths and tenths. If they are unable to visualise this, let them draw fraction strips to help them.

Before children begin part d), revisit ordering decimals by writing some with the same whole number parts on the board. Ask children to discuss with a partner how they will order these. Agree that they need to ignore the numbers that are the same and focus on those that are different, e.g. all the whole numbers are the same in each list so they are irrelevant when ordering. The number to focus on in list d) is the tenths. Children should be able to identify that 1.2 and 1.21 are higher than 1.02 and 1.12. To find the higher of the first two numbers they look at the hundredths. 1.2 doesn't have any but 1.21 does so this is the highest number. In lists e) and f) they need to examine the tenths, hundredths and thousandths. Let them make the lists as jottings and cross out the numbers as they list them in ascending order. Remind them that ascending means from smallest to largest. In g), h), i) and j) children are expected to order the fractions and decimal fractions. In order to do this, they must convert either the fractions to decimals or the decimals to fractions.

Evidencing mastery

If children can confidently order the fractions and decimals and can describe how they are doing this, they are showing mastery in this area of mathematics.

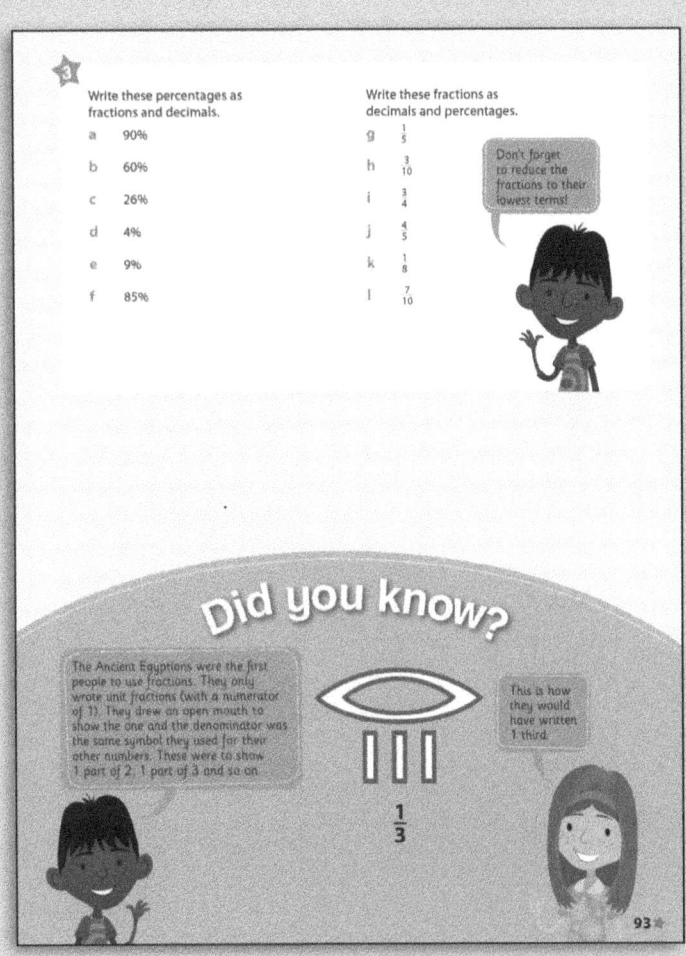

Concepts mastered

- ✓ Children can confidently and accurately explain and demonstrate how to compare and order fractions whose denominators are multiples of the same number.

- ✓ Children can confidently explain and demonstrate what improper fractions and mixed numbers are and can convert from one to the other.

- ✓ Children can confidently and accurately explain and demonstrate how to convert fractions to decimals.

- ✓ Children can confidently and accurately explain and demonstrate how to find simple fraction, decimal and percentage equivalences.

Assessment task 3

Running the task

This assessment task asks children to convert the percentages to equivalent fractions and decimals to show that they understand that percentages are parts of 100. Before they begin, recap the work they carried out on this in this unit. Write some percentages on the board and ask them to change these to fractions by turning the percentages into equivalent hundredths. They then change these hundredths to decimals. Discuss the idea of simplifying or reducing the fractions to their lowest terms by finding common factors to divide by.

Once you have rehearsed this, particularly with children who would benefit from this extra input, they can complete the task. Encourage children to reduce the fractions that can be reduced to their lowest term. This might mean finding a common factor to divide by and then another. The main focus of this activity is converting percentages to fractions and decimals. If children are unable to reduce the fractions, make a note of this, so that you can revisit this at a later date.

Evidencing mastery

If children can confidently convert the percentages to fractions and decimals and can explain why these are equivalent, they are showing mastery in this area of mathematics.

Did you know?

Explain to children that the word fraction actually comes from the Latin 'fractio' which means to break.

The Ancient Egyptians were the first people to write fractions. Their number system was a Base 10 system a bit like ours. They had separate symbols for 1, 10, 100, 1000, 10 000, 100 000 and 1 000 000. They had special pictures for all their numbers.

When writing fractions, they only wrote unit fractions (with a numerator of 1). They drew a picture of an open mouth to show the one and underneath the denominator was the same drawing or symbol that they used for their other numbers. These were to show one part of two, one part of three, one part of four, and so on

See the diagram in the Textbook for how they would have written one third.

Special numbers, operators and scaling

Mathematical focus

★ **Number: number and place value, multiplication and division, fractions**

★ **Measurements: length, capacity, mass, time, money**

Prior learning

Children should already be able to:

- identify multiples and factors, including factor pairs of a number, and common factors of two numbers
- identify square and cube numbers
- solve problems involving addition, subtraction, multiplication and division and a combination of these, including understanding the meaning of the equals sign
- multiply and divide numbers mentally drawing upon known facts.

Key new learning

- Know and use the vocabulary of prime numbers, prime factors and composite (non-prime) numbers.
- Recognise and use square numbers and cube numbers, and the notation for squared (^{2}) and cubed (^{3}).
- Solve problems involving multiplication and division including using their knowledge of factors and multiples, squares and cubes.
- Solve problems which require knowing percentage and decimal equivalents of $\frac{1}{2}$, $\frac{1}{4}$, $\frac{1}{5}$, $\frac{2}{5}$, $\frac{4}{5}$ and those fractions with a denominator that is a multiple of 10 or 25.
- Solve problems involving multiplication and division, including scaling by simple fractions and problems involving simple rates.

Making connections

- Multiplication links clearly with other areas of number, including square numbers and percentages.
- Multiplication and division have a whole variety of real-life applications. Use a variety of contexts to support understanding, including calculations involving money and length.
- If children have mastered strategies for multiplication and division, they will be able to attempt problems involving area with greater confidence.

Unit 8 Special numbers, operators and scaling

What do you notice about these bathroom tiles?

Look at the numbers on the football players' shirts. What have they got in common?

★94

Talk about

Discuss the fact that scaling up and scaling down are important models for multiplication and division. They link well with mental calculation strategies such as doubling, fractions and ratio. Ensure that children are comfortable using the word 'scaling' in this context. There should be no confusion between 'scaling' and 'weighing scales'. In a preliminary discussion, recap square and cube numbers. Can children remember what each is?

Engaging and exploring

You could ask children to look the pictures and the question that goes with each and discuss with a partner what they might be about. Focus on each picture in turn.

For the picture with the geometric tiles, you could discuss what children notice about the pattern on the tile. Take every suggestion and talk about it, e.g. it is repeating, it is made of squares. Focus on one section and ask children if they know the name for squares that appear to start small and get bigger from a common centre. Tell them that is the same name as is given for circles that create a similar pattern. Establish that the word is concentric, these are patterns of concentric squares.

Ask them what they notice about the size of each square in each section. Agree that they are increasing by one length of the smallest square each time. Establish that the pattern shows the first few square numbers. The first square is 1 unit by 1 unit, the second is 2 units by 2 units and so on.

For the picture of the football players you could ask children to look at the numbers on the football players' shirts. Ask them what is the same about the two numbers and then what is different. Listen to their suggestions, they may say that they are both odd numbers, one has two digits and the other has one. If someone says they are both prime numbers, focus on that. If they don't, ask them to find the factors of each number. Establish that they only have two factors, which are 1 and the number itself. Inform children that these are called prime numbers.

Ask children to work with a partner and to write down as many prime numbers as they can in 2 minutes. For each number, they need to check that they have only two factors.

For the chart with the buildings you could find out if children know any of the buildings shown. Ask them if they think these buildings are really this size. Establish that they are not but they have been made to look smaller. They have been scaled down. Ask children to tell you of other things they know of, maybe, in the classroom that have been scaled down. Photographs of children are a good example. Can they think of things that are scaled up? A good example could be items looked at under a microscope.

Tell children that scaling up is multiplication and the scaling down is division. Draw a rectangle on the board and then another underneath it that is twice the size. Ask them how much bigger they think the longer one is. Agree twice as big, double or it has been multiplied by 2. Reverse this and ask how much smaller the shorter one is. Agree half the size or it has been divided by 2. Add a third rectangle that is twice as big as the larger of the two. Repeat the questioning.

Give a value to the smallest rectangle, e.g. 10. Ask what the others must be. Give a value to the longest one and ask what the others might be. Repeat this a few times. Ask them to estimate how tall each building is in feet using the vertical axis and then to tell you roughly how much taller one building is than another. Encourage them to use terms such as twice as high, half the height, four times as high.

For the picture with the map you could ask children whether they have ever visited Spain. Can they identify where in the world Spain is?

Ask children to look at the scale. You could tell children that there are approximately 1.6 km in a mile or 0.6 miles in a kilometre. Ask children questions that involve converting from miles to kilometres and vice versa. To make their conversions, encourage them to use mental calculation strategies and scaling. Ask them to record the conversions they make. Aim to ask for conversions that lend themselves to these strategies, e.g. how many miles in 2 km (they double), 4 (double 2), 8 (double 4), 10 km (they multiply by 10), 14 (add 10 and 4).

Things to think about

How will you:

- Organise mixed attainment groupings?

- Plan activities for children who need extra reinforcement of the concepts taught?

- Use manipulatives to help develop conceptual understanding for multiplication and division with all children?

- Reinforce problem solving using strategies such as sometimes, always, never and tell me another and another and another?

- Provide opportunities for children to work practically with different aspects of measure?

Checking understanding

You will know children have mastered these concepts when they can explain and show properties of prime, composite, square and cube numbers and explain factor pairs related to these sets of numbers. They understand and can explain the relationship between multiplication, division, fractions and percentages. They use this understanding to derive facts and solve problems.

- Identify multiples and factors, including finding all factor pairs of a number, and common factors of two numbers.
- Know and use the vocabulary of prime numbers, prime factors and composite (non-prime) numbers.
- Recall primes up to 19.
- Recognise and use square numbers and cube numbers, and the notation for squared (^{2}) and cubed (^{3}).
- Solve problems involving multiplication and division including using their knowledge of factors and multiples, squares and cubes.

Homework 43 and 44   Practice Book pp 64–6   100 Squares

Representations and resources

100 squares, scissors, interlocking cubes, cm-squared paper, rulers.

Mathematical vocabulary

Multiply, divide, multiplication, division, factor, product, multiple, square number, cube number, prime number

Warming up

Take the opportunity to rehearse mental calculation strategies. Write some calculations on the board and ask children to discuss with a partner the most efficient way to answer them. You could begin with these examples: $4356 + 1998$ (add 2000, subtract 2), $3602 - 1999$ (subtract 2000, add 1), 2464×5 (multiply by 10 and halve), $3440 \div 20$ (divide by 10 and halve).

Background knowledge

Prime numbers are numbers that have only two factors, the number itself and 1. Composite numbers are numbers that are not prime numbers.

Note that 1 is, therefore, not a prime number because it only has one factor. 2 is a prime number because it has two factors: 1 and 2.

A prime factor is a factor of a number that is also prime, e.g. the prime factors of 12 are 3 and 2 because $3 \times 2 \times 2 = 12$

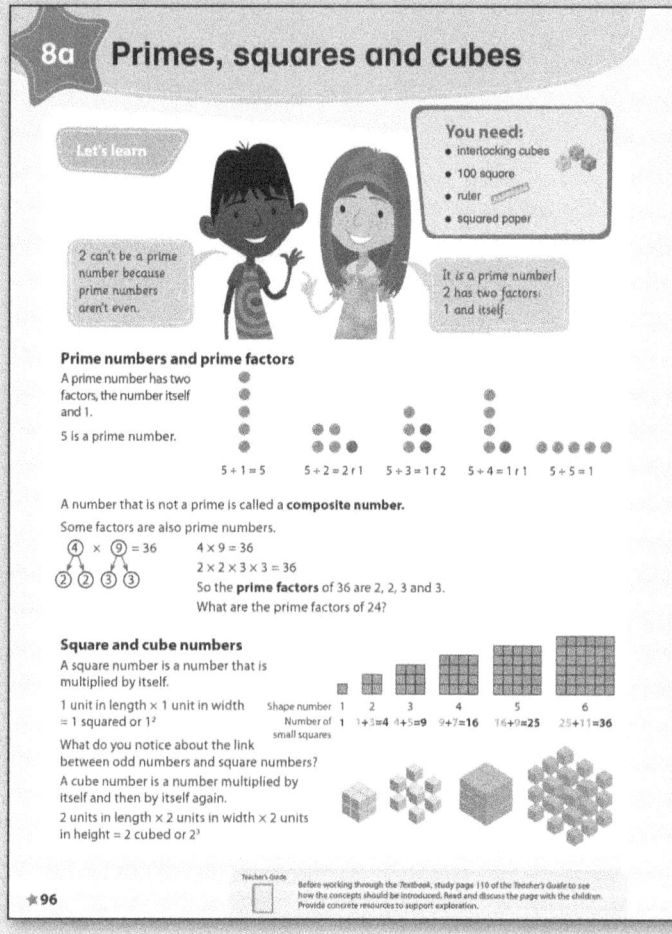

Let's learn: Modelling and teaching

Prime numbers and prime factors

- Discuss the comments made by the children in the Textbook. Establish that a prime number has two factors, itself and 1. Two has two factors, 2 and 1, so it is prime. It is the only even prime number. Numbers that are not prime are called composite numbers.

- Give children a 100 square. Ask them to cross out 1 because it only has one factor, all the multiples of 2 apart from 2 and all the multiples of 3 apart from 3. Repeat for multiples of 5 and 7, etc. This pattern is known as the Sieve of Eratosthenes.

- Use the example in the Textbook to explain what a prime factor is. Call out some numbers and ask them to find a factor pair and then find the factors of those until all the factors are prime numbers.

Square and cube numbers

- Introduce the square numbers diagram in the Textbook. Ask children to draw a similar model for 7, 8 and 9 squared. They may wish to use cubes to support them.

- Ask children to square some single-digit and 2-digit numbers, and then to write down their factors as factor pairs. What do they notice? (There are always an odd number of factors because the number has been multiplied by itself, so that factor makes the number of factors odd.)

- Ask children to work in small groups to explain the cube numbers diagram in the Textbook. As a class, write an explanation of what the diagram shows. Children could make cube numbers using interlocking cubes, writing down their dimensions and finding the total.

Let's practise: Digging deeper

Step 1

The task asks children to demonstrate that they know what square numbers are, by writing multiplication statements to show the square numbers up to and including 12. To confirm their understanding they should draw the squares to represent these as they do. For children who are less confident encourage them to work slowly through the first few square numbers.

As an extension you could ask children to find the squares of 20, 25, 50, 75 and 100. Observe whether they use a mental calculation strategy, the grid method or the written method. Most should be answered using a mental calculation strategy such as using known facts.

Step 2

Before children begin the task, recap cube numbers. Ask children to show you different cube numbers using interlocking cubes and to explain how these are made up. Ensure they talk about the dimensions that are multiplied together.

The task asks children to show that they know what cube numbers are, by working out the first five cube numbers. They should do this using mental calculation strategies for multiplication, such as multiplication facts, doubling and doubling again. They check their answers by making the cubes to see if their total matches the number of cubes they make. For children who are less confident, ask them to build the cubes first. You could ask children to write the multiplication statements to reinforce their conceptual understanding.

Finally, challenge children to identify which of their starting numbers are prime. What do they notice?

Step 3

Before children begin the task, revisit the definition, formula and measurements for area. Ask them to draw squares of different lengths and work out their areas.

The task asks children to apply their understanding of square numbers to find areas of squares from given clues. When they have worked out the areas, they draw the squares on cm-squared paper to check that they are correct.

Step 4

To show a deepening understanding, children need to use their knowledge of square and prime numbers to investigate whether they can make square numbers by adding two prime numbers together. Encourage them to work systematically by listing the squares of the numbers in order first. They might find it helpful to list the prime numbers to 100 on the same piece of paper.

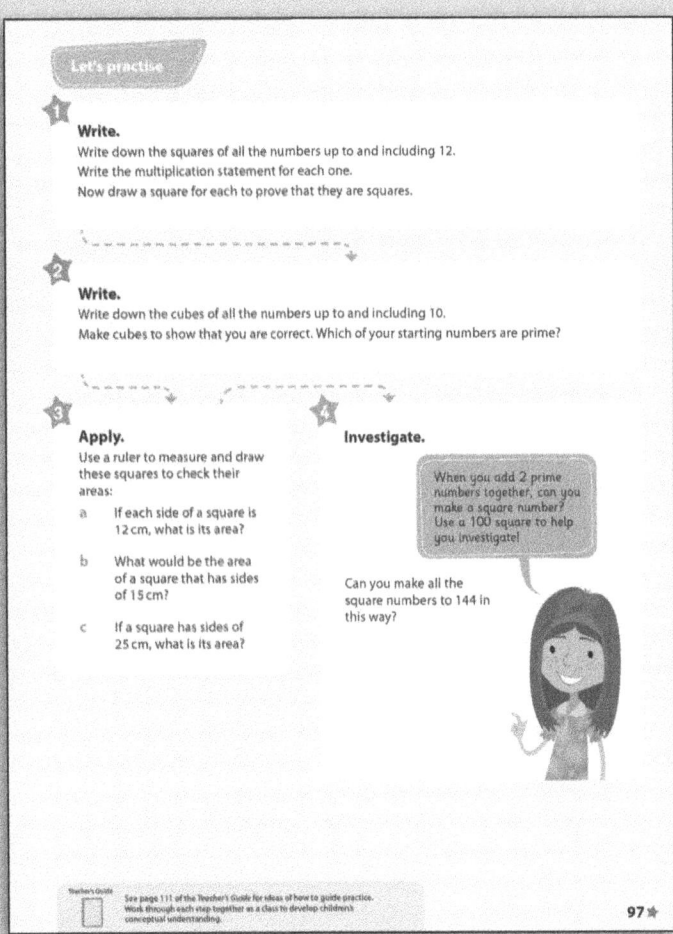

Ensuring progress

Supporting understanding

Work with focus groups of children who might not have understood the properties of these numbers previously. Work through each type of number again using squared paper and cubes to repeat activities that you have carried out with the class.

Broadening understanding

Provide opportunities for children to work out areas and volumes to reinforce that square and cube numbers are used in real life.

✓ Concept mastered

Children can explain and demonstrate prime numbers and recognise and use square and cube numbers..

Follow-up ideas

- Children could make up a dominoes game. Using playing card size of card, they divide it in half. They write a square number on one side and a number that is being squared on the other, e.g. 64 on one side and 5 on the other. The two need to be different and the square number should always be on the same side. On the second piece of card they write, e.g. 8 and 25. Once they have all the square numbers up to and including 144, they play dominoes.

- Ask children to use the Internet to find all the existing prime numbers that mathematicians have found. They could also research Eratosthenes, who was the mathematician who found an effective way to identify prime number using his 'sieve'.

Answers

Step 1

1, 4, 9, 16, 25, 36, 49, 64, 81, 100, 121, 144

Step 2

1, 8, 27, 64, 125, 216, 343, 512, 729, 1000

Step 3

a   144 cm²

b   225 cm²

c   625 cm²

Step 4

All numbers can be made by adding pairs of prime numbers except 121:
$4 = 2 + 2$, $9 = 2 + 7$, $16 = 5 + 11$, $25 = 2 + 23$, $36 = 13 + 24$, $49 = 2 + 47$, $64 = 17 + 47$, $81 = 2 + 79$, $100 = 3 + 97$, 121 impossible, $144 = 47 + 97$

Using fractions as operators for multiplication and division

- Solve problems that require knowing percentage and decimal equivalents of $\frac{1}{2}$, $\frac{1}{4}$, $\frac{1}{5}$, $\frac{2}{5}$, $\frac{4}{5}$ and those fractions with a denominator of a multiple of 10 or 25.

Homework 45 and 46   Practice Book pp 67–9   Fraction Wall

Mathematical vocabulary

Multiply, divide, multiple, factor, fraction, decimal fraction, percentage, numerator, denominator, operator

Representations and resources

Sets of digit cards (enough for 1 between 2), place-value grids (from thousands to hundredths), money, rulers, scales.

Warming up

Continue to practice mental calculation strategies this time involving finding percentages. Write 100% = £360 on the board. Give children 3 minutes to make up as many different percentages as they can from the statement. Encourage them to find 10% first and then double, halve, add, subtract, multiply and divide, e.g. 10% = £36, 5% = £18, 20% = £72, 30% = £108, 15% = £54, 45% = £162.

Background knowledge

There are strong links between multiplication, division and fractions. Fractions are operators. To find a fraction of an amount, children need to divide the amount by the denominator of the fraction and multiply by the numerator. This concept spread explores this and also the equivalences between fractions and decimals. It introduces finding percentages by finding 1% (so dividing an amount by 100 and multiplying by the percentage needed).

Let's learn: Modelling and teaching

Finding percentages

- Discuss that percentages are fractions that are out of 100, so you can find these by first dividing the amount by 100 (the denominator) to find 1% and then multiplying by the number of parts (the numerator) to find the percentage needed.

- Discuss why the Amy wrong about 20p being 2% of £1. What do children think she was thinking? Encourage them to link this to hundredths.

- Use place-value grids and digit cards to rehearse dividing by 100 to find 1%.

- Relate this to money, by looking at the grid in the Textbook. The grid represents 100% and each hole represents 1%. Discuss that 100% represents £1 and you could divide that by 100 to find that 1% represents 1p. To find 10% of £1, you could multiply 1p by 10 to give 10p. You could find 50% in the same way to have 50p, and 20% to have 20p.

- Ask children to find different percentages of amounts of money using this method. As they do, ask them to consider whether there was a more efficient method to use, e.g. finding 10% and manipulating that.

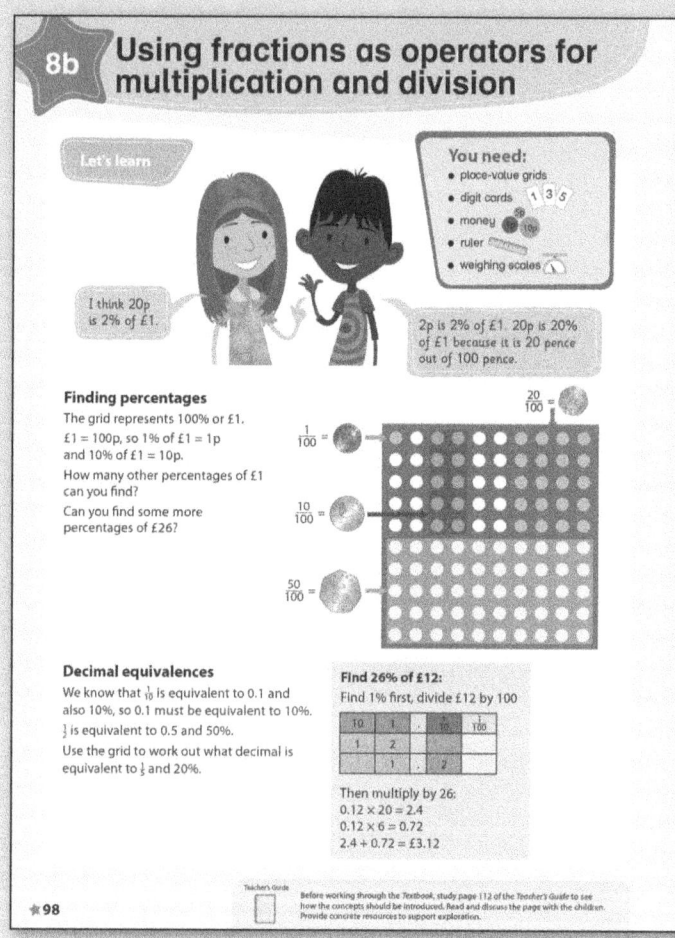

Decimal equivalences

- Ask children to tell you what they remember about fraction and decimal equivalences. Expect them to be able to tell you that to turn a fraction into a decimal they divide the denominator into the numerator, e.g. $\frac{1}{2} = 1 \div 2 = 0.5$.

- Ask them to make a list of the fraction and decimal equivalences that they know, e.g. $\frac{1}{10} = 0.1$, $\frac{2}{10} = \frac{1}{5} = 0.2$, $\frac{1}{4} = 0.25$, $\frac{3}{4} = 0.75$.

- Relate this to money and ask them to find different fractions and decimals of whole pound amounts, e.g. 0.1 of £10, $\frac{2}{5}$ of £50, 0.75 of £100, 0.01 of £120.

- Ask them to find amounts that are fractions with a denominator of a multiple of 10 or 25, e.g. $\frac{20}{25}$ of £250, $\frac{25}{75}$ of £750.

Let's practise: Digging deeper

Step 1

This is a more challenging activity and may need to work with a focus group. Explain that it can be simpler to find 10% and manipulate that using doubling, halving and addition. Work through a few examples with the group and then ask them to answer some of the questions independently. Remind children that it is not unusual to make mistakes. Ask them what they learn from any mistakes that they make.

Step 2

This activity provides a good opportunity for extra challenge. Remind them how to find fractions of an amount. To find the decimal, they divide the whole by the decimal given. Encourage them to consider converting the decimal to the equivalent fraction if they think a fraction might be simpler to work with. Some children may need extra guidance from you,

so work with them as a focus group and take them through one or two examples together, then give them simpler fractions and decimals to work on independently.

Step 3

In this task children find the percentages of the amounts. Encourage them to use the strategy discussed in the Textbook. For multiplying by the percentage needed, they should use long multiplication. If they are unsure of this method they could multiply by the tens number first, then the ones and add the two answers together. They could check their answers by finding 10% and manipulating that.

Once they have found the percentages provide them with suitable equipment to practically measure each amount.

Step 4

Before children begin the task, discuss what 15%, $\frac{1}{5}$ and 0.25 are and ask them to convert each to equivalent fractions, decimals and percentages as appropriate. Ask them to order the fractions from smallest to greatest. Discuss whether $\frac{3}{20}$ is always the smallest fraction. Establish that it depends what the whole is. In the task the amounts of money are different, so $\frac{3}{20}$ is not necessarily going to be smaller than $\frac{1}{4}$.

The task gives children the opportunity to apply what they have learned to solve a problem. They should work out each amount of money offered and show their working. They then decide which amount Sophie should opt for.

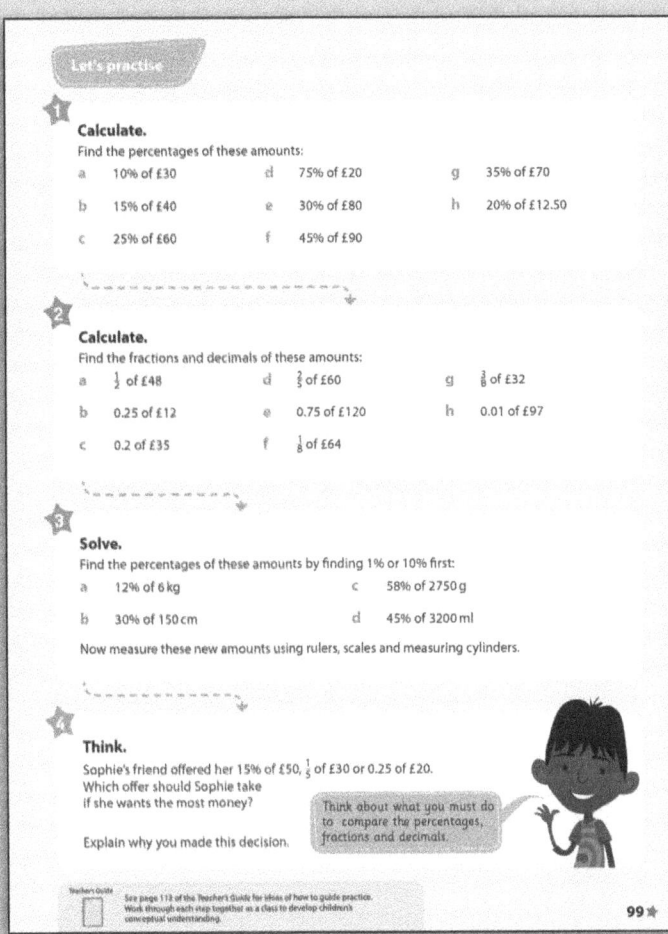

Follow-up ideas

- Children could make up problems that involve finding percentages of amounts of money for the rest of the class to solve.

- Children could use the Internet or toy catalogues to find details of sales and special offers, as these are often presented using fractions or percentages. Ask them to work out the new prices of items in the sale, using the equivalent fraction or percentage, whichever they find easiest to work with.

Ensuring progress

Supporting understanding

For the percentage tasks, some children may benefit from working with smaller numbers and also use digit cards and place-value grids to make the numbers they need and physically divide them by 100. You could also give them coins so that they can manipulate them to find the solutions.

Broadening understanding

Provide opportunities for children to make up their own problems in different contexts, e.g. time, length, mass, volume and capacity. You could provide opportunities to explain to another child how to find percentages. This will help you to assess their true understanding.

 Concept mastered

Children can explain and demonstrate how to find fractions, decimals and percentages of amounts of money and other measures.

Answers

Step 1		Step 2		Step 3	
a	£3	a	£24	a	0.72 kg
b	£6	b	£3	b	45 cm
c	£15	c	£7	c	1595 g
d	£15	d	£24	d	1440 ml
e	£24	e	£90		
f	£40.50	f	£8	**Step 4**	
g	£24.50	g	£12	15% of £50 = £7.50,	
h	£2.50	h	97p	$\frac{1}{5}$ of £30 = £6, 0.25 of £20 = £5. Sophie should accept 15% of £30	

- Solve problems involving multiplication and division, including scaling by simple fractions and problems involving simple rates.

Homework 47 and 48   Practice Book pp 70–3

Mathematical vocabulary

Multiply, divide, multiplication, division, scaling, scaling up, scaling down, rates

Representations and resources

Sets of digit cards (enough for 1 between 2), place-value grids (from thousands to hundredths), squared paper, counters.

Warming up

Write a multiplication number fact on the board, e.g. $9 \times 12 = 108$. Give children 3 minutes to come up with as many different facts as they can involving multiplication and division from the one on the board by doubling and halving, e.g. $108 \div 12 = 9$, $108 \div 6 = 18$, $108 \div 3 = 36$.

Background knowledge

Scaling is an important model for multiplication and division. In previous strategies and curriculums this usually related to ratio. Now the connection between ratio and multiplication and division has been made stronger. Early work on ratio before its introduction in Year 6 is encountered in this model. It is important that children develop a conceptual understanding in this area so that they will be successful when dealing with ratio in later years. If something is scaled up it is increased by a particular amount. The opposite happens for scaling down. This concept spread also explores the idea of simple rates. A rate is essentially a comparison of two quantities, often in different units. This will be the first time children have encountered this in mathematics. We begin simply, by relating this to exchange rates when dealing with currency. Children will explore this using scaling up and down.

Let's learn: Modelling and teaching

Scaling up and down

- Look at the diagram in the Textbook and ask children to explain to a partner what they think it shows. Establish that it shows an amount that has been scaled up by 4 and then scaled down to a quarter of the size. Explain that scaling up and down involves multiplication and division. To scale up, children multiply. To scale down, they divide. The division often involves finding fractions.

- Give children some squared paper. Ask them to shade 1 square. Tell them that it represents 12. Underneath ask them to colour 8 squares and to tell you the value of the line, if each square represents 12. Repeat this with other amounts where the squares represent 2- and 3-digit numbers.

Simple rates

- Ask children if they have ever heard of the term 'rates' before. Discuss exchange rates in terms of currency.

- Explain that they will explore this, using scaling up and down. Tell children that if they were travelling to most parts of Europe, they would need to change their money to Euros. At

the time of writing, 1 Euro was approximately 70p. Ask them to work out what 2, 4, then 8 and 16 Euros would be worth using doubling. Encourage them to record these like this:

1 Euro	=	70p
2 Euros	=	£1.40
4 Euros	=	£2.80
8 Euros	=	£5.60
16 Euros	=	£11.20

Emphasise the fact that, in doing this, they are scaling up. Ask children to illustrate their scaling using cubes, with one cube representing 70p.

- Next, ask them to combine different amounts from their list to find other amounts, e.g. 12 Euros = £8.40 (4 Euros + 8 Euros), 7 Euros = £4.90 (1 + 2 + 4 Euros).

Let's practise: Digging deeper

Step 1

For the first part of the activity, children need to scale up the amounts by multiplying each number by 4. They also need to explain how they did this. Encourage them to use a mental calculation strategy such as partitioning, doubling or using known facts. All of these can be answered in this way. For the second part they divide the numbers by 8 to find an eighth. Encourage them to use an efficient strategy to work these out, e.g. 272 can be partitioned into 240 and 32, 3 × 8 = 24, so 30 × 8 = 240. 32 ÷ 8 = 4, so the answer is 34. 2560 can be partitioned into 2400 and 160.

Step 2

In this task children are asked to solve problems that involve scaling up and down. Ask them to set these problems out using counters and then draw the representations on paper. They could use circles or squares as their representations. Once they have drawn these they solve the problems. For those that finish

this task quickly, ask them to make up their own problems for a partner to solve.

The last part of the task asks children to apply their understanding of scaling to find out how many dollars each friend is going to take with them on holiday. Encourage them to work systematically through this by writing what £1 would be in dollars, then £2, £4, £8 and £16. They then use this information by, e.g. adding and multiplying by 10 to find the correct conversions from pounds to dollars.

Step 3

In this task children are asked to scale down a recipe so that it makes four cheese scones. Encourage children to work out what to divide 12 by to give 4 and then scale the amounts down by dividing each by 3. Once they have done this, they weigh the dry ingredients into three different containers and the liquid into a bottle or jug. They could use, e.g. sand for the dry ingredients and water for the milk. Alternatively, you could provide the real items and they could then make the scones.

Step 4

Provide children with counters and ask children to set the problem out:

Dan's biscuits

Tom's biscuits

They then manipulate them so that the boys have the same amount:

If Tom gave Dan 10 biscuits then each counter is worth 5. They can now work out how many biscuits they had altogether.

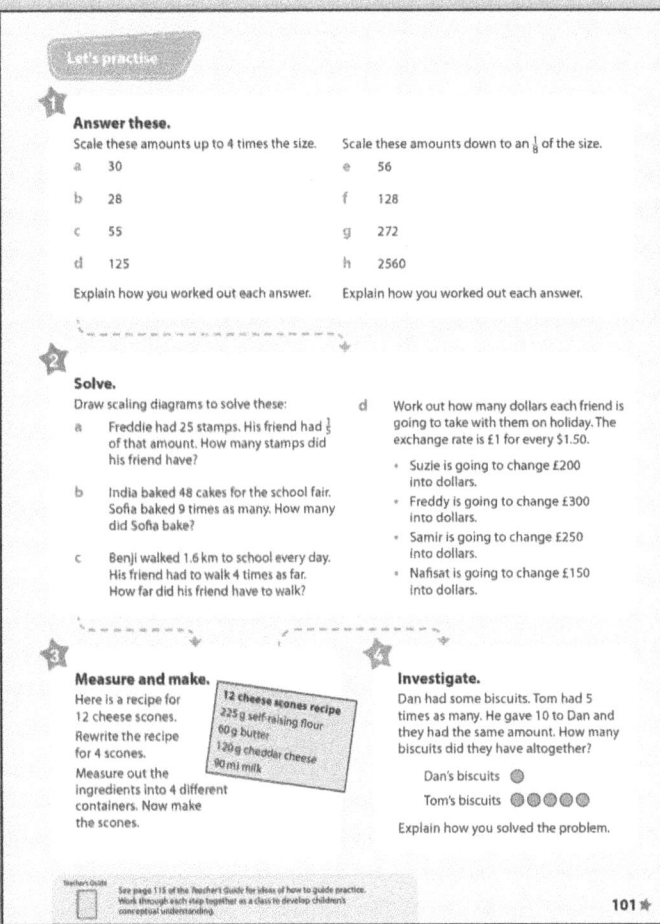

Follow-up ideas

- Children could make up problems that involve scaling up and scaling down for the rest of the class to solve.

- Ask children to use number cards to 100. They split them into two piles and place them face down on the table. They take it in turns to pick one care from each pile. One card represents the number of pounds and the other the amount it needs scaling up. Children work out the number when it has been scaled up and score that number of points. After 10 goes, the winner is the player with the most points.

- Children could look up cake recipes from books or on the Internet and scale them up and down for different numbers of people.

Ensuring progress

Supporting understanding

For all the questions, encourage children to use counters or draw rectangles so that they can see the structure of the mathematics that they are using. For some of the questions you may wish to use smaller numbers.

Broadening understanding

Provide opportunities for children to make up their own problems in different contexts, e.g. time, length, mass, volume and capacity. You could provide opportunities to explain to another child what scaling is and how it works. This will help you to assess their true understanding.

✓ Concept mastered

Children can confidently and consistently explain and demonstrate how scaling up and down work and are applied within a variety of contexts.

Answers

Step 1		g	34	Step 3
a	120	h	320	75 g self-raising flour, 20 g butter, 40 g cheese 30 ml milk
b	112	**Step 2**		
c	220	a	5 stamps	
d	500	b	432 cakes	**Step 4**
e	7	c	6.4 km	30 biscuits
f	16	d	$300, $450, $375, $225	

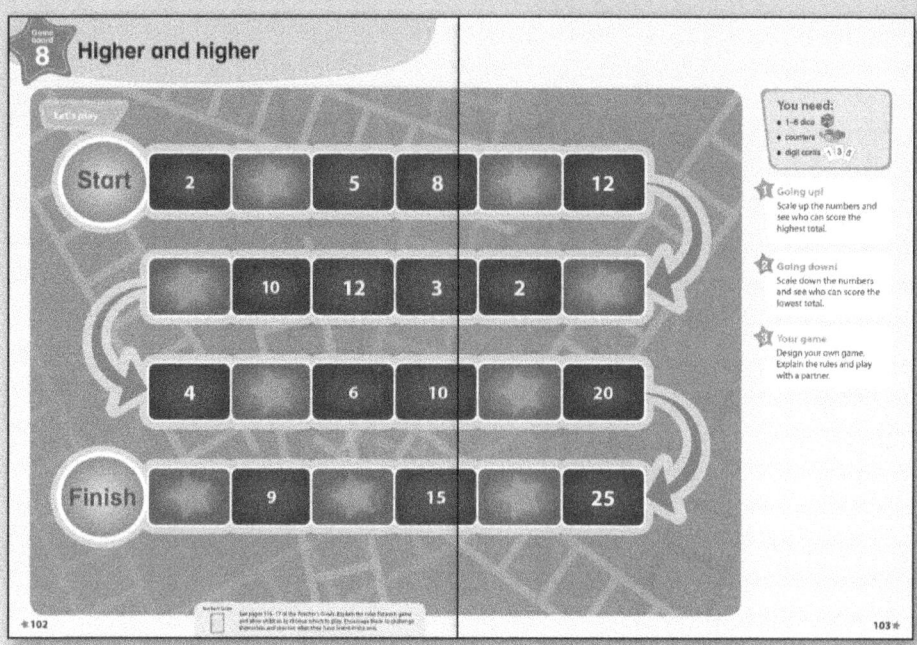

Game 1: Going up!

This game is to reinforce and rehearse scaling up. Children use digit cards to scale up the numbers they land on on the game board. They total their scores, and winner is the player with the highest score.

Maths focus

*   Scaling up

Resources

1 counter per player (1 colour per player), digit cards, 1–6 dice (1)

How to play

Children place their counters on Start. They take it in turns to throw the dice. They move that number around the board. If they land on a square containing a number, they pick up a digit card. They scale up the number on the digit card by the number they landed on. This is their score for that turn. If they don't land on a number they stay there until their next turn. When both players land on the Finish, they total their scores. The winner is the player with the highest total.

Making it easier

Children use digit cards from 1 to 5.

Making it harder

Children use number cards from 10 to 30.

Game 3: Your game

Children should invent their own game using rules that use the concepts covered in the unit. Challenge children to make their game easier or harder.

Game 2: Going down!

This game is to reinforce and rehearse scaling down. It is similar to Going up! Children follow the same rules, but they pick up a 2-digit number card and scale down this number by the number they landed on.

Maths focus

*   Scaling down

Resources

1 counter per player (1 colour per player), 2-digit number cards, 1–6 dice (1)

How to play

Children place their counters on Start. They take it in turns to throw the dice and move that number of spaces along the board. If they land on a number, they pick up a 2-digit number card and then scale it down by the number they had landed on. They can do this using a halving strategy or short division, it is up to them. Some of these numbers may involve remainders. These should be rounded up or down. The result is their score. If they don't land on a number, they stay where they are until their next go. When both players land on Finish, they total their scores. The winner is the player with the lowest total.

Making it easier

Give children number cards to 30. Encourage them to use grouping if they land on 15, 20 and 25 and to use known multiplication facts for the others.

Making it harder

Give children number cards from 50 to 100. Ask them to present any remainders as decimals.

Higher and higher

Choose a game to play.

Game 1: Going up!

You need:
- 1 counter per player (1 colour per player)
- digit cards
- 1–6 dice

How to play

- Each place your counter on Start.
- Take turns to roll the dice. Move your counter that number of spaces.
- If you land on a number, pick up a digit card.
- Scale up the number on your digit card by the number you have landed on.
- This is your score for that turn. If you don't land on a number, stay there until your next turn.
- When you have both landed on Finish, total up your scores.
- The winner is the player with the highest total.

Game 2: Going down!

You need:
- 1 counter per player (1 colour per player)
- 2-digit number cards
- 1–6 dice

How to play

- Each place your counter on Start.
- Take turns to roll the dice. Move your counter that number of spaces.
- If you land on a number, pick up a number card then scale the number on the card down by the number you have landed on.
- Some numbers may have remainders. You should round these up or down to find your score for the turn.
- If you don't land on a number, stay there until your next turn.
- When you have both landed on Finish, total up your scores.
- The winner is the player with the lowest total.

Game 3: Scale it!

- Make up your own game using the gameboard.
- Will you need to scale up or down in your game?
- How will you decide the winner?
- What are the rules for your game? Explain them to someone.

Please help your child by reading the instructions and playing the game together.

Assessment task 1

Running the task

Before children carry out the task, recap prime and square numbers. Ask children you particularly wish to assess to define them. Write some numbers to 100 on the board and ask them to identify which are prime, which are square and which are not, e.g. 11, 36, 42. Expect them to be able to tell you why they have made their decisions.

Recap factors and multiples. Ensure children can explain these and give examples. You could ask them to make up multiplication and division statements and highlight, using the correct vocabulary, which are factors and which are multiples.

Read each statement by children and ask the class to discuss whether they are always, sometimes or never true. They should prove their thinking by giving examples that fit the statement and a counter example if appropriate. From their experiences with prime numbers during this unit, they should be able to tell you that the first statement is sometimes true. Most prime numbers are odd, because all even numbers are multiples of 2. The only exception is 2. This is prime because it has only two factors.

They have had practice at investigating factors of different numbers and should be able to explain why the second statement is always true. There are always an odd number of factors because one factor is the number being squared and that is the single factor that makes an odd total.

Evidencing mastery

Look for children who can explain their thinking clearly and can give examples and counter examples as appropriate. If they can do this they are evidencing mastery in this area of mathematics.

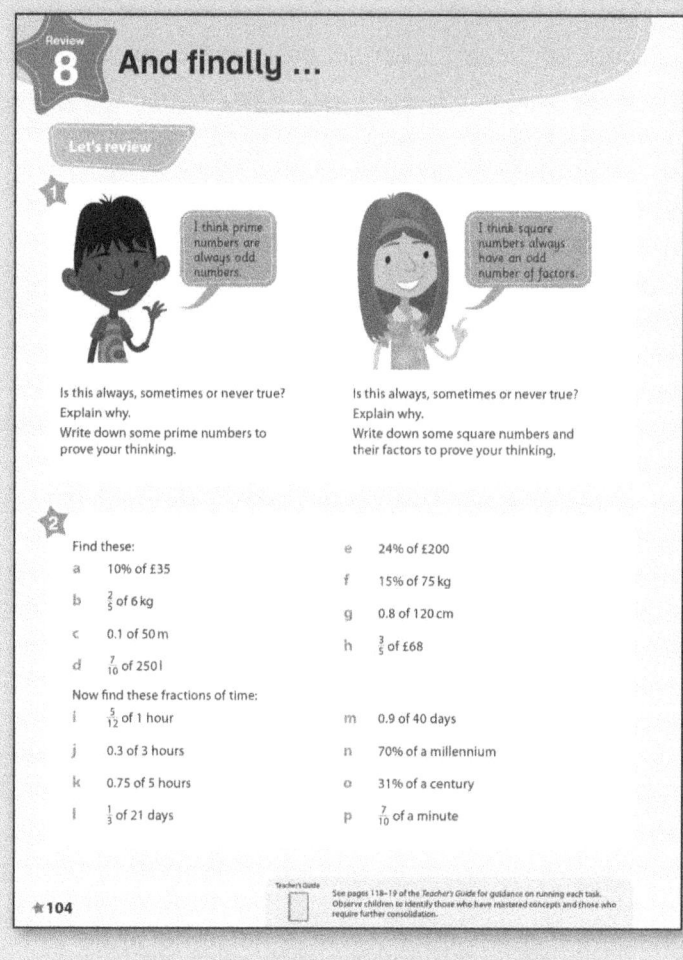

Assessment task 2

Running the task

Before children carry out this task, recap the link between fractions, decimals and percentages. Ensure that they understand that these are all the same type of number, they simply have a different appearance. Recap that decimals are always fractions with denominators that are powers of 10 and that percentages are always hundredths. Write a few fractions on the board, e.g. $\frac{1}{10}$, $\frac{3}{4}$ and $\frac{4}{5}$ and ask children to change these to decimals and percentages.

You could write decimals on the board for children to convert to fractions and percentages and then do the same with percentages.

For those that need extra support, work with them to ensure that they know how to find fractions, decimals and percentages of the given measurements by working through a few similar examples before they tackle the task.

Children should work on this task independently. Allow them to choose the methods of their choice. Discuss these methods with children you particularly wish to assess. Explanations can be in words or pictures. Some children may need manipulatives to help them.

The last part of this task is more challenging because it asks children to find fractions, decimals and percentages of units of time. You may decide to use this as an extension task.

Evidencing mastery

If children can confidently explain why fractions, decimals and percentages are the same type of number but have a different appearance, and also if they can demonstrate and explain with examples how to convert between fractions, decimals and percentages, they will be showing mastery.

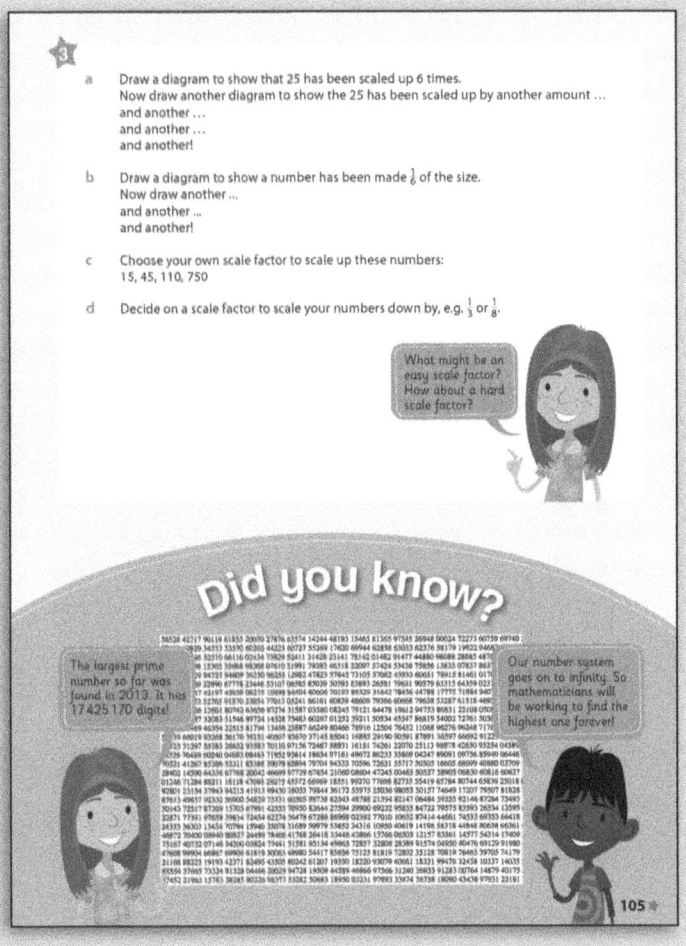

Concepts mastered

☑ Children can explain and demonstrate prime numbers and recognise and use square and cube numbers.

☑ Children can explain and demonstrate how to find fractions, decimals and percentages of amounts of money and other measures.

☑ Children can explain and demonstrate scaling up and scaling down

Answers

Step 2						
a	3.5	g	96 cm	l	7 days
b	2.4 kg	h	£40.80	m	36 days
c	5 m	i	25 minutes	n	700 years
d	175 l	j	54 minutes	o	31 years
e	£48	k	1 hour and 45 minutes/three-quarters or 225 minutes	p	42 seconds
f	11.25 kg				

Assessment task 3

Running the task

Before children begin the task ask them to explain what is meant by scaling up and scaling down. Encourage them to give examples.

You could work with children who need support before they begin to rehearse scaling up simple numbers by 2, 3 4 and 10 and scaling down by half and a quarter. Reinforce how to draw diagrams to show these. Then encourage them to work independently through this task.

You could recap scaling recipes up and down so that they are for different numbers of people. Discuss how much a recipe for two would need to be scaled up for a recipe for four and eight. How could they use this information for a recipe for 12?

You could also scale up for currency conversions and conversions from miles to kilometres and vice versa, e.g. 1 km is approximately 0.6 miles, how many miles would 2 km, 4 km and 8 km be? How could you use this information to work out how many miles are approximately equivalent to 6 km, 10 km, 12 km and 14 km?

Children need to work individually to draw scaling up and down diagrams as shown in the Textbook. Initially they are given numbers to scale up and down. Once they have done these they make up their own. Encourage them to challenge themselves. Some children may scale up 3- or 4-digit numbers and scale down to include fractions.

The last part of the task asks children to use their own scale factor to scale up four numbers. Establish that the scale factor in this case is the amount to scale up by. They then need to choose a scale factor to scale down by. Encourage them to choose their own fraction and to pick numbers that are multiples of the denominator of their fraction. You may wish to use this part of the task as an extension.

Evidencing mastery

Observe children when they make their drawings. If they work confidently and can explain scaling up and down accurately, they are evidencing mastery in this area of multiplication and division.

Did you know?

The largest prime number so far was found in 2013. It has 17 425 170 digits! Our number system goes on infinity. So mathematicians will be working to find the actual one forever! You could inform children that there are hints that the knowledge of prime numbers dates back to the Ancient Egyptians. The earliest known records date back to the Ancient Greeks when mathematician Euclid produced various theories on these.

2-D and 3-D shapes

Mathematical focus

★ **Geometry: properties of shapes, position and direction**

★ **Measurement: drawing and measuring angles**

Prior learning

Children should already be able to:

- compare and classify geometric shapes, including quadrilaterals and triangles, based on their properties and sizes
- draw given angles and measure them in degrees
- identify acute and obtuse angles, and compare and order angles up to two right angles by size.

Key new learning

- Identify, describe and represent the position of a shape following a reflection or translation, using the appropriate mathematical language, and know that the shape has not changed.
- Identify 3-D shapes, including cubes and other cuboids, from 2-D representations.
- Identify angles at a point (total 360°) and on a straight line (180°).

Making connections

- Examining patterns involving reflections and translations continues to develop children's appreciation of the beauty and usefulness of 2-D shapes in everyday life.
- 3-D shapes make up our world. An understanding of how to describe the properties of shapes helps children to make sense of the world.
- Today we have computers that enable us to draw shapes with a high degree of accuracy but thousands of years ago the Greeks were able to draw perfect circles and shapes simply using compasses and a ruler.
- Many aspects of physics involve the study of angles. Children will probably have studied light in their science lessons and could investigate the use of lens in spectacles for correcting sight defects.

Unit
9 2-D and 3-D shapes

I wonder what happens to shapes when they are reflected?

Are there translations in this patterned quilt?

I wonder what different faces and angles this beautiful diamond has?

★106

Talk about

The words 'reflex' and 'translate' that occur in this unit are also words used in everyday English. Ensure that children are clear about the mathematical meanings. A reflex angle is an angle that is greater than 180° but less than 360°. To translate an object means to move every point the same distance in the same direction.

Engaging and exploring

Give children some time to look at each photo in the Textbook and discuss the accompanying question in pairs before sharing ideas as a whole class.

Looking at the photo of the zebras, ask children how the object and the image are the same and how they differ. They should think about the size of the zebras and how the water is acting like a horizontal mirror line. Establish that the image is the same size but reversed. Extend this to thinking about mirror images. The image is the same distance behind the mirror as the object is in front of it; however, the image is reversed. The mirror makes the left-hand side of the object appear on the right. Children can test this by waving with their right hand in a mirror and observing that it is their left hand waving back.

In the photo of the patchwork quilt, individual patches could be considered as translations, moving in a horizontal (or a vertical) direction. Point out that the quilt has horizontal and vertical mirror lines, so there are reflections too.

Look at the picture of the cut diamond and ask children to describe its shape. Explain that faces on cut gems are known as facets, and ask children what different polygon faces they can see. Look at the different angles and estimate their sizes.

For the photo of the roofs, ask children if they can identify an acute and obtuse angle and to estimate their size in degrees. Discuss the meaning of the word 'pitch' in this context. Ask children if they can explain why some roofs are high pitched (with an angle of 90° or less) or low pitched (with an obtuse angle). The primary purpose of pitching a roof is to redirect water and snow. Thus, pitch is typically higher in areas of high rain or snowfall. Ask children if they can ascertain the likely weather conditions in Warsaw, the city shown in the photo.

The photo of the flan is a practical example of a reflex angle. Ask children to estimate the size of the reflex angle in degrees. If necessary, explain that a good way to do this is to estimate the size of the acute angle, which is much easier to do, and then take that angle away from 360°.

Checking understanding

You will know children have mastered these concepts when they can recognise reflections and translations, and describe the position of the vertices and identify 3-D shapes from 2-D representations.

They will also be able to discuss angle shapes using mathematical vocabulary and draw angles accurately, including reflex angles.

Things to think about

- Do the classroom and the outside area have an abundance of shapes?
- How will you organise groupings for discussions and activities?
- How will you check conceptual understanding?
- What support will you provide for left-handers or children with a degree of dyspraxia who find drawing angles very challenging?
- What opportunities will you provide to build fluency?

- Which problem-solving strategies are most appropriate for this unit, e.g.:
  - ▶ What is the same? What is different?
  - ▶ Always, sometimes, never
  - ▶ Another, another, another
  - ▶ Convince me
  - ▶ Odd one out
  - ▶ What else do we know?

9a Reflecting and translating 2-D shapes

- **Identify, describe and represent the position of a shape following a reflection or translation, using the appropriate language, and know that the shape has not changed.**

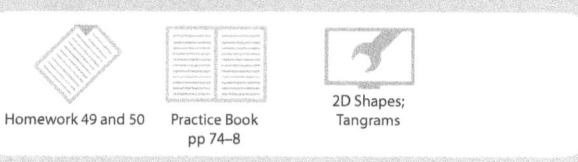

Homework 49 and 50 | Practice Book pp 74–8 | 2D Shapes; Tangrams

Mathematical vocabulary

Reflect/reflection, translate/translation, x- and y-axes, x- and y-coordinates

Representations and resources

cm-squared paper or cm-dotted paper, small mirror, 30 cm ruler, 1–10 dice, two 1-6 dice.

Warming up

Draw a quadrant with the x- and y-axes labelled 1–10. Divide the class into two teams, Red and Blue. A member of the Red team throws a 1–10 dice twice to determine a coordinate (first throw = x value; second throw = y value). The player marks the coordinate on the quadrant with a red cross. Then it is the Blue team's turn. The first team to get three coordinates in a straight line wins.

Background knowledge

This concept revisits translation. Mathematically this is where a shape is moved left or right and up or down but the properties of the shape remain unchanged.

When giving co-ordinates, the x-value (horizontal direction) is always given first, then the y-value (vertical direction). You can give children mnemonics to remember this, such as 'along the corridor and up the stairs' or 'walk before you fly'.

With practice, children will recognise that coordinates with the same x-value are on the same vertical line and those with the same y-value are on the same horizontal line.

Let's learn: Modelling and teaching

Reflecting 2-D shapes

- A reflection is a kind of transformation. It can be explained to children as a 'flip' over the line of reflection, or mirror line.

- Draw a horizontal mirror line on the floor and show them how a reflection flips a variety of 2-D shapes over the mirror line to a new position. Repeat with a vertical mirror line.

- Look back at the Textbook. Demonstrate how to check that a reflection is correct by counting the squares from the mirror line. Every point stays the same distance from the mirror line, so the shape stays the same size but faces the other way. Give children a mirror to reinforce understanding of this.

- Ask children to give the coordinates for the top vertex of the triangle before and after the reflection. In pairs ask them to do the same for the other vertices. Ask them what they notice about the coordinates and the triangles. Discuss the fact that when the triangle is flipped over the vertical mirror line $x = 5$, the y-coordinates have not changed nor has the size of the triangle. Repeat this for reflection in the y-axis.

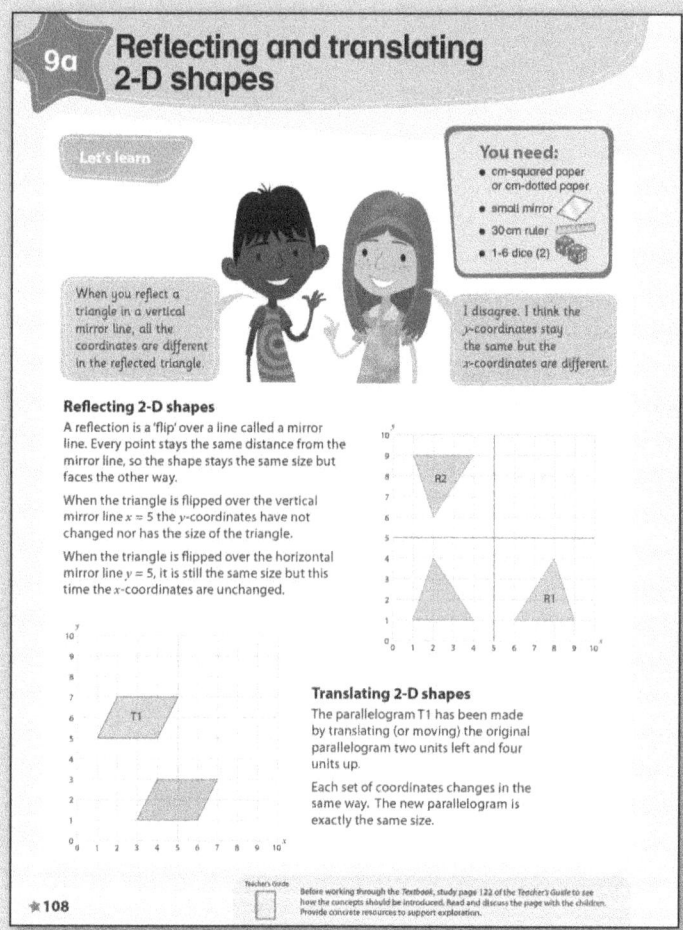

Translating 2-D shapes

- Using a square grid cut out 2-D shapes and demonstrate a translation. Explain that in geometry, translation means moving a shape without changing the size or shape. Every point of the shape must move the same distance in the same direction. A new position can be described by expressing it as moving a number of units to the left or right (the x-axis direction) and a number of units up or down (the y-axis direction).

- Talk children through the example in the Textbook, explaining that to to translate the point (3, 1), you decrease the x-coordinate by two, and increase the y-coordinate by four. The new coordinates for this point are (1, 5). The new parallelogram is exactly the same size.

Let's practise: Digging deeper

Step 1

Before carrying out the task, organise children into pairs and give them a 0–12 coordinate grid. Choose a mirror line, e.g. $x = 6$. Roll two 1–6 dice to give a set of coordinates. One child plots the point; the other plots to the position of the reflected point. They check with a mirror. Repeat, until the mirror is no longer required. Children can then complete the Textbook question independently.

Step 2

In this question children are reflecting each quadrilateral horizontally and vertically. They should see that the pattern looks 'right' and as they write down the coordinates, the same numbers will occur, in the x position and then the y.

Step 3

In this problem the mirror line is disguised as a garden path. Children are free to design their own gardens with flowerbeds and other features. Discuss how to record their design on a coordinate grid, beginning with the central path. Share and comment on each other's individual designs.

Step 4

Prepare a 0–12 coordinate grid and four identical right-angled triangles. Ask children to place them on the grid so that they are translations of each other and do not overlap. Label one of the triangles 'original'. Ask children to describe the translations from this triangle. Ask children what happens to the numerical values of the coordinates. Do they get bigger or smaller if they move to the left/right and up/down? Now children carry out the task with the L-shape. Encourage them to record the translations in a table to help them identify patterns.

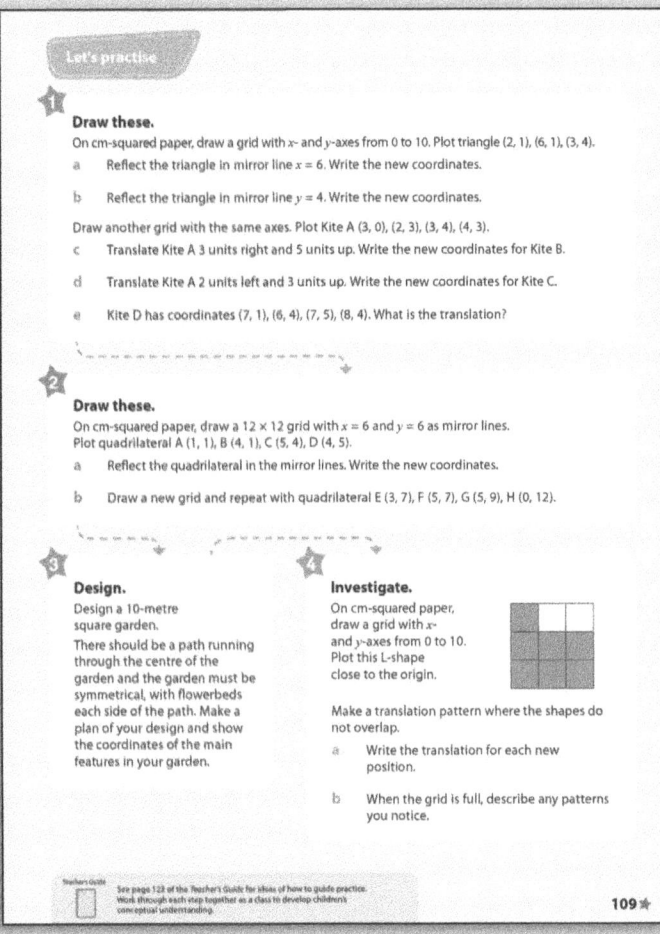

Follow-up ideas

- Draw large-scale grids in the playground so that children can play games translating shapes or reflecting them in a mirror line. Use a rope or coloured chalk line to represent a mirror.

- Investigate repeated patterns in everyday life and in art, including art from other cultures.

- Following on from the question on gardens, children can investigate the symmetry of formal gardens.

Ensuring progress

Supporting understanding

Encourage children to take care with the presentation of their work so that the coordinates are clear and easy to read. Children who find this challenging may benefit from using paper with larger squares or from having templates with the axes and coordinates pre-printed. They may enjoy playing coordinate games to strengthen their skills. Ensure that children have access to small mirrors when working on reflections.

Broadening understanding

Children will have explored letters that are symmetrical when you reflect them in horizontal or vertical mirror lines. Challenge them to find words that are unchanged when reflected in mirrors placed vertically or horizontally.

✓ Concept mastered

Children can identify and describe the new position of a shape following a reflection or translation using x- and y- coordinates.

Answers

Step 1

a (10, 1), (6, 1), (9, 4)

b (2, 7), (6, 7), (3, 4)

c (6, 5), (5, 8), (6, 9), (7, 8)

d (1, 3), (0, 6), (1, 7), (2, 6)

e 4 units right and 1 unit up

Step 2

a (1, 11), (4, 11), (5, 8), (4, 7); (11, 1), (8, 1), (7, 4), (8, 5)

b (3, 5), (5, 5), (5, 3), (0, 0); (9, 7), (7, 7), (7, 9), (12, 12)

Step 3

Individual answers

Step 4

a Individual answers

b Individual answers

- Identify 3-D shapes, including cubes and other cuboids, from 2-D representations.

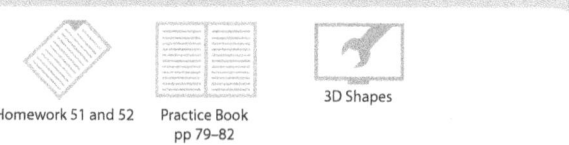

Homework 51 and 52   Practice Book pp 79–82   3D Shapes

Mathematical vocabulary

Face, edge, vertex, curved surface, apex, prism, pyramid, cross-section, parallel

Warming up

Choose a simple 2-D shape. Ask children to write the names of as many different 3-D shapes as possible that have the chosen 2-D shape as a face. Compare answers. Ask children to find the 3-D shapes from the solid shapes collection.

Background knowledge

Children will need to apply knowledge of the properties of geometric shapes (including quadrilaterals and triangles) to help them identify 3-D shapes. They may benefit from revising the properties of the most common regular 2-D shapes. Here is a summary of the polygons that are found most frequently in 3-D shapes:

Rectangle – a quadrilateral with four right angles. Both pairs of opposite sides are equal in length and parallel.

Square – a rectangle in which all four sides are equal in length.

Equilateral triangle – a triangle with three equal sides and angles (60°).

Isosceles triangle – a triangle with two equal sides and angles.

Regular polygon – a polygon with all the angles and sides equal. There is only one regular polygon for a given number of sides.

Representations and resources

2-D and 3-D shapes, cubes, isometric paper, straws, modelling clay.

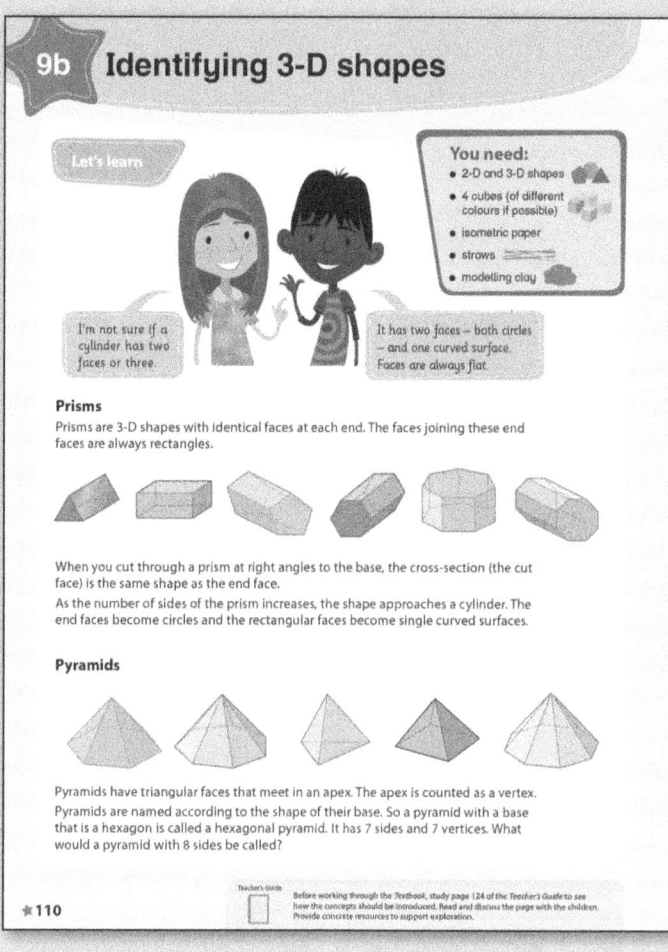

Let's learn: Modelling and teaching
Prisms

- Give children a variety of 3-D shapes. Ask them how they can recognise the prisms. Explain that they have identical faces at each end and a uniform cross-section. To help children understand this, ask them to make prisms from modelling clay and cut through the prism at intervals to check that the shape of the cross-section always matches the end face.

- Now choose certain prisms and ask children to name them and describe the faces, edges and vertices. Encourage discussion by asking: *What shape would the cross-section be? Are cubes prisms?*

- Can children suggest where prisms are seen in everyday life? There are many examples of cuboids and cubes but fewer of other types. They may suggest some biscuit packs and chocolate bars. Many pencils are long, narrow prisms. Revisit the misconception in the Textbook. Can children explain in their own words why Amy is wrong?

Pyramids

- Give children polyhedrons and ask them to make pyramids. As they do so, use questioning to draw out the concept: *What is special about a pyramid? Can you make a statement about pyramids that is always true?*

- Ask children to describe the pyramid that has an octagon as the base. Ask them to state how many sides and vertices it has. Repeat for a pentagon. Ask them if they can identify a pattern for the number of faces and vertices that pyramids have. (The number of faces is equal to the number of vertices. A pyramid with a base of n sides has $n + 1$ faces and $n + 1$ vertices.)

- Name the pyramids in the Textbook. Use these images to discuss pyramids in everyday life.

Let's practise: Digging deeper

Step 1

Using straws and modelling clay to make models helps children to understand how edges and vertices make faces, resulting in 3-D shapes. The models could form part of a classroom display.

Step 2

For part a) most children will know that cubes and cuboids have eight vertices. Elicit from them that there is only one shape that has four triangular faces – a tetrahedron (or triangular-based pyramid). As a result, the second possibility for part b) must have an additional face, and a square-based pyramid has one square face and four triangular ones. For part c) children will know that spheres and cylinders have curved surfaces, and for part d) that a cuboid has more than six vertices and is a prism with end faces that are rectangular. Help children to reason that any prism with end faces that have

four or more sides will therefore have more than six vertices. Similarly, pyramids that have a base with five or more sides will also satisfy part d.

Step 3

Show how a cube can be represented on isometric paper. Using cubes of different colours for the task will help children to see which arrangements are different. Explain that the orientation of a shape does not make it a different shape – four cubes joined vertically is the same shape as four cubes joined horizontally.

Step 4

The relationship that children are aiming to find is known as Euler's formula: the number of faces plus the number of vertices, minus the number of edges is always equal to two ($F + V - E = 2$). Suggest that children collect data for at least four 3-D shapes and then try to find a relationship. More able children will visualise the data, while others may benefit from using concrete materials so that they can physically count edges, vertices and faces. Support them to record their results in a table with headings F, V, $F + V$, and E. Once the results are in tabular form they should spot the relationship.

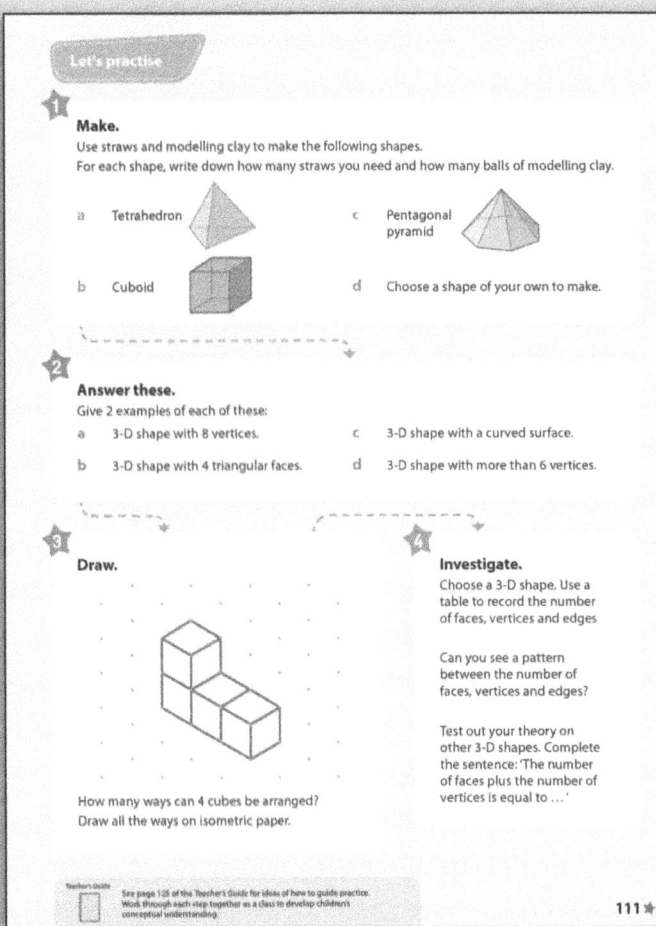

Follow-up ideas

- Leave out 3-D shapes and polydrons for children to use in free play. It will give them experience of handling and appreciating the properties of 3-D shapes.

- Ask children to investigate architectural drawings and computer-aided design (CAD). They may have experience of some simple CAD programs.

- Give children some isometric paper and help them to learn how to draw cubes, cuboids and other shapes.

Ensuring progress

Supporting understanding

The vocabulary in this topic will be quite challenging for some children. A display of the words with matching diagrams, or card games, may help children to remember the words and learn to spell them too.

Broadening understanding

Children who have good spatial awareness and understanding will enjoy tackling more challenging tasks, e.g. finding the number of arrangements possible with five or more cubes.

 Concept mastered

Children can identify 3-D shapes from 2-D representations. They can describe properties of 3-D shapes using appropriate mathematical vocabulary.

Answers

Step 1

a   6 straws, 4 clay pieces

b   12 straws, 8 clay pieces

c   10 straws, 6 clay pieces

d   Individual answers

Step 2

a   Cube, cuboid

b   Tetrahedron, square-based pyramid

c   Cone, cylinder, (sphere)

d   Hexagonal pyramid, heptagonal pyramid, octagonal pyramid, etc., pentagonal prism, hexagonal prism, heptagonal prism, etc.

Step 3

There are eight different arrangements.

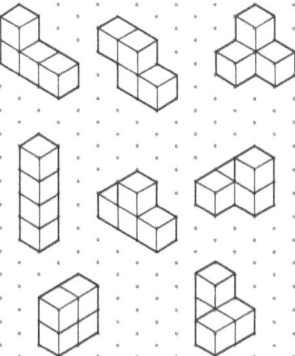

Step 4

The number of faces + number of vertices = number of edges + 2.

9c Angles

- Know angles are measured in degrees: estimate and compare acute, obtuse and reflex angles.
- Draw given angles, and measure them in degrees (°).
- Distinguish between regular and irregular polygons based on reasoning about equal sides and angles.
- Identify:
  ▶ angles at a point and 1 whole turn (total 360°)
  ▶ angles at a point on a straight line and half a turn (total 180°).

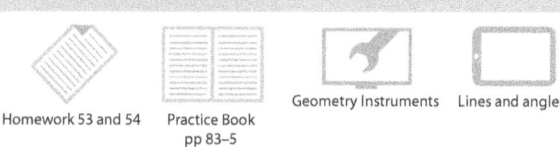

Homework 53 and 54   Practice Book pp 83–5   Geometry Instruments   Lines and angles

Representations and resources
Protractor, ruler, 0-9 number cards, geostrips.

Mathematical vocabulary
Acute, obtuse, reflex, protractor, estimate, accurate, visualise

Warming up
Practise estimating, and then measuring, the size of acute and obtuse angles.

Background knowledge
Angles are a measure of turn and can be measured as a fraction of a whole turn or in degrees. Children should know how to use a simple 180° protractor but it is worth letting them explore others. For example, circular angle measurers can help to eliminate confusion about which scale to use and emphasise the idea of an angle as an amount of rotation; other protractors show the two scale directions separately (one on each side of the protractor).
It is important that children estimate angles before measuring them. Making this practice automatic in children's minds will eliminate many errors in work on angles.

Let's learn: Modelling and teaching
Drawing and measuring reflex angles
- Reflex angles are seen and used less frequently, and can be more challenging to visualise. Ask children to stand up and make a $\frac{3}{4}$ turn clockwise. Ask the size of this angle and confirm it is 270°. Now ask them to think about turning 260° or 280°, and so on. Next, use 180° as a starting point and ask them to turn 180°, 190° or 200°. Repeat the exercise on mini-whiteboards, making sure that you ask children to draw reflex angles in both clockwise and anticlockwise directions.

- Use the example in the Textbook to demonstrate how to find reflex angles by subtracting from 360° or adding to 180°. Practise this using the whiteboards.

Calculating angles on a straight line
- Revisit the idea of a straight line as an angle. (It is two right angles or half a complete turn, equal to 180°.)

- Use 0–9 number cards to generate 2-digit angles. Ask children to show you these angles with geostrips and calculate mentally what the missing angle on a straight line would be.

- Discuss which mental calculation strategies might be the most effective. Selecting 0 and 1 (or other small digits) gives the opportunity of discussing the minute angle that 1° is – it is not an angle that usually appears in questions.

Let's practise: Digging deeper

Step 1

Children need practice measuring and calculating reflex angles. Enable them to discover that the quickest way to calculate reflex angles is to deduct the size of the known angle from 360°. Remind them that they can move the protractor (or even turn the book around) to make it easier to measure angles. Estimating the angles before measuring them helps to eliminate use of the incorrect scale on the protractor. If possible, mark children's work while they are doing parts d) and e), so that errors or bad practice can be corrected immediately.

Step 2

This step gives children practice in calculating and drawing all types of angles and measuring reflex angles. Before completing the task, ask children to visualise these angles: 90° (a right angle), 45° (half a right angle), 60° (the angle in

an equilateral triangle) and 135° (90° + 45°). Most other acute and obtuse angles can be sketched with reasonable accuracy by making them a bit smaller or bigger than these angles. Children could use geostrips to show you acute and obtuse angles and then practise subtracting multiples of 10 from 180. They should now be ready to do the task independently.

Step 3

This is an open-ended task. Finding good examples of reflex angles, especially ones that can be measured, can be challenging. Possible examples are open doors, parts of staircases or anything with an inverted kite shape. A teacher's or board protractor could help children to measure more accurately. Look carefully at how the children record their findings. Are they using a table? Have they grouped or organised the angles systematically? Encourage children to reflect on how accurately they estimated the angles and ensure that no child is consistently far off in their estimates.

Step 4

This is a low threshold, high ceiling task. Children who can draw shapes to fit in every box demonstrate mastery of the concepts, especially if they are able to see how polygons can grow in their number of sides and still fit into a particular section. Adding descriptions of the angles to the polygons reveals patterns. Encourage children to spot these by asking: *What do you notice?*

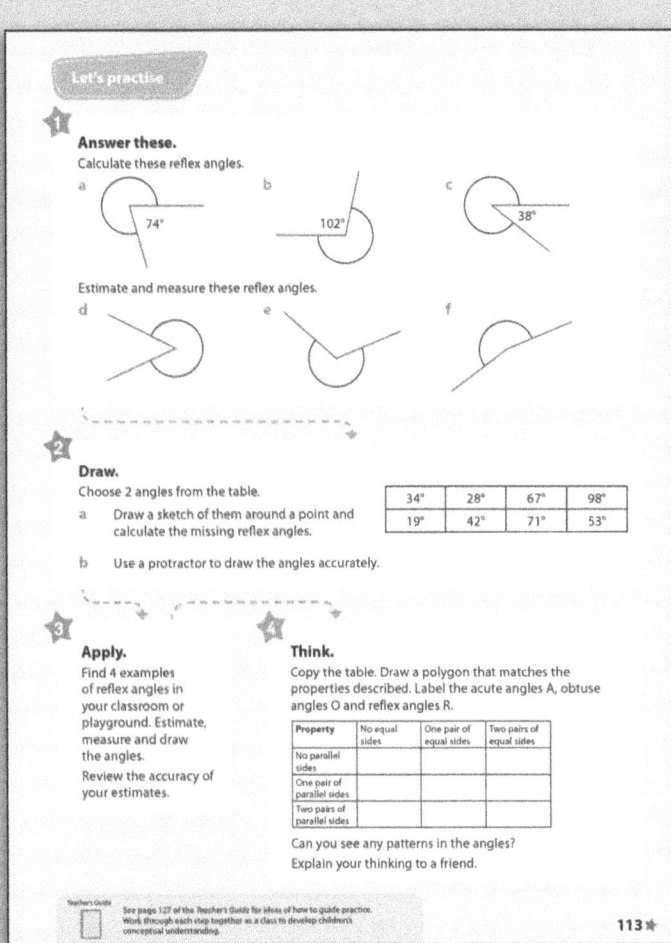

Ensuring progress

Supporting understanding

Ask children to use their arms to show you different angles. The ability to visualise angles accurately is only developed through practice. Using a protractor correctly and accurately is challenging for many children. Check that they are taking care to align it properly.

Broadening understanding

Children who have mastered these concepts will enjoy solving angle problems. Challenge them to make up some angle problems based on the angles that can be made using the hands on an analogue clock and then swapping with a partner.

✓ Concept mastered

Children can draw and measure angles, including reflex angles.

Follow-up ideas

- Investigate the pitch of roofs. The angle can vary from almost flat to very steep and will depend on the weather conditions in the area.
- Collect pictures of angles in everyday life. Sort them into acute, obtuse and reflex angles.

Answers

Step 1

a	286°
b	258°
c	322°
d	approx. 310°
e	approx. 240°
f	approx. 190°

Step 2

326°	332°	293°	262°
341°	318°	289°	307°

Step 3

Individual answers

Step 4

Property	No equal sides	One pair of equal sides	Two pairs of equal sides
No parallel sides	Scalene triangle or other irregular shape	Isosceles triangle or other irregular shape	Kite; Arrowhead
One pair of parallel sides	Trapezium	Isosceles trapezium or other irregular shape	Polygon with 6 sides or more that fits conditions
Two pairs of parallel sides	Possible for polygons with 7 or more sides	Irregular hexagon	Square; Rectangle (exactly 2 pairs)

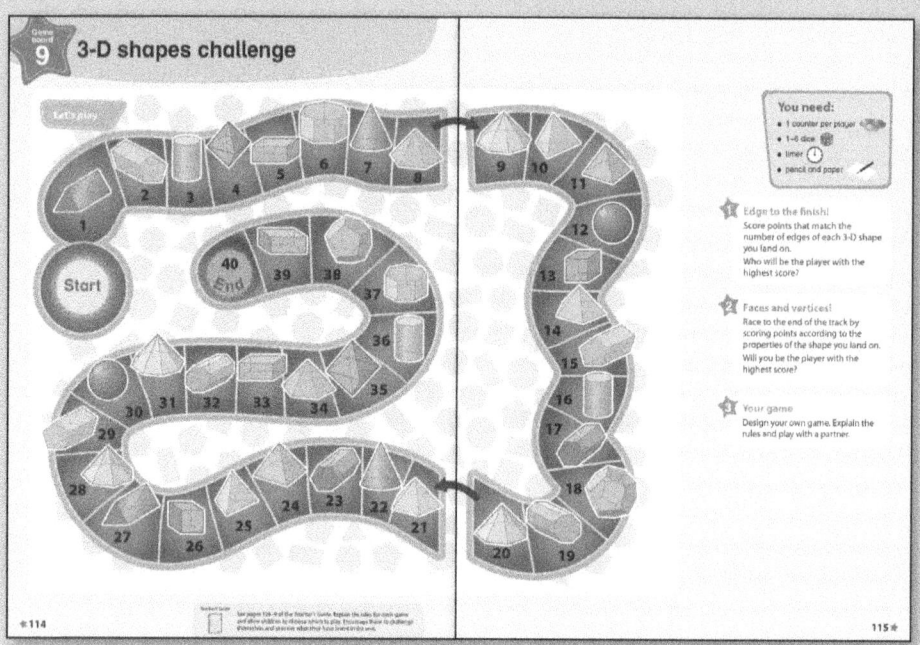

Game 1: Edge to the finish!

Children take turns to roll the dice and move their counter along the board. They score points that match the number of edges of each 3-D shape they land on.

Maths focus

- Identify 3-D shapes, including cubes and other cuboids, from 2-D representations.
- Visualise and describe the properties of 3-D shapes.

Resources

1 counter per player (1 colour per player), 1–6 dice (1).

How to play

This game is best played with two or three players. Children place their counter on Start. They take turns to roll the dice and move their counter along the board. Children score points that match the number of edges of each shape they land on. The game continues until a player reaches the End. The first player to finish scores 50 bonus points. The player with the highest score is the winner.

Making it easier

Have a box of 3-D shapes available that children can use to count the edges.

Making it harder

Ask children to name each shape they land on. Award a bonus point if they name the shape correctly.

Game 3: Your game

Children should invent their own game, designing rules that use the concepts covered in the unit. Challenge children to make their game easier or harder.

Game 2: Faces and vertices!

This game gives children practice in identifying and counting the number of faces and vertices of 3-D shapes. They score points according to the instructions that relate to their dice roll and the 3-D shape they land on.

Maths focus

- Identify 3-D shapes, including cubes and cuboids, from 2-D representations.
- Visualise and describe the properties of 3-D shapes.

Resources

1 counter per player (1 colour per player), 1–6 dice (1), timer, pencil and paper.

How to play

This game is best played by two or three players for a set period of time or until a player reaches the End. Children place their counter on End. Each player rolls the dice and moves that number of places along the board. They then look at the table to work out their score, which is determined by the properties of the shape they have landed on, e.g. if a player throws a two and lands on a cuboid, they score six points (because a cuboid has six rectangular faces). Children record their scores. The winner is the person with the highest score when time runs out or a player reaches the END.

Dice roll instructions:

Dice throw	Score
1	Number of triangular faces
2	Number of rectangular faces
3	Number of vertices
4	Number of faces
5	For a shape with a curved surface, score 5
6	Number of faces + number of vertices

Making it easier

Have a box of 3-D shapes available that children can use to count the faces and vertices.

Making it harder

If a four is thrown, move on by the number of edges.

3-D shapes challenge

Choose a game to play.

Game 1: Edge to the finish!

You need:

- 1 counter per player (1 colour per player)
- 1–6 dice

How to play

- Place your counter on Start.
- Take turns to roll the dice and move your counter along the board.
- Your score is the number of edges of each shape you land on.
- The first player to reach the End scores 50 bonus points.
- The player with the highest score is the winner.

Game 2: Faces and vertices!

You need:

- 1 counter per player (1 colour per player)
- 1–6 dice
- timer
- pencil and paper

How to play

- Place your counter on Start.
- Set the timer for an agreed time.
- Take turns to roll the dice and move along the board.
- Score according to the instructions in the table, e.g. if you throw a 2 and land on a cuboid, you score 6 (because a cuboid has 6 rectangular faces).
- Record your scores.
- The winner is the person with the highest score when the timer sounds or a player reaches the End.

Dice throw	Score
1	Number of triangular faces
2	Number of rectangular faces
3	Number of vertices
4	Number of faces
5	For a shape with a curved surface, score 5
6	Number of faces + number of vertices

Game 3: Your game

- Design your own game using the gameboard.
- Explain the rules and play with a partner.

Please help your child by reading the instructions and playing the game together.

And finally ...

Assessment task 1

Resources

- Cm-squared paper, protractor.

Running the task

Pair children appropriately and explain that first they are each going to be writing and answering their own question on reflection and translation. They will then give their question to their partner to work on, and finally they will compare their answers.

The question they write and answer enables children to show that they have mastered reflection and translation, and understand reflex angles. Getting children to reflect and translate one another's quadrilateral gives them the opportunity to check their work and help one another to self-correct if necessary. This will deepen their understanding.

Evidencing mastery

Children who have mastered these concepts will have no difficulty interpreting and completing the task without error. They will be able to estimate the reflex angle to within approximately 5°.

Children who are still working towards mastery may require support to draw a quadrilateral that fits the criteria and need reminding of the ways to estimate a reflex angle: by estimating the size of the remaining acute or obtuse angle and subtracting this from 360° or by estimating how much greater than a straight line angle it is and adding their estimate to 180°.

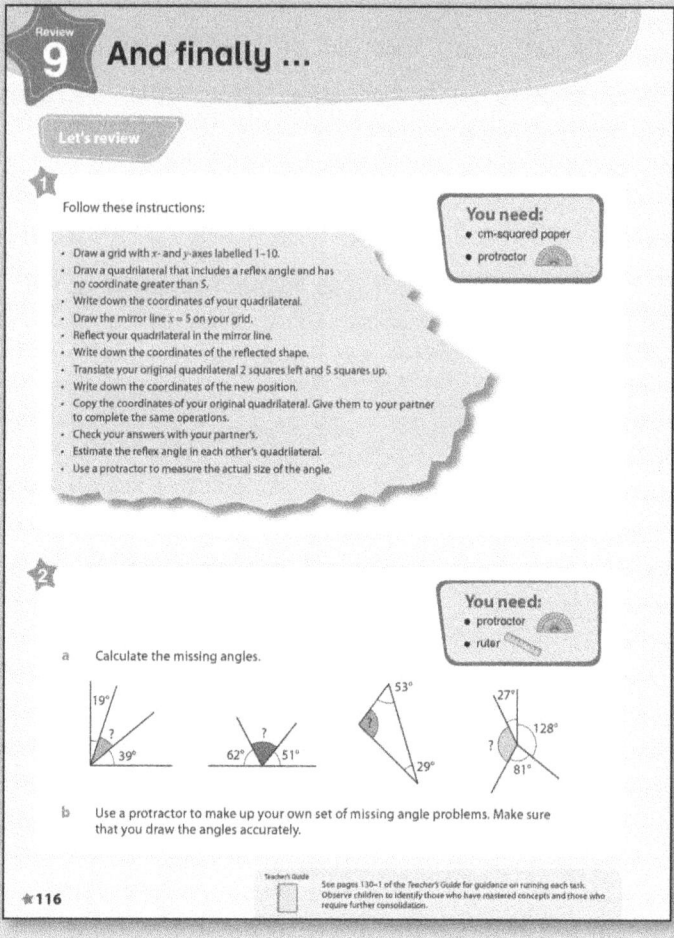

Assessment task 2

Resources

- Protractor, ruler.

Running the task

Discuss the mathematics involved in this task, including recapping angle facts. Remind children to estimate the size of the missing angle before starting the calculation. This is an important self-check procedure as if they miscalculate or use a wrong starting point a 'silly answer' is immediately apparent. Most children should be able to carry out the first part of the task with minimal support. The second part of the task challenges children to write their own examples. This aspect also assesses children's skill and dexterity as they use the protractor. If you see children who are still struggling with the correct placement and use of this instrument, try to arrange a small group session to support them.

Evidencing mastery

Children showing mastery can recall the entire range of angle facts and are able to calculate the missing angle competently. Ask children to explain their thinking to you as they work though the problem. They should be able to make statements such as 'I know the angles in a triangle add up to 180°, so I need to add the angles I have been given and subtract that total from 180°'.

Children will have mastered drawing and measuring angles if they consistently use the protractor proficiently and accurately.

Answers

a   32°; 67°; 98°; 124°

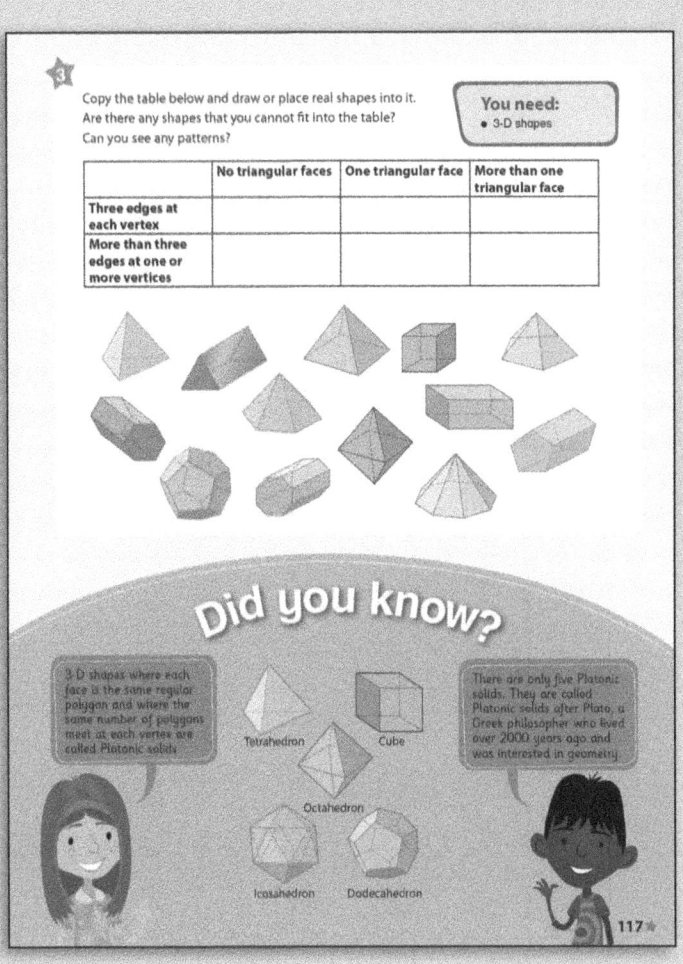

Concepts mastered

☑ Children can identify and describe the new position of a shape following a reflection or translation using *x*- and *y*- coordinates.

☑ Children can identify 3-D shapes from 2-D representations. They can describe properties of 3-D shapes using appropriate mathematical vocabulary.

☑ Children can draw and measure angles, including reflex angles.

Assessment task 3

Resources

- 3-D shapes, prepared worksheet

Running the task

Many children will be able to visualise the shapes but others may still value the support of handling 3-D shapes. A prepared worksheet grid will eliminate time to draw it where necessary. Tell children to consider and place shapes one at a time and to keep looking for patterns.

	No triangular faces	One triangular face	More than one triangular face
Three edges at each vertex	Pentagonal prism, hexagonal prism, etc. Cube/cuboid		Tetrahedron Triangular prism
More than three edges at one or more vertices	Dodecahedron		Square-based pyramid, pentagonal-based pyramid, etc.

Evidencing mastery

Children demonstrate mastery if they are able to consider and place each shape systematically and then spot that there are no shapes that fit the 'One triangular face' column.

Did you know?

There are some beautiful drawings of Platonic solids by Leonardo da Vinci. Children may enjoy making models of the Platonic solids from straws and modelling clay or by using construction apparatus such as polydrons. They may be familiar with the Platonic solids, using them as multi-sided dice.

Children may like to investigate Euler's formula ($F + V - E = 2$) for the solids, which some of them may have explored in 9b – Identifying 3-D shapes. Investigating how many faces meet at each vertex and the size of the angle can lead to an explanation of why there are only five Platonic solids.

Negative numbers, fractions and decimals

Mathematical focus

★ **Number: number and place value, fractions**

★ **Measurement: money, length, mass, capacity**

Prior learning

Children should be able to:

- read, write, order and compare numbers to at least 500 000 and determine the value of each digit

- understand that negative numbers mirror positive numbers across zero

- understand that fractions are a whole/part relationship

- compare and order fractions which have the same denominator

- write simple fractions as decimals, e.g. $\frac{1}{2}$ = 0.5.

Key new learning

- Read, write, order and compare numbers to at least 1 000 000 and determine the value of each digit.

- Interpret negative numbers in context, count forwards and backwards with positive and negative whole numbers, including through zero.

- Round any number up to 1 000 000 to the nearest 10, 100, 1000, 10 000 and 100 000.

- Compare and order fractions whose denominators are all multiples of the same number.

- Recognise mixed numbers and improper fractions and convert from one form to the other and write mathematical statements > 1 as a mixed number, e.g. $\frac{2}{5} + \frac{4}{5} = \frac{6}{5} = 1\frac{1}{5}$.

- Round decimals with two decimal places to the nearest whole number and to one decimal place.

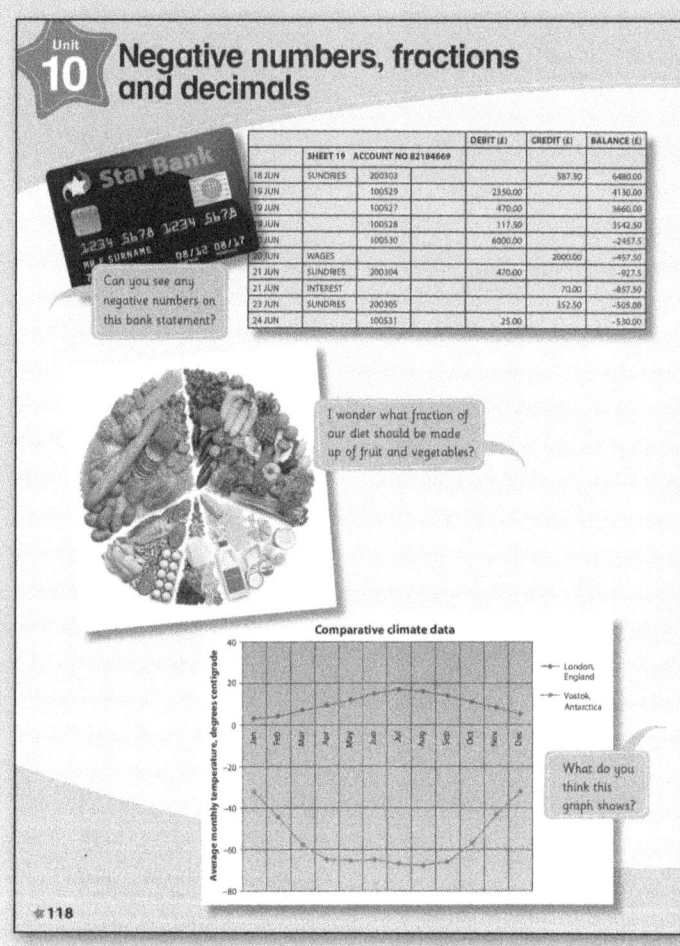

Making connections

- As negative numbers are abstract, it is important to apply them to real-life contexts, e.g. temperature and bank statements.

- Ordering, comparing and rounding decimal fractions can be used to support working with different units of measure.

- This topic includes plenty of opportunities to link to using measurements accurately, e.g. reading scales on thermometers, and measuring volume or capacity in litres and millilitres.

Talk about

It is important that children use the correct vocabulary when talking about fractions. Ensure that you use very precise mathematical vocabulary throughout your discussions with children, e.g. use vinculum when referring to the line separating the numerator and the denominator.

Engaging and exploring

Focus on each picture in turn. Use this as an opportunity to assess children's understanding about place value, negative numbers, fractions and decimals.

For the picture with the bank statement, you could discuss what a bank statement is. Have children ever seen one? You could provide copies of different bank statements for children to examine. Discuss bank accounts and how money goes into them when, e.g. people are paid, and out when people pay for things. Discuss how money can be spent, e.g. using cash, debit card, credit card and cheque.

Ask children about the parts of the bank statement in the Textbook. What do they think sundries, wages and interest are? Discuss the difference between credit and debit.

Focus on the balance. Establish that this is a running total to show the amount in the person's bank account on a daily basis. Agree that it goes up when something is credited to the account and it goes down when something is debited. Ask them to tell you when the amount is a negative amount and what has happened to make it like this. Agree that more money has been taken out of the account than is in there.

Focus on the debit card. Do children recognise it? A transaction is made and the card triggers a debit from the owner's bank account. Discuss the issue and expiry dates.

For the photo of the food discuss what is being shown. Establish that a healthy diet is mostly made up from carbohydrates, protein, fats, fruit and vegetables. Explain that a pie chart is a way of presenting information. Ask children to work out what fraction each of the parts is. Ask them to imagine a clock face. The fruit and vegetable section would go from 12 to 4 which is one third. The carbohydrate section is the same size and the other three food groups make up another third. Can they estimate what these are?

Ask children for some of their favourite foods, make a tally on the board and ask them to make up a pie chart to show the information. Encourage them to estimate the size of each part using fractions.

For the picture of the line graph you could ask children what information they think the graph shows. Can they identify the temperatures in different months in both places? Ask them to find the difference in temperatures between Vostok and London in different months. Find temperatures for the month before the one that you are working on this unit, write them on the board and ask children to create a line graph to show these.

Establish that the bus timetable tells people what times buses arrive at different bus stops. Have they ever seen a timetable, e.g. at a bus stop? Ask them to work out the time it takes to get from one stop to another. Which is the shortest/longest journey? The best way to do this would be by counting on from the earliest to the later time or counting on using a number line.

Ask them to make up their own timetable, e.g. for an imaginary bus or train.

For the picture of the sweets you could discuss the whole part relationship of the sweets. The whole is 11, the blue part is three, as are the green and pink. The orange part is two. Ask children what these would look like as a fraction. Agree, and model this on the board.

Give each child a selection of coloured counters and ask them to find the whole and write each colour as a fraction of the whole. Ask them to convert simple fractions to decimals, e.g. tenths, half, quarter.

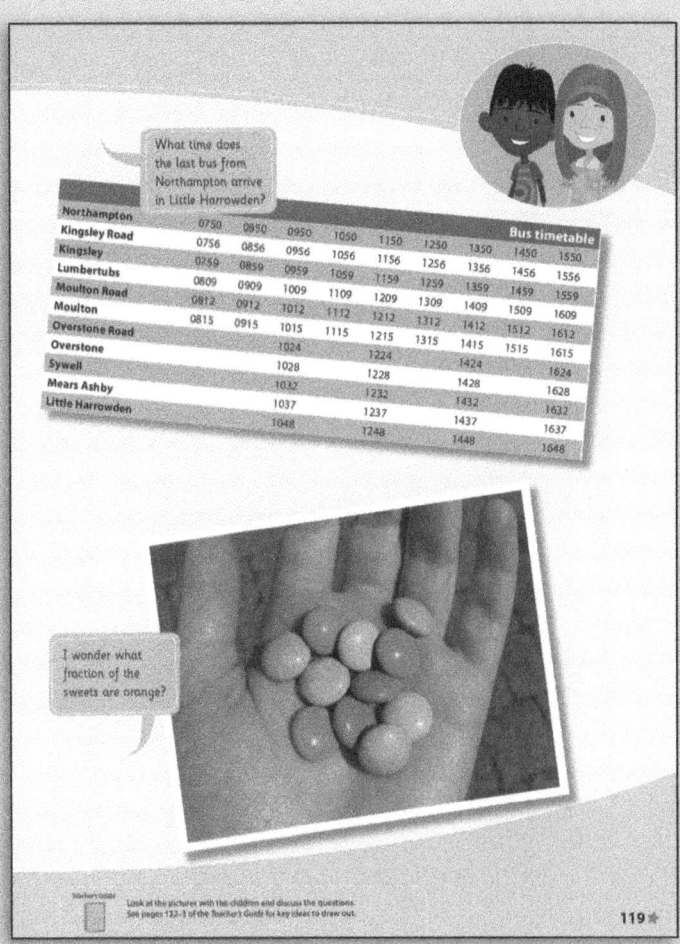

Things to think about

- How will you organise your class into mixed attainment groups of four and also give opportunities for paired talk?

- How will you plan focus group work?

- Which visual representations and manipulatives will ensure that all children are able to access their learning?

- What strategies will you use to develop reasoning through questioning and extra practice activities?

Checking understanding

You will know children have mastered these concepts when they can use their understanding of the multiplicative nature of the number system to convert between different units of measures, using how to multiply and divide by 10, 100 and 1000. They make appropriate decisions about when to use their understanding of counting (including in fractions), place value and rounding for solving problems including adding and subtracting.

10a Negative numbers and millions

- Read, write, order and compare numbers to at least 1 000 000 and determine the value of each digit.
- Count forwards or backwards in steps of powers of 10 for any given number up to 1 000 000.
- Interpret negative numbers in the context of temperature.
- Count forwards and backwards with positive and negative whole numbers, including through zero.
- Round any number up to 1 000 000 to the nearest 10, 100, 1000, 10 000 and 100 000.
- Solve number problems and practical problems that involve all of the above.

Homework 55 and 56   Practice Book pp 86–8   100 Squares; Place Value & Abacus; Number Line

Representations and resources

100 square (one per child), place-value grids (millions to ones as in Textbook).

Mathematical vocabulary

Million, place value, negative numbers, order, compare, round

Warming up

It is important to rehearse mental calculation strategies regularly. Give each child a 100 square. Ask them to put their finger on 4. Next give instructions for moving around the grid using the strategy of rounding to the nearest multiple of ten and adjusting, e.g. add 19 (add 20 and subtract 1), add 27 (add 30 and subtract 3), subtract 8 (subtract 10 and add 2), subtract 29 (subtract 30 and add 1) and so on.

Background knowledge

Place value is an incredibly important aspect of mathematics. Children need to be able to explain the positional, multiplicative, additive and Base 10 aspects. If needed, revisit the details of these elements of place value in Unit 1 so that you are prepared to extend these ideas to place value involving millions.. Children will also be exploring negative numbers in this concept spread. Negative numbers mirror positive numbers beyond zero. Negative numbers can be integers and also decimals.

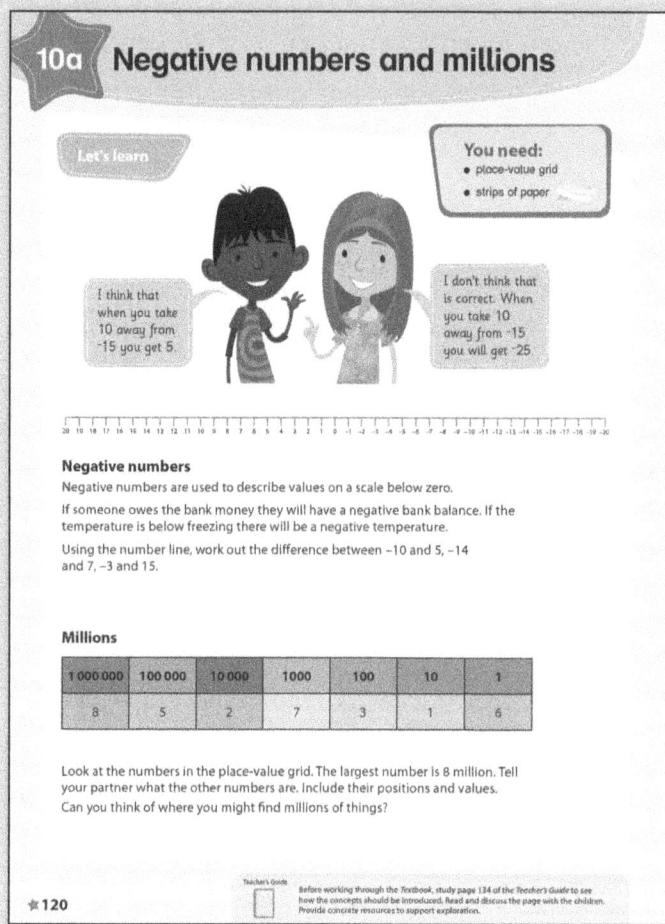

Let's learn: Modelling and teaching

Negative numbers

- Ask children to take their finger for a walk along the number line in the Textbook, e.g. start on zero, subtract 10, add 3, subtract 7. They could do this with a partner, giving each other instructions to follow.

- Give children numbers to add, subtract and order. They could compare them using >, < and =. You could write missing number questions on the board for them to answer.

- Discuss debt and negative bank balances. If possible give them some copies of bank statements and ask them to explore these, working out the differences in the balances they see.

- Ask children to tell you when else they might encounter negative numbers. Make up some simple activities around their suggestions , such as finding the difference between two temperatures on a thermometer..

- Recap positive and negative numbers within the context of temperature.

Millions

- Ask children to make millions numbers and place them in their place-value grid. They can tell a partner where each number is positioned and what its value is. Ask them to practise reading their numbers and write these in words.

- Ask children to round the numbers they make above to the nearest 10, 100, 1000, 10 000, 100 000 and 1 000 000.

- Ask problems which involve adding or subtracting different multiples of ten, e.g. in one town the population is 125 367. In the next door town there are 10 000 more people. What is the population of the second town?

Let's practise: Digging deeper

Step 1

Before children begin the task, rehearse counting forwards and backwards in ones and twos across zero. Then ask children to take their fingers for a walk along the number line in the Textbook as suggested on the Let's learn page. The first three questions involve children adding and subtracting positive and negative numbers. Encourage them to use the number line if they need to. The second half are missing number questions. Again, encourage them to use the number line to help them. Adapt the task for children who need extra support, so that the differences they find are smaller.

Step 2

Children make millions numbers from the given digits. Encourage them to make five in the first instance. When they make each one they record it in numbers and words, e.g. 3 567 248, three million five hundred and sixty seven thousand two hundred and forty eight. For children who may forget how to spell the key words, prepare a word bank for them to refer to. You could extend the question by asking children to round their numbers to the nearest thousand.

Step 3

Children need to work out the temperature increases and decreases and record whether they are negative or positive final temperatures. They could write down the original number and the new temperatures as well. If there is time, ask children to draw the thermometers to display the new temperature; alternatively, give them a ready-drawn thermometer on which they can mark the temperatures. If there is an opportunity, give children thermometers and ice in a cup and ask them to measure the temperature of the ice. If time allows they could make several readings during the day.

Step 4

Children need to explain why Amy is incorrect and write down the number. Do children notice that she wrote fifty nine thousand instead of five hundred and nine thousand? Ask them to explain the difference between the two numbers. Draw out that Amy left out the place holder and ask them to explain what the place holder is and to describe its job. Ensure that they can tell you the place holder is zero and it keeps the place of a position that has no numerical value. This will prepare children to create their own 7-digit numbers correctly.

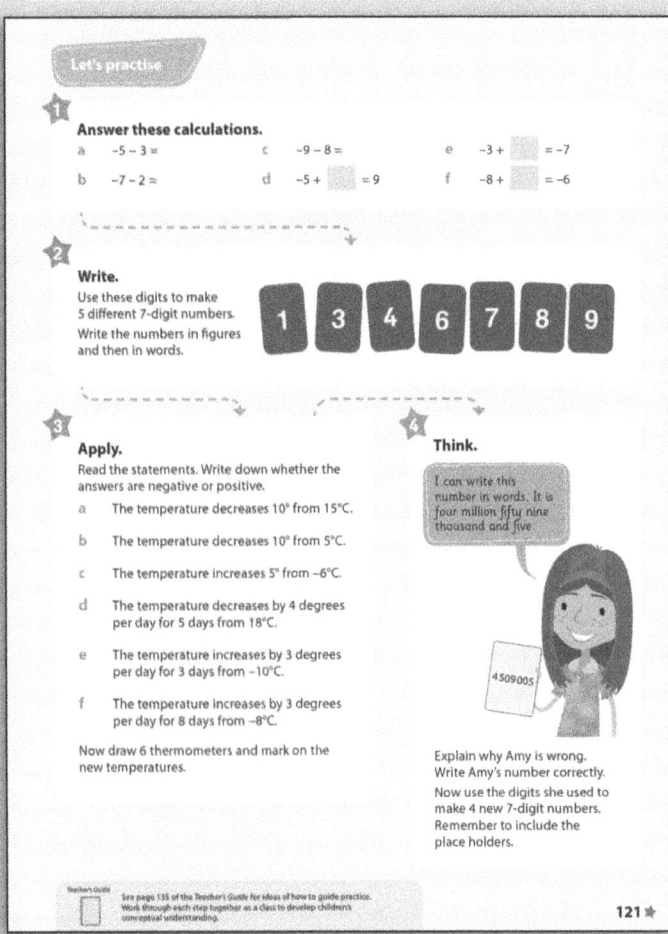

Ensuring progress

Supporting understanding

For children who struggle to read and write the 7-digit numbers, you could provide vocabulary cards or write the words they need on paper. For others you might want to focus on the first three questions in Step 3 and then, if ready, move on to the last three questions which are more challenging.

Broadening understanding

Encourage children to make up problems for others to solve. These should involve negative numbers and problems with adding and subtracting multiples of ten to other numbers. This will help you to assess their true understanding.

✓ Concept mastered

Children can explain and demonstrate negative numbers in context and the place value of millions numbers. They can order and compare both types of numbers.

Follow-up ideas

- Children could use the Internet to explore where they might encounter negative numbers and make a list of those they find.

- Children could use the Internet to find populations in cities around the world. They could read and record these.

- You could ask children to key a 3-digit number into a calculator and then change the numbers by adding and subtracting numbers. This will allow them to focus on place value, e.g. key in 245, put a 1 in front of the 2 (add 1000), put a 9 in front of the one (add 90 000), change the 4 to a 9 (add 50), put 16 in front of the first 9 (add 1 600 000).

Answers

Step 1

a   −8

b   −9

c   −17

d   14

e   −4

f   2

Step 3

a   positive (5 °C)

b   negative (−5 °C)

c   negative (−1 °C)

d   negative (−2 °C)

e   negative (−1 °C)

f   positive (16 °C)

Step 4

Explanations need to show that children understand that Amy has misread the position of the 0 placeholder. She has written 590 thousand when the figures show 509 thousands.

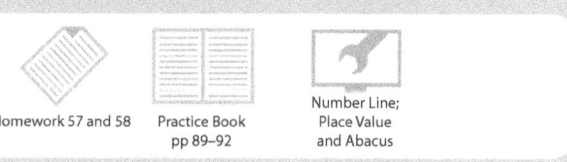

• Compare and order fractions whose denominators are all multiples of the same number.
• Recognise mixed numbers and improper fractions and convert from one form to the other and write mathematical statements > 1 as a mixed number, e.g. $\frac{2}{5} + \frac{4}{5} = \frac{6}{5} = 1\frac{1}{5}$.

Homework 57 and 58   Practice Book pp 89–92   Number Line; Place Value and Abacus

Representations and resources

Digit cards, interlocking cubes, rulers, scissors.

Mathematical vocabulary

Fraction, improper fraction, mixed number, equivalent, numerator, denominator

Warming up

It is important to rehearse mental calculation strategies regularly. Write up some calculations, e.g. 145 + 150, 137 + 99, 267 + 132, 156 – 99, 300 – 150. Ask children to talk to a partner about how they would solve these. Encourage them to think of the mental calculation strategies they could use. None of these should be calculated using a written method, they should be solved using, e.g. near doubling, rounding and adjusting, sequencing, counting on and knowledge of number facts.

Background knowledge

Children need to know that a proper fraction is part of a whole shape or quantity. They also need to know about mixed numbers and improper fractions and to have plenty of opportunities to explore these. They need to add and subtract fractions that have multiples of the same number. Equivalence is something that children have explored since their early experiences of fractions. It is important that they build on this foundation.

Let's learn: Modelling and teaching
Comparing and ordering fractions

• Ask children draw a bar 30 cm in length and about 2 cm wide on to plain paper using a ruler. They then draw one underneath and draw a vertical line to show half. They repeat this for quarters, eighths and sixteenths. They can then make up comparison and equivalent statements using these fractions.

• Repeat the above suggestion for fifths, tenths, fifteenths and twentieths and then thirds, sixths, ninths and twelfths.

• Give children digit cards and ask them to use them to make proper fractions. Once they have done this ask them to make comparison statements using >,< and =. Encourage them to make some addition and subtractions statements for =.

• Provide opportunities for children to estimate and measure fractions of kilograms and litres within the concepts of mass, capacity and volume.

Improper fractions

• Ask children to use the number line in their Textbooks

to count in fifths from zero to five. At different points ask them to tell you how many fifths they have counted and invite a child to write this on the board as an improper fraction and mixed number equivalence, e.g. at $4\frac{3}{5}$, they would write $4\frac{3}{5} = \frac{23}{5}$. Ask them what they notice about these fractions and how they could calculate converting a mixed number to an improper fraction (multiply the whole number by the denominator and add the numerator). Ask them to discuss with a partner what they would do to convert an improper fraction to a mixed number (the inverse, divide the denominator into the numerator).

• Ask problems which involve adding or subtracting different fractions, e.g. Sam ate $\frac{4}{5}$ of his pizza. Dan ate $\frac{3}{5}$ of his. How much of the two pizzas did they eat altogether?

Let's practise: Digging deeper
Step 1

This task asks children to choose pairs of fractions to add. They must convert them to fractions with the same denominator first. They can then add them and convert the answer to a mixed number. An example is modelled in the Textbook. Encourage children to use the fraction bar model to help them. Ask: *What does ascending order mean?* Then can then order their fractions correctly.

Step 2

This task asks the children to use a set of digit cards to make improper fractions. For each the numerator must be higher than the denominator. Once they have made about five they can convert them to mixed numbers recording their work in equivalent number statements. Encourage children to make one whole and work out how many parts are left. Some may

divide the numerator by the denominator. Whichever way they work, make sure that children explain their method clearly. Children should complete the task by comparing their fractions using < and >.

Step 3

Give children some paper, a ruler and some scissors. They need to measure and cut 10 strips of paper to 20 cm in length. They work out the fractions of the strips (these are given as mixed numbers in centimetres). They first take the appropriate number of whole strips and then fold their strips to find half, a quarter and an eighth. They then measure to find fifths and tenths. They can then show the length in centimetres.

Step 4

Children need to write an explanation as to why Theo is correct. Encourage them to explain how to convert the improper fraction to a mixed number. Once they have done this they can work out five other fractions that are equivalent to $4\frac{1}{2}$, e.g. $\frac{45}{10}$, $\frac{27}{6}$.

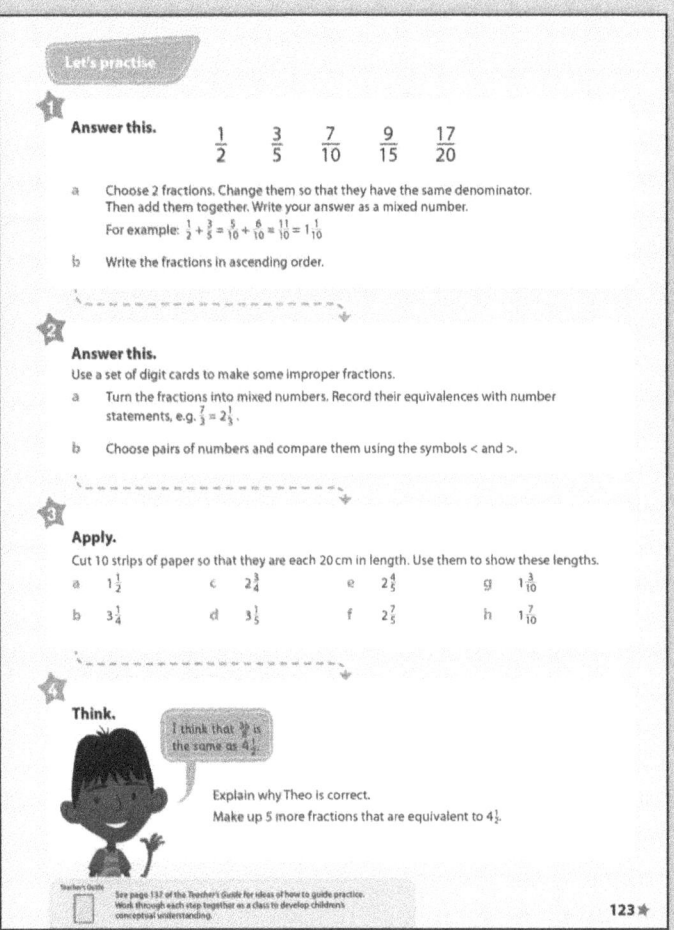

Ensuring progress
Supporting understanding

You might want to give some children specific pairs of fractions to add together. These could be combinations of halves, quarters and/or eighths. In Step 2, you might want to ask children to make improper fractions with denominators of 2, 4 and 8.

Broadening understanding

For Step 2, encourage children to make fractions with 2-digit numerators. In Step 3, you could ask children to measure a strip of paper to 40 cm, work out the fractions listed and then find the other fractions they can make. Encourage children to make up other statements similar to the one in Step 4 that are a mixture of correct and incorrect for a friend to answer.

✓ Concept mastered

Children can explain and demonstrate how to order and compare fractions including improper and mixed numbers. They will also show how they can convert an improper fraction to a mixed number and vice versa.

Follow-up ideas

- Children could make a pairs or snap game. They make cards with improper fractions and matching mixed numbers. When they play the game, they could share out the cards equally and take it in turns to place a card face up on the table. If they place two cards that are equivalent, they say 'snap'. The player who says 'snap' first wins all the cards on the table.

- In pairs, children could take it in turns to pick pairs of digit cards and make five proper fractions. They then work together to order these from smallest to highest.

Answers
Step 4

Explanations need to show that children understand that Oli is correct because if you divide 8 into 36 there are 4 wholes and $\frac{4}{8}$ left over. $\frac{4}{8}$ is equivalent to one half.

- Recognise and use thousandths and relate them to tenths, hundredths and decimal equivalents.
- Round decimals with two decimal places to the nearest whole number and to one decimal place.
- Read, write, order and compare numbers with up to three decimal places.
- Solve problems involving numbers up to three decimal places.

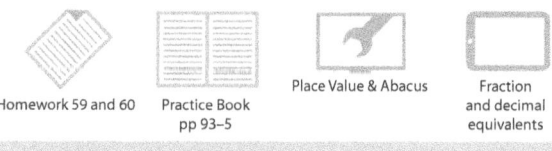

Homework 59 and 60   Practice Book pp 93–5   Place Value & Abacus   Fraction and decimal equivalents

Representations and resources

Base 10 apparatus, digit cards, place-value grid (100 000 to 1000th), digital scales.

Mathematical vocabulary

Decimal fraction, tenth, hundredth, thousandth

Warming up

Continue to rehearse mental calculation strategies. Write up some multiplication and division calculations, e.g. 245 × 4, 234.1 × 100, 124 × 5, 125 ÷ 25, 147 ÷ 7, 200 ÷ 20. Ask children to talk to a partner about how they would solve these. Encourage them to think of the mental calculation strategies that they could use. None of these should be calculated using a written method, they should be solved using, e.g. doubling, partitioning and knowledge of number facts.

Background knowledge

Children need to know that ten tenths are equivalent to one whole. 100 hundredths and 1000 thousandths are also equivalent to one whole. They need to explore the relationship between these fractions, developing an understanding that ten hundredths are equivalent to one tenth and ten thousandths are equivalent to one hundredth and 100 thousandths are equivalent to one tenth. From here you can develop children's understanding of the equivalence between these fractions and decimal fractions.

Let's learn: Modelling and teaching

Tenths, hundredths and thousandths

- Give children a set of digit cards and a place-value grid. Ask them to make a 6-digit number with three decimal places. They can explain to a partner the position each digit is in, its value and then read what the whole number is.

- Ask children to use their digit cards to make a 2-digit number with two decimal places in their place-value grid. Ask them to multiply their number by ten and then divide it by 1000 and describe what is happening.

- Give children some Base 10 apparatus. The thousands cube represents one, the hundreds flat represents one tenth, the ten stick represents one hundredth and the ones cube represents one thousandth. Ask them to explain why each represents what it does. Ask them to make these numbers: 2.351, 4.186 and 3.216.

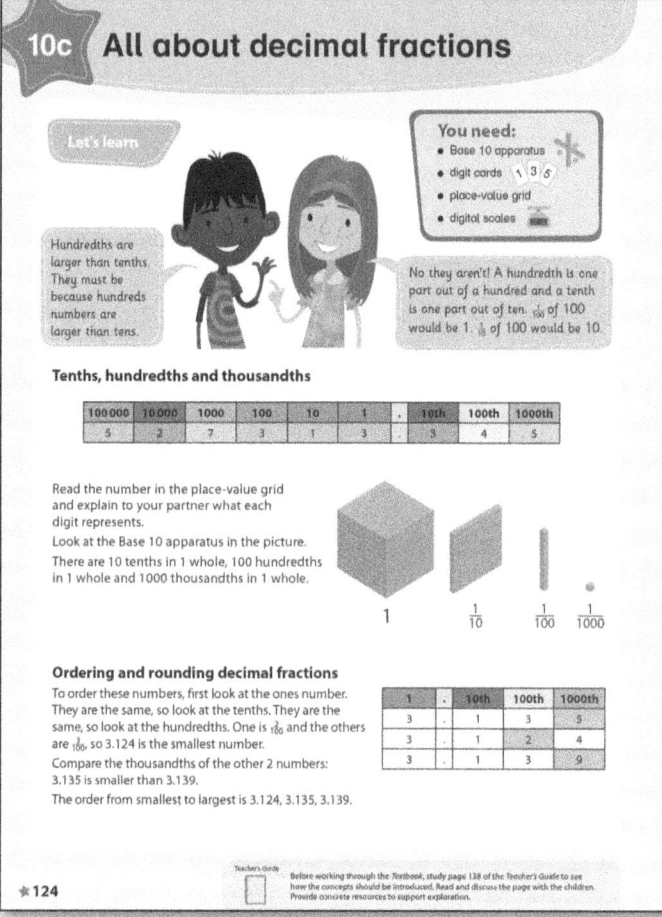

- Ask children to make up some numbers using the Base 10 apparatus and then to ask a partner what their number is.

Ordering and rounding decimal fractions

- Write a selection of numbers with one decimal place for children to order. Keep the whole numbers the same so that they focus on the tenths. Repeat for hundredths and then thousandths. They can then make comparison statements using > and <.

- Write some masses on the board and ask children to order these. Give them in different units and ask children to convert them all to kilograms, e.g. 2175 g, 2 kg 186 g, 2.1 kg. Ask children to round them.

Let's practise: Digging deeper

Step 1

Children need to explain the value of each digit in each number. One way that they could do this is to draw a place-value grid and place the digits in the correct position in it. They then explain what they have done and why. Another way would be to write the numbers in words.

Step 2

Using the Base 10 apparatus in the Textbook as a guide, children draw pictures of each number. You could give them Base 10 apparatus so that they can make each number before drawing it. The thousands cube should represent one, the hundreds flat one tenth, the tens stick one hundredth and the ones cube one thousandth. Encourage children to make their representations as accurate as possible yet simple, so that the drawing doesn't take too much time. They can use a combination of the concrete and pictorial to order their decimal fractions.

Step 3

Help children to find items or provide them with items to weigh. Alternatively, you could measure out different masses of sand in plastic bags or give them modelling material to weigh. Children weigh each item using digital scales and record its mass then round the masses to the nearest hundredth, tenth and whole number.

Step 4

Children need to write an explanation to prove that Amy is incorrect. They should show that they have an understanding that thousandths are smaller than hundredths because one thousandth is one out of one thousand thousandths and one hundredth is one out of one hundred hundredths and so the latter is the larger unit. They will need to give examples as proof.

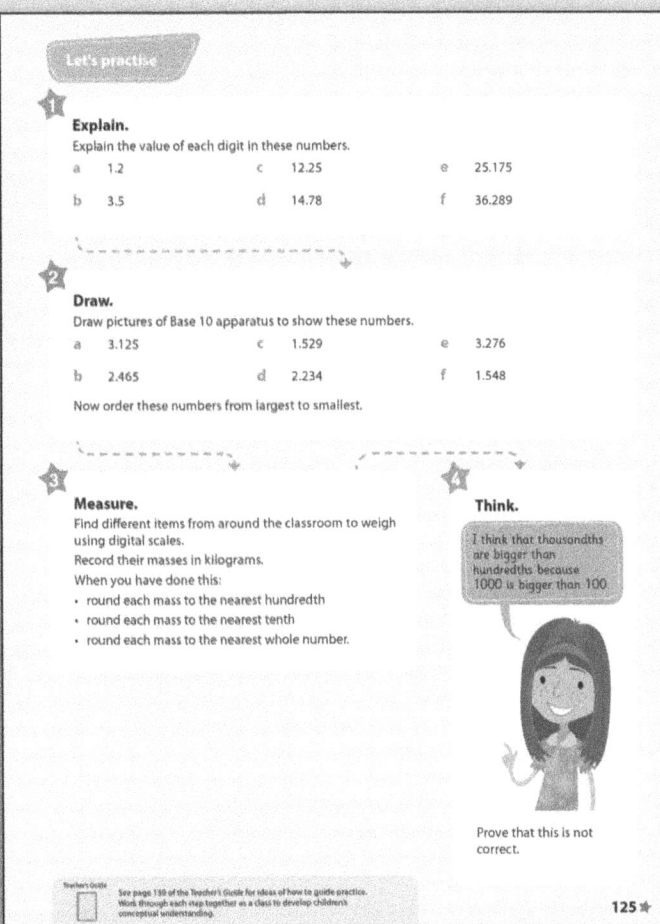

Ensuring progress

Supporting understanding

Some children will need physical Base 10 apparatus and place-value grids to help answer the questions in Step 1. This will also help to further their conceptual understanding of decimal fractions. Some children might work with tenths until they have mastered these and then move on to hundredths and thousandths.

Broadening understanding

In Step 1, you might like children to focus on numbers with three decimal places, so adapt the questions. You could ask children to make up some statements similar to Step 4, that are incorrect and correct, and then work in pairs to explain why.

✓ Concept mastered

Children can explain and demonstrate the position and value of tenths, hundredths and thousandths and can order and compare numbers with up to three decimal places.

Answers

Step 1

a 1 one and 2 tenths

b 3 ones and 5 tenths

c 1 ten, 2 ones, 2 tenths and 5 hundredths

d 1 ten, 4 ones, 7 tenths and 8 hundredths

e 2 tens, 5 ones, 1 tenth, 7 hundredths and 5 thousandths

f 3 tens, 6 ones, 2 tenths, 8 hundredths and 9 thousandths

Step 2

a 3 blocks, 1 flat, 2 sticks and 5 cubes

b 2 blocks, 4 flats, 6 sticks and 5 cubes

c 1 block, 5 flats, 2 sticks and 9 cubes

d 2 blocks, 2 flats, 3 sticks and 4 cubes

e 3 blocks, 2 flats, 7 sticks and 6 cubes

f 1 block, 5 flats, 4 sticks and 8 cubes

Step 4

Children understand that Amy is incorrect because one thousandth is one out of a thousand and one hundredth is one out of a hundred. So, e.g. $\frac{1}{1000}$ of 2000 is two and $\frac{1}{100}$ of 2000 is 20.

Follow-up ideas

- Children could work with a partner and play the 'ladder' game. They take it in turns to pick digit cards or throw a dice and make a single-digit number with three decimal places. They draw a ladder with ten rungs and position their number on to it. The idea is that they fill the ladder with the numbers they make so that they increase in size from the bottom of the ladder to the top. They discard any number they make that won't fit on a rung. The winner is the player with the most numbers on the ladder.

- Children could use digit cards to generate four numbers which represent grams. They write the grams down on paper and then convert them to kilogram amounts. They could repeat this for millilitres converting them to litres and then metres to kilometres.

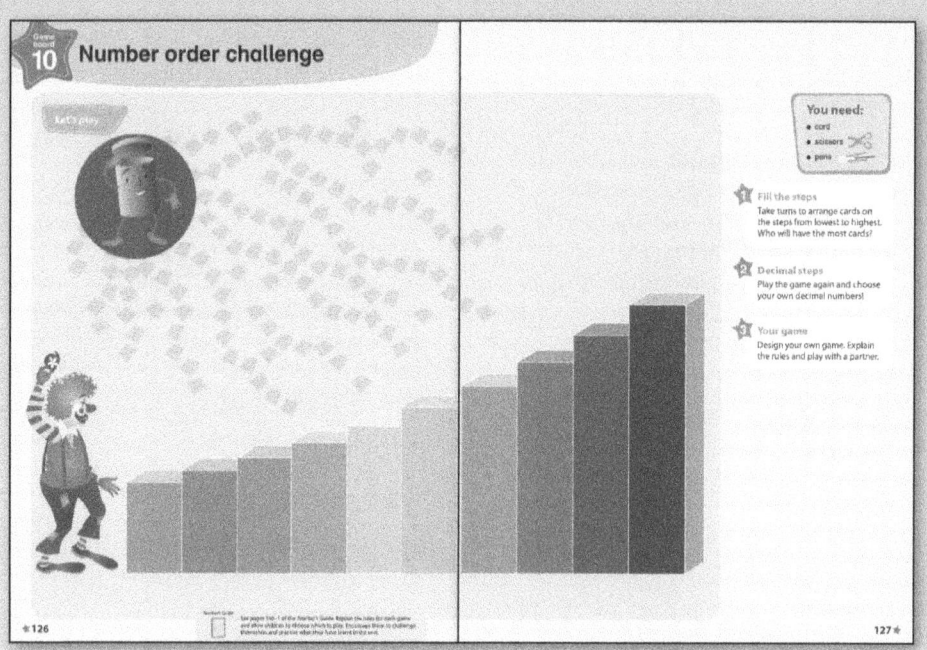

Game 1: Fill the steps

In this game children will practise ordering numbers from −15 to 15.

Maths focus

- Ordering positive and negative numbers

Resources

Card, scissors, pens.

How to play

Each player needs to cut out ten cards that will fit on to the steps. They write five positive numbers on five cards and five negative numbers on the other five cards. Numbers should go from −15 to 15. They each shuffle their cards and lay them in a pile, face down, in front of them. They then take it in turns to pick a card and place it on a step. The numbers go up the steps in order from lowest to highest. If a player picks a card that is the same as the other player's and is already on a step it is placed in the 'bin'. If they can't fit any of their numbers on a step because there are no spare steps where it will go, goes in the 'bin'. When all the cards have been used, the winner is the player with the most cards on the steps.

Making it easier

Make cards with specific numbers for children to use, ranging from −10 to 10. You could also provide a number line from −10 to 10 to help them order.

Making it harder

Ask children to write numbers that are positive and negative multiples of a particular multiplication table.

Game 2: Decimal steps

In this game children order numbers with decimal places.

Maths focus

- Ordering numbers to three decimal places

Resources

Card, scissors, pens.

How to play

This game has the same rules as Fill the steps, left. The difference is that children write numbers with three decimal places. The whole number of each should be one, they can choose their own tenths, hundredths and thousandths numbers.

Making it easier

Children could make ten numbers with one decimal place to enable them to focus on tenths. If they have mastered tenths their numbers could have two decimal places so that they are focusing on hundredths.

Making it harder

Ask children to be sure that they write numbers with different digits in the tenths, hundredths and thousandths and that there are no repeated numbers in each position.

Game 3: Your game

Children should invent their own game, designing rules that use the concepts covered in the unit.

Challenge children to make their game easier or harder.

Number order challenge

Choose a game to play.

Game 1: Fill the steps

You need:
- card
- scissors
- pens

How to play

- Each cut out 10 cards that will fit on to the steps in the game. Write 5 positive numbers on 5 cards and five negative numbers on the other 5 cards. The numbers should go from –15 to 15.
- Shuffle your cards and place them face down in front of you.
- Take turns to pick a card and put it on a step. The numbers go up the steps from lowest to highest.
- If you pick a card that is already on a step put it in the bin!
- If there is no space to fit your number, put it in the bin!
- When all the cards have been used, the winner is the player with the most cards on the steps.

Game 2: Decimal steps

You need:
- card
- scissors
- pens

How to play

- Use the same rules as Fill the steps, above, but this time use numbers with 3 decimal places on your cards.
- The whole number of each should be 1, but you can choose your own tenths, hundredths and thousandths numbers.

Game 3: Your game

- Make up your own game using the gameboard.
- Can you think of a way to use the steps – perhaps you could use fractions?
- How will you use the bin?
- What are the rules for your game? Explain them to someone.

Please help your child by reading the instructions and playing the game together.

Assessment task 1

Resources

Place-value grids, digit cards.

Running the task

Before they begin this task, work with any children who lack confidence. Write some different masses on the board, e.g. 1 kg and 20 g, 1.2 kg, 3005 g and ask children to write each in two different ways and to explain the value of each of the digits that they have written. You could provide some children with place-value grids and digit cards so that they can make the number if you think this would be of benefit.

During the task listen to groups of children discuss the statement and explain to each other why it is incorrect. They should be able to tell you that because there are 1000 grams in a kilogram, 1.04 kg is equivalent to 1040 g and 1 kg 40 g. Encourage them to explain why 1 kg 4 g and 14 grams are incorrect. You may wish to work with small groups of children and tease out full explanations from them. Once they have explained, they can write the extra masses as kilograms and grams and then grams, e.g. 5.25 kg = 5 kg 250 g = 5250 g. Again, expect them to describe the place value as they explain why they have recorded their amounts.

Once they have completed this part of the task, children convert the millilitre volumes, represented as improper fractions, to litres. E.g. they should convert 2500/1000 ml to 2.5 l. If needed, revisit the visual representations used in the lessons on improper fractions and decimal fractions to help children tackle this task.

Evidencing mastery

If children are able to convert one unit of measure confidently to another and explain the place value of the digits in each position of the kilogram decimal number and the grams whole number, they are evidencing mastery in this particular area of mathematics.

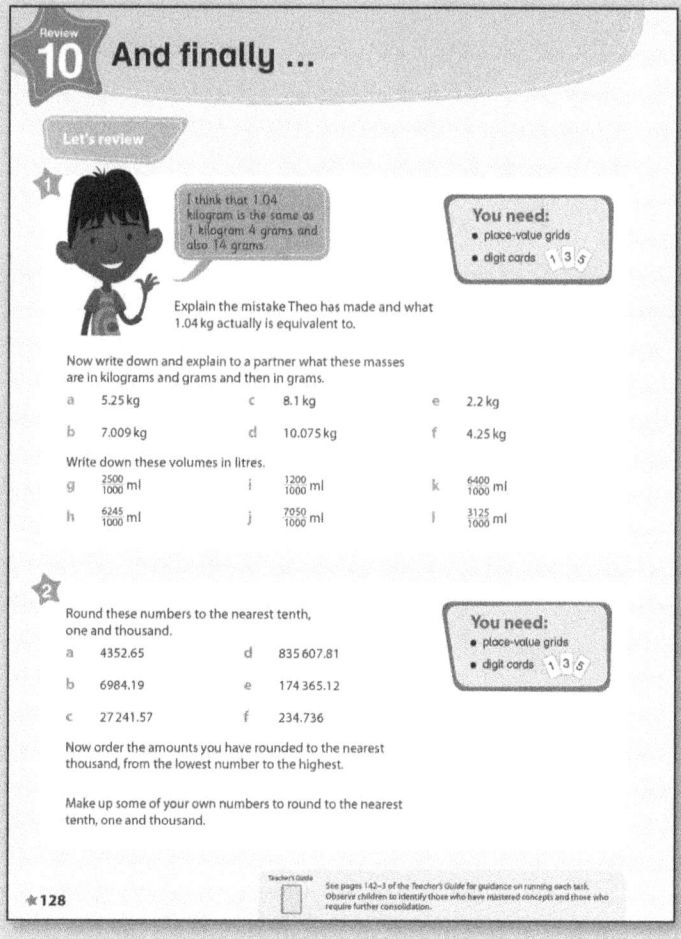

Assessment task 2

Resources

Place-value grids, digit cards.

Running the task

Before children begin the task, spend some time with those who need extra support in this area, recapping rounding to tenths, one and a thousand. When these children work through the task, you may wish them to focus on rounding to one first. If they cope well with this move on to thousands and then tenths. The aim is that they should be able to do all three. Make a note of any areas that they may be weak in and arrange a time to re-teach this outside the maths lesson.

Children need to round each number to the nearest tenth, one and thousand. They will need to write each number down and then write the rounded amounts. Encourage them to identify which digit is in each of these positions before rounding. You may wish to work with small groups of those children who you particularly wish to assess. Expect them to be able to tell you

the position of each digit and what to do to get its true value. When they round, they should be clear as to why to round up or down. You could ask some children to round to the nearest hundredth, ten and hundred after they have rounded as the instructions require.

If you think some children would benefit from making the numbers in place-value grids using digit cards before they round them, provide these resources for them to use.

Children then order the numbers that they have rounded to the nearest thousand in ascending order. Once they have answered the questions, encourage them to make up their own numbers to round to the nearest tenth, one and thousand.

Evidencing mastery

If children can confidently find the position of the tenth, one and thousand and round them to the closest higher number, then they are evidencing mastery of this concept.

Assessment task 3

Running the task

The first part of this task asks children to write 7-digit numbers in numerals and then in words. Before they begin, rehearse this with similar examples, ensuring that you position the place holders so that they represent different numbers. Once they have completed the task, they could make up their own numbers to write in numerals and words.

The second part of the task asks children to solve problems that involve working with positive and negative numbers. If any have trouble accessing the problems, read them aloud. If some children would benefit from using the number line, then allow this. However, you must bear in mind that if they need the number line, they have not yet mastered this concept.

Once they have solved the temperature problems encourage them to make up their own to solve.

Evidencing mastery

If children can confidently and accurately write numbers in both numerals and words, they are showing mastery in this area of mathematics. They are also showing mastery of place value.

If they can solve problems that involve adding and finding differences between negative and positive numbers, without using the number line, they are evidencing mastery at this stage of their learning.

Did you know?

It is thought that negative numbers were first introduced in 200 BCE by the Chinese. They used them to show how much people owed other people. Negative numbers appeared in India around 620 CE for the same reason. The first use of negative numbers in Europe was by the Frenchman Nicolas Chuquet during the 15th century. He used them as exponents, but referred to them as absurd numbers. Most European mathematicians didn't think that negative existed!

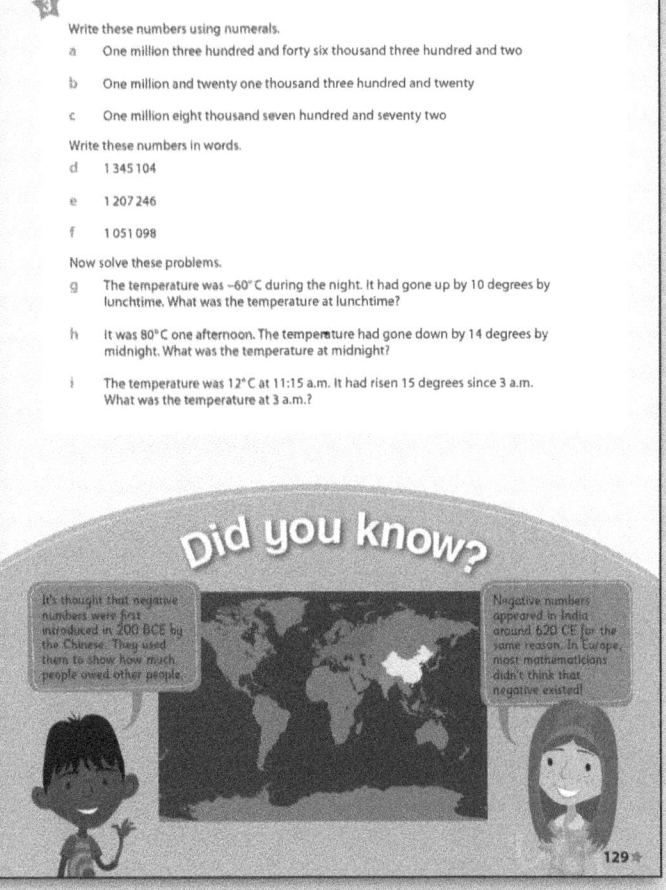

Concepts mastered

☑ Children can explain and demonstrate negative numbers in context and the place value of millions numbers. They can order and compare both types of numbers.

☑ Children can explain and demonstrate how to order and compare fractions including improper and mixed numbers. They will also show how they can convert an improper fraction to a mixed number and vice versa.

☑ Children can explain and demonstrate the position and value of tenths, hundredths and thousandths and can order and compare numbers with up to three decimal places.

Mathematical focus

★ **Number:** number and place value, addition and subtraction, fractions

★ **Measurement:** capacity, mass, time

★ **Statistics:** solve problems, interpret data

Prior learning

Children should already be able to:

- add and subtract numbers mentally with increasingly large numbers

- add and subtract whole numbers with four digits, including using formal written methods (columnar addition and subtraction)

- use rounding to check answers to calculations and determine, in the context of a problem, levels of accuracy

- solve addition and subtraction multi-step problems in contexts, deciding which operations and methods to use and why.

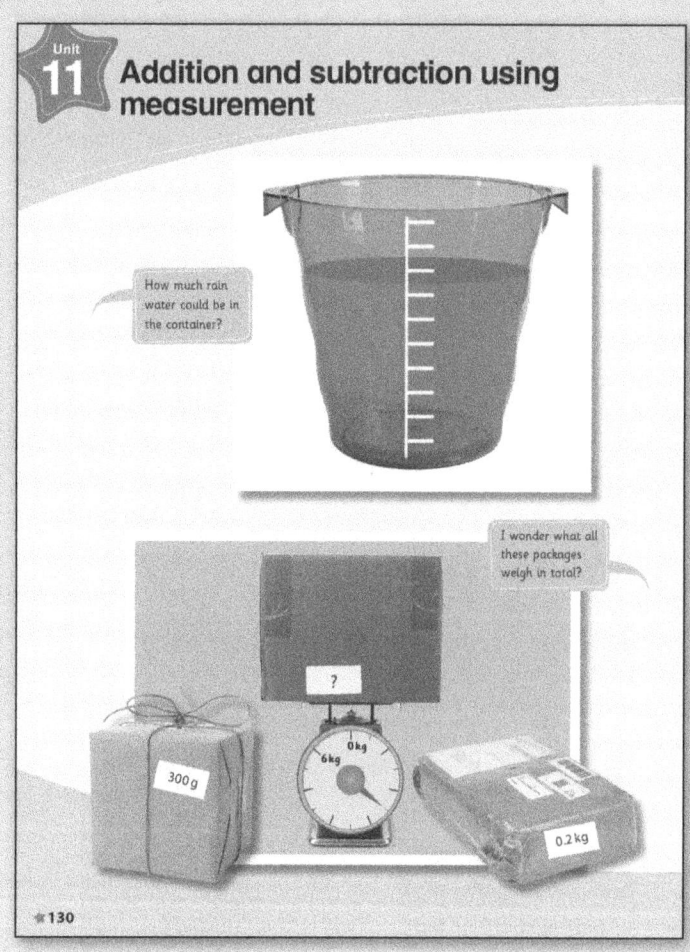

Key new learning

- Add and subtract whole numbers with more than four digits, including using formal written methods (columnar addition and subtraction).

- Add and subtract numbers mentally with increasingly large numbers.

- Use rounding to check answers to calculations and determine, in the context of a problem, levels of accuracy.

- Solve addition and subtraction multi-step problems in contexts, deciding which operations and methods to use and why.

- Solve problems involving number up to three decimal places.

- Recognise mixed numbers and improper fractions and convert from one form to the other and write mathematical statements >1 as a mixed number.

- Add and subtract fractions with the same denominator and denominators that are multiples of the same number.

Talk about

It is important to use precise mathematical vocabulary from the beginning and make connections to language that supports understanding, e.g. equivalence or the equals sign should be seen as 'has the same value but may look different'. Also, explore the language of measurement to reinforce units and their relationship to each other, e.g. 'milli' means thousandth so a millilitre is $\frac{1}{1000}$ of a litre .

Making connections

- Addition and subtraction problems involving measure provide an opportunity to revisit converting units of metric measure so that, e.g. children give the answer to 1.75 km + 200 m as 1750 m + 200 m or 1.75 km + 0.2 km, not 201.75 km or m.

- Connect solving comparison, sum and difference problems using information presented in a line graph, with work in science.

Engaging and exploring

You could ask children to look at each picture and the question that goes with each and discuss them with a partner. Focus on each picture in turn.

For the picture of the rain gauge, you could:

Discuss what children notice about the container and the level of the water. Encourage them to use the language of capacity and fractions, e.g. the container is more than half full; the water level is $\frac{3}{4}$ of the way up the scale.

Suggest that the container holds one litre of water. Children should draw on knowledge of litre and millilitre conversion and recognise that the scale can be labelled as 0.1 l, 0.2 l, 0.3 l, etc. or as 100 ml, 200 ml, 300 ml, etc., so the value shown is 750 ml or 0.75 litres.

Revisit the place-value grid to support converting litres to millilitres and vice versa.

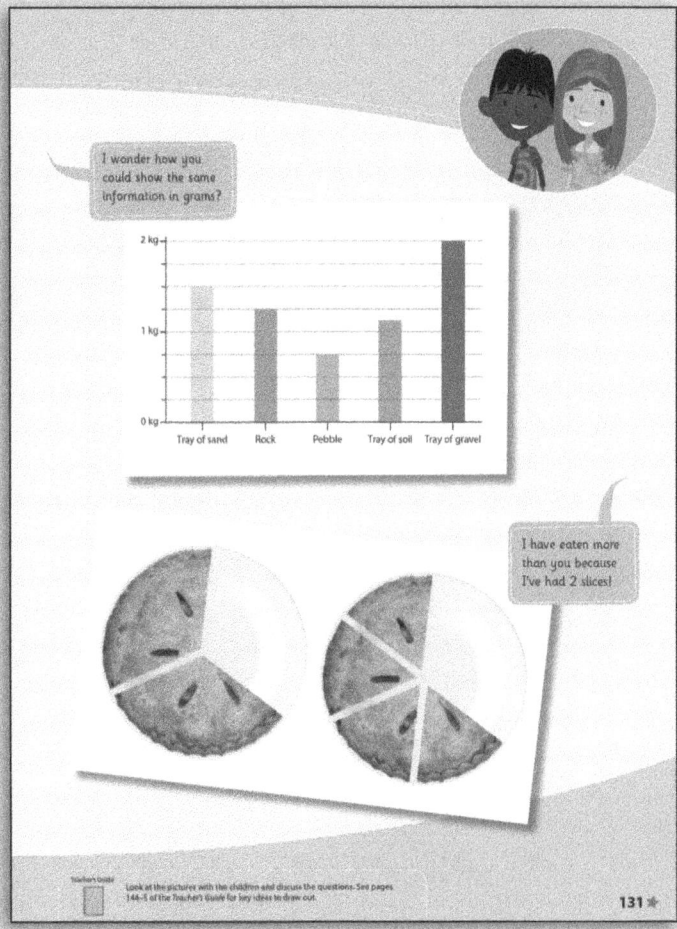

Things to think about

- How will you raise the profile of mental calculation?

- How will you organise groupings for discussions and activities?

- Which manipulatives will help to develop conceptual understanding for addition and subtraction?

- What opportunities will you provide to children to carry out practical tasks that develop their fluency when working with measure and statistics?

- How will you provide opportunities to develop problem solving strategies outlined in the introduction, which will be appropriate for your Year 5 children?

Encourage children in pairs to make up their own scale for the container starting from zero and write the value of the water level. You might like to use a rain gauge to collect rain water and revisit these activities in a hands-on, real-life way.

For the picture of the weighing scales you could:

Discuss the use of kilograms on the scale here rather than grams. Children should use their experience from previous activities to identify the scale using the information given.

Establish the mass of the parcel and consider the ways that this can be written, i.e. 2.5 kg or $2\frac{1}{2}$ kg. Ask them to decide whether 2.50 kg and 2.500 kg are also equivalent.

Focus just on the 0.2 kg parcel and challenge children to reason about and describe the new position of the arrow when the parcel is also put on the weighing scales.

Discuss what is different about the 300 g parcel. What is different about the mass of this parcel? Look at converting between kilograms and grams, revisiting the language as before.

Suggest that you would have found the total mass of the two smaller parcels first. Children should then explain why you may have done this. Other number bonds can be explore here that total 1 kg. You might like to use real weighing scales to support these tasks.

For the bar chart you could:

Discuss what children notice about the bar chart, e.g. bars are horizontal, the scale is in kilograms but with intervals of 0.25 kg.

Suggest they give you 'silly' answers when asked the mass of the tray of soil and explain their reasoning each time.

Challenge children to describe each of the masses using fractional language, e.g. two whole kilograms, $1\frac{1}{8}$ kg, etc.

Ask children to compare the masses and describe them, e.g. the tray of sand is 0.25 kg heavier than the rock.

Make up questions for children to answer, including finding difference using the bar model.

For the picture of the pies you could:

Ask children to discuss the statement and decide whether they agree. They should use representations to prove their thinking and should refer to equivalent fractions.

Discuss what the mistake is and perhaps describe a third pie that has three pieces missing but still an equivalent fraction of pie remains, i.e. ninths with three pieces eaten and six remaining. Can they make a generalisation about the possible number of slices?

Challenge children to calculate how much of the two pies children have left in total. Is there more than one whole pie left? Look at the calculation, focusing on the fact that the denominators are not the same.

Checking understanding

You will know children have mastered these concepts when they can solve addition and subtraction problems (including with fractions) in different contexts, appropriately choosing and using number facts using their understanding of place value and mental and written methods. They can explain their decision making and justify their solutions.

Applying addition and subtraction

- Add and subtract numbers mentally with increasingly large numbers.
- Add and subtract whole numbers with more than four digits, including using formal written methods (columnar addition and subtraction).
- Solve addition and subtraction multi-step problems in contexts, deciding which operations and methods to use and why.
- Convert between different units of metric measure.
- Use addition and subtraction to solve problems involving measurement using decimal notation.
- Solve problems involving units of time.

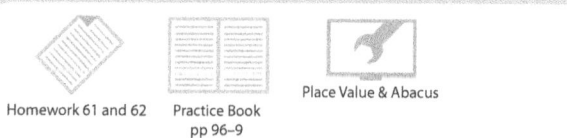

Homework 61 and 62   Practice Book pp 96–9   Place Value & Abacus

Representations and resources

Base 10 apparatus, place-value grids and digit cards.

Mathematical vocabulary

Place value, add, subtract, total, sum, difference, partitioning, counting on, sequencing hours, minutes, gram, kilogram, millilitre, litre, convert

Warming up

Challenge children to complete the diagram in as many ways as they can to show part-part-whole. This will reinforce multiplication facts, place value and the inverse relationship between multiplication and division.

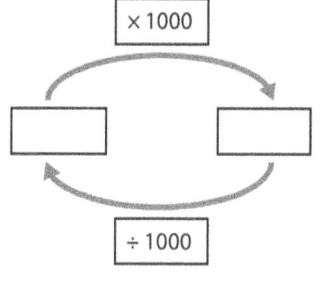

Background knowledge

Continue to practise mental and written calculation strategies to increase fluency. Throughout, children must make decisions. Be sure to challenge inappropriate methods.

This concept provides an opportunity to apply methods of addition and subtraction to measurement. An understanding of place value and the effect of multiplying and dividing by 10, 100 and 1000 is important to support converting between units of metric measurement.

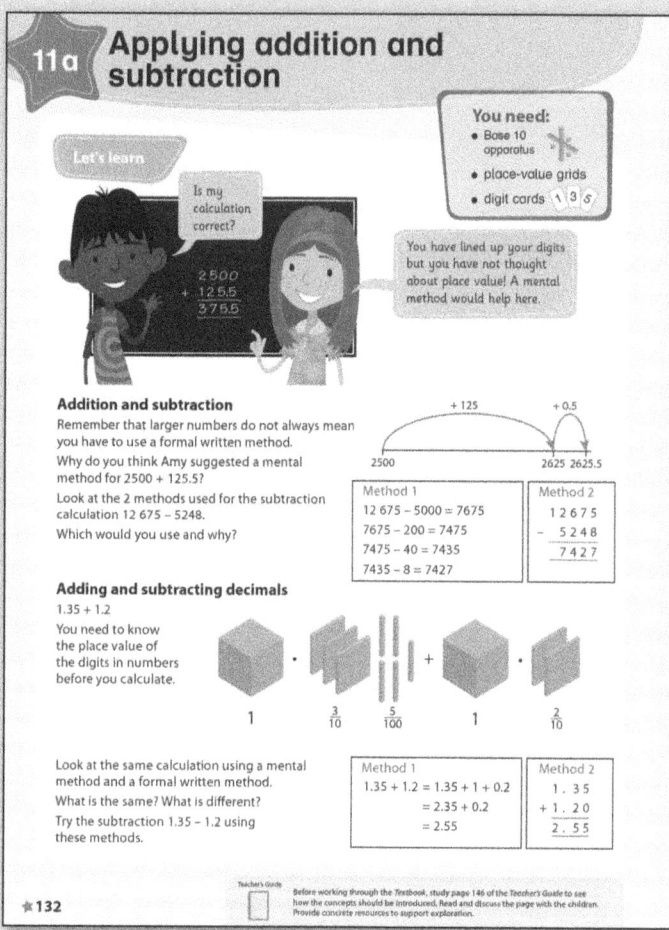

Let's learn: Modelling and teaching

Addition and subtraction

- Discuss the comments made by Amy and Theo focusing on the mistake that has been made and why this has happened. Consider using estimates.

- Look at the number line method used and discuss why this has been suggested as a better method. Children should suggest other calculations where a mental method is more appropriate, linking back to previous units.

- Discuss the methods used for 12 675 – 5248, reasoning about any choices that are made. Model the calculation, focusing on decomposition when subtracting 8 from 5, etc.

Adding and subtracting decimals

- Use Base 10 apparatus to represent the calculation as shown in the Textbook and discuss how this helps us to avoid place value errors. Refer back to Theo's mistake.

- Children could physically use the apparatus to help secure conceptual understanding.

- Suggest that children make up other calculations, e.g. ▨ . ▨ ▨ + ▨ . ▨ using the apparatus and practising mental methods, e.g. 1.46 + 0.2

- Ask why we must write decimals to the same number of decimal places when using a formal written method. Consider other errors that may occur with calculations, such as 10.5 + 1.23 as both have the same number of digits.

Let's practise: Digging deeper

Step 1

These calculations require children to add or subtract whole numbers using a method of their choice. They are encouraged to consider mental methods first and make estimates. The calculations include a mix of 4- and 5-digit numbers.

Step 2

Children should apply the same thinking to work on the next calculations involving decimal numbers. Encourage them to discuss the most efficient calculation strategies for each question. Some children may wish to use Base 10 apparatus to help them ensure accuracy of place value.

Step 3

Children are presented with a set of different masses shown either in grams or kilograms and are required to draw on knowledge and skills of conversion to support calculations.

Place-value grids and digit cards can be used to ensure that pairs of masses are written to the same unit of measurement each time before calculation. Mental and written methods should be selected appropriately.

Step 4

Using the masses shown in the grid, children must use the information about Opal's estimate to identify the addition calculation she has written. The masses are shown in kilograms or grams to encourage conversions before estimating and calculating.

This task provides opportunities to practise written methods.

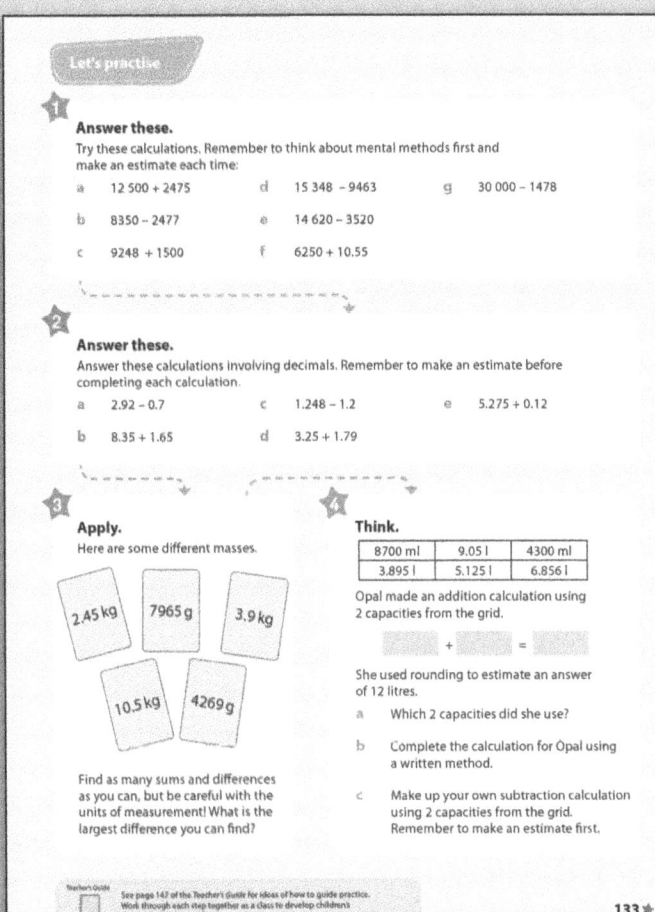

Ensuring progress

Supporting understanding

All children should look for a mental method first before adopting a written method. You might need to work with some children in a focus group to provide additional practice of partitioning, multiplying and dividing by powers of ten, counting on and back in steps of a constant size. This will ensure that they develop fluency and will provide them with the tools necessary to work mentally.

The place-value grid and Base 10 apparatus are invaluable in this unit to support conversion.

Broadening understanding

Puzzles and two-step or multi-step word problems involving addition and subtraction should be used to encourage children to make decisions about which methods to use. Inappropriate use of written methods should be challenged so that mental strategies continue to have a high profile.

Problems should require children to persevere and break down questions into simpler steps. Try to ensure that there are a range of problems that have more than one answer and require a generalisation.

✓ Concept mastered

Children can make and explain their choices when selecting a mental or written method of addition and subtraction.

Follow-up ideas

- Set problems that involve adding or finding the difference using a variety of mathematical language, e.g.
  - ▶ How much heavier is a box weighing 4.785 kg than a box weighing 3752 g?
  - ▶ Explore the timetables to prove whether the following statement is always true, sometimes true or never true. A coach journey from Bristol to Birmingham is more than 30 minutes longer than the same journey by train.

By train			
Bristol	13:00	13:30	14:00	14:30
Birmingham	14:24	14:56	15:23	15:56

By coach			
Bristol	13:15	13:30	16:00	20:00
Birmingham	15:35	15:25	18:05	22:15

Answers

Step 1

a   14 975

b   5873

c   10 748

d   5885

e   11 100

f   6260.55

g   28 522

Step 2

a   2.22

b   10 (10.00)

c   0.048

d   5.04

e   5.395

Step 3

Children's own pairings for sums and differences, e.g. 3.9 kg + 1500 g showing a conversion to either grams or kilograms as 3900 g + 1500 g. Largest difference is 8.05 kg.

Step 4

a   5.125 l and 6.856 l

b   Any sensible written method for 5.125 litres + 6.856 litres with an answer of 11.981 litres, e.g. a column method of addition

c   Open ended

- Recognise mixed numbers and improper fractions and convert from one form to the other and write mathematical statements >1 as a mixed number.
- Add and subtract fractions with the same denominator and denominators that are multiples of the same number.
- Start to solve comparison, sum and difference problems using information presented in a line graph.
- Start to solve problems involving units of time.

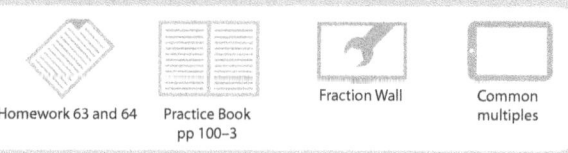

Homework 63 and 64   Practice Book pp 100–3   Fraction Wall   Common multiples

Representations and resources

Fraction bars, number lines, shapes, contextual images (e.g. pizzas, a clock face).

Mathematical vocabulary

Fraction, numerator, denominator, vinculum, equivalent, improper fractions, mixed numbers, add, subtract, total, sum, difference, counting on, sequencing, estimate

Warming up

You could begin by counting on and back in steps of 25 from zero and from any multiple of 25. Agree facts, such as there are four lots of 25 in 100 so there are eight lots of 25 in 200, etc. Link this count and the use of place value to counting in steps of 0.25, again establishing similar facts using what they already know. Children should recognise this count as steps of a quarter.

You could also present line graphs or bar charts (as in the unit opener) with intervals of 25 and 0.25 to make connections with these counts.

Background knowledge

Children should have plenty of experience of counting on and back in fraction steps. Ensure that, when counting, they use knowledge of equivalents where appropriate. Counting helps to reinforce fractions as numbers and also introduces the idea of adding on and subtracting.

Varying representations, such as fraction bars, will help children make connections, particularly when working with improper fractions and mixed numbers.

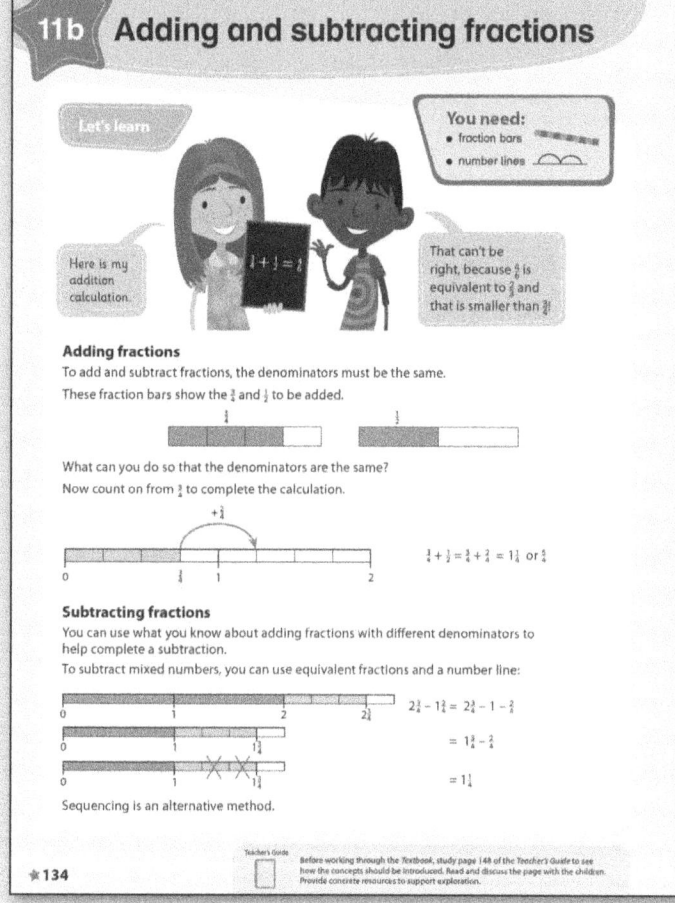

Let's learn: Modelling and teaching

Adding fractions

- Focus on Amy and discuss the error she has made. Discuss Theo's thinking and decide whether children agree. Encourage them to make a sensible estimate, e.g. $\frac{3}{4}$ is more than $\frac{1}{2}$ so the answer must be more than 1.

- Consider different ways of representing $\frac{3}{4}$ and $\frac{1}{2}$. Discuss which images are more useful for counting and perhaps link this to the number line.

- Focus on fraction bars and number lines to represent the fractions to be added. Discuss what is the same and what is different about the bars, i.e. two equal parts and four equal parts can both show a half but look different.

- Look at how improper fractions can also be used to support crossing boundaries:
  $3\frac{1}{4} - 1\frac{3}{8} = 3\frac{2}{8} - 1\frac{3}{8} = \frac{26}{8} - \frac{11}{8} = \frac{15}{8}$ or $1\frac{7}{8}$

Subtracting fractions

- Discuss how equivalent fractions can also help in the calculation $\frac{7}{8} - \frac{1}{4}$. Children could use fraction bars or sketches to establish that $\frac{1}{4}$ is equivalent to $\frac{2}{8}$.

- Model the written method of $\frac{7}{8} - \frac{1}{4} = \frac{7}{8} - \frac{2}{8}$ and ask children to follow the calculation using fraction bars or number lines.

- Practise other subtractions that also require children to use equivalent fractions, e.g. $\frac{5}{6} - \frac{1}{3}$ or $\frac{9}{10} - \frac{1}{2}$ or $\frac{9}{10} - \frac{3}{5}$

- Use fraction bars and the number line to model the subtraction of mixed numbers, linking this to the written method. Focus on the use of sequencing, e.g. $2\frac{3}{4} - 1 - \frac{2}{4} = 1\frac{1}{4}$

Let's practise: Digging deeper

Step 1

These sets of addition and subtraction calculations predominantly require children to calculate within one whole as calculations involving different denominators is new for Year 5. This allows children to focus on equivalents.

Fraction bars should continue to be used to secure conceptual understanding and confirm equivalence between two fractions. Some children may prefer to sketch their own visual representation of the bar model to confirm their calculations.

Children should be encouraged to simplify any familiar fractions and to reflect on the representations and strategies that they are using.

Step 2

All calculations in this section involve mixed numbers and also require children to use equivalent fractions. They should use

the sequencing method to add or subtract amounts. Again, fraction bar representations would support here.

Encourage children to use the language of fractions and convince others that two fractions are equivalent.

Step 3

These word problems require children to use what they know about adding fractions to find out the duration of bus and train journeys. They should use equivalent fractions or simply refer back to the calculation $\frac{3}{4} + \frac{1}{2}$ at the beginning of this spread to fluently add.

Encourage the use of fraction bars and a clock face to represent the problem so that they can clearly see the connections. Children should explain what each whole represents, i.e. a whole hour, and therefore, what $\frac{3}{4}$ and $\frac{1}{2}$ represent.

Step 4

Children can complete this puzzle on their own, with a partner or in a group. This would make a useful group activity as children work together to find a starting point and convince each other about the value of the missing numbers using calculations to help them.

They should make estimates and also consider ways to check that a value is possible drawing on knowledge of the inverse or related facts.

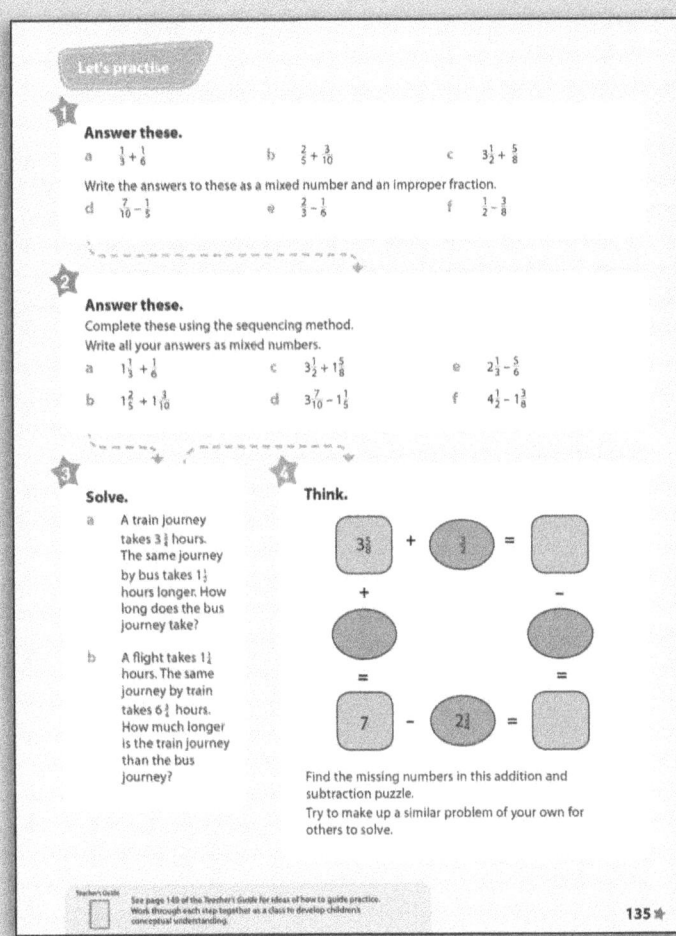

Ensuring progress

Supporting understanding

Children may need more practice adding and subtracting fractions with the same denominator before moving on to examples where denominators are different. They should use representations to support work on fractions. It may be useful to use a context to help develop understanding.

Broadening understanding

The concept of using improper fractions to aid calculation can be further explored, particularly to support subtraction where boundaries need to be crossed. Children should explain how each improper fraction relates to the original fraction and begin to look at ways of using multiplication to fluently convert between mixed numbers and improper fractions, e.g:

$3\frac{3}{4} = (\frac{4}{4} \times 3) + \frac{3}{4}$ where $\frac{4}{4}$ represents each whole
$= \frac{12}{4} + \frac{3}{4}$
$= \frac{15}{4}$

Follow-up ideas

• Children could make up a set of 'Follow me' cards that focus on equivalent fractions or calculation. They could, of course, focus on both:

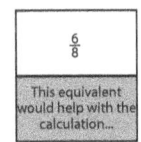

$1\frac{1}{2} - \frac{3}{4}$
A fraction that is equivalent to $\frac{1}{2}$ is...

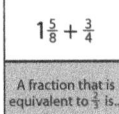

$\frac{6}{8}$
This equivalent would help with the calculation...

$1\frac{5}{8} + \frac{3}{4}$
A fraction that is equivalent to $\frac{3}{4}$ is...

• Use further examples of statistical representations that require children to add and subtract. Children could also re-label an axis with intervals of 100 ml as tenths of a litre, recognising that $\frac{2}{5}$ litre is equal to $\frac{4}{10}$ litre. This also means that 300 ml can be described as $\frac{3}{10}$ litre or even as $\frac{1}{5}$ litre + $\frac{1}{10}$ litre or $\frac{2}{5}$ litre – $\frac{1}{10}$ litre. How many different ways can they show 700 ml?

Concept mastered

Children can fluently use equivalent fractions so that all parts of a calculation share the same denominator.

Answers

Step 1	Step 2	Step 3
a $\frac{3}{6}$ ($\frac{1}{2}$)	a $1\frac{3}{6}$ ($1\frac{1}{2}$)	a $5\frac{1}{4}$ hours
b $\frac{7}{10}$	b $2\frac{7}{10}$	b $5\frac{1}{2}$ hours
c $4\frac{1}{8}$ ($\frac{9}{8}$)	c $5\frac{1}{8}$	**Step 4**
d $\frac{5}{10}$ ($\frac{1}{2}$)	d $2\frac{5}{10}$ ($2\frac{1}{2}$)	Top row: $5\frac{1}{8}$
e $\frac{3}{6}$ ($\frac{1}{2}$)	e $1\frac{3}{6}$ ($1\frac{1}{2}$)	Middle row: $3\frac{3}{8}$ and $\frac{7}{8}$ Bottom row: $4\frac{1}{4}$
f $\frac{1}{8}$	f $3\frac{1}{8}$	

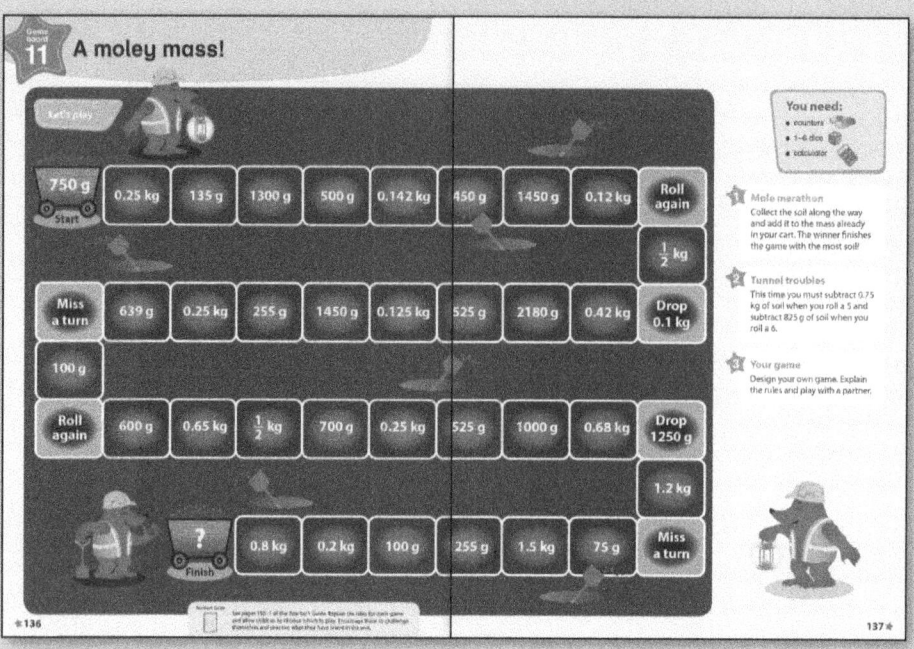

Game 1: Mole marathon

The moles are digging a tunnel. Each starts with 750 g of soil in their cart. This is a race to collect the greatest mass of soil by the end of the game. Ask children to look at the measurements shown and discuss what they may have to do as part of the game.

Maths focus

* Addition and subtraction of mass using decimals up to three decimal places

Resources

1 counter per player (1 colour per player), 1-6 dice (1), calculator.

How to play

This game can be played in pairs or in small groups so children can discuss calculations. Players take it in turns to roll the dice and move on this number of spaces. They collect the mass of soil shown where their counter lands, converting as necessary to add it to the mass of soil already in their cart.

Children should be encouraged to estimate first and consider a mental method. The game also requires them to use a calculator to check each other's calculations.

The winner is the mole who finishes the game with the greatest mass of soil in their cart.

Making it easier

Play in groups so a player has a partner to work with. The game could be adapted by changing any masses that are shown to three decimal places to only one or two places.

Players could also convert all the kilogram masses to grams before they start. This would mean that all calculations can be completed using whole numbers.

Making it harder

Introduce two dice so that children make decisions about which number to use, e.g. at the beginning of the game, are they better choosing a three or a six? The six moves them further around the board, the three results in collecting more soil.

Game 2: Tunnel troubles

This is an adaptation of Mole Marathon and will require players to subtract given masses of soil when a five or six is rolled. Again it is a race to collect the greatest mass of soil by the end of the game.

Maths focus

* Addition and subtraction of mass using decimals up to three decimal places

Resources

1 counter per player (1 colour per player), 1-6 dice (1), calculator.

How to play

This game is an adaptation of Game 1 but this time will involve more subtractions as rolling a five results in subtracting 0.75 kg and rolling a six means that 825 g should be subtracted.

Making it easier

Again, children could work with a partner to discuss strategies or the game could be adapted as suggested for Mole Marathon.

Making it harder

Change the aim of the game so that the winner is the mole who has the least soil at the end of the game. Introduce two dice so that children can make decisions about which number to use so that they drop more soil or only collect smaller masses along the way.

Game 3: Your game

Children should invent their own game designing rules that use the concepts covered in the unit. Challenge children to make their game easier or harder.

A moley mass!

Choose a game to play.

Game 1: Mole marathon

You need:
- 1 counter per player (1 colour per player)
- 1–6 dice
- calculator

How to play

- Place your counters on Start. You start with 750 g of soil in your cart.
- Take it in turns to roll the dice and move your counter this number of spaces.
- Collect the mass of soil shown where your counter lands, converting it if you need to and add it to the mass of soil already in your cart.
- Use a calculator to check each other's calculations.
- The winner is the player who finishes the game with the greatest mass of soil in their cart.

Game 2: Tunnel troubles

You need:
- 1 counter per player (1 colour per player)
- 1–6 dice
- calculator

How to play

- Follow the same rules as Game 1: Mole Marathon.
- This time you must subtract 0.75 kg of soil when you roll a 5 and subtract 825 g of soil when you roll a 6.

Game 3: Your game

- Make up your own game using the gameboard.
- What are the rules to your game? Explain them to a someone.
- How could you make it easier or harder?
- Will your game involve adding or subtracting the masses?

Please help your child by reading the instructions and playing the game together.

Assessment task 1

Resources

Pencil and paper or a whiteboard.

Running the task

Listen to groups of children discuss the statement and suggest different mental strategies that can be used. Encourage them to spot number bonds or identify calculations where it may be easier to use the finding the difference strategy for subtraction, e.g.:

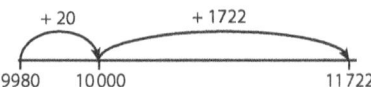

Look for those who immediately recognise that they will need to convert between units of measurement for all calculations. Encourage them to consider all the different strategies that would be efficient here and look for those who recognise a good opportunity to round and adjust, which is a strategy that has been used in previous units. Ask them to explain why these methods are more efficient than the formal written method for many of the calculations here, but why the last calculation would best be solved using the written method.

Look for those who appropriately choose to work in grams/millilitres or kilograms/litres to avoid decimals or to avoid much larger whole numbers.

Evidencing mastery

If children are able to do this easily and explain what they are doing, they have a good understanding of different mental calculation strategies and when to use them. Look for those than refer to the proximity of numbers when making a decision about a finding the difference method.

Look for those who use place value to fluently convert grams to kilograms and vice versa, or millilitres to litres and vice versa.

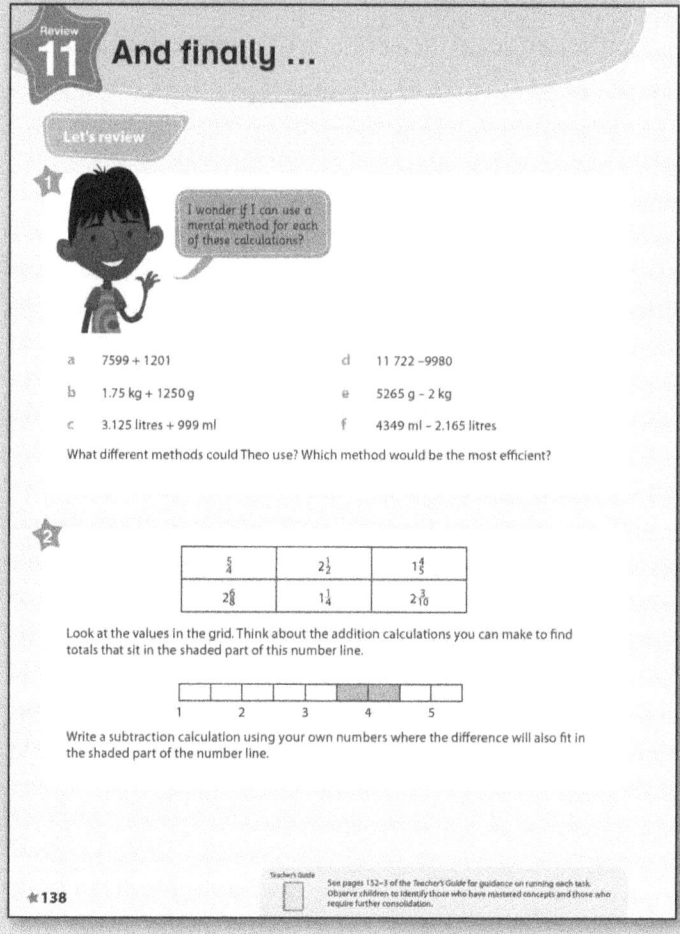

Assessment task 2

Resources

Pencil and paper or a whiteboard, fraction bars.

Running the task

This is a more open task where children are required to estimate and reason about different sums that can be made from the mixed numbers or improper fractions in the grid. They could work with a partner to discuss possible solutions and find a starting point. However, they must first identify the value of the shaded part of the number line.

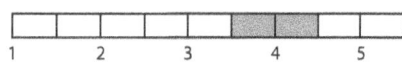

Children can also use fraction bars or make sketches to check their thinking, especially when later making up subtractions using their own numbers.

Encourage them to convince you or their peers of their solutions using mathematical language and reasoning, e.g. $\frac{5}{4}$ is equivalent to $1\frac{1}{4}$ and I know that $\frac{1}{2}$ and $\frac{1}{4}$ is equal to $\frac{3}{4}$ so $2\frac{1}{2} + \frac{5}{4}$ is $3\frac{3}{4}$. This fraction is more than $3\frac{1}{2}$ and less than 4.

Evidencing mastery

Look for children who quickly recognise that the totals must fit within a range of $3\frac{1}{2}$ to $4\frac{1}{2}$ on the number line. Children who explain why certain pairs would not result in a total of this size are showing how they can use estimates to help make decisions and have a secure understanding of mixed numbers. Look for those who fluently draw on knowledge of equivalents to aid additions and use the fraction bar or other representations to reason about or check a solution.

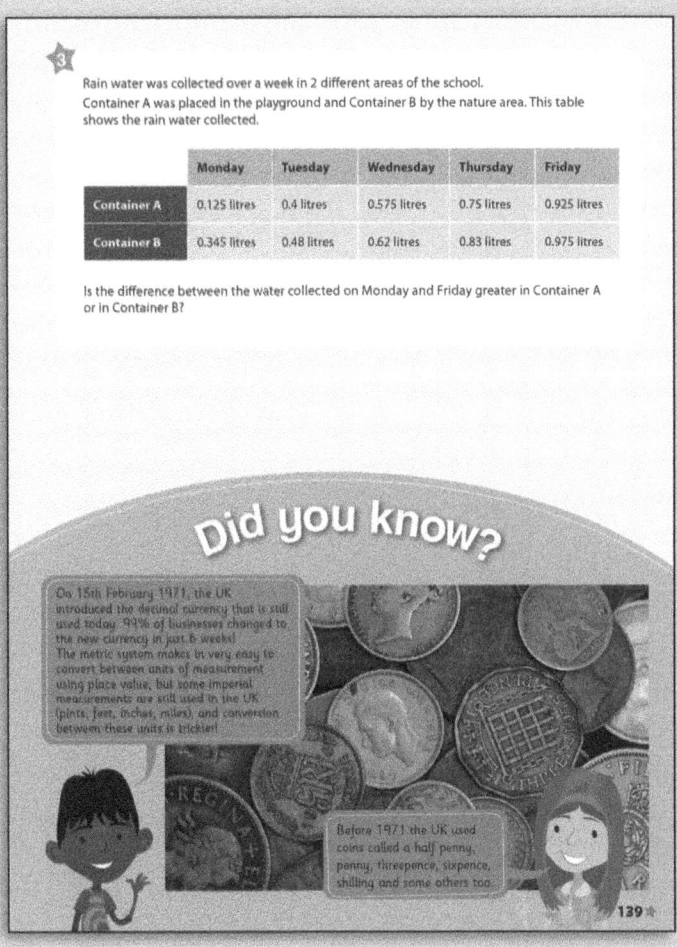

> ③ Rain water was collected over a week in 2 different areas of the school.
> Container A was placed in the playground and Container B by the nature area. This table shows the rain water collected.
>
> | | Monday | Tuesday | Wednesday | Thursday | Friday |
> |---|---|---|---|---|---|
> | Container A | 0.125 litres | 0.4 litres | 0.575 litres | 0.75 litres | 0.925 litres |
> | Container B | 0.345 litres | 0.48 litres | 0.62 litres | 0.83 litres | 0.975 litres |
>
> Is the difference between the water collected on Monday and Friday greater in Container A or in Container B?
>
> **Did you know?**
>
> On 15th February 1971, the UK introduced the decimal currency that is still used today. 99% of businesses changed to the new currency in just 6 weeks! The metric system makes in very easy to convert between units of measurement using place value, but some imperial measurements are still used in the UK (pints, feet, inches, miles) and conversion between these units is trickier!
>
> Before 1971 the UK used coins called a half penny, penny, threepence, sixpence, shilling and some others too.
>
> 139

Assessment task 3

Resources

Pencil and paper or a whiteboard.

Running the task

This task will help to assess both fluency and problem solving skills. Ask children to suggest what they need to do to solve the problem. Discuss their initial thoughts as a class and use questioning to ensure that children are thinking about efficient strategies. Look for children who simply identify the amount of water in Container B on Friday and assume that this is the greatest difference because it is 0.975 litres as opposed to 0.925 litres. You could later discuss how the question would need to change so this was the case.

Children should complete the task independently, using an efficient mental or written calculation strategy. Be aware that if any children require the use of concrete apparatus, they will not be showing mastery.

Evidencing mastery

Children who recognise that they will need to calculate the difference for both containers and not just look at the final amounts show an understanding of comparison and how subtraction can be used to solve the problem. Children demonstrating mastery will fluently apply knowledge of place value to calculate with decimals up to three decimal places, or use conversion to show each capacity in millilitres so that the calculations can be carried out using whole numbers.

Concepts mastered

- ✓ Children can make and explain their choices when selecting a mental or written method of addition and subtraction.

- ✓ Children can fluently use equivalent fractions so that all parts of a calculation share the same denominator.

Did you know?

Discuss with children how on 15th February 1971, the UK introduced the decimal currency that is still used today. A survey showed that 99% of businesses changed to the new currency in just six weeks! However, the changeover to other metric measurements did not go as smoothly. Discuss how we still use pints, feet, inches and miles today and ask children if their weighing scales at home show pounds and ounces. Explain that these are called Imperial measurements and that, while the metric system makes in very easy to convert between units of measurement using place value, conversion between units of Imperial measurement is not quite as easy. Talk about how calculating with times is also challenging because we to remember lots of different information.

Children need to know why the metric system came about (a practical business decision) and how the uniformity using tens, hundreds and thousands makes it easier to convert between different units. They should understand that calculations should be completed when the measurements are shown in the same unit.

This is also true for time, but children should recognise that time does not use a metric system to relate one unit of measurement to the next.

Exploring fractions, decimals and percentages

Mathematical focus

★ **Number: number and place value, fractions**

★ **Measurement: money, length, mass, capacity**

Prior learning

Children should already be able to:

- compare and order halves, quarters and eighths
- recognise mixed numbers and improper fractions and convert from one form to the other
- add and subtract fractions with the same denominator
- understand tenths, hundredths and thousandths and find decimal equivalents
- understand percentage as one hundredth.

Key new learning

- Compare and order fractions whose denominators are all multiples of the same number.
- Recognise mixed numbers and improper fractions, convert from one form to the other and write mathematical statements > 1 as a mixed number (e.g. $\frac{2}{5} + \frac{4}{5} = \frac{6}{5} = 1\frac{1}{5}$).
- Multiply fractions by whole numbers.
- Read and write decimal numbers as fractions (e.g. $0.71 = \frac{71}{100}$).
- Multiply and divide whole numbers and those involving decimals by 10, 100 and 1000.
- Recognise and use thousandths and relate them to tenths, hundredths and decimal equivalents.
- Recognise the per cent symbol (%) and understand that per cent relates to 'number of parts per hundred', and write percentages as a fraction with denominator 100, and as a decimal.
- Identify, name and write equivalent fractions of tenths and hundredths.

Unit 12 — Exploring fractions, decimals and percentages

I wonder what these volumes would look like as litres?

Special offer!
3 for the price of 2

White mushrooms
Mass: 200 g
Price: £1.00 per 100 g

White grapes
Mass: 220 g
Price: £1.20 per 100 g

Apples
Mass: 475 g
Price: 80p per 100 g

How much would it cost altogether to buy the mushrooms, grapes and apples?

★140

Making connections

- Build on the real-life applications that you have made in previous units on fractions, decimals and percentages by making connections to new practical contexts. These might include cross-curricular contexts, such as science.
- Percentages are found all around us. Provide pictures of, e.g. sale prices in shops, takeaway menus, holiday brochures and magazines so that the children can identify real-life percentages.
- This unit provides an opportunity to revisit time. Explore how fractions are used when talking about time.
- Throughout the unit, develop and extend the connections between fractions, decimals and measures of length.

Talk about

Remind children that fraction is from the Latin word 'fractio'. Demonstrate by drawing the line or vinculum separating the numerator and denominator first to indicate breaking into parts. Next write a denominator to show the number of parts and then the numerator to show how many parts are needed. Be sure to be consistent when using the vocabulary of vinculum, denominator and numerator. Develop the discussion to include tenths, hundredths and thousandths. Expect children to be able to tell you how these relate to fractions and to discuss the place value of each.

Engaging and exploring

You could ask children to look at each picture and the questions that go with it and discuss with a partner what each might be about. Use this as an opportunity to assess children's understanding of fractions, decimals and percentages. Focus on each picture in turn.

For the picture with the measuring jugs, you could remind children what volume and capacity are. Ensure that they understand that volume is the amount in a container and capacity is the amount that the container can hold.

Discuss the scales on the measuring jugs. Can children tell you what intervals they each go up in? Establish that one goes up in steps of 100 ml and the other 20 ml. Ask children to tell you the volume in each jug in mililtres and litres. Ask children to explain how they know their answers are correct.

Ask questions such as:

- How much do I need to add for the first jug to have a volume of 0.75 l?

- If I take 0.13 l out of the second jug, how much will be left?

Write different volumes in millilitres on the board and ask children to convert them to litres and then vice versa.

Talk about the fruit and vegetables shown. Are children familiar with them? Do they know how and where they are grown? You could ask them to choose their favourite of the three and show the information as a tally for children to turn into a table and then a representation, such as a pie chart.

Ask children to tell you the mass of each packet. Can they write these in kilograms? Give them different masses to convert to kilograms and grams.

Each food is priced per 100 g. Ask children to use a mental calculation strategy to work out how much it costs for the actual packets. You could give them money and ask them to make these amounts using, e.g. the fewest number of coins. Ask them to find the price of pairs of items and then all three and tell you what the change would be from different amounts.

Discuss the 'three for the price of two' offer. What do they think this means? Do they think this offer is always a good one? You could consider the positive and negative aspects of such an offer. Then ask them to work out the cost of the items in the photo.

For the picture of the sweets ask children to estimate the number of sweets in the bag. Write these on the board. Pick or make an estimate of an amount that children can explore the fractions of.

Give children counters or sweets and ask them to arrange them in groups of different sizes. They can then use these to make and write different improper fractions and mixed numbers. E.g. if they have ten counters they might have a line or pile of six to represent one whole and four left over. This would give $\frac{10}{6}$ or $1\frac{4}{6}$. Ask them to use these to make up some addition and subtraction number sentences.

For the picture of the shop sale you could discuss what the percentage signs in the photo indicate. Agree that they are discounts in the prices of the items. Ask children to explain what a percentage is: a fraction which is always a part out of 100.

Give them counters. Set problems e.g. '20% has been taken off the price of rollerblades. One set now costs £36. What was the original price?' Ask them to set out five counters to show 100% (each counter represents 20%). Once one counter (20%) has been taken away, the remaining four counters represent £36. So each represents £9. Therefore the discount is £9 and the original price was £45. This problem, or similar problems, will encourage children to apply known knowledge to percentages.

Look at the pictures with the children and discuss the questions. See pages 154–5 of the Teacher's Guide for key ideas to draw out.

141

Things to think about

- How will you plan focus group work?

- What will you do to plan tasks with challenge to deepen understanding?

- What kind of visual representations and manipulatives will you provide to ensure that all children are able to access their learning?

- How will you develop problem solving and reasoning through questioning and the extra practice activities you give to children?

Checking understanding

You will know children have mastered these concepts when they can explain and demonstrate their understanding of fraction, decimal and percentage equivalences, and use them to solve problems in different contexts.

Exploring fractions

- Compare and order fractions whose denominators are all multiples of the same number.
- Recognise mixed numbers and improper fractions and convert from one form to the other and write mathematical statements > 1 as a mixed number (e.g. $\frac{2}{5} + \frac{4}{5} = \frac{6}{5} = 1\frac{1}{5}$)
- Multiply fractions by whole numbers.

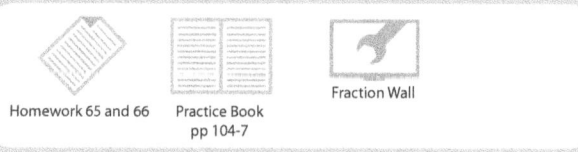

Homework 65 and 66   Practice Book pp 104-7   Fraction Wall

Representations and resources

Strips of paper, clock faces, rulers.

Mathematical vocabulary

Million, place value, negative numbers, order, compare, round

Warming up

Write pairs of numbers on the board which can be added and subtracted using number pairs to ten, e.g. 346 + 264 (6 + 4 = 10, 40 + 60 = 100, so 346 + 264 = 500 + 100 + 10 = 610), 572 − 135 (500 − 100 = 400, 72 − 35: 72 − 2 − 3 = 67, 67 − 30 = 37, so 572 − 135 = 437). You can encourage children to make jottings if they would find this helpful.

Background knowledge

It is important that children understand what equivalent fractions are and how to use common multiples to find them. If they can convert fractions to those that are equivalent they will find it easier to compare and order them. This will also help their understanding of how many parts of a fraction make a whole and they will be able to transfer this knowledge when working with improper fractions and mixed numbers.

Let's learn: Modelling and teaching

Comparing and ordering fractions

- Ask children to find ten equivalent fractions from the fraction wall in the Textbook, e.g. $\frac{3}{3} = 1$, $\frac{6}{15} = \frac{2}{5}$, $\frac{5}{15} = \frac{1}{3}$, $\frac{2}{5} = \frac{4}{10}$. Ask children to compare the fraction equivalences they have made.

- Give children five strips of 2 cm-wide A4 paper each. Ask them to keep the first strip whole and write 1 in the middle. They can then use rulers to measure and label fifths, tenths, fifteenths and twentieths on the other strips. They can use these to find equivalent fractions.

- Direct children to the two clocks in the Textbook and ask them to tell you what fraction the shaded parts are. Give children 12 copies of clock faces, ask them to cut these into different fractions and record, e.g. $\frac{1}{12}$ = five minutes.

Multiplying fractions by whole numbers

- Ask children to explain the number pattern they see in the Textbook to a partner. Can they make the link that $\frac{1}{2} \times 2 = 1$ is the same as finding $\frac{1}{2}$ of 2?

- Give children strips of paper. They label each with a 2-digit number. They multiply $\frac{1}{2}$ and then $\frac{1}{4}$ by the amounts, folding the paper in two and then four parts. Repeat this for other fractions and numbers.

- Together work through the idea that you can turn the whole number into a fraction, e.g. 9 is $\frac{9}{1}$ (9 divided by 1) and then the numerators and denominators can be multiplied, e.g. $\frac{1}{3} \times 9 = \frac{1}{3} \times \frac{9}{1} = \frac{9}{3} = 3$. Model this using paper strips. Give children 9 strips of paper of the same length. They fold them into thirds. They shade one third on each strip, then find the total which is 9 thirds or three. Repeat for other numbers.

Let's practise: Digging deeper
Step 1

Children need to choose pairs of the fractions given and convert them so that they have the same denominator. Once they have done this they compare them using the symbols > and <. Encourage children to use the fraction wall in the Textbook if they would like support. They could also make fraction strips for halves, quarters and eighths.

Step 2

The task asks children to multiply different fractions and whole numbers together. Encourage them to label strips of paper with the whole numbers and fold them to find the fractions as in the whole-class suggestion. Draw out the link between multiplication and repeated addition as they add the fractions together.

Step 3

The task asks children to multiply fractions by lengths. When they have done this they can draw lines the same length as their answers.

Step 4

Children need to write an explanation to show they understand why $\frac{2}{5}$ and $\frac{6}{15}$ are equivalent. You could also write some fractions that can be reduced on the board, e.g. $\frac{8}{20}$, $\frac{10}{15}$. Ask children to explain how they would reduce these to their simplest form, e.g. they could say what each part of the fraction can be divided by to give an equivalent fraction that uses smaller numbers. Repeat this for increasing the numerator and denominator. Ask them to compare pairs that they made using < and >.

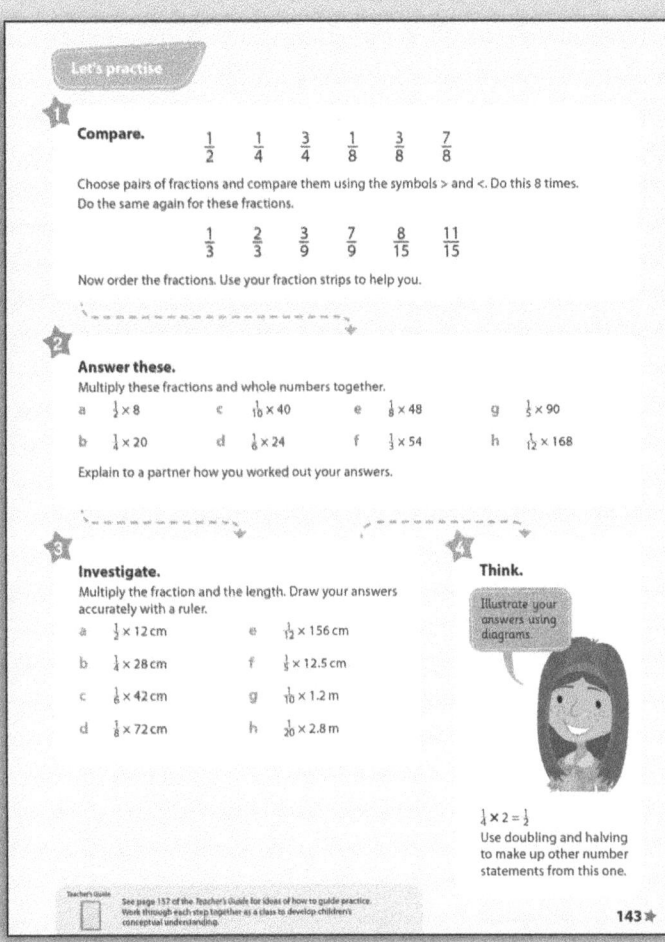

Ensuring progress
Supporting understanding

For the first step children could compare halves, quarters and eighths by folding their strips. They could compare unit fractions initially and, if coping well, move on to comparing non-unit fractions. For Step 2 ask children to focus on multiplying by two. They could use fraction strips again. Consistent use of this manipulative will help to secure their conceptual understanding.

Broadening understanding

For the first step encourage children to make more complicated combinations of fractions, e.g. thirds, quarters, sixths and ninths, and compare non-unit fractions. If children can successfully multiply unit fractions by whole numbers ask them how they can use division to check that they are correct. This should lead them towards thinking that they are essentially changing an improper fraction to a whole number.

✓ Concept mastered

Children can explain and demonstrate how to find equivalent fractions and also to convert improper fractions to mixed numbers and vice versa.

Follow-up ideas

- Give children scales, plastic bags and sand. Ask them to measure 500 g of sand. Then they measure out fractions of this amount, e.g. $\frac{4}{5}$, $\frac{3}{10}$, $\frac{3}{4}$. Encourage them to fill five bags and label each with the fraction they made and its mass. They then order these from smallest to greatest and write the order of the fractions on paper.

- Give children a length statement, e.g. 1 km represents one whole. They write this in the middle of a piece of paper, then find as many fractions of this amount as they can in three minutes. Encourage them to be creative and find, e.g. fifths, eighths, twentieths, hundredths.

- Write a volume statement on the board, e.g. 1 l 200 ml represents $\frac{1}{2}$. Children then use this to make different statements, e.g. $\frac{1}{4}$ = 600 ml, $\frac{3}{4}$ = 1 l 800 ml, $\frac{1}{8}$ = 300 ml, $1\frac{1}{8}$ = 2 l 700 ml.

Answers

Step 1

Children's own correct pairs showing correct ordering, e.g.
$\frac{1}{8} < \frac{1}{4} < \frac{3}{8} < \frac{1}{2} < \frac{3}{4} < \frac{7}{8}$ etc.

$\frac{1}{3} = \frac{3}{9} < \frac{8}{15} < \frac{2}{3} < \frac{11}{15} < \frac{7}{9}$

Step 2

a 4
b 5
c 4
d 4
e 6
f 18
g 18
h 14

Step 3

a 6 cm
b 7 cm
c 7 cm
d 9 cm
e 13 cm
f 2.5 cm
g 12 cm
h 14 cm

Step 4

Explanations need to show that children understand that because five is a factor of 15 or 15 is a multiple of three, they can multiply the numerator and denominator by three to convert it to $\frac{6}{15}$.

Answers include $\frac{1}{2} \times 4$, $\frac{1}{8} \times 4$, $\frac{1}{16} \times 8$, $\frac{1}{32} \times 16$ etc.

- Multiply and divide whole numbers and those involving decimals by 10, 100 and 1000.
- Read and write decimal numbers as fractions (e.g. $0.71 = \frac{71}{100}$).
- Recognise and use thousandths and relate them to tenths, hundredths and decimal equivalents.

Homework 67 and 68   Practice Book pp 108–10   Fraction Wall   Fraction and decimal equivalents

Representations and resources

Whiteboards and pens, place-value grids (thousands to thousandths), digit cards, coloured counters, ruler.

Mathematical vocabulary

Fractions, proper fractions, decimal fractions, equivalence, tenths, hundredths, thousandths, powers of 10, reduce, lowest term, positional, multiplicative, additive

Warming up

Practise doubling and near doubling. Use digit cards to generate 3-digit numbers. As you make a number, children write it on their whiteboards and then double it again and again, e.g. 234: 468, 936. Repeat this for 4-digit numbers (3527: 7054, 14108) and numbers with one or two decimal places. Next, call out pairs of numbers that can be added using the near double strategy, e.g. 245 + 247, 2.34 + 2.37. At this stage, start to introduce decimals, as a lead in to the Let's learn section.

Background knowledge

Children need to understand that when multiplying and dividing by 10, 100 and 1000 the digits of the number become 10, 100 and 1000 times bigger or smaller. The digits move to the left if multiplying or the right if dividing. They need to understand that the decimal place doesn't move but remains constant. It would be helpful to introduce the term 'powers of ten' into children's vocabulary as shown in the Textbook when talking about multiplying and dividing by multiples of ten in this context.

Let's learn: Modelling and teaching
Multiplying and dividing decimals by powers of 10

- Give children place-value grids from thousands to thousandths and a set of digit cards. Ask them to make the first number in the place-value grid in the Textbook and place it in their grid. They multiply the number by 10, then 100. Ask children to explain what happens to the digits each time. Expect them to tell you that they become 10 and 100 times bigger. If any mention adding zeros address this misconception. Next ask them to divide the number by 10 and 100.

- Ask children to look at the Gattegno chart in the Textbook and to tell you what is happening in each row (increasing by one of each value). Discuss what is happening in the columns. Ensure you ask them to explain what happens to the number as it moves down from, e.g. 0.3 to 3 (×10), then 3000 (×1000), then 30 (÷100) and 0.03 (÷1000).

- Ask children to choose a number from each row and make up a millions number with three decimal places. They explain

to a partner what each digit represents using the language of positional, multiplicative and additive place value.

Decimal numbers as fractions

- Call out different decimals, beginning with tenths, e.g. 0.6, 0.7. Ask children to write these down as fractions. Continue with hundredths, e.g. 0.12, and then thousandths, e.g. 0.783. Ask them to reduce any fractions they can to their lowest term. Discuss how this is done.

- Give children five different-coloured counters. Each colour should represent different number values, e.g. white could be tens, red ones, blue tenths, yellow hundredths and green thousandths. Call out some numbers for children to make using the counters, e.g. 41.368, 86.824. Once they have made them, they write the decimal part as a fraction.

Let's practise: Digging deeper

Step 1

You could rehearse this task before children carry it out, particularly for those who are less confident. Call out some 2-digit numbers with one or two decimal places and ask children to multiply them by 10, 100 and 1000 and write their answers on their whiteboards. They explain what is happening to the numbers. Next call out multiples of 1000 and ask children to divide these by 10, 100 and 1000 and to explain what is happening this time. Provide digit cards, place-value grids and Gattegno charts to support children as they carry this out.

Children multiply the first set of numbers by 10, then 100 and 1000 and explain to a partner what happens to the digits each time. Ask some to give a written explanation. Repeat this for the second set of numbers, but dividing by 10, 100 and 1000.

Step 2

In this task children convert the decimals of each number to fractions. Encourage those who would benefit to make the numbers in their place-value grids so they can see what the fractions would look like. They then reduce as many as they can to their lowest terms.

Step 3

Children convert measurements to their decimal equivalents. Once they have done so, you could add a more practical element to the activity and ask them to weigh or measure different lengths, masses and volumes, converting and recording them as decimals, e.g. 3m 9cm to metres (3.09m), 1kg 150g to kilograms (1.15kg), 2l 75ml to litres (2.075l).

Step 4

Children need to work out the Theo's number. Encourage them to do this by working backwards. They start with the only number given and do the opposite each time, e.g. they begin with 276.8, multiply it by 10, double it, add 1000 and divide by 100. Once they have done this they work it through from the beginning to see if the instructions from the starting number give 276.8.

Ask similar questions to this so that children can practise this type of problem solving.

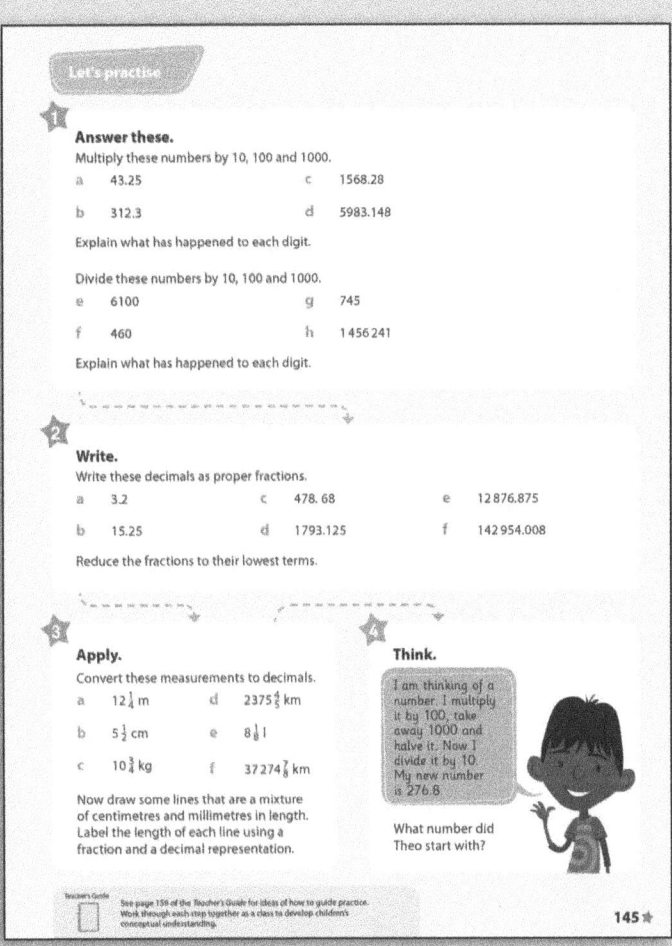

Ensuring progress

Supporting understanding

Provide digit cards and place-value grids for Steps 1 and 2. Work with children in a focus group to reinforce understanding of multiplying and dividing by 10, ensuring they understand that when multiplying the digits become 10 times bigger and when dividing they become 10 times smaller.

Broadening understanding

In Step 1 ask children what they would need to do if they were multiplying or dividing by 20, 200 and 2000. Give them numbers to multiply and divide by these amounts. Repeat for other multiples of 10, 100 and 1000. You could also ask them to make up problems within the context of measures for a partner to solve.

✓ Concept mastered

Children can explain and demonstrate how to convert fractions to decimals and vice versa and also explain the value of the digits in a number with three decimal places.

Follow-up ideas

- You could ask children to work with a partner. They make up a 3-digit number. They take it in turns to throw a dice. If they throw an even number they multiply it by 100. If they throw an odd number they divide it by 10. Once they have thrown the dice ten times each the game ends and the winner is the player with the highest or lowest number. They can decide this.

- Children could use a set of digit cards to generate decimal numbers. They make as many single-digit numbers with three decimal places as they can. Once they have found them all they order them from smallest to largest number.

- Children could make an information poster about all they have learnt during this unit.

Answers

Step 1

a 432.5, 4325, 43 250

b 3123, 31 230, 312 300

c 15 682.8, 156 828, 1 568 280

d 59 831.48, 598 314.8, 5 983 148

e 610, 61, 6.1

f 46, 4.6, 0.46

g 74.5, 7.45, 0.745

h 145 624.1, 14 562.41, 1 456.241

Step 2

a $3\frac{2}{10}$ or $3\frac{1}{5}$

b $15\frac{25}{100}$ or $15\frac{1}{4}$

c $478\frac{68}{100}$ or $478\frac{17}{25}$

d $1793\frac{125}{1000}$ or $1793\frac{1}{8}$

e $12876\frac{875}{1000}$ or $12876\frac{7}{8}$

f $142954\frac{8}{1000}$ or $142954\frac{1}{125}$

Step 3

a 12.25 m

b 5.5 cm

c 10.75 kg

d 2375.8 km

e 8.125 l

f 73 274.875 km

Step 4

65.36

- Recognise and use thousandths and relate them to tenths, hundredths and decimal equivalents.
- Recognise the per cent symbol (%) and understand that per cent relates to 'number of parts per hundred', and write percentages as a fraction with denominator 100, and as a decimal.
- Identify, name and write equivalent fractions of tenths and hundredths.

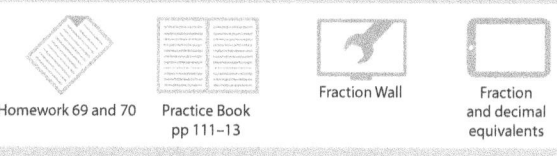

Homework 69 and 70   Practice Book pp 111–13   Fraction Wall   Fraction and decimal equivalents

Representations and resources

Strips of paper, counters, ruler.

Mathematical vocabulary

Fractions, proper fractions, decimal fractions, per cent, percentage, equivalence, factor, multiple, lowest term

Warming up

Ask children to rehearse the mental calculation strategy of multiplying by five by multiplying by ten and halving. Call out some two-digit even numbers such as 48, 62 and 96. Children should either halve them first and multiply by ten or multiply by ten and halve. They can write their answers and show you. Next, you could ask them to do this for 2-digit odd numbers and then 3-digit numbers and those with one decimal place. Repeat this for multiplying by 20 by multiplying by ten and doubling or doubling and then multiplying by ten. You could then divide by five by dividing by ten and doubling and divide by 20 by dividing by ten and halving.

Background knowledge

The symbol % means per cent which comes from the Latin per centum, out of 100. We see percentages in many different contexts and it is important that children are aware of this. You could provide visual representations that show this, e.g. food packaging and holiday brochures. Also provide opportunities to put percentages into contexts, e.g. money and other measures.

Let's learn: Modelling and teaching

Working out a percentage

- Refer to the fraction wall in the Textbook. Tell children that the 100% bar represents £200. Ask them to work out the value of the other parts of the wall.

- Discuss how to find percentages of numbers. Encourage children to think about finding 10% first and then halving, doubling, adding, subtracting, multiplying and dividing to find other amounts. Write '100% is equivalent to £150'. Ensure that they are clear about the meaning of 'is equivalent to'. Give children three minutes to find as many different percentages as they can.

- Discuss the comments by Amy and Theo. Write different amounts of money on the board and ask children to find 10%, then other percentages.

- Ask problems, e.g. *A DVD was reduced by 20% in a sale. It was originally £12. How much is it now?* Use counters to

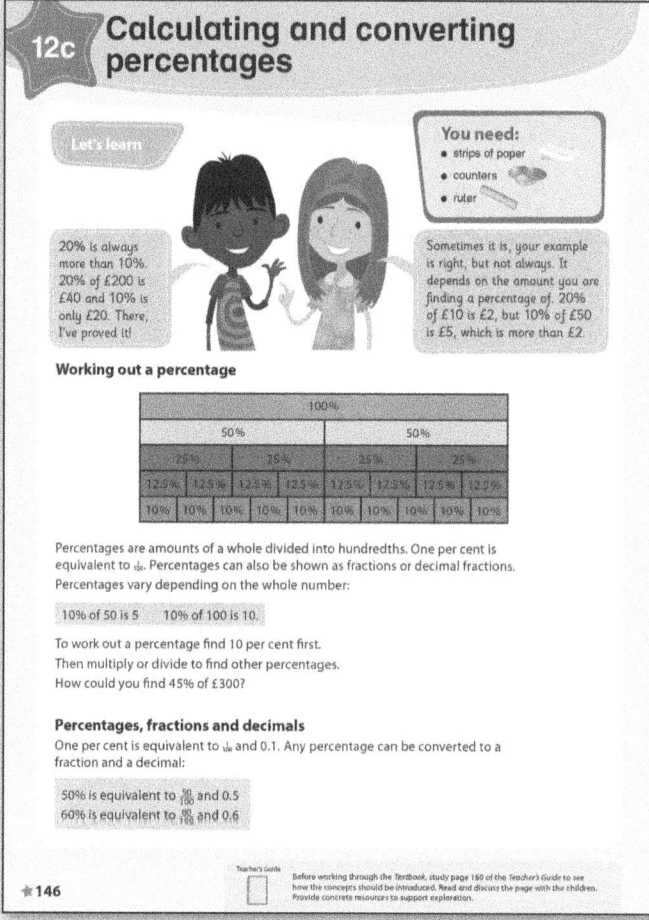

set these problems out. For each they should use five counters each representing 20%. If the original cost was £12, each part is worth £2.40. So the discount is £2.40. The sale price is therefore £12 – £2.40 = £9.60.

Percentages, fractions and decimals

- Remind them about the work they did on converting decimals to hundredths and liken this to writing percentages as fractions, e.g. 0.25 is equivalent to $\frac{25}{100}$ and because 25% is out of 100, this would also be $\frac{25}{100}$. Write some percentages for children to convert to fractions and decimals. Ask them to reduce the fractions.

- Write trios of percentages, fractions and decimals on the board. Children can order these from greatest to smallest. To do this, they convert the trios to the same unit. e.g. 15%, $\frac{1}{10}$, 0.3.

Let's practise: Digging deeper

Step 1

Children need to work out percentages of different amounts of money and explain their methods. They should do this in written format. Once they have completed this task, they could repeat it for different lengths, kilograms and litres.

Step 2

In this task children convert percentages to fractions and decimals. Encourage them to reduce the fractions to their lowest terms.

Step 3

Before children tackle the task give them strips of paper measuring 15cm in length and ask them to keep one whole and label it 100%. They fold a second in half. Discuss what percentage they have made. Agree that, because each part

is half, each part will be half of 100%. They label each part 50%. Ask them to fold the next strip in half and half again and repeat the previous discussion. Repeat for folding in half three times. Tell children that the whole strip labelled 100% is worth 1 m. Ask them to find the values of all the parts of the strips they folded above.

For the task provide children with strips of paper measuring 15 cm in length. They then need to find the percentages listed and cut strips of paper to these lengths. When they have done this, they work through the other tasks in which 100% represents 24 km, 32 kg and 16 l. You could challenge some children to find 93% and/or 97% of the amounts by finding 1%, multiplying by seven and/or three and subtracting the amount from 100%. It would be worth sharing this with the rest of the class.

Step 4

Children need to explain how Amy can find 12.5% by finding 10%, halving and adding. You might need to give them an amount to work with, e.g. £100 as 100%.

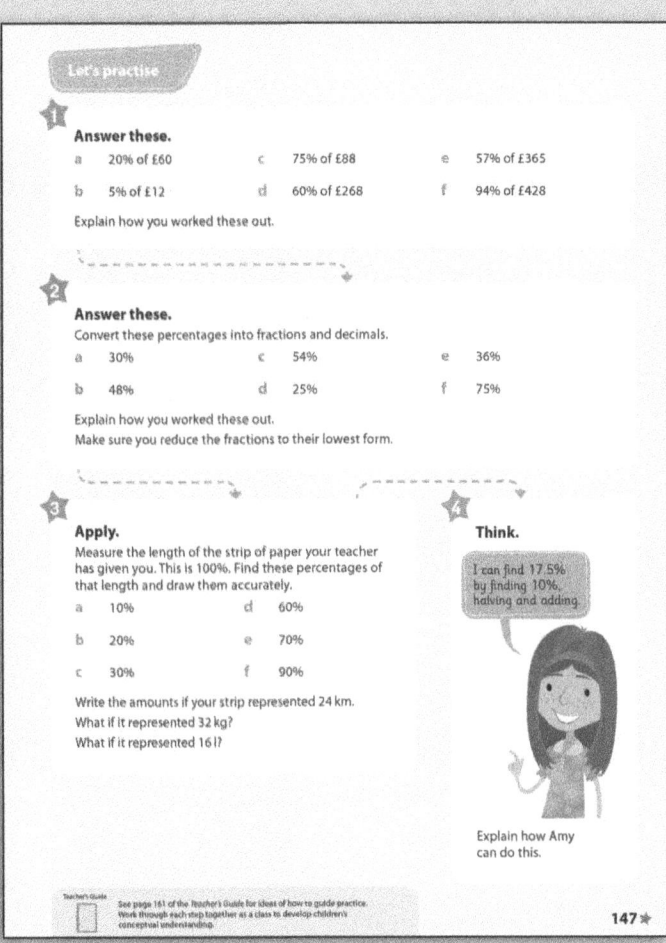

Ensuring progress

Supporting understanding

Observe children as they work through the activities. If any struggle they should focus on percentages that are multiples of ten initially and master this. You could also give them simpler numbers to work with.

Broadening understanding

Assess children as they work through the activities. If they appear to have mastered this area of maths, they should attempt finding more complicated percentages, such as 12.5% or 120%. Even if children are not yet able to work out these percentages, it would be valuable for them to discuss how they might approach working them out. Encourage them to use precise mathematical vocabulary as they discuss possible strategies.

Concept mastered

Children can explain and demonstrate how to find percentages of different amounts and explain and demonstrate equivalences between percentages and fractions.

Follow-up ideas

- You could give children takeaway menus, or similar. They should find all the different types of numbers they can, noting any percentages, fractions and decimals. They then convert these to the other linked units.

- Children could make up a matching game by writing a percentage on a piece of card and then the equivalent fraction and decimal on two other pieces of card. They do this ten times. They could make up their own rules for the game.

- You could ask children to make two sets of cards: a set of percentages and a set of amounts of money. They take it in turns to pick one of each. They find the percentage of the amount of money and write it down.

Answers

Step 1

a £12

b 60p

c £66

d £160.80

e £208.05

f £402.32

Step 2

a 30%: $\frac{3}{10}$, 0.3

b 48%: $\frac{12}{25}$, 0.48

d 54%: $\frac{27}{50}$, 0.54

e 25%: $\frac{1}{4}$, 0.25

f 36%: $\frac{9}{25}$, 0.36

g 75%: $\frac{3}{4}$, 0.75

Step 3

a 1.5cm

b 3cm

c 4.5cm

d 9cm

e 10.5cm

f 13.5cm

If 24km: a 2.4km, b 4.8km, c 7.2km, d 14.4km, e 16.8km, f 21.6km

If 32kg: a 3.2kg, b 6.4kg, c 9.6kg, d 19.2kg, e 22.4kg, f 28.8kg

If 16l: a 1.6l, b 3.2l, c 4.8l, d 9.6l, e 11.2l, f 14.4l

Step 4

Finding 17.5 can be found by dividing by ten to give 10%, halving that amount for 5% and halving that amount for 2.5%. These three amounts are then added to give 17.5%.

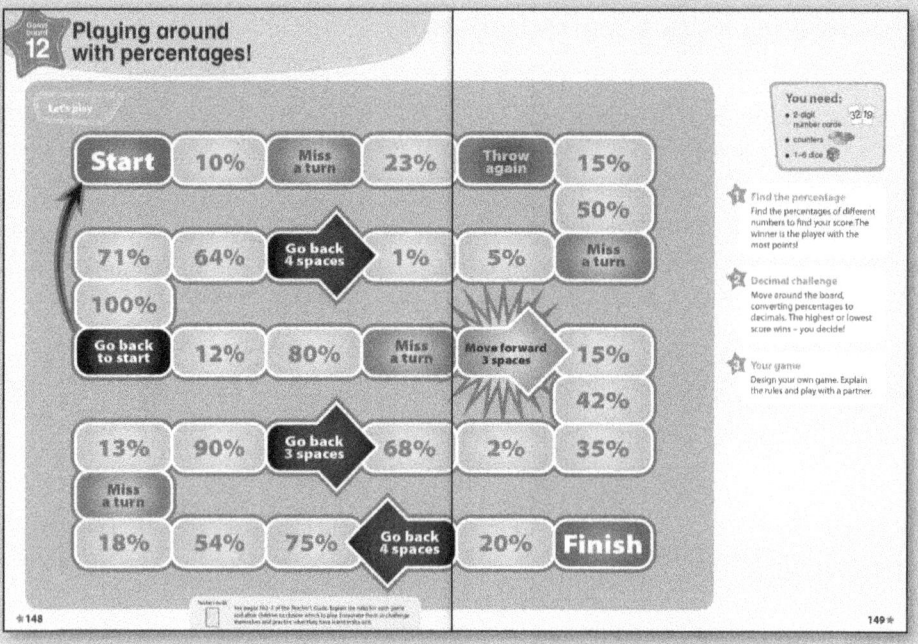

Game 1: Find the percentage

Children use the skills that they have learnt about percentages in this unit and apply them to the game.

Maths focus

- Finding percentages of number

Resources

2-digit number cards, 1 counter per player (1 colour per player), 1–6 dice (1).

How to play

Each player begins on Start. They take it in turns to throw the dice and move the number thrown around the gameboard. If they land on a percentage space they pick a number card and find the percentage of that number. Encourage them to find ten per cent of the number first and then use doubling, halving, multiplying and dividing by ten and simple addition and subtraction to find the different percentages.

When they have found the percentage of the number, they write it down, and this indicates the number of points they have scored. If they land on another space, they follow the instructions written.

When they land on Finish, they total their points. The winner is the player with the most points.

Making it easier

Give children number cards to 40 to use in the game. You could also simplify the percentages that they need to find to, e.g. 10%, 5%, 20% and 1%.

Making it harder

Give children 3-digit number cards to use in the game.

Game 2: Decimal challenge

This game reinforces children's understanding of how to convert a percentage to an equivalent decimal.

Maths focus

- Equivalent percentages and decimals

Resources

1–6 dice (1), 1 counter per player (1 colour per player).

How to play

Children take it in turns to throw the dice. They move around the board according to their dice throw. If they land on a percentage space they convert it to a decimal and write it down. Encourage them to make the link between percentages and their equivalent hundredths. If some children need to use place-value grids to help them as they play, ensure that these are provided.

When they reach the Finish they total the decimals. The highest or lowest score wins – let children decide.

Making it easier

Children could focus on converting percentages that are multiples of ten.

Making it harder

You could ask children to convert to fractions instead of decimals and add these.

Game 3: Your game

Children should invent their own game designing rules that use the concepts covered in the unit. Challenge children to make their game easier or harder.

Choose a game to play.

Game 1: Find the percentage

You need:
- 2-digit number cards
- 1 counter per player (1 colour per player)
- 1–6 dice

How to play
- Take it in turns to throw the dice and move around the board.
- If you land on a percentage space pick a number card and find the percentage of that number. Write it down – this is the number of points you have scored.
- If you land on another space, follow the instructions.
- When you get to Finish, total your points.
- The winner is the player with the most points!

Game 2: Decimal challenge

You need:
- 1 counter per player (1 colour per player)
- 1–6 dice

How to play
- Take it in turns to throw the dice and move around the board.
- If you land on a percentage space convert it to a decimal and write it down.
- When you get to Finish, total the decimals.
- The highest or lowest score wins – you decide!

Game 3: Your game

- Make up your own game using the gameboard.
- Perhaps you could use money instead of number cards?
- You could continue the game back to the Start or do something else.
- What are the rules for your game? Explain them to someone.

Please help your child by reading the instructions and playing the game together.

Assessment task 1

Running the task

Before they begin this task, write a mixture of fractions on the board. Ask children to write these down and beside them the appropriate equivalent decimals and percentages. Repeat this, writing decimals on the board and then percentages. Each time children can write them down and find the appropriate equivalences.

During the task, listen to groups of children discuss the statement and explain to each other why it is correct. Expect them to be able to tell you that decimals and percentages are both fractions but represented in different ways. Also expect them to talk about tenths and hundredths and their connection to multiples of $\frac{1}{10}$ and $\frac{1}{100}$. They should be able to tell you that one per cent is equivalent to $\frac{1}{100}$. They could refer to the fact that it is a special fraction.

You could ask children where they have heard the word 'cent' before. Agree in different currencies and establish that there are 100 cents in a dollar and in a Euro. Explain that this is the same for percentages, there are 100 in a whole. Once you have had this conversation, ask them to write an explanation as to why Theo is correct. They then convert the percentages listed to decimals and fractions. You could also give them an amount of money, a length, mass, capacity or volume and ask them to find the percentages of these amounts.

Evidencing mastery

If children are able to explain and demonstrate how to convert between fractions, decimals and percentages and can confidently and efficiently show examples, they are showing mastery in this area of mathematics.

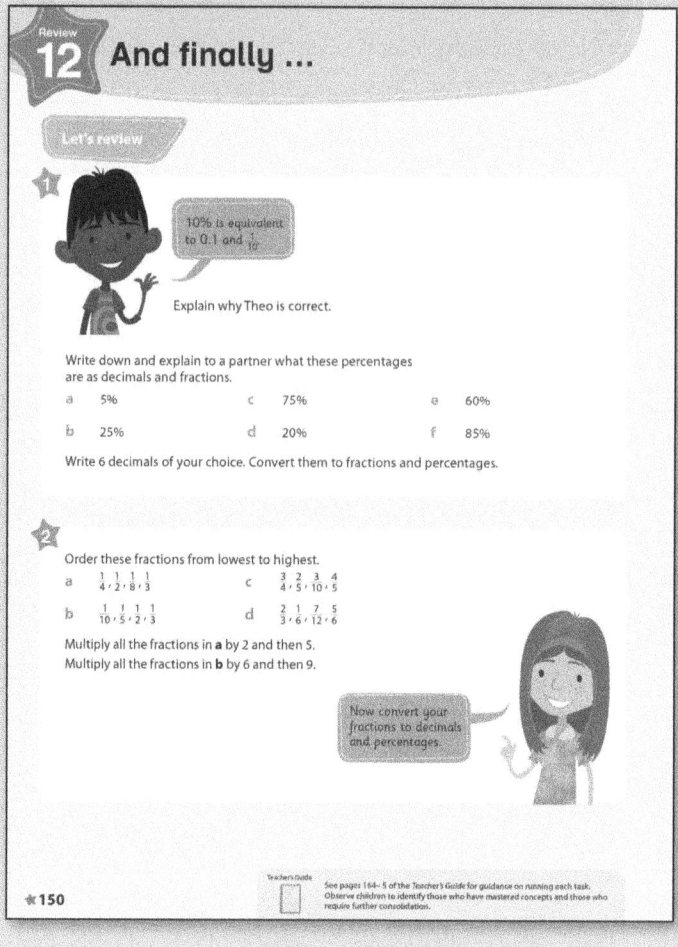

Assessment task 2

Running the task

Before beginning the task, ask groups of children to tell you how they would order fractions. Which part of the fraction would they consider first? Do they need to worry about the numerators? They should be able to tell you that the denominator is the part they need to consider and that the larger the denominator the smaller the fraction, because that means it is divided into more parts. You could ask children if this is always the case. Expect some to be able to tell you that it depends on the size of the whole. If they are the same then it is always smaller. If the size or quantity varies then it won't necessarily be smaller.

Agree that if it is a unit fraction they don't need to worry about the numerator but if it is a non-unit fraction they do. Discuss how they could convert the fractions to a common equivalent

and then ordering will be straightforward, e.g. in d) all the fractions can be turned into twelfths.

Once you have had this discussion, children can carry out the task which is to order sets of unit and non-unit fractions. Observe any children that you particularly wish to assess.

Children must then multiply the fractions in parts a) and b) by different whole numbers. They should attempt this without referring back to the concept spreads.

Observe whether children challenge themselves further by converting the fractions to decimals and percentages.

Evidencing mastery

If children can confidently explain and demonstrate how to order unit and non-unit fractions they are evidencing mastery in this area of mathematics.

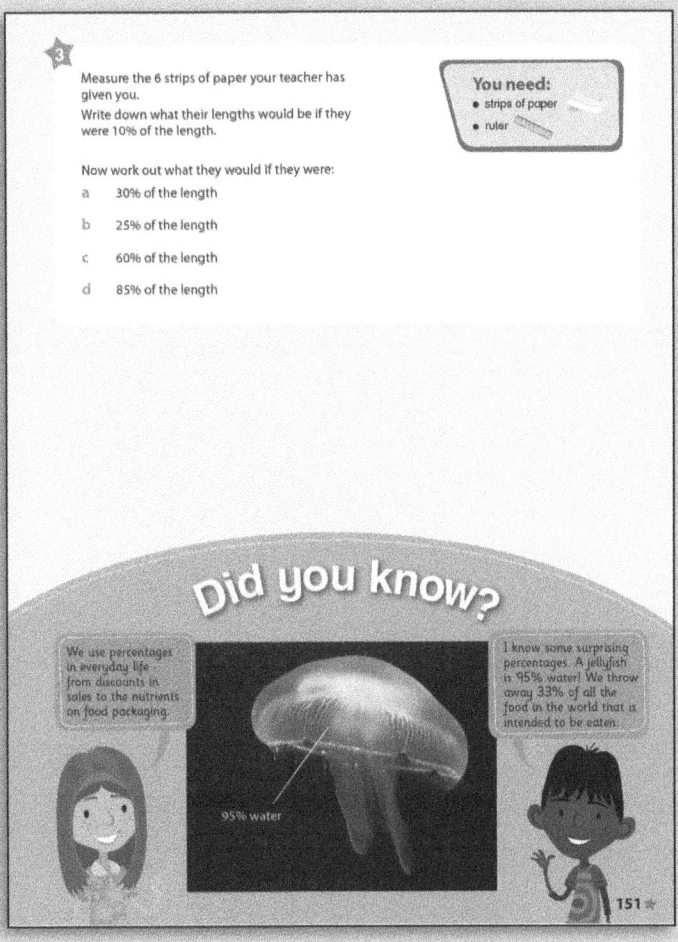

Did you know?

We use percentages in everyday life from discounts in sales to the nutrients on food packaging.

I know some surprising percentages. A jellyfish is 95% water! We throw away 33% of all the food in the world that is intended to be eaten.

95% water

151 ★

Assessment task 3

Resources

Strips of paper, rulers

Running the task

Prepare strips of paper of different lengths in whole centimetres. Give six strips to each child. Their task is to measure each and then record what the length would be if it was 10% of the length. They can record these as millimetres. Once children have found the length when 10% smaller they are asked to find lengths when smaller by different percentages.

Before the task, allow children to practise by drawing lines with a ruler to whole centimetre lengths and, working out 10% of the length and drawing the new length. It might help some children to convert the centimetres to millimetres.

Observe children as they complete the task and assess them to see how confident they are. As they work ask them to explain what happens when finding different percentages. It is important that they talk about dividing by ten for 10%. They could use this to find other percentages. Some may divide by 100 and multiply by the percentage. Encourage them to tell you what the new values of the numbers are.

Evidencing mastery

If children can explain and demonstrate confidently how to multiply and divide by ten and 100, they are showing mastery in this area of mathematics.

Did you know?

Ask children where they have seen percentages in real life. You might like to provide take away menus, catalogues, travel brochures and food packaging and ask them to find examples and to explain them.

You could explain that percentages add a common meaning to results. You could say, e.g. that 25% of children in school have school dinners, which means one in four children. This is a lot easier to understand than saying 120 out of 480 children have school dinners.

Go through the interesting percentages highlighted by Theo in the Textbook. You could challenge children to research more amazing percentages of their own, using the Internet.

Concepts mastered

✓ Children can explain and demonstrate how to find equivalent fractions and also to convert improper fractions to mixed numbers and vice versa.

✓ Children can explain and demonstrate how to convert fractions to decimals and vice versa and also explain the value of the digits in a number with three decimal places.

✓ Children can explain and demonstrate how to find percentages of different amounts and explain and demonstrate equivalences between percentages and fractions.

Mathematical focus

★ **Number: multiplication and division, fractions**

★ **Measurement: length, mass, volume, capacity**

Prior learning

Children should already be able to:

- recognise multiples and factors

- recognise square and cube numbers

- know what is meant by a prime number, prime factor and composite number

- use known facts to multiply and divide

- understand how to use the short method for multiplication of 3-digit numbers by single digits

- understand how to use the short method for division of 3-digit numbers by single digits.

Unit 13 Factors, scaling and long multiplication and division

I wonder what this mass is in pounds?

78p per cake

How much would it cost me in total to buy 15 cupcakes?

★152

Key new learning

- Identify multiples and factors, including finding all factor pairs of a number, and common factors of two numbers.

- Multiply and divide numbers mentally, drawing upon known facts.

- Solve problems involving addition, subtraction, multiplication and division and a combination of these.

- Solve problems involving multiplication and division, including scaling by simple fractions and problems involving simple rates.

- Multiply numbers up to four digits by a single- or 2-digit number using a formal written method, including long multiplication for 2-digit numbers.

- Divide numbers up to four digits by a single-digit number using the formal written method of short division and interpret remainders appropriately for the context.

Making connections

- This unit draws together a range of areas of mathematics, including multiplication and division, factors and prime factors.

- Scaling up and scaling down is used frequently in real life, for example currency conversion and converting between imperial and metric units of measure. Draw in as many real-life contexts as possible to engage children.

Talk about

It is important to reinforce the fact that the written methods are not always the most appropriate methods to use for calculating. Sometimes mental calculation strategies (with jottings if appropriate) are more efficient. For the calculation 238×5, the strategy $\times 10$ and halve is more appropriate.

Discuss the metric and imperial systems, particularly the latter. Most will know miles as we still use these to measure distance. Some may be familiar with feet and inches because parents sometimes use these to measure height. Some may know stones and pounds as these are often still used to measure weight.

Engaging and exploring

You could ask children to look at each picture and the comments or questions that go with it and discuss with a partner what it might be about. Focus on each picture in turn.

For the picture with the bathroom scales, you could ask children what units we usually use to measure mass. Agree kilograms and grams. Explain that these are metric measurements. Inform them that before we used metric measurements we used something called imperial measurements. Ask them if they know of any.

Ask children to look at the scales in the Textbook and to read the mass shown, reminding them, if necessary, that there are 14 pounds in a stone. Tell children that there are approximately 2.2 pounds in a kilogram. You could ask them to convert different numbers of pounds to kilograms and

vice versa. It is helpful to use a scaling model to do this, e.g. 1 kg = 2.2 lbs, 2 kg = 4.4 lbs, 4 kg = 8.8 lbs, 8 kg = 17.6 lbs. Once they have these facts they can manipulate them to get many different amounts, e.g. 6 kg, 16 kg and 20 kg. You could use real scales and a variety of objects to generate the different masses for conversion.

For the photo of the cupcakes you could ask children what their favourite type of cake is. You could display their choices as a tally chart and ask them to make a pictogram, bar or pie chart to show the information.

Ask them to find what fraction of the total each type of favourite cake makes up, e.g. $\frac{2}{3}$, $\frac{4}{5}$ and $\frac{7}{15}$. They could order the fractions from smallest to largest.

Ask children to tell you all the ways they can think of to find the price of 15 cupcakes. Invite individuals to share the methods that they thought of. Expect them to use partitioning, the grid method, the short written method and mental calculation strategies, i.e. multiplying by 10, halving and adding the two numbers together. Discuss which they think is the most efficient strategy. Agree that the latter is the most efficient strategy for many people.

For the picture of the milk carton you could ask children to tell you what 2.6 l is in millilitres and litres and millilitres. Call out some volumes for children to convert between litres and millilitres.

Ask children if they know what imperial measurements are used to measure volume and capacity. Establish that pints and gallons are used. Inform children that 568 ml is equivalent to one pint. Call out some millilitres for children to convert to pints and vice versa. Use the scaling model for this as suggested above.

Ask children how they could work out how much drink would be in a glass if 2.6 l were shared equally into eight glasses. Agree that they could divide 2.6 by 8. They could do this using a halving strategy or the short method for division. Model how to do this using coloured counters to represent the different values of the digits. See Unit 3 for details of how to do this. The answer is 0.325 l. Ask children what that would be in millilitres. Agree 325 ml.

For the picture with the present you could discuss how to find the volume of a cube. Agree that you multiply the length by the width and then by the height. Agree that a cube has lengths, widths and heights that are the same. Call out some dimensions for a cube. Children work out the volume. Agree that they are multiplying the same number twice, so finding cube numbers.

Spend some time considering factors and multiples. You could ask children to list all the factors of the cubes they found. They could pick one of these factors and write down some of its multiples. They could find a number that has two or three common factors.

Things to think about

- How will you organise your class into mixed attainment groups of four and also give opportunities for children of similar attainment levels to work together?

- What will be the most effective way to plan focus group work?

- How can you ensure that all children are able to access their learning?

- What strategies will you use to develop reasoning through questioning?

- How will you use visual representations to help conceptual understanding with all children?

Checking understanding

You will know children have mastered these concepts when they can explain and demonstrate appropriate methods for multiplication and division, including within the context of measure.

- Identify multiples and factors, including finding all factor pairs of a number, and common factors of two numbers.
- Solve problems involving multiplication and division including using their knowledge of factors and multiples, squares and cubes.

Homework 71 and 72   Practice Book pp 114–17   100 Squares

Representations and resources

Individual clocks, time number lines, rulers.

Mathematical vocabulary

Multiply, divide, multiplication, division, multiplicand, multiplier, product, dividend, divisor, quotient, factor, multiple, prime factor

Warming up

Give each child a clock. Ask them to find different times and show you them. Recap the importance of moving the hour hand between the hour numbers because it moves slowly to the next hour as the time changes. Call out analogue times for them to find and ask them to write the 12- and then 24-hour digital times. Ask questions that involve finding time durations and differences. You could encourage children to use a time number line to do this.

Background knowledge

Children need to be aware that our number system is infinite; no one has ever found the highest number. This means that there are an infinite number of multiples of all the numbers and these numbers all have different numbers of factors. Children need to know that a factor is the multiplicand and multiplier of a multiplication and the divisor and quotient of a division. They need to understand that a common factor is a factor of two or more multiples and that a prime factor is a factor that is a prime number. They will need to know about square and cube numbers for some of the Textbook activities, so be sure to recap these when appropriate.

Let's learn: Modelling and teaching

Factors

- Ask : *What do you know about factors?* Bring out these facts: two factors multiplied together create a product; a factor is the multiplicand and multiplier of a multiplication and the divisor and quotient of a division. Ask them to write multiplication and division statements circling the factors.

- Ask them to look at the multiplication table in the Textbook and to identify the factors of 24, 48 and 96. Give the children 24 counters and ask them to prove that it has factors of 2, 3, 4, 6, 8 and 12 by sharing them into piles of those sizes. Can they find all of them, including those not on the table? Ask them to choose other numbers and to find all their factors.

- Recap prime factors. Agree that they are factors that are prime numbers. Ask children to find the prime numbers on the multiplication table in the Textbook.

- Call out some numbers and ask children to find a factor pair

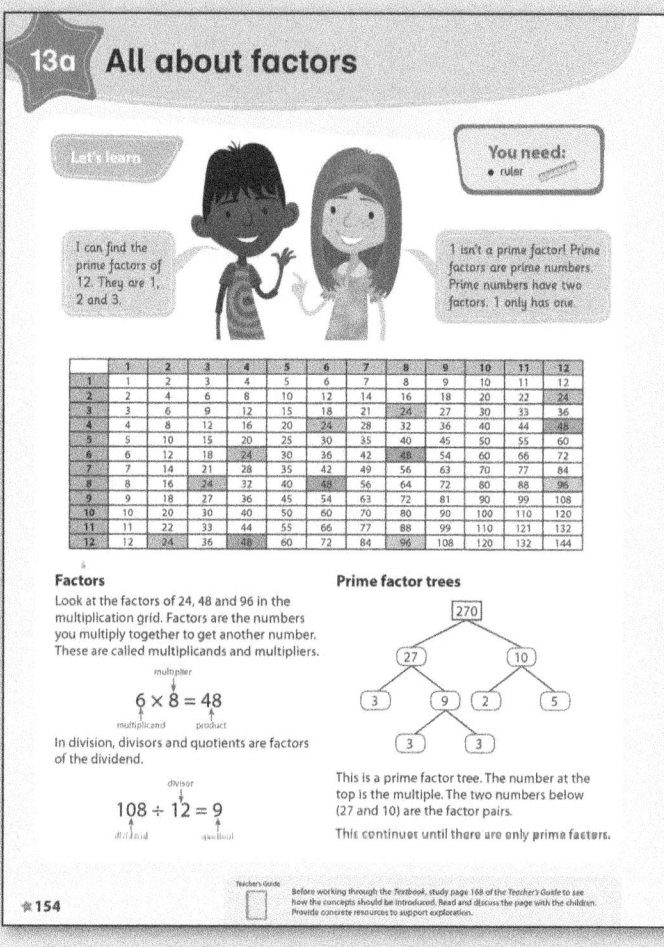

and then find the factors of those until all the factors are prime numbers, e.g. for 18 the factor pair could be 2 and 9.

Prime factor trees

- Ask children to look at the factor tree in the Textbook. Can they suggest reasons why it is called a factor tree? They might suggest that it looks like a root system or branches.

- Ask them to talk to a partner about what is happening on the tree. Establish that the number at the top is the multiple and the two numbers below are a factor pair that make it, in this case 27 and 10. Then the other numbers under 27 and 10 are their factor pairs and this continues until only prime factors are left.

- Explain that this is a useful model to use to find prime factors of different numbers. Ask children to make some up.

Let's practise: Digging deeper

Step 1

To show their understanding that a factor is the multiplicand or multiplier of a multiplication and the divisor or quotient of a division children make up pairs of multiplication and division statements and circle the factors. You could ask them to make more than two statements. Listen carefully to to ensure children are using precise mathematical vocabulary.

Step 2

Before children begin the task, recap what multiples and factors are. Expect them to explain that a multiple is the product of two factors and to give examples, e.g. 56 is a multiple of the factor pair 7 and 8. Expect children to explain that a factor is either the divisor or product of a multiple and again give examples, e.g. 9 is a factor of 81. You could invite children to write multiplication and division statements on the board and highlight which numbers are the multiples and factors.

The task asks children to create prime factor trees. They can choose their own factor pairs to make all the multiples. If any children need the support of the factor tree in the Textbook, let them use it.

Step 3

Before the task ask children to explain what a prime number is and to give examples. Expect them to tell you that they are numbers with two factors, the number itself and one. Write a selection of numbers on the board between 20 and 50. Ask children to identify the primes. The task asks children to draw lines the length of all the prime numbers to 20. Encourage them to measure accurately.

Step 4

To show a deepening understanding children need to use their knowledge to find the number Theo is thinking of. The key clue here is that it has an odd number of factors. Children should by now know that the number must either be a square or cube number. This reduces their options considerably.

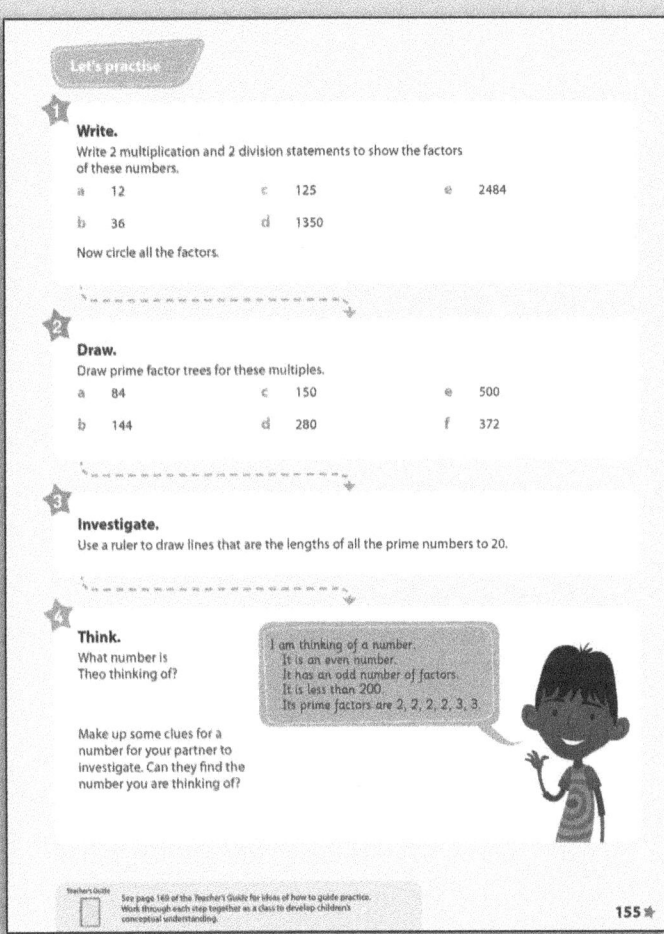

Ensuring progress

Supporting understanding

Children who need support would benefit from using the multiplication grid in the Textbook for many of the suggested activities. You may wish to work with them as a focus group to ensure they have a developing understanding. If they are struggling to grasp the concept, you could accept fewer multiples and factors for the first three steps.

Broadening understanding

You could provide opportunities for children to solve problems and investigations using multiples and factors and also square, cube and prime numbers. As they work through some, encourage them to devise problems of their own to give to other members of the class to solve.

 Concept mastered

Children can explain and demonstrate factors, factor pairs, prime factors and multiples.

Answers

Step 3

Lines length: 2 cm 3 cm, 5 cm, 7 cm, 11 cm, 13 cm, 17 cm, 19 cm.

Step 4

It has an odd number of factors which means that it is a square number. If you multiply the prime factors you get 144 which fits all the criteria.

Follow-up ideas

- Children could make up a two-criteria Carroll diagram, with headings: square numbers/not square numbers and multiples of 4/not multiples of 4 or similar. They then populate each section with appropriate numbers. They could also do this without labelling the headings and ask a partner to work out what they should be.

- You could time children for two minutes and have a competition to find who has generated the most multiples of a number that the class chooses.

- Children could make up an information poster about multiples, factors and square, cube and prime numbers, including prime factors. They should include all they have learnt over the year, use correct vocabulary and give examples.

- Multiply and divide numbers mentally drawing upon known facts.
- Solve problems involving addition, subtraction, multiplication and division and a combination of these.
- Solve problems involving multiplication and division, including scaling by simple fractions and problems involving simple rates.

Homework 73 and 74   Practice Book pp 118–20

Representations and resources

Sets of digit cards, squared paper, counters, sand, scales, plastic bags.

Mathematical vocabulary

Multiply, divide, multiplication, multiplicand, multiplier, product, dividend, divisor, quotient, numerator, denominator, operator

Warming up

Write a multiplication statement on the board, e.g. $6 \times 7 = 42$. Give children two minutes to generate as many other facts as they can by multiplying and dividing by ten, doubling and halving and adding and subtracting, e.g. $60 \times 7 = 420$, $60 \times 3.5 = 210$.

Background knowledge

It is important to give children opportunities to explore mental calculation strategies for multiplication and division. This concept explores another model for multiplication and division called scaling up and down. Scaling down also links well to fractions and they are both a form of ratio. Developing children's conceptual understanding of this in order to help them when they look at ratio as a topic in Year 6.

Let's learn: Modelling and teaching

Mental calculation

- Discuss the strategy Theo suggests for multiplying by 15. Give numbers for them to multiply by 15 using this strategy.

- Discuss the other strategies mentioned in the Textbook. Give each child a set of digit cards. They can generate 2-, 3- or 4-digit numbers and multiply them by 5, 20 and 4 in the ways suggested. Ask children to draw bar models (as modelled in the Textbook) to show that they understand this.

- Agree that division is the inverse operation to multiplication and therefore these strategies can be used to divide. The opposite procedure should be used, e.g. when dividing by five, they need to divide a number by ten and double. Ask children to use digit cards to generate numbers to divide by 5, 20 and 4. Children should consolidate their understanding by drawing a bar model.

- Emphasise the importance of knowing multiplication tables. Give an example such as $8 \times 7 = 56$ and ask children to generate as many facts as they can in two minutes.

- Provide data for time and distance or temperature, e.g.

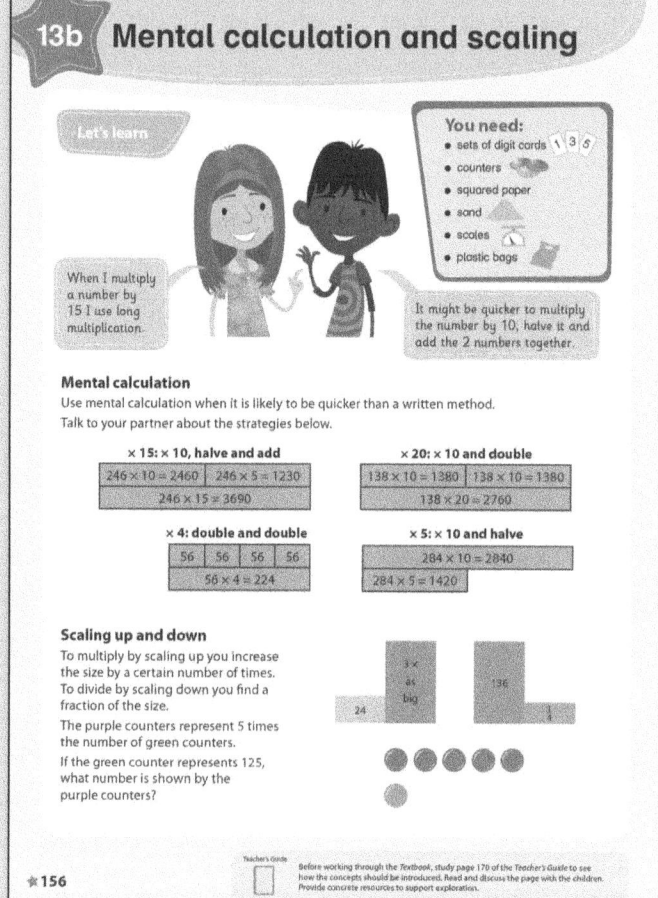

distance travelled over a period of a number of hours, average monthly temperatures over a year. Children create line graphs to show the information where the vertical axis has intervals increasing in a particular multiplication table.

Scaling up and down

- Ask children to tell a partner all they can remember about scaling up and down.

- Give children counters and ask them to use these to demonstrate the model for scaling up and down that is shown in the Textbook. Give them similar problems to those given to model in this way.

- Give children squared paper and repeat the above. This time they can draw bar models to show scaling up and down.

Let's practise: Digging deeper

Step 1

Remind children of the strategies they looked at in the lesson for multiplication and division, with several examples of each to answer.

Children need to multiply the amounts using the mental calculation strategies discussed during the lesson. They need to explain what they did. They could use bar models to do this.

In the second part they divide the amounts using mental calculation strategies for division. Again, they explain their methods.

Step 2

In this task children solve problems by scaling up and down. They could use counters before they draw the bar models. Encourage them to read the questions carefully. Once they have solved the problems, they can make up some of their own. Encourage them

to make these up within the context of measures.

Step 3

In this task, children will put what they have learned about scaling up into a practical context. You will need to provide small groups of children with sand, plastic sandwich bags and weighing scales. Children take it in turns to measure out the correct amount of sand and place it in one of the bags. Encourage them to be as accurate as possible.

Once they have their bags, they work out how heavy the bags would be if the mass is scaled up six times. They need to show how they work out the new amounts using counters and then by drawing the bar model. Encourage them to write the amounts in kilograms and grams as appropriate. They weigh these amounts of sand on the scales, fill some more bags and then compare to see the difference in sizes. Ask children if their results are a surprise or as expected.

Step 4

Children create a pictorial representation (bar model) and use it to find a value. You could give children squared paper. They draw a rectangle and another three times the size. They record its value. They then draw more bars and find their values by scaling up and down. Ask them to record their answer using abstract symbols and mathematical notation.

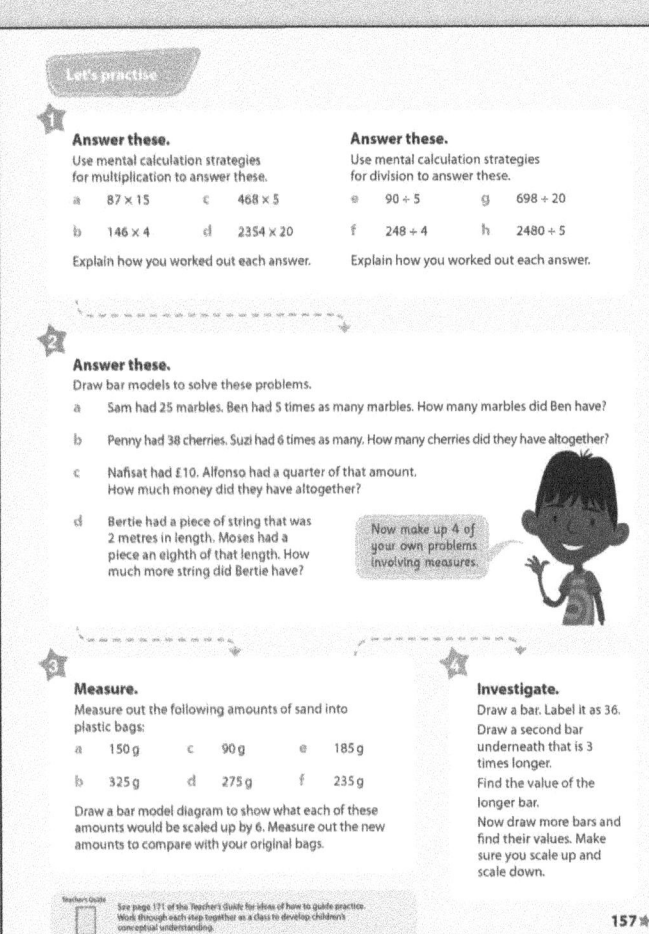

Ensuring progress

Supporting understanding

For the first task, work with children in a focus group. Give them options for possible mental calculation strategies and ask them to choose which they think is the best one. Then give them 2-digit numbers to multiply independently.

Broadening understanding

Ask children to explain scaling up and down and the links to fractions to a child who needs their understanding of this concept reinforcing.

 Concept mastered

Children can explain and demonstrate mental multiplication and division and why these are more efficient than written methods. They are also able to explain and demonstrate scaling up and down.

Follow-up ideas

- Give children a set of digit cards. They put these in a pile face down on the table. They make up a 2-digit number and pick a digit card. They then scale their number up by the amount on the card. They repeat this with other digit cards. After about four goes, the child with the highest number wins.

- Give children millimetre measurements. They draw these and then scale them up by six times and draw the new lengths.

- Children give each other problems to solve involving measurement. The problems should involve multiplying or dividing using a mental calculation strategy.

Answers

Step 1

a   1305

b   584

c   2340

d   47 080

e   18

f   62

g   349

h   496

Step 2

a   125

b   266

c   £12.50

d   1 m 75 cm

Step 3

a   150 g scaled up to 900 g

b   325 g scaled up to 1950 g or 1 kg 950 g or 1.95 kg

c   90 g scaled up to 540 g

d   275 g scaled up to 1650 g or 1 kg 650 g or 1.65 kg

e   185 g scaled up to 1110 g or 1 kg 110 g or 1.11 kg

f   235 g scaled up to 1410 g or 1 kg 410 g or 1.41 kg

Step 4

Children should first draw a bar labelled 108. They should then draw other scaled bars showing correct multiples of 36, e.g. 72, 144, 180 etc.

4-digit and long multiplication

- Multiply numbers up to four digits by a single- or 2-digit number using a formal written method, including long multiplication for 2-digit numbers.

Homework 75 and 76   Practice Book pp 121–5

Mathematical vocabulary

Multiplication, division, factor, multiplicand, multiplier, product, dividend, divisor, quotient

Representations and resources

Counters (different colours), digit cards, money (coins).

Warming up

Practise converting between units of measure. You could write an amount, e.g. 2 kg 450 g on the board for children to convert to grams and then kilograms. You could do this for any measure including money with pounds and pence and time with hours, minutes and seconds.

Background knowledge

The written method for multiplication should be taught and practised in a way that helps children to develop their conceptual understanding and procedural fluency. Manipulatives are an important tool in aiding their understanding. When they multiply encourage children to make arrays and understand how these can be translated into the grid method and then the short method. For long multiplication explore the links between the grid methods, using first two calculations and then one calculation.

Let's learn: Modelling and teaching

4-digit multiplication

- Ask children to tell you what they think is the same about the three models in the Textbook. Then ask them to tell you the differences between them. Agree that they all show the same calculation but in different ways. Ask children to find 9000, 1500, 120 and 18 in each of the models.

- Set some 4-digit by single-digit multiplication calculations for children to set out in arrays using coloured counters, each colour representing a different value. As you write them on the board tell children the name of each number (multiplicand and multiplier). Remind children that product is the answer. They can record what they do using both the grid and short written method.

Long multiplication

- Write the example from the Textbook on the board, i.e. 567 x 24. Explain that children could make an array but would need a lot of counters to do this. So instead they will use the grid and explore how to write two multiplication calculations. Ask them to find similarities between the two in the Textbook. Ask questions such as: *Where can you see 11 340 in the grid? What about in the written method? What about 2268?*

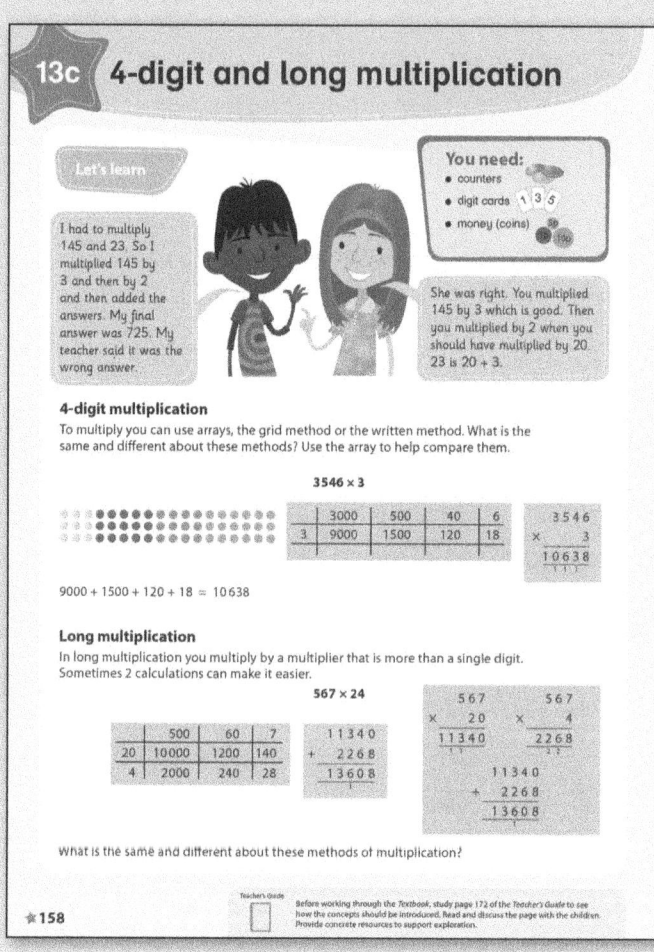

- Set more calculations like this one for children to answer using the grid method. As you do this recap the vocabulary.

- Explore a long multiplication, which is basically the two shorter methods put together. Set some calculations for children to work through using this method.

- Ask children to use five or six digit cards to make up calculations. They can use three or four cards to create the multiplicands and one or two cards for the multipliers. Encourage them to use the short written method and check their answers using the grid method. If creating long multiplication calculations, you could ask them to solve these using the two part method as described in the Textbook.

Let's practise: Digging deeper

Step 1

Recap the written method with some 4-digit examples. Encourage children to begin by setting out the calculations as arrays to reinforce their conceptual understanding. This will prepare them to write the appropriate grid method. They check using the short written method. During the task ask children to work with a partner and take turns to explain what they are doing. It is important that children experience all three methods because this is the first time they have multiplied 4-digit numbers. This will help to develop their conceptual understanding.

Arrays are very cumbersome when it comes to setting out a long multiplication. For the second part of this step begin by rehearsing some examples of the methods for long multiplication beginning with the grid method, then the two written calculations and adding the two products together, finally the actual long multiplication calculation. Ensure that children can explain what is happening in each method and that they can make the links between them. In this part of the task, children need to answer the calculations using the long multiplication method and then check their solutions using the grid method.

Step 2

This task requires children to make up their own 4-digit long multiplication calculations using digit cards to generate their numbers. They do this five times. They can use the grid method, written method or make two calculations and total them. This will give you some idea of their confidence in answering these types of calculation. You could discuss with them why they chose the particular method they used.

Step 3

Children work in pairs. Provide them with a pile of pound coins, ten pence coins and pennies. They make an amount between £5 and £10. They then work out how much money they would have if the amount was scaled up 15 times. Again, they can choose their method for finding the total. After they have found this, they scale the amount up by 16 and then 24.

Step 4

Children need to work out how Amy could have solved her multiplication. Strategies could include an array, the grid method, the short written method and the mental calculation strategy of doubling, doubling and doubling again.

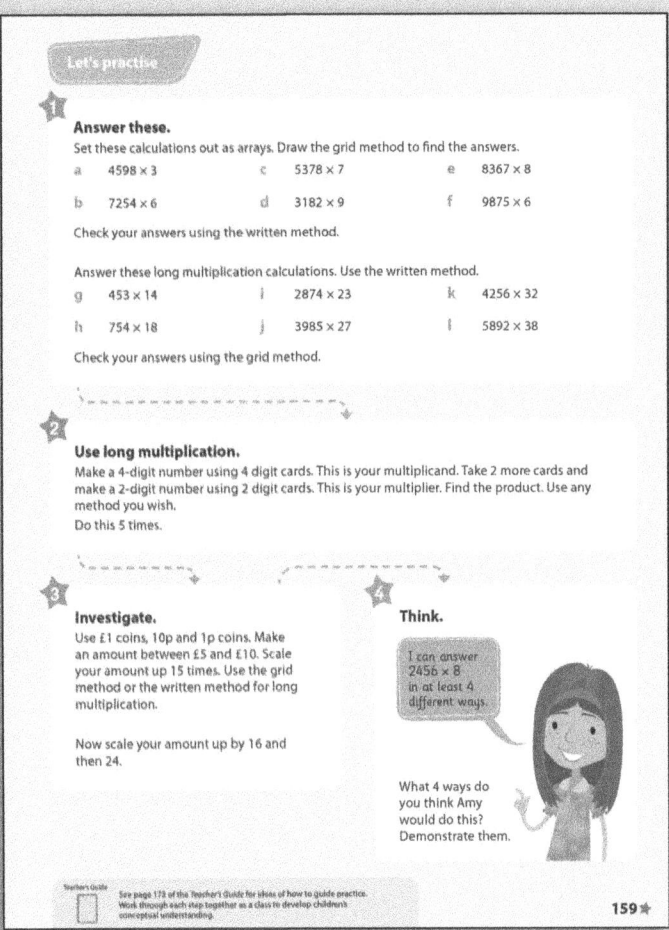

Ensuring progress

Supporting understanding

It is important that all children continue to develop a conceptual understanding of the written methods and do not simply learn rules. Some children might need the use of manipulatives for longer than other children. Some children may benefit from being encouraged to make two calculations for long multiplication.

Broadening understanding

Provide opportunities for children to explain the written methods for multiplication to their peers using manipulatives or the grid method and then translate these to the written methods. They could make up and solve word problems within different contexts such as length, mass and money. Encourage them to solve long multiplication calculations using one step.

Follow-up ideas

- You could ask children to make an information poster to explain how to answer long multiplication calculations.

- You could encourage children to make up a game that involves multiplication. They could create their own gameboard and make up calculations that need answering, e.g. 459 × 14.

- Ask children to look at shopping websites and to find the cost of different food items. They can then work out how much these items would cost for varying amounts.

 Concept mastered

Children can explain and demonstrate how the long multiplication method works.

Answers

Step 1

a	13 794	d	28 638	g	6 342	j	107 595
b	43 524	e	66 936	h	13 572	k	136 192
c	37 646	f	59 250	i	66 102	l	223 896

Step 4

Children should be able to demonstrate an array (by drawing coloured counters), the grid method, the short written method and the mental calculation strategy of doubling, doubling and doubling again.

- Divide numbers up to four digits by a single-digit number using the formal written method of short division and interpret remainders appropriately for the context.

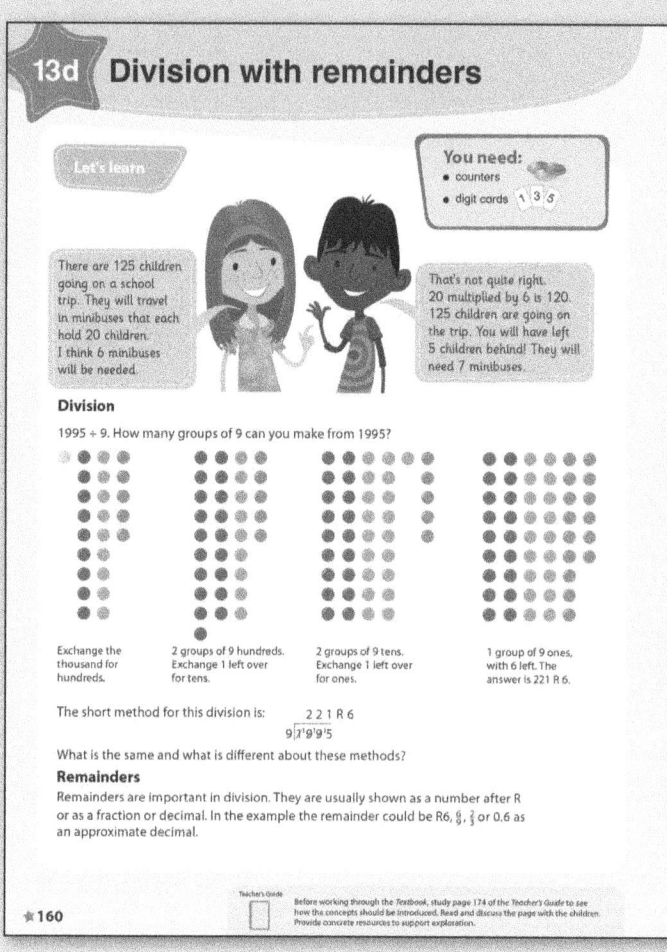

Homework 77 and 78   Practice Book pp 126–7

Representations and resources
Counters (different colours), digit cards.

Mathematical vocabulary
Division, division bracket, factor, dividend, divisor, quotient

Warming up
Write a multiplication statement on the board. Give children two minutes to work out and write down as many new facts as they can from this, e.g. $8 \times 9 = 72$, $80 \times 9 = 720$, $80 \times 4.5 = 360$. Encourage them to use doubling and halving and multiplying and dividing by 10. After two minutes, take feedback inviting children to write their ideas on the board. You could give them another two minutes. They can use some of the examples given to generate new facts. You could repeat this for a division statement, e.g. $42 \div 7 = 6$.

Background knowledge
The written method for division.should be taught and practised in a way that helps them to develop their conceptual understanding and procedural fluency. Manipulatives are an important aid to understanding. Remainders link to work on fractions and decimals and also interpret remainders according to context.

Let's learn: Modelling and teaching
Division
- Encourage children to explore similar calculations to the one described in the Textbook. They can use four sets of different-coloured counters and assign their own values to them. They set out, e.g. 5736 with their counters. Ask them to demonstrate to their partner what happens when they divide this by four.

- Together, model the written method. Write the calculation $1615 \div 5$ and $5\overline{)1\,615}$. Ask children what is the same about these calculations and what is different. Draw out the difference between the division symbol and the division bracket. Ask them to tell you which is the dividend, which is the divisor and what the answer is called. Agree that you need to find out how many groups of the divisor they can make from the dividend. Ask them to hold up the thousand counter. Agree that it needs to be exchanged for hundreds. Now there are 16 hundreds. Agree they can make three groups of five hundreds and one will be left over. This needs exchanging for tens. There are now 11 tens. These make two groups of five tens with one left over. This is exchanged for ones. This will now make three groups of ones, giving 323.

- Give children examples to work with that have no remainders. Children model with counters and write the appropriate stages of the calculations as they work.

Remainders
- Model the problem that the Amy is talking about using counters representing the different values.

- Give children calculations to solve that will have remainders. They can choose whether to use manipulatives or simply the written method only. They represent the remainders as fractions.

Let's practise: Digging deeper
Step 1
The task asks children to show how the remainder to the division calculations can be represented as a fraction and then a decimal. The solutions to the divisions have been provided, so that they can focus on the remainders. Encourage them to work out the lowest term for the fraction remainders. The second part of the task asks children to solve the calculation and then represent any remainders as fractions. You might like to reinforce conceptual understanding by first asking children to model the division using counters, and then to draw what they have done. Ask them to explain how the counters, drawing and formal written method show the same calculation.

Step 2
Children need digit cards for this task. They use these to generate numbers. They pick four cards and make the dividend. They then

pick a fifth card which needs to be between 5 and 9. This card is the divisor. They set their calculation out and answer it, writing any remainders as a fraction or decimal. It would be a good idea to model an example before they begin. They can choose whether to use manipulatives or not. They do this five times.

Step 3
This task gives a problem in context. The aim is to encourage children to consider what to do with the remainder. In this case, there will be books left over and so they need to go on an additional shelf. Therefore the answer is rounded up. Encourage children to explain why. They should then make up some of their own problems for the class to solve.

Step 4
Before this task explore the rules of divisibility. Children should know that any even number can be divided by two; that an even number that is also a multiple of four can be divided by four; a multiple of five and ten can be divided by five and a multiple of ten can be divided by ten.

Ask them to write down some multiples of three and to notice what they all have in common (the digit total will be 2, 6 and 9). Next ask them to complete the task.

Theo knows there will be no remainder because a number that can equally be divided by nine has a digit total of nine $(2 + 4 + 6 + 6 = 18, 1 + 8 = 9)$.

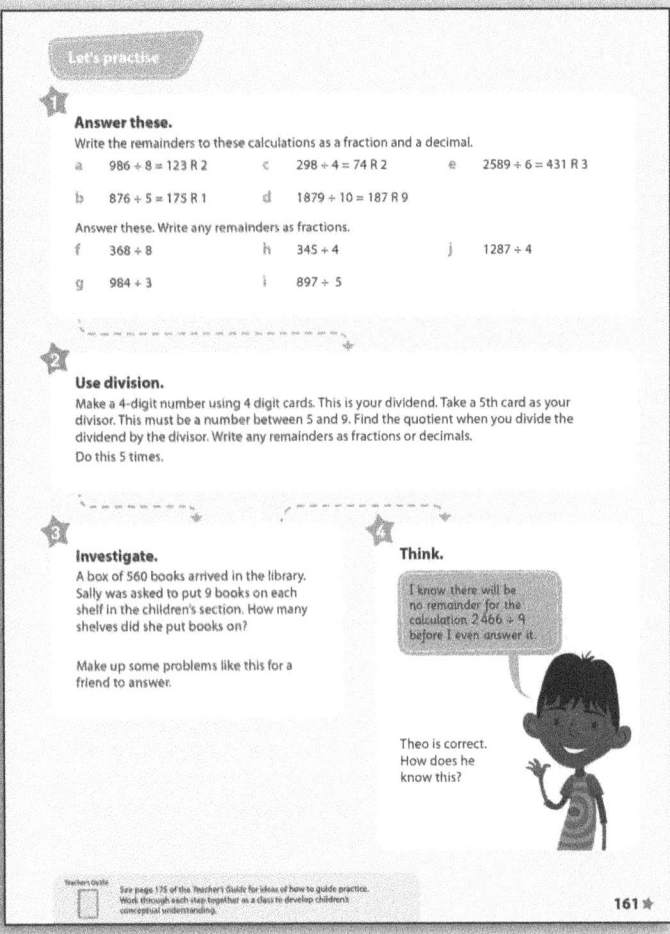

Ensuring progress
Supporting understanding
Some children might need the use of manipulatives for longer than other children. You might need to take them back to working with 2-digit numbers initially and build up to 3- and then 4-digits.

Broadening understanding
Provide opportunities for children to explain the written method for division to their peers using manipulatives. They could make up and solve word problems within different contexts such as length, mass and money.

✓ Concept mastered
Children can explain exactly how a division calculation works to show conceptual understanding. They will also have mastered the concept of remainders if they can explain what one is, what they would need to do with one in a problem and how these appear as fractions and decimals.

Follow-up ideas
- You could ask children to make an information poster to explain how to answer division calculations.
- You could encourage children to make up a game that involves division. They could create their own game board and make up calculations that need answering, e.g. 365 ÷ 5.
- Ask children to look at shopping websites and to find the cost of different food items per kilogram. They then work out how much these items would cost for varying amounts, e.g. 200g, 375g.

Answers
Step 1
a $\frac{2}{8}$ or $\frac{1}{4}$ and 0.25
b $\frac{1}{5}$ and 0.2
c $\frac{2}{4}$ or $\frac{1}{2}$ and 0.5
d $\frac{9}{10}$ and 0.9
e $\frac{3}{6}$ or $\frac{1}{2}$ and 0.5
f 46
g 328
h $86\frac{1}{4}$
i $79\frac{2}{5}$
j $321\frac{3}{4}$

Step 3
63 shelves

Step 4
Children should be able to explain that, according to the rules of divisibility, all numbers that are divisible by 9 have digits that total 9 or a multiple of 9. Check children understand that they need to keep summing digits until they have a 1-digit answer.

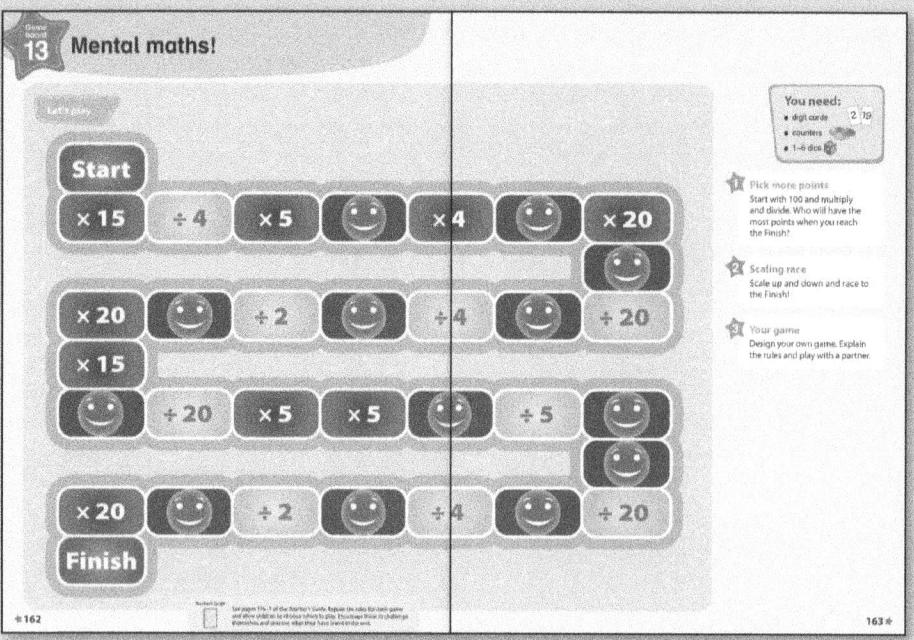

Game 1: Pick more points

This game is designed to help children reinforce, rehearse and consolidate the mental calculation strategies that they have learned for multiplication and division.

Maths focus

- Mental calculation strategies for multiplication and division

Resources

1 counter per player (1 colour per player), 1–6 dice (1), digit cards.

How to play

Before they play the game, ask children to tell you efficient mental methods for multiplying by 2, 4, 5, 15 and 20 and to demonstrate these with numbers that they choose for themselves. Repeat this for dividing by 2, 4, 5 and 20. Remind children that these are often more efficient ways to multiply and divide than carrying out a written method.

Each player puts their counter on the Start. They begin the game with 100 points. They take it in turns to throw the dice. If they land on an operation they do what it says to their points. If they land on a smiley face they miss a turn. The winner is the player with the highest number of points when all the players land on Finish.

Making it easier

Children could just focus on one operation, e.g. × 5.

Making it harder

You could give children a different starting number of points, e.g. 175.

Game 2: Scaling race

This game is designed to help children reinforce, rehearse and consolidate the work that they covered on scaling up and down by doubling, halving or multiplying, or dividing by ten and adjusting.

Maths focus

- Scaling up and down

Resources

1 counter per player (1 colour per player), digit cards, 1–6 dice (1).

How to play

Each player puts their counter on the Start. They pick two digit cards and make a 2-digit number. They take it in turns to throw the dice. If they land on a space with a multiplication, they scale their number by the amount it says. Encourage them to use doubling whenever possible or multiplying by ten and halving or doubling. If they land on a division they scale the number down. Encourage them to use halving and dividing by ten. If they land on a smiley face they miss a turn. The first player to reach Finish is the winner.

Making it easier

Children could use single-digit cards and focus on scaling up only.

Making it harder

Children could use three or four digit cards to make 3- or 4-digit numbers.

Game 3: Your game

Children should invent their own game, designing rules that use the concepts covered in the unit. Challenge children to make their game easier or harder.

Mental maths!

Choose a game to play.

Game 1: Pick more points

How to play
- Each place your counter on Start.
- Each player starts the game with 100 points.
- Take it in turns to throw the dice and move around the board.
- Do what it says to your points. If you land on a smiley face miss a turn.
- The winner is the player with the highest number of points when everyone gets to Finish.

You need:
- 1 counter per player (1 colour per player)
- 1–6 dice

Game 2: Scaling race

How to play
- Pick 2 digit cards and make a 2-digit number.
- Each place your counter on Start.
- Take it in turns to throw the dice and move around the board.
- If you land on a space with a multiplication, scale your number by that amount.
- If you land on a division, scale your number down.
- If you land on a smiley face, miss a turn.
- The first player to reach Finish is the winner.

You need:
- 1 counter per player (1 colour per player)
- 1–6 dice
- digit cards

Game 3: Your game

- Make up your own game using the gameboard.
- Will your game be a race or about having the most points?
- Perhaps the player with the lowest number of points could win?
- What are the rules for your game? Explain them to someone.

Please help your child by reading the instructions and playing the game together.

Assessment task 1

Running the task

Before beginning this assessment task, recap with the class the mental calculation strategies they learnt about for multiplication and division. Agree that the main ones were:

- multiplying by four by doubling and doubling
- multiplying by five by multiplying by ten and halving
- multiplying by 20 by multiplying by ten and doubling
- dividing by four by halving and halving again
- dividing by five by dividing by ten and doubling
- dividing by 20 by dividing by ten and halving.

Write a few calculations on the board for children to solve using these methods.

Next, write a multiplication statement on the board, e.g. $9 \times 5 = 45$. Ask children to write as many other multiplication statements as they can in two minutes from this. Encourage them to double, halve and multiply or divide by powers of 10, e.g. $18 \times 5 = 90$, $36 \times 5 = 180$, $36 \times 2.5 = 90$, $36 \times 1.25 = 45$, $36 \times 0.125 = 4.5$, $900 \times 5 = 4\,500$, $900 \times 50 = 45\,000$.

Read the first statement by the Theo in the Textbook. Ask children in pairs to explain how Theo can multiply by five in the way stated. They should be able to explain that five is half of ten and therefore they could multiply a number by ten and halve it.

Repeat the above for Amy's statement. They should be able to tell you that doubling is the same as multiplying by two, so doubling again is multiplying by four.

Theo's second statement talks about using known facts and asks children to make up 10 from $8 \times 7 = 56$. Remind them about what they did above. Take suggestions for what they could do to these numbers to generate different multiplications. Encourage children to be creative and make decimal statements.

Evidencing mastery

Look for children who can competently use mental calculation strategies to multiply and divide and can explain their thinking clearly, giving appropriate examples. If they can do this they are evidencing mastery in this area of mathematics.

Assessment task 2

Running the task

Scaling up and down is a very useful strategy for everyday life. To use scaling effectively children need to be able to think flexibly and often use mental calculation strategies to help them. Scaling is useful for many things, e.g. currency conversion, converting between units of measure and converting between imperial and metric units. Before children begin this assessment task, recap scaling up and down. Ask children what they know about each one. Invite children to demonstrate on the board, using diagrams. They may draw circles to represent counters or bars. Both are acceptable if they are able to talk about x times the size or a fraction of the size. They should choose their own values for the smaller quantity and the class work out what the larger quantity is. They then choose a value for the larger quantity and the class work out the smaller.

During the task encourage children to challenge themselves. Some children may scale up 3- or 4-digit numbers. Encourage them to look for multiples of the denominator of the fraction they scale down.

Evidencing mastery

Observe children when they make their drawings. If they work confidently and accurately and can explain scaling up and down, they are evidencing mastery in this area of multiplication and division.

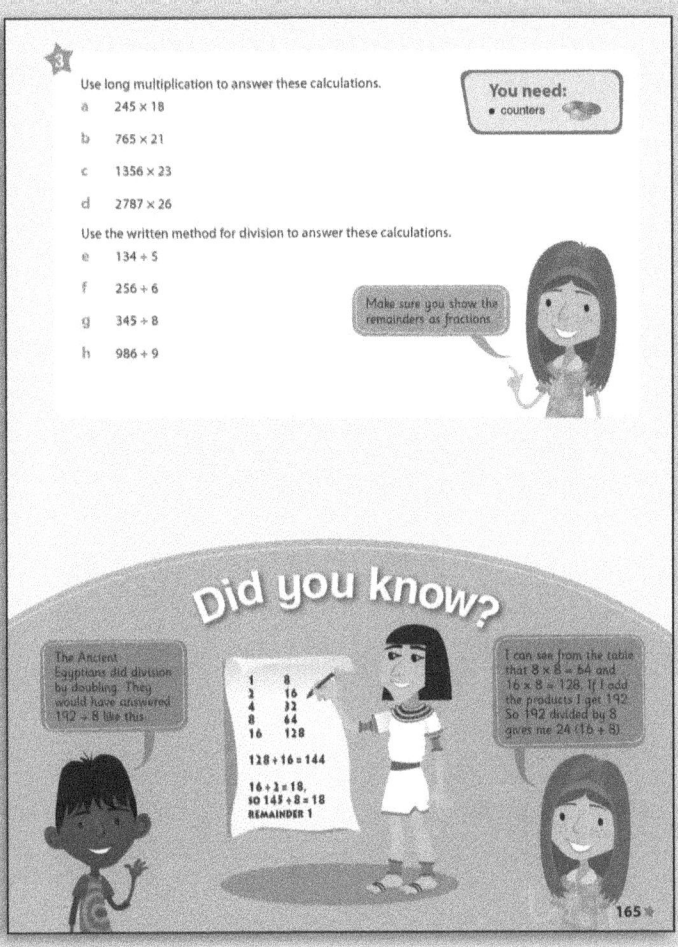

Concepts mastered

- ☑ Children can explain and demonstrate factors, factor pairs, prime factors and multiples.

- ☑ Children can explain and demonstrate mental multiplication and division strategies and why these are more efficient than written methods. They can also explain and demonstrate scaling up and down.

- ☑ Children can explain and demonstrate how the long multiplication method works.

- ☑ Children can explain exactly how a division calculation works to show conceptual understanding. They will also have mastered the concept of remainders if they can explain what one is, what they would need to do with one in a problem and how these appear as fractions and decimals.

Assessment task 3

Resources

Sets of coloured counters to which children assign their own values.

Running the task

Remind children that when mental calculation strategies cannot be used quickly and efficiently they should use written methods. Before children begin the task, recap the written methods for division and multiplication. By this stage children should have had plenty of opportunities to use manipulatives, so most should be able to explain exactly what is happening when they use these methods. Invite individuals to demonstrate to the class.

For the task children should work independently. They should focus on using the long multiplication method for multiplying and the short method for division. If any children need resources, allow them to be used. If children are still at the stage of needing to use the grid method or two separate calculations to total, let them do this, but make a note that they have not yet mastered this aspect of mathematics.

Evidencing mastery

If children can confidently and efficiently demonstrate and explain the written methods for multiplication and division, they are showing mastery.

Did you know?

Egyptian division is basically Egyptian multiplication in reverse.

The divisor is repeatedly doubled to give the dividend.

192 divided by 8.

powers of two (doubling)	divisor and repeated doubling
1	8
2	16
4	32
8	64
16	128

Look for the combination of numbers that add up to 192 in the divisor column.

We can see from the table that $8 \times 8 = 64$ and $16 \times 8 = 128$. If we add the products we will get 192. So 192 divided by 8 gives us 24 (16 + 8). This Egyptian method reinforces the links between multiplication and division.

Give children opportunities to solve multiplication and division calculation the Egyptian way! Ask them what they notice about this ancient method. Establish that the Egyptians basically used scaling up.

Mathematical focus

★ Geometry: properties of shapes
★ Measurement: volume, capacity, length, area, perimeter

Prior learning

Children should already be able to:

- compare and classify geometric shapes based on their properties and sizes
- use the properties of rectangles to find missing lengths and angles
- distinguish between regular and irregular polygons.

Key new learning

- Calculate the perimeter of a rectangle and develop understanding of the formula $P = 2(l + w)$ or $P = 2l + 2w$.
- Calculate the perimeter of a composite rectangle, using the properties of rectangles to deduce missing lengths.
- Calculate the area of a rectangle and develop understanding of the formula $A = l \times w$.
- Calculate the area of a composite rectilinear shape by separating the shape into rectangles.
- Compare the perimeter of shapes with the same area and develop an understanding that the shape with the smallest perimeter will be the rectangle closest to a square.
- Calculate and compare the area of rectangles (including squares) including using standard units, square centimetres (cm²) and square metres (m²) and estimate the area of irregular shapes.
- Estimate the volume of cuboids, e.g. using 1 cm cubes, and capacity, e.g. using water.

Unit
14 Perimeter, area and volume

What do you have to measure to find the area of each tennis court?

How can you compare the size of these carpets?

※166

Making connections

- Finding different shapes with the same area involves identifying factor pairs and common factors. If children can readily recall factor pairs, or know how to find them, this will make the task easier.
- Scale drawings, such as maps and plans, are practical examples of where the concepts of area and perimeter are used. Discuss with children their experience of using them, the units that they are drawn in and the idea of scale.
- Another practical application is in home DIY projects. Children may have visited DIY stores to purchase flooring or garden fencing. Discuss how to calculate the cost of materials from the area and perimeter.

 ### Talk about

Take particular care to use the words 'volume' and 'capacity' accurately, as children will often use them interchangeably. Volume is the measure of the three-dimensional space, i.e. space taken up by something. We use different units depending on whether we are measuring the volume of a liquid (litres or millilitres) or the volume of a solid (metres cubed: m³ or centimetres cubed: cm³). Capacity is the amount a container can hold. Capacity is always measured in millilitres or litres.

A five-litre bucket has a capacity of five litres and contains five litres when full. Volume is the measure of the space taken up by something, so if the bucket has only two litres of water in it, then we say the volume of water is two litres.

Engaging and exploring

Allow children time to look at the photos in the Textbook and to discuss them with a partner before engaging with them. This gives them the chance to focus on the maths content of the unit.

The first photo shows an aerial shot of a tennis club with a number of tennis courts. The question asks: *What do you have to measure to find the area of each tennis court?* Children may suggest that you need to measure the dimensions of the court, i.e. its length and width. In Year 4 they learned to find the perimeter of rectilinear shapes and some children may recall this term. Working together, establish that the perimeter of the court is equal to the total of twice the length plus twice the width. It is measured in metres and centimetres. (The perimeter of a full-size tennis court is always exactly the same because the length and width have been fixed by the Lawn Tennis Association.) In Year 4

children learnt to find the area of simple rectilinear shapes by counting squares. They might suggest estimating the number of metre squares in the tennis court. Ask them when you might need to measure the area and perimeter of outdoor spaces. Some children may have experience, e.g. of measuring a new patio at home.

The next photo shows a display of carpets of different shapes and sizes and asks how you can compare the sizes. Children may explain that because the lengths and widths of the carpets differ, they will have different areas. They will be learning to calculate area in this unit. Ask them whether they think that it is true to say the larger the carpet, the higher the cost or do they think that there are other factors involved, e.g. the type of material, the pattern, the design?

The photo of footprints of a small child and an adult poses the question of how the area of the footprints can be estimated. Clearly these shapes are irregular and cannot be broken down into rectangular shapes. In Year 4 children measured areas by counting squares; drawing on this experience, they may suggest using centimetre-squared grid paper. If you place a transparent grid over the photo you can identify and count the squares that are complete and see the partly-covered squares. Explain that one method of estimating partly-covered squares is to count those that are more than half covered and ignore those where the coverage is less than half. Make it clear that the final area calculated in this way is not entirely accurate but a very good estimate.

Ask children if they can think of real-life situations where you need to find the area of irregular shapes. Some suggestions might be the area of a pond or an island.

The next photo shows a partly-filled glass of water and a bottle of water that is half full. The question opens up conversations on units of measure. Collect children's estimates of the amount of water in the glass and the bottle which will give a good indication of their ability to visualise amounts. You can discuss the capacity of the glass and the bottle, i.e. the amounts they contain when full, and compare this amount with the actual volume in them as shown in the photo. You might like to reinforce this task with real glasses or other containers.

The final photo shows formal gardens and paved areas and the question asks how you could make a copy of it. You would need to make a scale plan of the garden, showing the area of the beds, grass and paved areas. Ask children to think about what measuring would be required, e.g. you would need to find the area of the small beds and measure the perimeters so that you could calculate the number of small hedging plants required to plant around the outside. Challenge children to calculate the number of paving stones and turf squares required for the checkerboard foreground. Discuss with children their experience of plans and scale drawings.

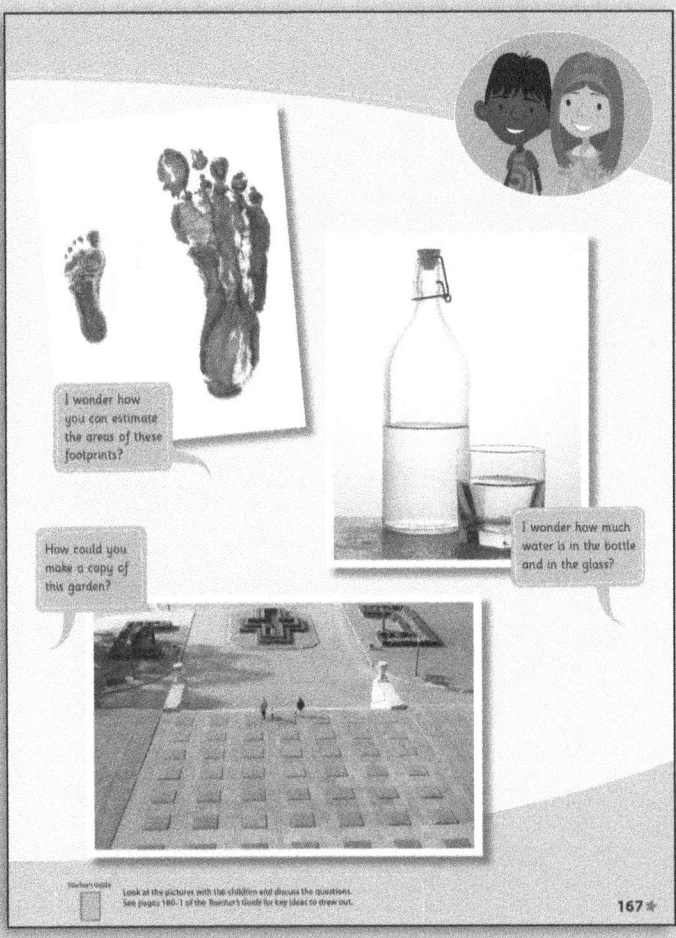

I wonder how you can estimate the areas of these footprints?

How could you make a copy of this garden?

I wonder how much water is in the bottle and in the glass?

Teacher's Guide
Look at the pictures with the children and discuss the questions.
See pages 180–1 of the Teacher's Guide for key ideas to draw out.

167

Things to think about

- Is practical measuring of perimeters and areas possible in both the classroom and outside areas?

- How will you organise groupings for discussions and activities?

- How will you check conceptual understanding of perimeter, area, volume and capacity?

- What opportunities will you provide to build fluency so that children show efficiency, accuracy and flexibility in their approach?

- Which problem-solving strategies are most appropriate in Year 5?

Checking understanding

You will know that children have mastered these concepts when they can calculate perimeters of composite rectangular shapes, working out missing lengths. They can also draw rectangles of the same area with different perimeters and make sensible predictions of the shape that will have the largest/smallest perimeter. They will know how to estimate the area of irregular shapes. They can estimate the volume and capacity of simple cuboids (including cubes).

- **Measure and calculate the perimeter of composite rectilinear shapes in centimetres and metres.**
- **Use the properties of rectangles to deduce related facts and find missing lengths and angles.**

Homework 79 and 80   Practice Book pp 128–31

Mathematical vocabulary

Perimeter, rectangle, formula

Representations and resources

Squared paper, ruler, 0–9 dice, individual whiteboards, tape measures, trundle wheels.

Warming up

Practise doubles up to 100. This could be done using two 0–9 dice. Roll the dice and make a 2-digit number to double. Reverse the digits and double this number. Repeat with new dice rolls.

When children understand the formula for determining the perimeter of a rectangle, the usefulness of fluency in calculating doubles will be evident.

Background knowledge

In this concept children are revisiting the concept of perimeter introduced in Year 4 and learning the formula. The perimeter of a rectangle can be expressed algebraically as $2(l + w)$ where l and w are the dimensions expressed in the same unit. Children will be extending their understanding to include finding the perimeter of composite rectilinear shapes by separating them into rectangles in order to determine missing lengths.

Children should have practical opportunities to appreciate the importance of rectangles in everyday objects from paper to doors, from faces of buildings to football pitches. They should understand that a square is a special rectangle.

Let's learn: Modelling and teaching
Finding missing lengths

- Look at the first diagram in the Textbook. Establish that the perimeter of a shape is the distance around the outside of it. Ask children how many sides this polygon has (6) and how many of those sides they know (4). *Can you see how this shape can be divided into two shapes? What are the two shapes?* Agree that the shape is made from two rectangles. Ask children to copy the shape, cut it out and fold it to reinforce the shape of the two rectangles. Ask children to tell you what they know about the lengths of sides in a rectangle (they are equal) and from this elicit the missing lengths. Confirm that if you know the length of one of a pair of equal sides, you know what the other length is.

- Draw the two diagrams (below) and ask children to find the missing lengths and the perimeter of each shape. Remind them to remember the units!

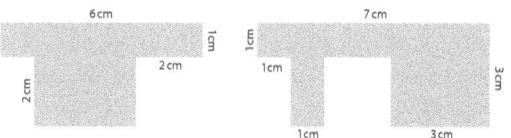

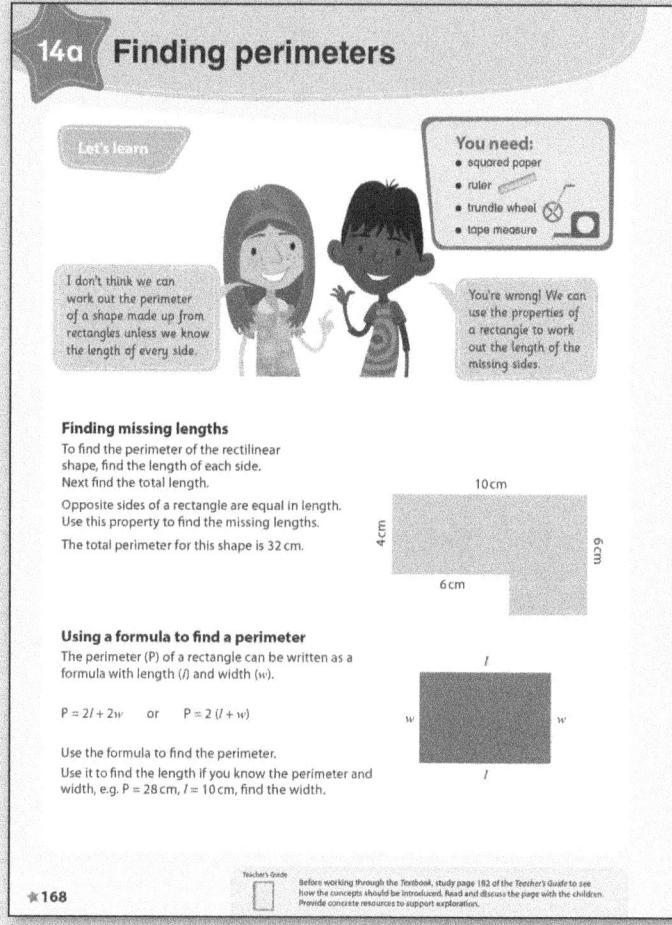

Using a formula to find a perimeter

- Ask children to tell you the definition of perimeter. It is the distance around a 2-D shape. In this unit the focus is on rectangles and composite rectangular shapes. Ask children to tell you the total of the sides as you move around the rectangle in the Textbook., i.e. $l + w + l + w$. Help them to work out the formula for themselves. It can be written as $P = 2l + 2w$ or $P = 2(l + w)$.

- Using this can provide a quick method of finding an answer and enable children to find a missing length of a rectangle in problems where they know the perimeter and the length of one side.

Let's practise: Digging deeper

Step 1

In this step children find the missing lengths using the properties of rectangles to work out the perimeter of a composite rectilinear shape. A common misconception is the belief that when finding the perimeter of a compound shape, which has been split into rectangles, internal lengths should be added. Help children to understand that the perimeter is only the outside measurements by tracing the perimeter with their finger and counting the number of sides. They can check that the number of sides matches the number of measurements.

Step 2

These can be solved in a number of ways, e.g. by working backwards or by substituting the numbers in the formula.

Working backwards through the first problem, they know one side is 4 cm and by recalling the properties of a rectangle, they know the side opposite must also be 4 cm. If they take 8 cm (4 cm + 4 cm) away from the known perimeter, 28 cm, there is 20 cm left. This is the total of both the remaining sides, so each side must be half that, i.e. 10 cm. Some may be able to use the formula to solve the problem.

Step 3

In this practical task children measure an outdoor area such as a patio or sports pitch. They are asked to estimate the perimeter first. Observe whether children are making sensible estimations and recording measurements systematically. Children who are confident using the formula for perimeter will simply measure the length and width and then work out the perimeter, rather than measuring the entire perimeter.

Step 4

This investigative task demonstrates the many ways that the two rectangles can be positioned to make new shapes. One way to approach this systematically is to cut out the two rectangles from squared paper, then keep one of the rectangles in a fixed position and place the second rectangle in positions around it. Move the second rectangle one square at a time and then repeat this with the shape rotated through 90°. Record each new composite shape. Remind children to look out for shapes that are the same but simply rotated.

Some children may recognise that the one with the smallest perimeter is the shape closest to a square which has a perimeter of 22 cm. Encourage children to reflect on their predictions and discuss or write them down.

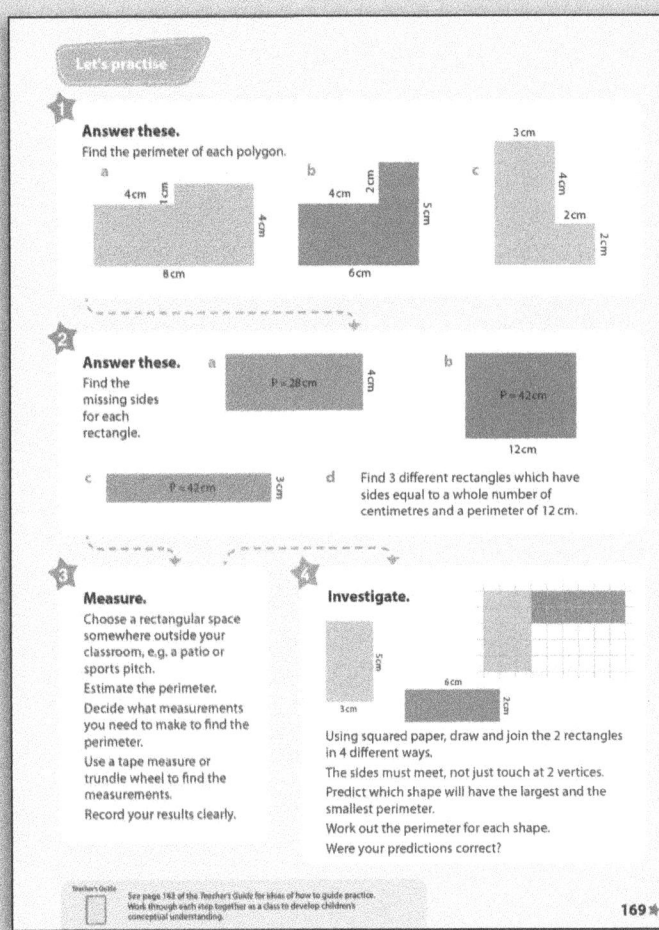

Ensuring progress

Supporting understanding

Work with children in a guided group to ensure that they understand what they need to measure (they do not need to measure 'internal' lengths). Being able to draw diagrams carefully is becoming an increasingly useful skill and those children who find this challenging should be encouraged and supported. Ensure that they are using a transparent ruler and a sharp pencil. Remind them to take time to ensure that the ruler is in the correct position before they draw a line.

Broadening understanding

Using the perimeters of, e.g. their sports pitch or patio, children can work how much it would cost to enclose the area with fencing.

Follow-up ideas

- Challenge children to make up word problems involving perimeter. Possible scenarios are calculating the amount of fencing required for gardens or swimming pools or determining the distance covered by a security guard patrolling the outside of a building.

- You could ask children to investigate the cost of framing some paintings from their art lessons. Give them a selection of differently-priced frames.

- If all the Year 5 children in your school sat in one square and each child had 50 cm, ask them to calculate the size of the square they would make, showing how they worked it out.

 Concept mastered

Children can calculate the perimeter of rectangles and composite rectangles. They can use the formula for perimeter, $P = 2(l + w)$ to calculate possible dimensions for a given perimeter and, given the perimeter and the length of one side, calculate the missing one.

Answers

Step 1		Step 2		Step 4
a	24 cm	a	Length = 10 cm	Many possible answers.
b	22 cm	b	Width = 9 cm	
c	22 cm	c	Length = 18 cm	The smallest perimeter is 22 cm.
		d	5 cm × 1 cm; 4 cm × 2 cm; 3 cm × 3 cm	The largest perimeter is 28 cm.

- Measure and calculate the perimeter of composite rectilinear shapes in centimetres and metres.
- Calculate and compare the area of rectangles (including squares), including using standard units, square centimetres (cm²) and square metres (m²), and estimate the area of irregular shapes.
- Identify multiples and factors, including all factor pairs, and common factors of two numbers.

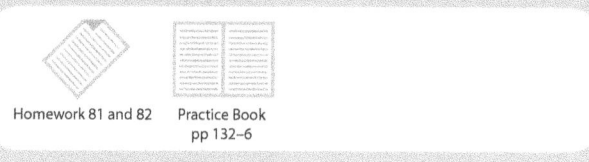

Homework 81 and 82   Practice Book
pp 132–6

Representations and resources
Squared paper, ruler.

Mathematical vocabulary
Perimeter, area, factor, factor pair

Warming up
Ask children to give factor pairs of 2-digit numbers, e.g. 8, 32, 48, 30, 54, 80, 63, 64, etc. Check that they have all the pairs. Explain that finding factor pairs is useful when you have a given area and are looking for possible dimensions.

Background knowledge
Measuring area and using square units is new for children although they are familiar with the idea of an amount of surface and counting squares.

Children sometimes muddle the terms perimeter and area. Use visual cues to show that perimeter is a single dimension while area measures two dimensions; point with your finger around the perimeter and sweep the surface with the flat of your hand to show area.

To find the area of a rectangle multiply the length by the width. This can be written as A = l × w, where A = area, l = length and w = width.

Let's learn: Modelling and teaching
Finding area using a formula

- Ask children to draw a rectangle, 5 cm × 2 cm on squared paper. Ask how many squares are in the rectangle. There are ten which is 5 × 2. Area is 5 cm × 2 cm = 10 cm². Repeat with other rectangles, e.g. 4 cm × 3 cm and elicit that the area is 4 cm × 3 cm = 12 cm². Ask children to work out the perimeter of these two rectangles (both 14 cm).

- Ask children to find the area and perimeter of a rectangle, 6 cm × 2 cm and a square, 4 cm × 4 cm. These have the same perimeter, 16 cm, but the rectangle has an area of 12 cm² while the area of the square is 16 cm². Shapes with the same area may not have the same perimeter.

- With practice children start to realise as they count squares to find the area of a rectangle that it would be quicker to find area by counting the number of squares in one row and multiplying this by the number of rows. Ask them to think about whether they always need squared paper in order to find the area.

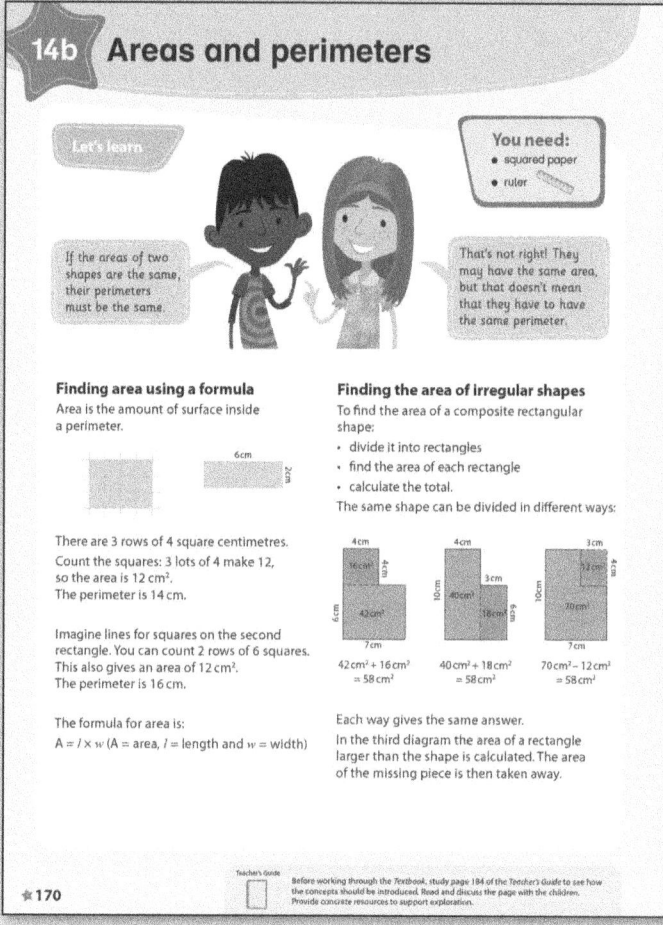

Finding the area of irregular shapes

- Explain that you can find the area of composite rectangular shapes by dividing them into rectangles, finding the area of each rectangle and calculating the total. You can also calculate the area of a rectangle larger than the composite shape and then take away the area of the missing piece. Model the approach in the Textbook using squared paper, then introduce another example on plain paper and work with children to find the area.

- Demonstrate that you can estimate the area of irregular areas that are not composed of rectangles using the following method: count the number of complete squares and add the number of incomplete squares where half the square or more is part of the shape. Ignore the squares that are less than a half. This gives a good estimate of the area.

Let's practise: Digging deeper

Step 1

Children practise calculating the area and perimeter of both simple rectangles and irregular shapes. They also reinforce their understanding that shapes with the same area may or may not have the same perimeter and vice versa. For parts b) and c) give children an opportunity to explain their steps using correct mathematical language.

Step 2

In this task children know the area and the length of one side and they need to deduce the length of the missing side using algebraic thinking. Encourage children to model the questions using sketches if needed.

In the first problem, the area is 20 m² and one side is 4 m. To find the length of the other side, divide 20 by 4, to give 5. The length of the missing side is 5 m. Encourage children to check that this

is correct by multiplying 4 × 5 to give 20. The perimeters of the other shapes can be calculated in the same way.

In the final section encourage children to draw a diagram of the flowerbed using squared paper to visualise the problem clearly. They need to decide on a sensible width for the beds, probably 1 or 2 m.

Step 3

Children find the perimeter and the top surface area of some common small items. You could ask them to estimate first. Check that they include the units in their answer and that they are setting out their workings systematically..

Step 4

Explain to children that a hexomino is a polygon of six equal-sized squares. Ask children to write down their predictions using accurate mathematical vocabulary. Return to these at the end of the activity. How many children predicted correctly? Write down the correct statement on the whiteboard. Encourage them to set their findings out in a systematic manner. You may choose to tell them that there are 35 different hexominoes and challenge them to find as many as possible. Some children may benefit from using paper to model the arrangements.

As an additional activity children may like to work out which hexominoes will fold to make a cube. There are only 11 that do.

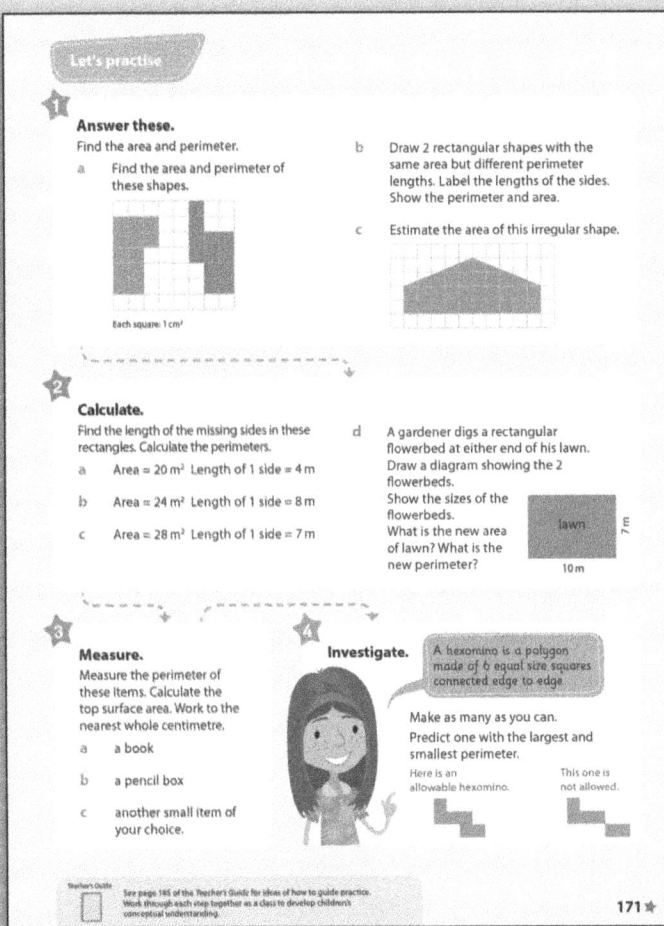

Ensuring progress

Supporting understanding

A common confusion is to use incorrect units for perimeter, cm and area, cm². Use 2-D representations and 3-D shapes to reinforcethat perimeter is a one-dimensional attribute, i.e. the total of the lengths of the sides measured in centimetres and area a two-dimensional one, i.e. found by multiplying centimetres by centimetres, giving cm². This should help eliminate the problem.

Broadening understanding

Look at plans of the school and its grounds and analyse the areas of different parts. An interesting investigation can be carried out looking at metric paper sizes, from A1 to A6.

Concept mastered

Children understand why area is measured in square units such as cm² and m². They can calculate the area of rectangles and understand the formula $A = l \times w$ for the area of a rectangle and composite rectangles.

Follow-up ideas

- Investigate the perimeter and area of sports pitches. The dimensions for a tennis court were agreed when imperial measurements were in use and so the sizes appear very clumsy when expressed in metric units, e.g. the full width of the court is 10.97 m.

- Give children squared paper and ask them to draw their initials using whole squares and then calculate the area and perimeter of them.

- Ask children to research jobs that involve measuring area and perimeter, e.g. builders, architects, painters, farmers, gardeners and interior designers.

Answers

Step 1

a   A Area = 12 cm²
      Perimeter = 16 cm
      B Area = 12 cm²
      Perimeter = 18 cm

c   51 cm² 88 cm²

d   30 cm²

Step 2

a   Missing side = 5 cm P = 18 cm

b   Missing side = 3 cm P = 22 cm

c   Missing side = 4 cm P = 22 cm

Step 4

There are 35 possible hexominoes which can be found using the Internet.

Smallest perimeter 3 cm × 2 cm rectangle – 10 cm.
Largest perimeter 14 cm – lots of the shapes have this perimeter.

14c Volume and capacity

- **Estimate the volume of cuboids, e.g. using 1cm cubes, and capacity, e.g. using water.**

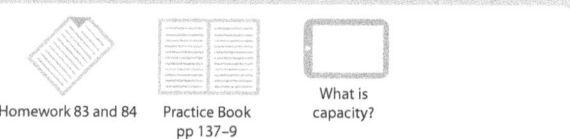

Homework 83 and 84   Practice Book pp 137–9   What is capacity?

Mathematical vocabulary

Volume, capacity, cuboid, hollow

Representations and resources

1 m cubes (centicubes), hollow litre cube, measuring cylinders and measuring jugs, variety of unmarked containers, stones, 1 cm-squared paper.

Warming up

Practise dividing 2-digit and 3-digit multiples of ten by 1000, e.g. $330 \div 1000 = 0.33$. Extend this to changing millilitres to litres, e.g. $330 \, ml \div 1000 = 0.33 \, l$.

Background knowledge

Volume measures the amount of space taken up by an object. It is a 3-D measurement. It follows on from length (1-D and measured in cm) and area (2-D and measured in cm²).

When we measure the volume of a liquid, we use litres or millilitres; when we measure the volume of a solid we use metres cubed (m³) or centimetres cubed (cm³).

Capacity is defined by the amount a container can hold. Capacity is always measured in millilitres or litres. A bucket with a capacity of ten litres contains ten litres of liquid when full. If, however, the bucket is only half full (with five litres of liquid), we say that the volume of liquid in the bucket is five litres.

The volume of a cuboid can be estimated by working out how many centimetre cubes would be needed to make it. A cuboid measuring 4 cm long × 3 cm wide × 2 cm high can be made by arranging two layers of cubes; each layer of 12 cubes is arranged in a 4 × 3 array. So the volume of this cuboid is 24 cm³. Remember that in Year 5, children are only asked to estimate volume; they do not calculate volume until Year 6.

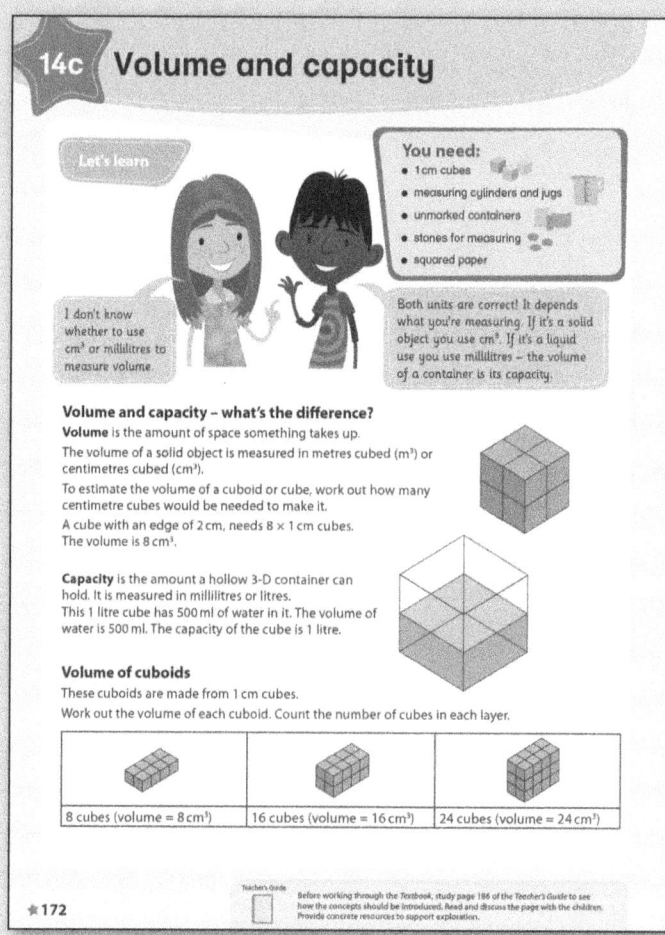

Let's learn: Modelling and teaching

Volume and capacity – what's the difference?

- Carefully explain the difference between volume and capacity.

- Explain to children that to measure the volume of a solid object we use metres cubed (m³) or centimetres cubed (cm³). We can estimate the volume of a cuboid or cube by working out how many centimetre cubes would be needed to make it. The Textbook shows a cube with an edge of 2 cm. 8 × 1 cm cubes are required to make it so the volume of the cube is 8 cm³. Give children cubes to build it.

- Explain that the capacity of containers is measured in millilitres or litres. Capacity usually measures liquids. Remember volume is the measure of the space taken up by something, so if a 1 litre cube has 500 ml of water in it, then we say the volume of water is 500 ml but the capacity of the cube has not changed, it is still 1 litre. In this case the volume is also used to describe an amount of liquid.

- Set up an activity base with containers and water outside

the classroom so that children gain experience of capacity using concrete materials.

Volume of cuboids

- Cuboids are 3-D shapes with length, width and height. Cuboids are measured in cubic units such as m³ or cm³.

- Give children cubes to build the cuboids shown in the Textbook. Extend this by building cuboids of different shapes and building successive layers, e.g. 3 cm × 5 cm as a single layer (15 cm³), two layers of 3 cm × 5 cm (30 cm³). *How many cubes do you think there are in a cuboid with four layers?*

- Examining how cuboids are constructed will help children to develop their understanding of volume and build a sound foundation for understanding the formula for calculating volume that they will learn in Year 6.

Let's practise: Digging deeper
Step 1

Children visualise or build the smallest cuboid that includes irregular shapes made from cubes. Give children access to cubes to build the shapes. Tell them to look at the bottom layer and think how many cubes are required to make that single bottom layer. Then look at the next layer and so on. Ensure that children recall the correct units for volume. Ask: *What do you notice about the number of cubes and measurement in cm³?*

Step 2

Children measure the capacity of a variety of containers. Remind children that to read the scale on a measuring cylinder or measuring jug accurately, they should make sure that it is on a flat surface. Then they should bend down so that their eyes are on the same level as the surface of the water. Provide plenty of opportunities to discuss the children's estimates and results.

Step 3

Children measure the volume of an irregularly shaped object. The Textbook suggests using a stone but you could use any object of a suitable size providing it sinks in water. The Textbook explains how to carry out the experiment. Use questioning throughout to ensure that children are thinking carefully about the mathematics that is being revealed. The number of millilitres is equal to the volume of the stone in cm³ because in the metric system 1 ml of water takes up 1 cm³ space. Encourage children to record the experiment so someone else could try it.

Step 4

Give children squared paper; they need a separate piece to make each box. Unit cubes from Base 10 apparatus could be used if the class does not have, e.g. centicubes. The results may be expressed in different ways but encourage children to record them systematically. They could record their results in a table. Children could work in pairs to encourage plenty of 'maths chat' during the investigation.

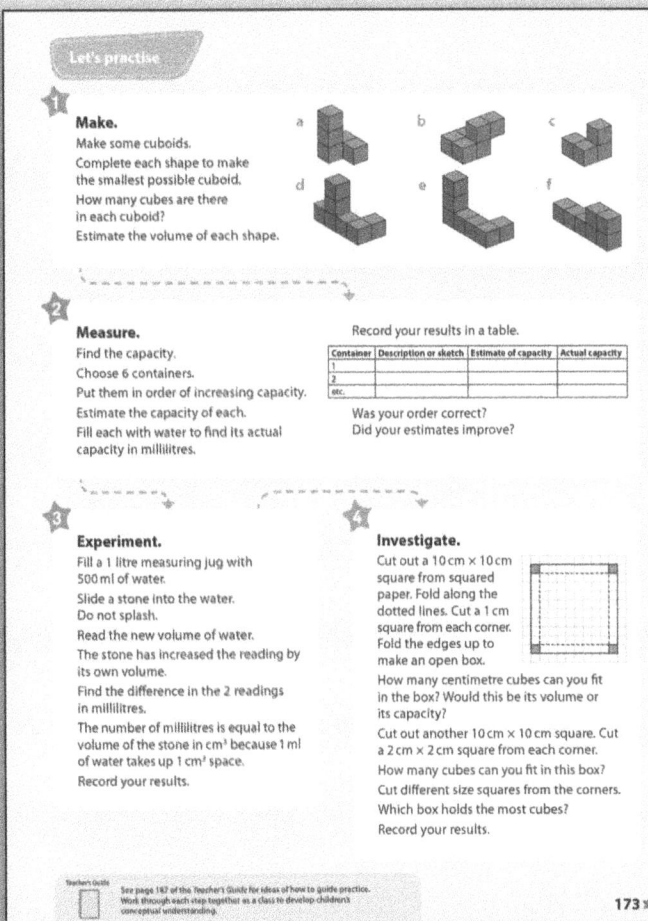

Ensuring progress
Supporting understanding

Conservation of volume is difficult for many children to appreciate because of the 3-D nature of volume. Children may think that a tall thin container has a greater capacity than a short wide one. Show them containers of very different shapes and ask them to predict the total capacity. Set up an activity area with water for children. Give them a selection of containers and ask them to put 250 ml in each of them. This will allow them to actively test comparative capacities.

Broadening understanding

Children can try starting Step 4 with a larger paper square. Encourage them to set out their findings systematically to look for patterns. The volume increases and then drops away.

You could suggest that children investigate Archimedes' 'Eureka!' moment.

 Concept mastered

Children can estimate volume and capacity and explain the difference between them.

Follow-up ideas

- Use the school buildings and classroom items to investigate larger volumes, e.g. the classroom, the school hall, cupboards, boxes.

- Suggest to children that they use the Internet to research the volume of containers on container ships. When they have found the volume of one container, they could investigate how many can be transported on different-sized ships and work out which ships hold the largest volume of goods.

- Encourage children to take any opportunities to cook at school or home where they will use measuring jugs in real-life situations.

Answers
Step 1

a	12 cubes – 12 cm³		d	24 cubes – 24 cm³
b	12 cubes – 12 cm³		e	24 cubes – 24 cm³
c	8 cubes – 8 cm³		f	10 cubes – 10 cm³

Step 4

Answers may be expressed in different ways. The columns in italics are beyond the expectations for Year 5 children.

Size of square removed	Dimensions of cube	Number of cubes	Volume of cube
1 cm²	8 cm × 8 cm × 1 cm	64	*64 cm³*
2 cm²	6 cm × 6 cm × 2 cm	72	*72 cm³*
3 cm²	4 cm × 4 cm × 3 cm	48	*48 cm³*
4 cm²	2 cm × 2 cm × 4 cm	16	*16 cm³*

For whole number values a cut out square of 3 cm gives the largest volume.

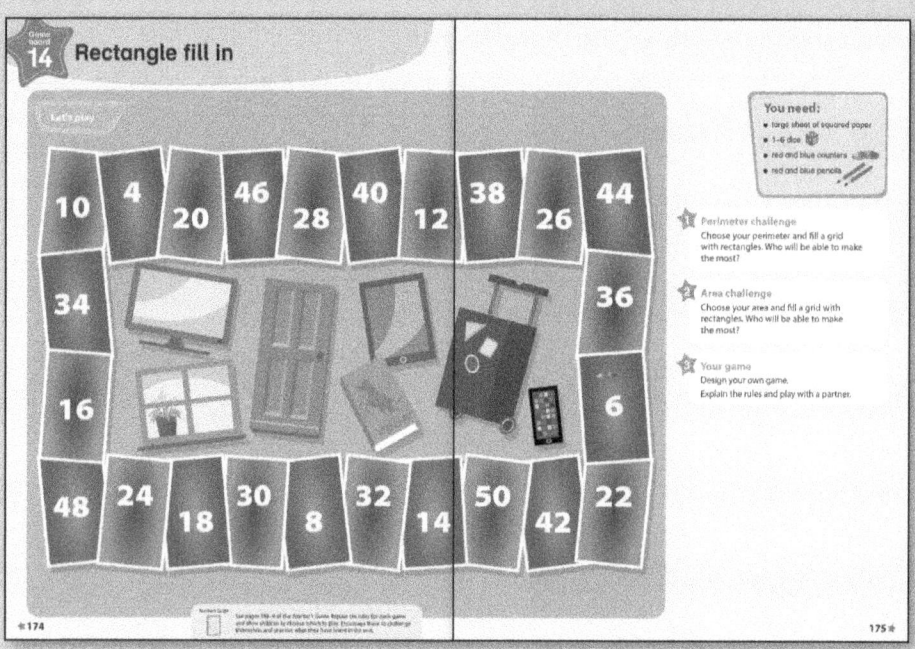

Game 1: Perimeter challenge

Children use their knowledge of perimeters to fill a grid with rectangles. As they move around the board the squares they land on determine the size of the rectangles they draw.

Maths focus

- Determine the lengths and widths of possible rectangles for a given perimeter

Resources

A4 squared paper (e.g. 0.7 cm squares), 1–6 dice (1), 1 red counter and 1 blue counter, red and blue coloured pencils.

How to play

Ask children to prepare the A4 squared paper by marking a large rectangle on it, e.g. 20 × 30 squares. Children choose to be red or blue and place their counter on a starting square of their choice on the gameboard. They take turns to roll the dice and move clockwise. On the squared paper, children make a rectangle (or square) which has a perimeter equal to the number they land on, e.g. for 12, they could make a rectangle 5 × 1, 4 × 2 or 3 × 3. They choose where to draw it within the main rectangle and colour it in. The game continues so the paper is gradually filled with rectangles. The game is over when no rectangle can be drawn in the available space for three consecutive turns. The winner is the child with the most rectangles.

Making it easier

Give children extra paper to draw possible rectangles.

Making it harder

The winner is the player with the most small squares coloured.

Game 2: Area challenge

Children have to work out the possible measurements of rectangles for a given area to fill a grid. As they move around the board the squares that they land on determine the size of the rectangle they can draw.

Maths focus

- Determine the lengths and widths of possible rectangles for a given area

Resources

A4 squared paper (e.g. 0.7cm squares), 1–6 dice (1), 1 red counter and 1 blue counter, red and blue coloured pencils.

How to play

Play the game in the same way as Game 1. This time, however, children draw a rectangle which has an area equal to the number they land on, e.g. for 12, they could make a rectangle 12 × 1, 6 × 2 or 4 × 3. They choose where to draw it and colour it in. The game continues with each child filling in a rectangle so that the paper is gradually filled with different-sized rectangles. Towards the end of the game, landing on square with a high number may mean that none of the possible rectangles will fit into the remaining space. The game is over when no rectangle can be drawn for three consecutive turns. The winner is the child with the most rectangles.

Making it easier

Give children extra squared paper to try drawing the possible rectangles.

Making it harder

Change the scoring so that the winner is the player with the most small squares coloured at the end of the game.

Game 3: Your game

Children should invent their own game, designing rules that use the concepts covered in the unit. Challenge children to make their game easier or harder.

Rectangle fill in

Choose a game to play.

Game 1: Perimeter challenge

How to play

- Decide who is red and blue. Place your counter on a square of your choice.
- Both roll the dice. The player with the higher score goes first.
- Take turns to move clockwise around the gameboard.
- Draw a rectangle (or square) with a **perimeter** equal to the number you land on, so for 12, you could make a rectangle that is 5×1, 4×2 or 3×3.
- Choose where to draw it within the main rectangle on the squared paper. Colour it in to match your counter.
- Continue filling the paper with different-sized rectangles.
- The game is over when no rectangle can be draw for 3 consecutive goes.
- The winner is the player with the most rectangles!

You need:

- A4 squared paper with a large rectangle marked on it, e.g. 20×30 squares
- 1–6 dice
- 1 red and 1 blue counter
- red and blue coloured pencils

Game 2: Area challenge

How to play

- Play this game the same way as for Game 1.
- This time, draw a rectangle (or square) with an **area** equal to the number you land on, so for 12, you could make a rectangle that is 12×1, 6×2 or 4×3.
- The winner is the player with the most rectangles!

You need:

- A4 squared paper with a large rectangle marked on it, e.g. 20×30 squares
- 1–6 dice
- 1 red and 1 blue counter
- red and blue coloured pencils

Game 3: Your game

- Make up your own game using the gameboard and squared paper.
- Can you find a different way to decide on the winner?
- What are the rules for your game? Can you explain them to someone?

Please help your child by reading the instructions and playing the game together.

Assessment task 1

Resources

Squared paper, ruler.

Running the task

The task asks children to calculate the area of two different patios and to do the calculation in two different ways. Before they begin the task, you could draw some L-shapes on the board so that children can practise different ways of dividing shapes into rectangles. If they do not suggest it, remind them that they can make a larger rectangle and take away the missing part.

To find the area of each rectangle, they use the formula for area, $A = l \times w$. They then add the area of the separate rectangles together. Once they feel confident, they can work on the task.

Encourage children to draw careful diagrams of the shapes with the given lengths, and those that they have deduced, marked on the diagram.

Their calculations will be one of the following.

For the first patio, $55\,m^2 + 21\,m^2 = 76\,m^2$, or $56\,m^2 + 20\,m^2 = 76\,m^2$, or $88\,m^2 - 12\,m^2 = 76\,m^2$.

For the second patio, $84\,m^2 + 6\,m^2 = 90\,m^2$, $27\,m^2 + 63\,m^2 = 90\,m^2$, or $108\,m^2 - 18\,m^2 = 90\,m^2$.

Evidencing mastery

Children who show mastery will approach the task with confidence and be able to divide the shape in two different ways. Their answers will be same whichever way they divide the shape and if the answers do not match, they will know that they have made a computational error and check their working to find it. Children showing mastery will record their results clearly and use the correct units (m^2) in their answers.

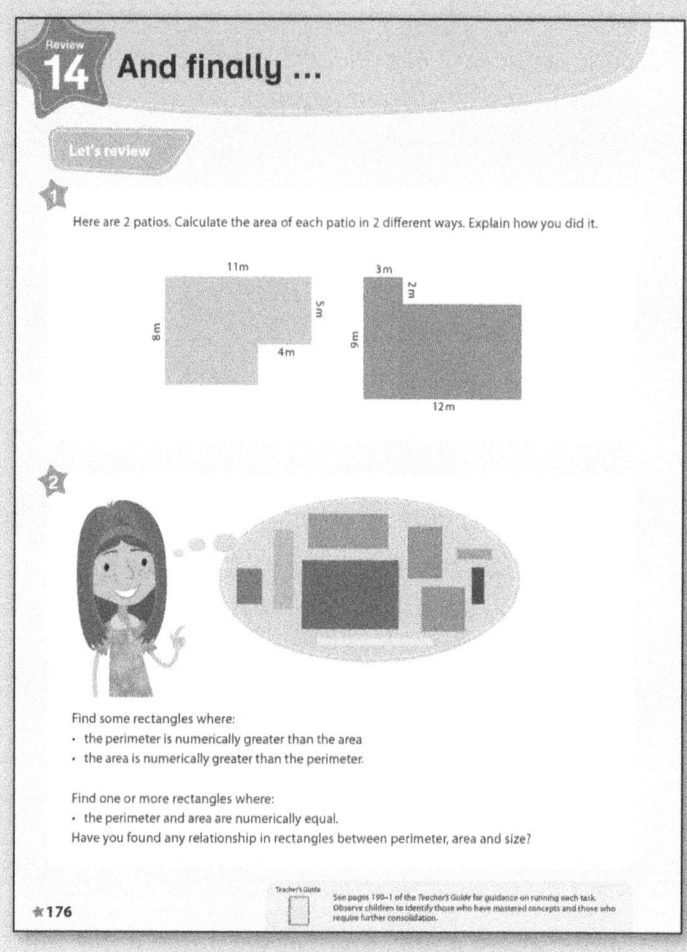

Assessment task 2

Resources

Squared paper, ruler.

Running the task

Check children's understanding of the task. They can begin the investigation with any rectangle. There are two solutions for rectangles with perimeter and area numerically equal, a 4 cm square and a 3 cm × 6 cm rectangle. Children may discover these by trial and error.

If children need support, suggest that they investigate the perimeter of shapes with a fixed area, e.g. 24 cm² or the area of shapes with a fixed perimeter, e.g. 24 cm.

Area	Dimensions	Perimeter	Relationship
24 cm²	1 cm × 24 cm	50 cm	P > A
24 cm²	2 cm × 12 cm	28 cm	P > A
24 cm²	3 cm × 8 cm	22 cm	P < A
24 cm²	6 cm × 4 cm	20 cm	P < A

Long thin rectangles have bigger perimeters than rectangles that are closer to a square.

One strategy to suggest to children who are finding the task challenging, would be tell them to examine squares of increasing size. Doing this will give one of the two solutions.

Area	Dimensions	Perimeter	Relationship
1 cm²	1 cm × 1 cm	4 cm	P > A
4 cm²	2 cm × 2 cm	8 cm	P > A
9 cm²	3 cm × 3 cm	12 cm	P > A
16 cm²	4 cm × 4 cm	16 cm	P = A
25 cm²	5 cm × 5 cm	20 cm	P < A
36 cm²	6 cm × 6 cm	24 cm	P < A

Evidencing mastery

Children showing mastery will construct tables similar to those shown above. They will recognise a square as a rectangle. Those who are less secure may see it as a different shape. Children may be able to make some generalisations. There is no direct relationship between area and perimeter but for a given area, the smallest perimeter is always the one closest to a square.

Assessment task 3

Resources

Collection of items for estimating the capacity, e.g. can of fizzy drink, washing-up bowl, litre bottle of squash, coffee mug, bucket, individual carton of fruit juice, kettle , teaspoon.

Running the task

You could make a collection of everyday items ranging in capacity and ask children to estimate the capacity of each. Suitable items are illustrated in the Textbook but it will be a better assessment if you can show them real items, substituting alternative items as necessary. You will need to check the capacity of items like the washing-up bowl, as there are bowls of very different capacities.

Evidencing mastery

Children showing mastery will be able to give good estimates for the items within a reasonable error margin for the size of the item. They will use litres for items like the bucket and washing-up bowl and probably millilitres for those with smaller capacities or they will be able to express volumes like 200 ml as 0.2 l competently.

Did you know?

The legend of Queen Dido builds on the concept that the same area can be divided into pieces that have a completely different perimeter. Conservation of area is a challenging concept for some children. However, children who fully understand the concept will appreciate that every time the width of the strip is halved the length of the strip is doubled. Theoretically this can be done again and again although in practice of course there is a limit to cutting the ox hide or paper!

Suggest to children that they cut a sheet of A3 paper into strips to make the largest rectangle that they can. They can then measure the perimeter and calculate the area of their new very long, thin rectangle.

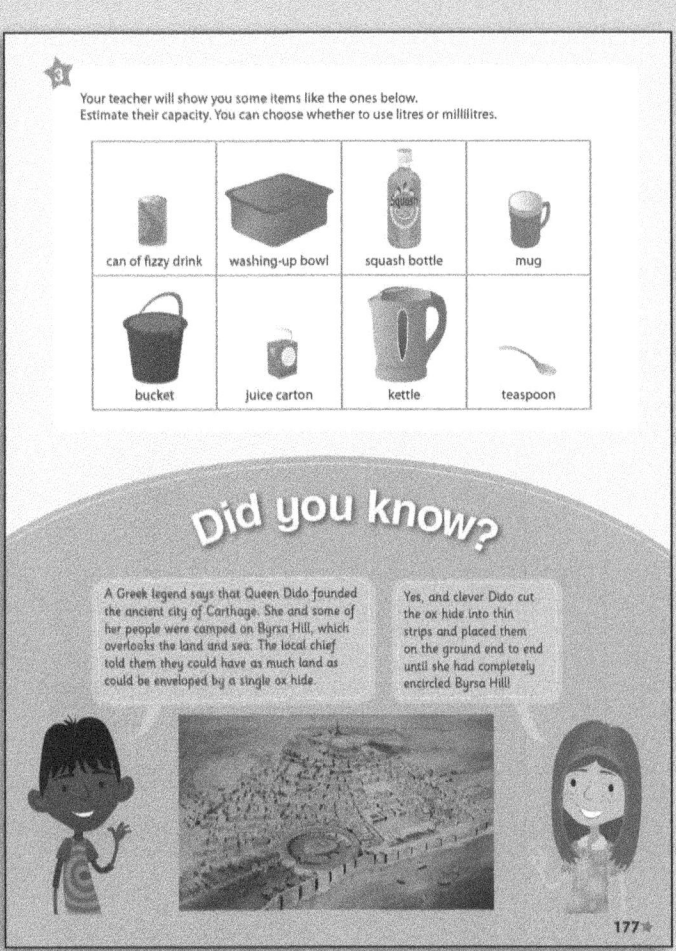

Concepts mastered

- ✓ Children can calculate the perimeter of rectangles and composite rectangles. They can use the formula for perimeter, $P = 2(l + w)$ to calculate possible dimensions for a given perimeter and, given the perimeter and the length of one side, calculate the missing one.

- ✓ Children understand why area is measured in square units such as cm² and m². They can calculate the area of rectangles and understand the formula $A = l \times w$ for the area of a rectangle.

- ✓ Children can estimate volume and capacity and explain the difference between them.

Comparing and rounding 6-digit numbers

100 000	10 000	1000	100	10	1

You need:
- place-value grid
- 1–6 dice
- pencil and paper

- Sketch a place-value grid like the one shown here.
- Roll the dice. Write the digit you roll into any position on the grid.
- Do this 6 times until the grid is full.
- Read the number you have made.
- Now rearrange the digits to make at least 5 other numbers. List them in order of size.
- Will any number in your list round to 400 000?
- Roll the dice again until you can make a 6-digit number that will round to 354 000. Count how many times you needed to roll the dice to make your number.

Please help your child by reading the instructions and doing the activity together.

Rising Stars Mathematics Year 5 © Rising Stars UK Ltd 2015

Holiday distances

- Choose 4 holiday destinations from around the world.
- Find the distance in kilometres from your home town to each destination.
- Which is the nearest? Which is the furthest?
- Now round each distance to the nearest 100 km. Compare the distances using inequality and equals signs (<, =, >).

You need:
- mileage maps from the Internet or an atlas
- pencil and paper

Does it always take longer to travel to destinations that are further away?

Please help your child by reading the instructions and doing the activity together.

Rising Stars Mathematics Year 5 © Rising Stars UK Ltd 2015

1b Multiplying and dividing by 10, 100 and 1000

- Cover each number on the grid with a coin. Put the paper slips face down.
- Player 1 picks a paper slip and removes any coin. Multiply the numbers, e.g. 293 × 100. Say the answer out loud.
- Player 2 checks the answer. If correct, Player 1 keeps the coin. If incorrect, replace the coin.
- Take turns until all the coins have gone. The winner is the player with the most coins.
- Draw your own grid. Use numbers between 1000 and 500 000 rounded to the nearest thousand. Write ÷10, ÷100, ÷1000 on paper slips. Play the game again.
- What range of numbers is needed on the grid to use all 6 paper slips (×10, ×100, ×1000, ÷10, ÷100, ÷1000) and always make whole number answers?

You need:
- 12 counters (or 5p coins)
- ×10, ×100, ×1000 written on paper slips
- pencil and paper
- a partner

147	293	317	449
528	635	794	813
975	584	274	863

 Please help your child by reading the instructions and doing the activity together.

Rising Stars Mathematics Year 5 © Rising Stars UK Ltd 2015

1b Time conversions

Alice 2 h 36 min

Jon 160 minutes

Katy 8100 seconds

Fraser 140 min

Kaseem 9600 sec

Lucy 2½ hours

You need:
- pencil and paper
- clock, watch or stopwatch with seconds

These are the times taken by the 6 runners in a race.

- Who was the winner?
- Think about what you need to do to the times first so that you can compare them.
- Now rank the runners in order from 1st to 6th.
- Time yourself on your journey home from school. Write the time in minutes and seconds.

How could you make your journey home quicker?

Please help your child by reading the instructions and doing the activity together.

Matching decimals and fractions

1c

You need:
- pencil and paper
- scissors

- Make a set of cards like the ones below.

- Shuffle the cards. Place them face down on the table.

- The aim is to match any decimals and fractions which are equivalent. Turn over 2 cards at a time, looking for a decimal and fraction match.

- Make your own set of decimal and fraction cards showing different numbers. Play the game again.

- You could use the same digits on all the cards but move their positions in the decimal number, e.g. 34.58, 5.438 or 853.4. Make cards for the equivalent fractions too.

15.26	27 and $\frac{4}{10}$	3.728	43 and $\frac{31}{100}$
43.31	0.543	921.3	15 and $\frac{26}{100}$
3 and $\frac{728}{1000}$	921 and $\frac{3}{10}$	27.4	$\frac{543}{1000}$

Please help your child by reading the instructions and doing the activity together.

Rising Stars Mathematics Year 5 © Rising Stars UK Ltd 2015

Decimal masses

1c

You need:
- pencil and paper
- weighing scales and measuring jugs for reference
- cookery books

- How much of each ingredient is needed to make enough cake for 100 people?

- First show the amount of each ingredient needed in grams, e.g. 1200 g butter.

- Now show each as a decimal, e.g. 1.2 kg butter.

- Next show each as whole numbers and proper fractions, e.g. 1 $\frac{2}{10}$ kg butter.

- Calculate the ingredients needed for 500 people.

- Look through your cookery books and make a cake together!

Apple cake

Serves 10 people

120 g butter

350 g chopped apples

275 g flour

75 g sugar

175 ml milk

2 eggs

Remember

1 kg = 1000 g

1 l = 1000 ml

Please help your child by reading the instructions and doing the activity together.

Rising Stars Mathematics Year 5 © Rising Stars UK Ltd 2015

Comparing and rounding decimals

1d

You need:
- digit cards 0–9
- pencil and paper
- a partner

- Shuffle your digit cards. Place them face down on the table.
- Choose 3 each. Use them to make a number with 2 decimal places.

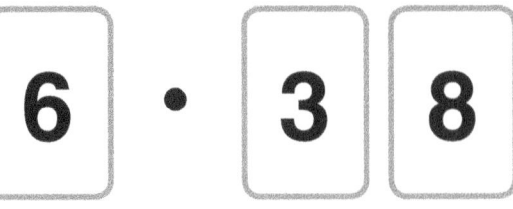

- Round your decimal to the nearest whole number, e.g. 6.38 rounds to 6.
- Record this number as your score.
- The first person to reach an agreed total is the winner.
- Make some changes to the rules of the game and play again, e.g.:
  ▶ you have to place the digits in the order they were picked up
  ▶ round the decimals to the nearest tenth to make your score
  ▶ the winner is the person with the lowest total after 5 turns.

Please help your child by reading the instructions and doing the activity together.

Rising Stars Mathematics Year 5 © Rising Stars UK Ltd 2015

Capacity

1d

You need:
- pencil and paper
- measuring jug with scale in millilitres

Rainwater has been collected in 3 different places over the weekend.

	Saturday	Sunday
Park	1.46 litres	2.51 litres
Town	1.72 litres	1.34 litres
Garden	1.29 litres	2.47 litres

- Round each capacity to the nearest litre. Which place had the most rain each day?
- If the capacities were rounded to the nearest tenth of a litre, would your answer be the same?
- Record how much liquid your family drinks over 2 days. Round your answer to the nearest tenth of a litre.
- Are you surprised by how much or how little you drink? Who drinks the most? Who drinks the least? How much does each person drink on average?

Please help your child by reading the instructions and doing the activity together.

Rising Stars Mathematics Year 5 © Rising Stars UK Ltd 2015 **195**

⭐ 2a Addition routes

£11.96 £13.04 £16.98 £17.02 £23.99 £22.01 £27.96 £29.04 £32.97 £39.04 £35.96 £37.03 £41.99 £44.01 £42.97 £45.03

You need:

- pencil and paper

- Choose routes across or down the board which jump on 4 different money amounts.
- Add the amounts you jump on.
- Find the highest possible money total and the lowest possible money total.
- Use rounding to help you add. Don't forget to adjust the total afterwards.
- Investigate routes which jump on more than 4 different money amounts.
- Which route will give a total nearest to £100?

Please help your child by reading the instructions and doing the activity together.

Rising Stars Mathematics Year 5 © Rising Stars UK Ltd 2015

⭐ 2a Population differences

You need:

- pencil and paper
- calculator
- a partner
- Internet access

	Worcester	Durham	Hereford	Stirling	Lichfield	Bangor
Population	93245	87350	55670	45200	30820	20175

- Pick 2 cities. Challenge your partner to find the population difference between them.
- It might help to count up from the smaller to the larger of the 2 populations using the bar model or a number line.
- Check their answer using a calculator. Award 1 point for a correct answer.
- Take it in turns. See who scores the most points.
- Which 2 cities have a population difference closest to 40000?
- Use the Internet to find the population of your own city or town.
- Compare it to the population of Durham. How much larger or smaller is your city's population?

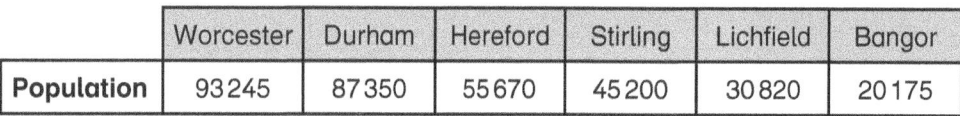

Please help your child by reading the instructions and doing the activity together.

Rising Stars Mathematics Year 5 © Rising Stars UK Ltd 2015

2b Subtraction reversed

- Write a 4-digit number with consecutive digits, e.g. 4567.
- Reverse the digit order to create another number, e.g. 7654.
- Use a subtraction method to find the difference between the 2 numbers.
- Repeat this with other 4-digit numbers. What patterns do you notice? Can you predict answers?
- Does this work for 5-digit and 6-digit numbers?

You need:
- pencil and paper

Explore decimal numbers too.

 Please help your child by reading the instructions and doing the activity together.

Rising Stars Mathematics Year 5 © Rising Stars UK Ltd 2015

2b A new fence

A gardener needs to buy enough fencing to go around the perimeter of this plot.

You need:
- pencil and paper
- tape measure

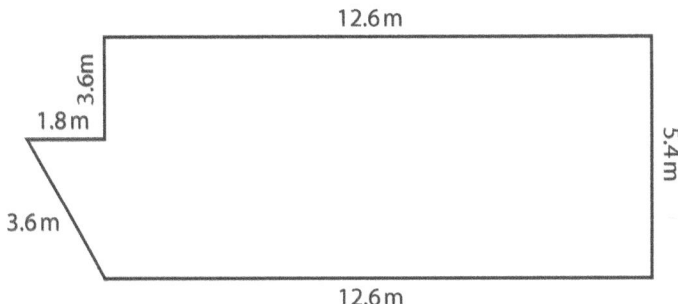

12.6 m

3.6 m

1.8 m

3.6 m

5.4 m

12.6 m

Not drawn to scale

Fence panels come in lengths of 1.8 m. Each panel costs £34.99.

If you buy 5, the price of each panel reduces to £30.99.

- How many panels does the gardener need to buy? What will the total cost of the panels be?
- Measure your own garden. If you don't have a garden, plan your dream garden!
- Draw your garden to scale where 1cm represents 1m.
- Calculate the number of panels needed and the total cost to fence it.

 Please help your child by reading the instructions and doing the activity together.

3a Square and cube numbers

- Last year Jamie's age was a square number. Next year it will be a cube number. How old is he this year?

- If you need help to solve this problem, you could download a 1–100 number square from the Internet. Then highlight square and cube numbers on it. Use 2 different colours.

- Remember, multiply a number by itself to get a square number. Multiply a number by itself and then again by itself to get a cube number.

- When will Jamie's age be **both** a square and a cube number?

- When will your age be a square number, a cube number, and both a square and cube number at the same time?

a squared $= a \times a$
a cubed $= a \times a \times a$

Please help your child by reading the instructions and doing the activity together.

Rising Stars Mathematics Year 5 © Rising Stars UK Ltd 2015

3a Multiples and factors

- Put the digit cards face down on the table. Each player chooses and reveals a number.

- Both players work out a common multiple of the 2 numbers. The player who says the lowest common multiple wins a point.

Both answers are multiples of 3 and 9, but 18 is lower and scores the point.

- What strategies can you use to quickly work out common multiples?

- How can you check if you have the lowest possible common multiple?

- Play again. This time turn over 3 digit cards. Find the lowest common multiple of all 3 numbers.

- Do the strategies you used with 2 numbers work with 3 numbers?

Please help your child by reading the instructions and doing the activity together.

Rising Stars Mathematics Year 5 © Rising Stars UK Ltd 2015

⭐ 3b Multiplying by 5 and 20

A carpet fitter must calculate the cost of carpet for his new hotel project.

The carpet he uses costs £14 per square metre.

One hotel room measures 6.4 m long by 4 m wide.
All the rooms are the same size.

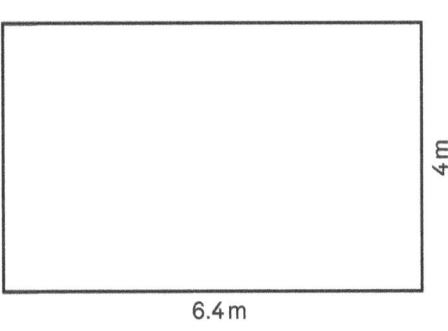

6.4 m

- Work out the cost to carpet 1 room.
- How much would it cost to carpet 10 rooms?
- Work out the cost to carpet 5 rooms and 20 rooms.
- Work out the cost of carpeting your bedroom.

You need:
- pencil and paper
- tape measure

How could you use your answer for 10 rooms to help you work out the answers for other numbers of rooms?

 Please help your child by reading the instructions and doing the activity together.

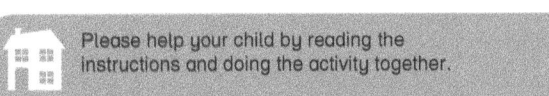

⭐ 3b Multiplication facts

Jessica, Robert and Kyla collect football cards.
They all have the **same** number of cards.
They keep them in special albums.

Jessica has 5 full pages and 12 spare cards.

Robert has 6 full pages and 3 spare cards.

Kyla has 4 full pages and 21 spare cards.

You need:
- pencil and paper
- multiplication square or lists of times tables as support

- How many cards are needed to complete one full page?
- How many cards in total (including spares) does each child have?

Please help your child by reading the instructions and doing the activity together.

Multiplication arrays

You need:
- pencil and paper
- 1–6 dice
- a partner

- Write down any 3-digit number.

- Show this number as an array with one symbol for hundreds, another for tens and a third for ones, e.g.

253 = ⊘ ⊘ ⊘ ⊘ ⊘ ⊘ ⊘ ◯ ◯ ◯

- Roll the dice to choose a multiplier, e.g. 4.
  Make 4 rows of the array in total to show 4 lots of 253.

253 = ⊘ ⊘ ⊘ ⊘ ⊘ ⊘ ⊘ ◯ ◯ ◯
253 = ⊘ ⊘ ⊘ ⊘ ⊘ ⊘ ⊘ ◯ ◯ ◯
253 = ⊘ ⊘ ⊘ ⊘ ⊘ ⊘ ⊘ ◯ ◯ ◯
253 = ⊘ ⊘ ⊘ ⊘ ⊘ ⊘ ⊘ ◯ ◯ ◯

- Find the answer to 4 × 253 by counting the hundreds, tens and ones.

- Repeat this for other 3-digit numbers. Use the dice to choose the multiplier.

- Show 2 other methods for calculating answers to multiplications like these.

- Challenge someone else to see who can reach the correct answer first.

Please help your child by reading the instructions and doing the activity together.

Rising Stars Mathematics Year 5 © Rising Stars UK Ltd 2015

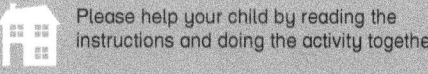 

Division practice

You need:
- pencil and paper
- 1–6 dice

- Roll the dice 3 times to create a 3-digit number.

- Divide this 3-digit number by 2. Use the division methods you have been practising in class. Write the answer.

- Now divide it by 3. Write the answer.

- Keep going until you have divided the 3-digit number in turn by 2, 3, 4, 5 and 6.

- Can you see any patterns in your answers? Try looking at any remainders.

- Create a different 3-digit number and repeat the investigation. Are similar patterns created?

- Investigate what happens when a 4-digit number is divided in turn by 2, 3, 4, 5 and 6.

	÷ 2	÷ 3	÷ 4	÷ 5	÷ 6
251					

Please help your child by reading the instructions and doing the activity together.

Rising Stars Mathematics Year 5 © Rising Stars UK Ltd 2015

Parallel pairs

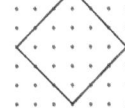

You need:
- pencil
- ruler

- Draw different regular and irregular polygons on the dotty paper.

- Label them to show which have 1, 2 or 3 pairs of parallel sides.

- Are there more polygons with 1 pair of parallel sides than with 3 pairs of parallel sides? Investigate.

Please help your child by reading the instructions and doing the activity together.

Rising Stars Mathematics Year 5 © Rising Stars UK Ltd 2015

Making shapes

- Fold a small piece of paper in half and then in half again.

- Hold the corner. Cut two straight lines around the corner.

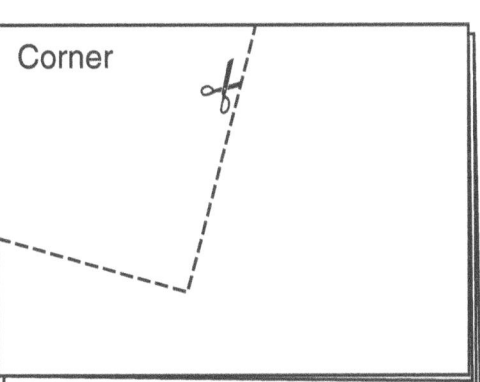

Corner

You need:
- pencil and paper
- scissors
- ruler

- Open up the paper to see the shape you have made.

- How many sides does it have? Does it have any parallel sides? Can you name the shape?

- Now try to make another shape using the same folding technique. What is the total length of its sides?

- Is it possible to make other shapes with the same side length?

- Try cutting 3 straight lines around the corner to make other shapes.

Please help your child by reading the instructions and doing the activity together.

4b Unknown angles

- Here are some triangles. Each has an unlabelled angle.
- Can you calculate the missing angles? Remember that the sum of the 3 angles in a triangle is 180°.

A 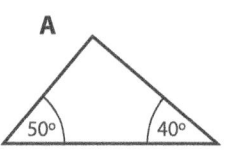 50° 40°

B 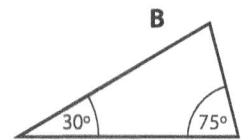 30° 75°

C 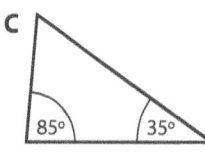 85° 35°

D 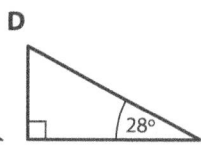 28°

E 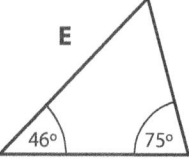 46° 75°

F 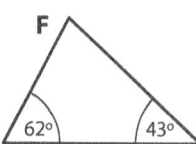 62° 43°

- These isosceles triangles have **2** unlabelled angles. Explain how you can still work these out.

A 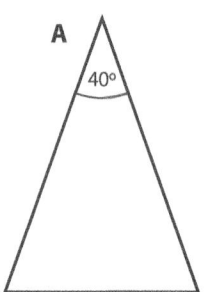 40°

B 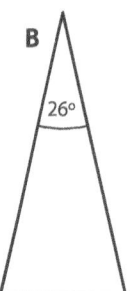 26°

C 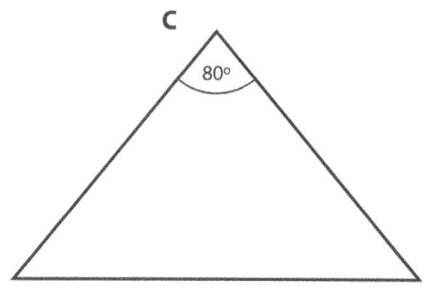 80°

 Please help your child by reading the instructions and doing the activity together.

Rising Stars Mathematics Year 5 © Rising Stars UK Ltd 2015

4b Making triangles

- Arrange your 15 strips to make a triangle.
- Sketch the triangle. Record the length of each side.
- Is it a scalene, isosceles or equilateral triangle? Does it have a right angle?
- Make as many different triangles as you can. Draw each one.
- Sort your triangles into groups.
- Explain any patterns you discover.

Please help your child by reading the instructions and doing the activity together.

Rising Stars Mathematics Year 5 © Rising Stars UK Ltd 2015

Isosceles stretch

You need:
- pencil
- ruler

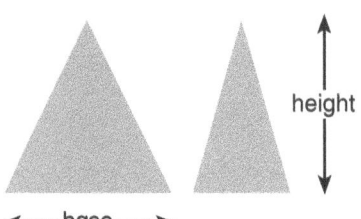

height

- Use the dotty paper. Draw 5 isosceles triangles which have the same height but different base lengths.

- Cut them out and stand them all on their bases.

←base→

- Order the triangles. Put the one with the shortest base first.

- As the base length increases, how does the angle at the top change to keep the isosceles shape?

- Do the side lengths change as well? Measure them with a ruler and record any patterns.

- Can you predict the changes that would happen if you draw another isosceles triangle of the same height with a longer base?

Please help your child by reading the instructions and doing the activity together.

Rising Stars Mathematics Year 5 © Rising Stars UK Ltd 2015

Split the grid

You need:
- ruler
- coloured pencils

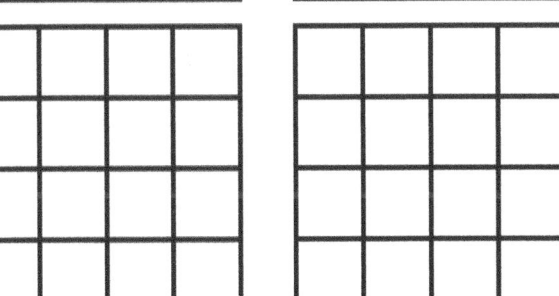

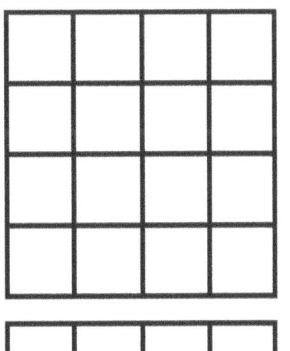

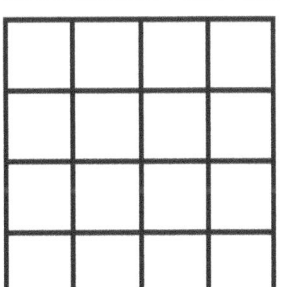

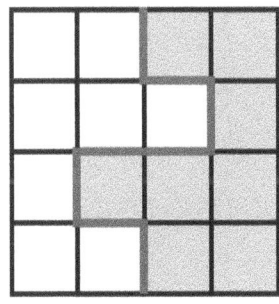

Example

- Find different ways to split the grid into 2 parts.

- Each part must show the **same** shape and have the **same** area.

- Draw a coloured line across the grid to show how you have split it.

Please help your child by reading the instructions and doing the activity together.

5a Target number

100 000	10 000	1000	100	10	1

- Sketch a place-value grid like the one shown here.
  Leave plenty of room underneath each heading for counters.

- Place your 15 counters onto the place-value grid to create
  different numbers, e.g. 5 counters placed in the 10 column represents 50 or 3 counters
  placed in the 10 000 column represents 30 000.

- What is the largest number you can make using all 15 counters?
  What is the smallest number?

- Now roll the dice 4 times. Use the digits you roll to make a 4-digit number, e.g. 5346.
  This is your target number.

- Place all 15 counters on the place-value grid to try to make the target number.
  If it is impossible, make the nearest number you can.

- Now make a 5-digit or 6-digit target number. Compete with a partner.
  Who can get closest to the target?

Please help your child by reading the instructions and doing the activity together.

Rising Stars Mathematics Year 5 © Rising Stars UK Ltd 2015

5a Mass comparisons

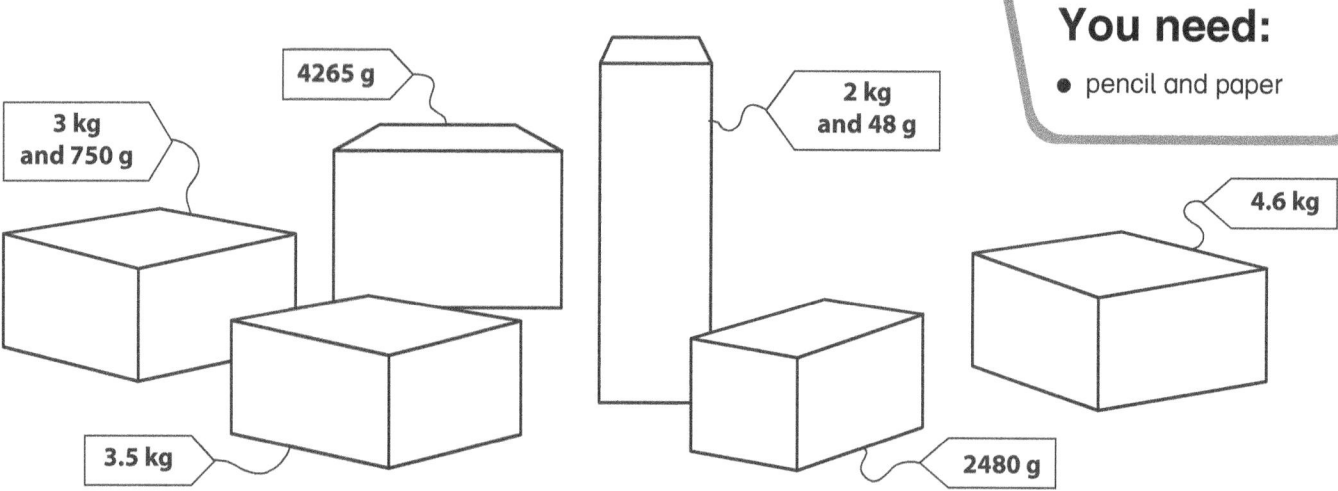

- Convert each parcel's mass to grams so you can compare them easily.

- Number the parcels in order of mass: Parcel 1 = lightest and Parcel 6 = heaviest.

- The postman carries **3** of these parcels.
  Their combined mass is more than 11 kg, has a 3 in the hundreds column
  and is a multiple of 5 g. Which parcels could he be carrying?

- Draw and label a 7th parcel. It must weigh more than Parcel 3 but less than Parcel 4.

Please help your child by reading the instructions and doing the activity together.

Rising Stars Mathematics Year 5 © Rising Stars UK Ltd 2015

Positive and negative numbers

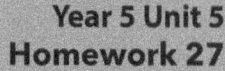
- Shuffle the digit cards. Stack them in a pile face down.

- The aim is to fill the empty boxes you have drawn with 5 numbers in order, e.g. –5, –3, 0, 2, 6.

- Player 1 turns over a digit card and chooses which empty box to place it on. Once a number has been placed, it cannot be moved.

- Your turn ends when you cannot place any more numbers in order. Player 2 takes over.

- The player who places the last of the 5 digit cards is the winner.

You need:
- digit cards –8 to +8
- 5 empty boxes drawn in a line on paper
- a partner

> Think of ways to make the game easier and harder.

Please help your child by reading the instructions and doing the activity together.

Rising Stars Mathematics Year 5 © Rising Stars UK Ltd 2015

Temperatures

Average minimum and maximum temperatures in Reykjavik, Iceland

○ Max. temp.
● Min. temp.

You need:
- pencil and paper
- encyclopaedia or Internet to look up weather temperatures

> Where would you rather live? There are advantages and disadvantages to both!

- What is the maximum temperature during the hottest month?

- How much colder than this can it get in January?

- Which month has the largest temperature range from maximum to minimum? Calculate it.

- Look up maximum and minimum temperatures for a hot country.

- Calculate the difference between the temperatures in Iceland each month and the temperatures in your chosen country.

Please help your child by reading the instructions and doing the activity together.

Rising Stars Mathematics Year 5 © Rising Stars UK Ltd 2015 **205**

⭐ 5c Train timetables

You need:
- pencil and paper
- Internet access or a train timetable

- The train for London leaves Edinburgh at 10:00 a.m. It stops at 5 places on the way. Write each stopping time in digital format underneath each clock.

- Calculate the journey times from Carlisle to Crewe, Lancaster to Milton Keynes, and Edinburgh to Birmingham.

- A direct train takes 4 hours and 23 minutes to travel from Edinburgh to London. How much quicker is this than the train shown here?

Edinburgh	Carlisle	Lancaster	Crewe	Birmingham	Milton Keynes	London
: a.m.	: a.m.	: p.m.	: p.m.	: p.m.	: p.m.	: p.m.

- Look up some other train times on the Internet.

- Can you show the times on an analogue clock using Roman numerals? Look out for clocks like these on station platforms.

Please help your child by reading the instructions and doing the activity together.

Rising Stars Mathematics Year 5 © Rising Stars UK Ltd 2015

⭐ 5c Roman calculations

You need:
- pencil and paper
- a partner

- Each player chooses a Roman numeral from each of the 4 rows to create a 4-digit number. Write both numbers on a piece of paper in place-value columns.

- Working together, add these 2 numbers. Write the answer in Roman numerals.

	I 1	II 2	III 3	IV 4	V 5	VI 6	VII 7	VIII 8	IX 9
Ones	I 1	II 2	III 3	IV 4	V 5	VI 6	VII 7	VIII 8	IX 9
Tens	X 10	XX 20	XXX 30	XL 40	L 50	LX 60	LXX 70	LXXX 80	XC 90
Hundreds	C 100	CC 200	CCC 300	CD 400	D 500	DC 600	DCC 700	DCCC 800	CM 900
Thousands	M 1000	MM 2000	MMM 3000	$\overline{IV}$ 4000	$\overline{V}$ 5000	$\overline{VI}$ 6000	$\overline{VII}$ 7000	$\overline{VIII}$ 8000	$\overline{IX}$ 9000

Example

	Th	H	T	O
Player 1	MMM	C	L	III
Player 2	V	DCC	LX	V
Answer				

Please help your child by reading the instructions and doing the activity together.

Rising Stars Mathematics Year 5 © Rising Stars UK Ltd 2015

6a Choosing addition methods

- Here you will write some tricky calculations.
  One person will use a written addition method
  to solve them. The other will use a sequencing strategy
  for addition.

- Put some stickers on the dice so that it shows
  numbers 4–9 instead of 1–6.

- Each player rolls the dice 4 times to generate a 4-digit number.

- Race to add the 2 numbers using your
  chosen method.

- Repeat 3 times.

- Who got the correct answers first?
  Check the answers using a calculator.

- Swap methods and play again.

- Did one method always win?

You need:
- paper and pencil
- 1–6 dice
- calculator
- a partner

Explore which additions suited each method best.

Please help your child by reading the
instructions and doing the activity together.

Rising Stars Mathematics Year 5 © Rising Stars UK Ltd 2015

6a Higher and higher

This table shows the heights of some very tall buildings
around the world.

Jin Mao Tower	Petronas Towers	Empire State Building	John Hancock Centre
421 m	452 m	381 m	344 m

You need:
- pencil and paper
- Internet access or encyclopaedia

- Choose 2 buildings. Add their heights using a number line or
  sequencing method.

- Find the total height of all 4 buildings using a compact written method.

- Which 3 heights of buildings, when added, make a total that can be
  rounded to 1150 m?

- Find out the height of the 'Tapei 101' building in Taiwan.

- Calculate how much taller it is than each of the 4 buildings in this chart.

- Think carefully about a suitable calculation method for the heights involved.

Please help your child by reading the
instructions and doing the activity together.

6b Subtraction trail

- Start at the top of each column. Work your way down by finding differences.
- Choose a method each time that suits the numbers.

You need:
- pencil and paper

Start	9542	8346	9137	8698
	−8431	−5283	−8993	−3000
Subtotal				
	−1	−63	−132	−4375
Final answer				

Rising Stars Mathematics Year 5 © Rising Stars UK Ltd 2015

6b Record breakers

Here are some record-breaking swimming times (in seconds) for men and women.

You need:
- pencil and paper
- clock, watch or stopwatch with seconds

	100 m freestyle	100 m butterfly	100 m backstroke	100 m breaststroke
Men	44.94	48.48	48.94	55.61
Women	51.01	55.05	55.23	1:02.36
Difference				

- Use a counting on strategy to find the difference between the men's and women's times for each event. Use number line jottings to help.
- If each athlete swam 3.21 seconds faster next year, what would the new records be?
- Time yourself doing a sporting challenge. This might be running round the garden, bouncing a ball 10 times or jumping across the room.
- Repeat the challenge 5 times. Do your times get better or worse?

Rising Stars Mathematics Year 5 © Rising Stars UK Ltd 2015

7a Ordering fractions

- Write all the possible proper fractions which have the denominator 2, 3, 4 or 6. They must be less than 1, e.g. $\frac{1}{2}$.

- How many are there?

- Try to put them in order from smallest to largest.

- Now convert all the fractions so that their denominators are 12, e.g. $\frac{1}{2} = \frac{6}{12}$.

You need:
- pencil and paper
- a partner

Is it easier to order fractions with the same denominator? Explain why to a partner.

Please help your child by reading the instructions and doing the activity together.

Rising Stars Mathematics Year 5 © Rising Stars UK Ltd 2015

7a Equivalent pairs

- In this challenge, you can use any of the numbers from 1–20. You can only use each number once.

- Make a pair of equivalent fractions, e.g. $\frac{1}{2} = \frac{6}{12}$.
  This example has used the numbers 1, 2, 6 and 12.

- Make another pair using the numbers 1–20.
  Don't repeat the numbers you have already used.

You need:
- pencil and paper

How many different equivalent pairs can you make?

Please help your child by reading the instructions and doing the activity together.

Rising Stars Mathematics Year 5 © Rising Stars UK Ltd 2015 **209**

7b Improper fractions to mixed numbers

You need:
- pencil and paper
- other players

- First write a set of 10 improper fractions on separate pieces of paper. The numerator must be larger than the denominator and the fraction value is more than 1, e.g. $\frac{23}{7}$.

- Put them face down on the table.

- Each player chooses one improper fraction card.

- Each player converts their improper fraction to a mixed number, e.g. $\frac{23}{7} \rightarrow 3\frac{2}{7}$.

- Compare your answers. Any player with a fraction part (e.g. $\frac{2}{7}$) which is less than $\frac{1}{2}$ scores a point.

- Return the improper fractions to the table face down. Shuffle the fractions and play again.

- The winner has the most points after an agreed number of turns.

Please help your child by reading the instructions and doing the activity together.

Rising Stars Mathematics Year 5 © Rising Stars UK Ltd 2015

7b Measuring and converting lengths

Remember

1 millimetre = $\frac{1}{10}$ of a centimetre

You need:
- pencil and paper
- ruler
- a partner

This line measures 6 mm or $\frac{6}{10}$ cm.

This line measures 18 mm or $\frac{18}{10}$ cm or 1 cm and 8 mm.

- Measure the lines making up this boat picture. Write each measurement in millimetres, as an improper fraction of a centimetre and as a mixed number.

- Draw your own picture using a ruler. Show someone else how to measure the lengths and convert them to improper fractions of a centimetre and to mixed numbers.

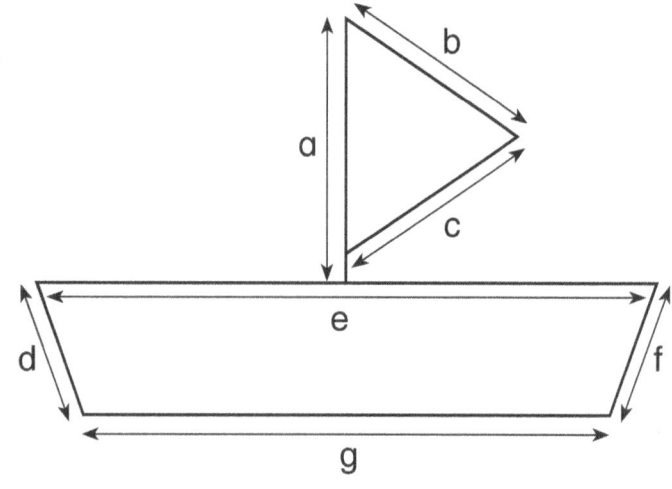

Please help your child by reading the instructions and doing the activity together.

Rising Stars Mathematics Year 5 © Rising Stars UK Ltd 2015

7c Grams and kilograms

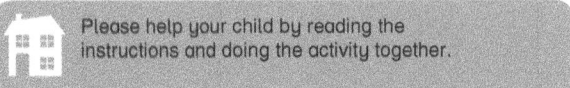

Chocolate cake
Makes 16 slices

150 g margarine
150 g caster sugar
110 g self-raising flour
40 g cocoa powder
1 teaspoon vanilla extract

3 medium eggs
165 g icing sugar
100 g butter, softened
35 g chocolate

You need:
- pencil and paper
- recipe books or recipes on the Internet

- You need to make enough cake for 320 wedding guests to have a slice each!

- Calculate the ingredients you would need.

- Now write each gram measurement in kilograms and as an improper fraction of a kilogram, e.g. 2350 g = 2.350 kg = $\frac{2350}{1000}$ of a kilogram.

- Look at other recipes and gram/kilogram measures on food packets.

Please help your child by reading the instructions and doing the activity together.

7c Decimal stepping stones

smallest  largest

You need:
- a large sheet of paper
- pencils and small pieces of paper
- 1–6 dice
- other players

- Draw the picture of stepping stones on a large sheet of paper.

- Each player writes down 5 decimal numbers.
  Each number must have a unit and 3 decimal places,
  e.g. 2.734. Keep your numbers a secret from the other players.

- Roll a dice to decide who goes first.

- Player 1 places one of their numbers face up on any one of the stepping stones.

- The next player places one of their numbers on another stepping stone. Numbers must be placed in order from smallest to largest.

- A player is out if they are 'stuck' because they cannot place one of their numbers on the stepping stones in the correct order.

- Keep going until only 1 player is left or all the stepping stones have been filled.

- Play again with different decimals or with more stepping stones.

Please help your child by reading the instructions and doing the activity together.

7d Finding percentages

You need:
- pencil and paper
- 1–6 dice

- Roll the dice to make a 3-digit number. Write this number in the middle box. Remember, 100% = this number.

- Start at the top. Work clockwise to calculate the other percentages of your number.

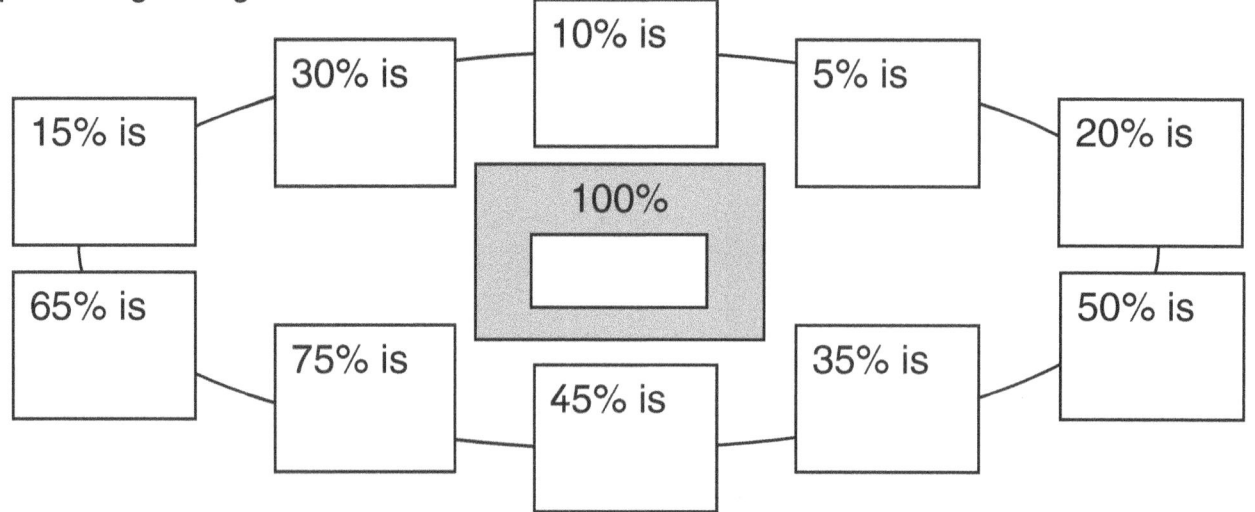

- How does finding certain percentages help you to calculate the others?

- Which percentages are helpful to work out first?

Rising Stars Mathematics Year 5 © Rising Stars UK Ltd 2015

7d Percentage, decimal, fraction

- Make 8 sets of percentage, decimal and fraction equivalent cards.

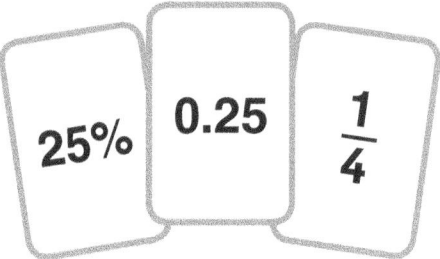

You need:
- small pieces of paper
- pencils
- 2 or more players

- The aim is collect sets of 3 equivalent cards.

- Shuffle all 24 cards and deal 6 to each player. Put the rest face down in a pile.

- Take turns to turn over a card from the centre pile.
  Decide whether to keep it or discard it. If you keep it, you must discard another from your hand so that you still have 6 cards.

- Discarded cards are placed face up in a separate pile. They can be taken by another player during their turn instead of turning over a card from the main pile.

- The winner makes 2 complete sets first.

- Change the rules to include more players or make the game harder or easier.
  You could also make more equivalent sets.

Rising Stars Mathematics Year 5 © Rising Stars UK Ltd 2015

8a Square areas

- A garden company specialises in putting artificial grass in play areas. Work out the square metres of artificial grass needed for each play area.

Play area 1: 15 m wide by 15 m long

Play area 2: 35 m wide by 35 m long

Play area 3: 20 m wide by 20 m long

- What shape are all the play areas?
- How many square metres of artificial grass are needed in total?
- Draw a diagram of your own garden. If you don't have a garden, design your dream one!
- Measure the length and width of any grassy areas in metres.
- Calculate how many square metres of artificial grass you would need.

Please help your child by reading the instructions and doing the activity together.

8a Prime investigation

Here is the list of prime numbers between 1 and 100.

2, 3, 5, 7, 11, 13, 17, 19, 23, 29, 31, 37, 41, 43, 47, 53, 59, 61, 67, 71, 73, 79, 83, 89, 97

- Choose a prime number greater than 3 and square it (multiply it by itself). Now subtract 1 from your answer.
- Write your answer in the table.
- Repeat for other prime numbers.
- Do you notice any patterns? If you work systematically you will see any patterns more clearly.

Prime number	Square it	Subtract 1
7	49	48

Please help your child by reading the instructions and doing the activity together.

8b Finding fractions of amounts

- Place the number cards face down on the table.

- Each player writes down a fraction. The fractions must be halves, quarters or eighths, e.g. $\frac{5}{8}$ or $\frac{3}{4}$.

- Give your fraction to another player. Look at the fraction you have been given.

- When it is your turn, choose a number card from the table. Find the fraction you have been given of that amount, e.g. $\frac{5}{8}$ of 280.

- Remember to divide by the denominator (bottom number) to find one part, e.g. $\frac{1}{8}$. Then multiply by the numerator (top number) to calculate the number of parts you need, e.g. 5 for $\frac{5}{8}$.

- Take turns.

You need:
- pencil and paper
- number cards 240, 280, 320, 360, 400 and 440
- a partner

Which fractions are harder to calculate? Which are easier?

 Please help your child by reading the instructions and doing the activity together.

Rising Stars Mathematics Year 5 © Rising Stars UK Ltd 2015

8b Which deal is best?

A
85

B
60

C
72

You need:
- pencil and paper

- As a special treat, Jack can choose some sweets from one of the jars.

- His dad says he can have:

30% of Jar A  85 **or** 0.4% of Jar B 60 **or** $\frac{3}{8}$ of Jar C  72

- Which deal will give Jack the **greatest** number of sweets?

- Make up another puzzle like this for someone else to solve.

Please help your child by reading the instructions and doing the activity together.

Rising Stars Mathematics Year 5 © Rising Stars UK Ltd 2015

8c Growth rate of plants

Ali has been growing some plants in a warm greenhouse.

Amy has been growing her plants in the garden.

You need:

- pencil and paper
- Internet access or books on plants

	Week 1	Week 2	Week 3	Week 4
Ali's plants	1 cm	4 cm	7 cm	10 cm
Amy's plants	1 cm	2 cm	4 cm	8 cm

- Look at the different growth rates. Whose plants are the tallest by week 4?

- What is the weekly growth rate for Ali's plants?

- Describe the growth rate of Amy's plants.

- Both sets of plants continue to grow at these rates. What height will Ali's and Amy's plants be by week 10?

- Find out the growth rate of different plants on the Internet or in books.

- Which plants grow faster than others? What can a gardener do to increase the growth rate?

Please help your child by reading the instructions and doing the activity together.

8c Scaling the cost of flowers

- Thomas bought some flowers for his Mum.

- Roses cost £1.60 each and lilies cost £2.40 each.

- He bought a beautiful bouquet using these flowers. He spent exactly £24.

- How many of each flower might Thomas have included? Use scaling up to help you solve the problem.

You need:

- pencil and paper

Is there more than 1 possible combination?

Please help your child by reading the instructions and doing the activity together.

Reflection game

- Draw a grid on the squared paper with the x-axis 0 to 8 and y-axis 0 to 8.

- Use a ruler and a coloured pencil. Draw a vertical line at $x = 4$ and a horizontal line at $y = 4$. These are the 'mirror lines'.

- Player 1 places a counter on the grid and writes its coordinate.

- Player 2 places another counter on the grid and writes its coordinate. It must be positioned to be a reflection of the first counter about one of the mirror lines.

- Player 1 places another counter as a reflection of 1 of the counters already on the grid, and writes the new coordinates.

- Keep taking turns until the grid is full.

- Look at the coordinates you have written down. Can you see any patterns?

Please help your child by reading the instructions and doing the activity together.

Symmetrical arrangement

- Draw a 10 × 10 grid on the squared paper. Label the y-axis 1 to 10 and x-axis 1 to 10. Draw a vertical line at $x = 5$. This will be the line of symmetry.

- Your task is to position a set of 10 pieces of artwork on the grid. The final arrangement must be symmetrical about the line you have drawn.

- There are 5 different canvas shapes (2 of each). They can be placed in any orientation.

> The shapes are:
>
> 2 × equilateral triangle: base 2 squares wide
>
> 2 × rectangle: 1 square wide and 5 squares long
>
> 2 × square: sides 2 squares long
>
> 2 × rectangle: 1 square wide and 2 squares long
>
> 2 × rhombus: parallel sides 2 squares long

Please help your child by reading the instructions and doing the activity together.

9b Shape maker

You need:
- straws
- adhesive tack
- construction kit
- a partner

- Explore the range of 3-D shapes you could make using straws joined together with adhesive tack. The straws are the edges of the shape. The adhesive tack holds them together at the vertices.

- Sketch any shapes you make.

- Challenge each other to make different shapes.

- If you have a construction kit at home, you could try using that too.

Which shapes are the most difficult to construct?

Please help your child by reading the instructions and doing the activity together.

Rising Stars Mathematics Year 5 © Rising Stars UK Ltd 2015

9b 3-D constructions with cubes

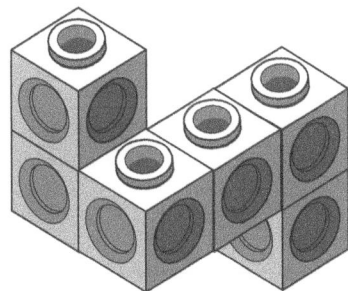

You need:
- pencil and paper
- interlocking cubes (borrow from school)

- Use 6 cubes. Find ways to join them together into different 3-D shapes.

- Sketch each shape you find.

- Is there a maximum number of ways to arrange 6 cubes? Don't include repeats.

- Does the number of ways increase if you increase the number of cubes used? Investigate this with your cubes.

Please help your child by reading the instructions and doing the activity together.

9c Finding triangles

- Look at this picture. Write down the names of any shapes you can see.

You need:
- pencil and paper
- protractor (borrow from school)

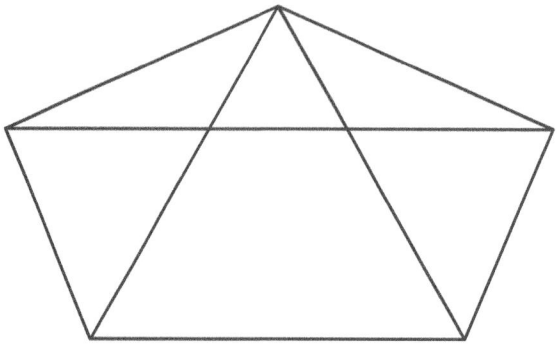

- How many triangles can you see?

- Sort them into isosceles, equilateral, right-angled scalene and scalene.

- Use a protractor to measure some of the angles you can see.

- Are any of the same angles found in more than 1 position? Why is this?

✂ -

9c Guess my shape

- Together draw some 2-D and 3-D shapes. Draw each on a separate piece of card.

You need:
- pencils
- ruler
- card
- other players

- Think of 1 fact about each shape. Write this on a separate piece of card. Also note on the card which shape this fact is about.

- Place the shape pictures on the table face up.

- Player 1 chooses a fact to read out to the other players. Take turns to read out the facts.

- The other players try to identify which shape is being described. They score 1 point for a correct answer.

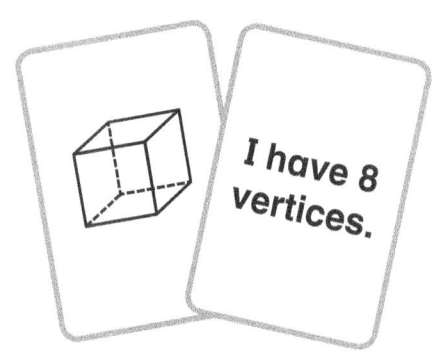

I have 8 vertices.

- Is it always obvious which shape the description matches? How could you make the descriptions link more clearly to 1 specific shape?

- Adjust the descriptions and play again.

Making millions

- Each player draws a place-value grid on a piece of paper.
- The aim of the game is to make the largest number.
- Take turns to roll the dice. Choose where to place that digit in your grid.
- Keep going until all the places on both grids are filled. Read out your big numbers.
- Play 3 rounds. Record your final numbers in each round.
- Together put the 6 different numbers in order from largest to smallest.
- Choose 1 of the numbers and rearrange its digits to create an even larger total. Which number did you choose to rearrange? Explain why.

You need:
- pencil and paper
- 1–6 dice
- a partner

1 000 000	100 000	10 000	1000	100	10	1

 Please help your child by reading the instructions and doing the activity together.

Comparing areas

Here are the areas in square kilometres of various countries.

You need:
- pencil and paper
- Internet access or reference books

UK	Singapore	Jamaica	Monaco	US	Vatican City	Turkey
244 818	692	4244	2.6	9 631 365	0.44	780 575

- Write the countries in order of size from largest to smallest.
- Approximately how much bigger is Jamaica than Singapore?
- Find the difference in area between Turkey and the UK.
- Round the areas of the UK, Jamaica, the US and Turkey to the nearest thousand.
- Use the Internet or books to find a country with a larger area than the US.
- Canada and China are similar sizes. Research their areas and find the difference between them.

Please help your child by reading the instructions and doing the activity together.

10b Fractions of amounts

> Ben won a prize of £21,375.
>
> He gave $\frac{1}{3}$ of it to his children.
>
> Of the amount left, he spent $\frac{3}{5}$ on a new car.
>
> He used $\frac{2}{3}$ of the remainder to pay off some bills.
>
> Finally left he bought 12 necklaces at £150 each.

- How much money did Ben have left?

What would you do with £21,000?

Please help your child by reading the instructions and doing the activity together.

Rising Stars Mathematics Year 5 © Rising Stars UK Ltd 2015

10b Equivalent fractions

- Cut 4 strips of paper measuring exactly 12 cm long and 1 cm wide.

- Divide each strip equally into blocks by drawing vertical lines on the strips to show the divisions. Divide the strips into 3, 6, 9 and 12 blocks. The one below has been divided into 6 (sixths) as an example.

- Use these fraction bars to make some fractions that are equivalent to $\frac{2}{3}$. Write them in order from the smallest denominator to the largest.

- Look at how the numerator and denominator increase in size. Is there a pattern? Can you explain it?

- Look at fractions equivalent to $\frac{3}{4}$ in the same way. Do the same patterns emerge?

- Continue investigating other equivalent fraction chains.

Please help your child by reading the instructions and doing the activity together.

Rising Stars Mathematics Year 5 © Rising Stars UK Ltd 2015

Rounding decimals

10c

You need:
- 2 sets of digit cards 0–9
- some decimal point cards
- other players (optional)

- Shuffle the digit cards. Deal out 3 to each player.

- Each player uses the digit cards and a decimal point card to make a number to 2 decimal places, e.g. 2.45.

- How many different numbers can you make with your 3 cards?

- This time deal out 5 digit cards to each player. Explore the numbers you can make now. Use 3 of the digit cards each time, e.g. 2.45.

- Round each number you have made to the nearest whole number.

- Is there 1 whole number that lots of the decimals round to? Are there any whole numbers that none of the decimals will round to? Explain any findings.

Please help your child by reading the instructions and doing the activity together.

Rising Stars Mathematics Year 5 © Rising Stars UK Ltd 2015

Calculating decimal mass

10c

You need:
- pencil and paper
- kitchen weighing scales

- Some geologists have been collecting different rocks and recording them by mass. The labels have got muddled up and the scales are now broken!

- Can you work out the mass of each rock using the geologists' notes?

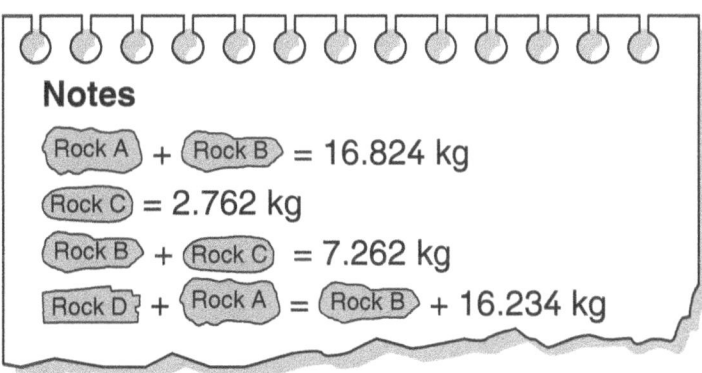

Notes

Rock A + Rock B = 16.824 kg

Rock C = 2.762 kg

Rock B + Rock C = 7.262 kg

Rock D + Rock A = Rock B + 16.234 kg

- Find some stones in your garden or at the park.

- Use the kitchen scales to weigh them. Record the mass of each in grams and kilograms.

Please help your child by reading the instructions and doing the activity together.

11a Adding and subtracting measurements

3.21 litres	1.140 litres	2.64 litres
3.7 litres	4.239 litres	1.71 litres

You need:
- pencil and paper
- measuring jug
- cups

- Make up some additions using these numbers.

- Find out which addition makes a total nearest to 5 litres.

- Now find out how many subtractions you can make with an answer of 1.5 litres.

- Do all the cups in your house hold the same amount of liquid?

- Measure their capacities to find out.

Which cup holds the most?

Please help your child by reading the instructions and doing the activity together.

11a Slush machines

The Slush Company provides slush drinks machines for parties and events.

Each machine is filled with 10 litres of liquid.

This liquid expands by 20% when it is frozen, making even more to drink!

The cups are provided with the machine.
Each one holds 200 millilitres of slush.

You need:
- pencil and paper

- How many cups of slush can 1 machine fill?

- Milly is having a party and inviting 180 guests.
  She wants to give everyone 1 drink.

  How many machines must Milly hire?

- Josef is having 72 guests to his party.
  He wants everyone to have 2 drinks.

  How many millilitres of slush will Josef need? How many machines will he need? Will there be any slush left over? How much?

Please help your child by reading the instructions and doing the activity together.

11b Fraction puzzle

$2\frac{6}{16}$	+	=	$3\frac{7}{8}$

+   +   +

| | + | $4\frac{4}{8}$ | = | |

=   =   =

| $3\frac{1}{2}$ | + | | = | |

- Find the missing fractions to complete the grid.

- Find the total of each row and each column.

- What do you notice about the combined row totals and the combined column totals?

- Make up another fraction puzzle for a friend to solve.

 Please help your child by reading the instructions and doing the activity together.

11b Fraction conversions and calculations

$\frac{2}{3}$	$\frac{4}{6}$	$\frac{5}{12}$	$\frac{9}{12}$	$\frac{8}{24}$
$\frac{3}{24}$	$\frac{21}{24}$	$\frac{17}{6}$	$\frac{10}{3}$	$\frac{15}{12}$

- Shuffle the cards. Put them face down in a pile.

- Each player is dealt 2 cards.

- Each player must add the fractions and find the difference between them.

- Check each other's answers. Correct answers score 1 point.

- The first player to score 6 points is the winner.

Please help your child by reading the instructions and doing the activity together.

12a Fractions of time

- Shade the fractions on the clocks to show how much of an hour they represent.

- Complete the boxes to show how many minutes each fraction is.

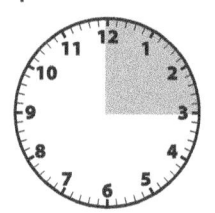  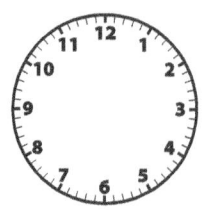 

$\frac{1}{4}$ hour = 15 min $\frac{3}{5}$ hour = ☐ min $\frac{5}{6}$ hour = ☐ min $\frac{2}{3}$ hour = ☐ min

  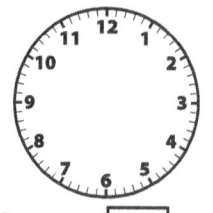 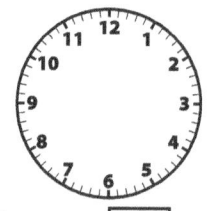

$\frac{17}{20}$ hour = ☐ min $\frac{4}{15}$ hour = ☐ min $\frac{10}{12}$ hour = ☐ min $\frac{9}{30}$ hour = ☐ min

- Write the fraction of an hour you spend eating breakfast, travelling to school, having a bath, reading a book and playing games. How many minutes does each of your fractions represent?

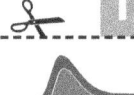 Please help your child by reading the instructions and doing the activity together.

Rising Stars Mathematics Year 5 © Rising Stars UK Ltd 2015

12a Weighing and finding fractions

- Use weighing scales to measure 400 g of dry rice.

- Put it into a bag. We'll call this '1 whole bag of rice'. Label the bag.

- Now measure out the following fractions of rice. Put each into its own bag. Label the bags with the fractions.

$\frac{1}{2}$ of a bag of rice

$\frac{6}{8}$ of a bag of rice

$\frac{3}{5}$ of a bag of rice

$\frac{1}{4}$ of a bag of rice

$\frac{4}{10}$ of a bag of rice

- Complete these calculations:

$\frac{6}{8} + \frac{1}{4} =$ ☐ grams $\frac{3}{5} + \frac{4}{10} =$ ☐ grams $\frac{1}{2} + \frac{6}{8} =$ ☐ grams

- Now check your answers by weighing the bags.

  Please help your child by reading the instructions and doing the activity together.

Rising Stars Mathematics Year 5 © Rising Stars UK Ltd 2015

12b Multiply and divide by multiples of 10, 100 and 1000

You need:
- 1–6 dice
- a partner

- Play this multiplying and dividing game using place value.
- Each number on the dice represents a multiplication or division.

| 1 | ×10 | 2 | ÷10 | 3 | ×100 | 4 | ÷100 | 5 | ×1000 | 6 | ÷1000 |

- Start at 5000. One player wins if the number reaches 5 000 000. The other player wins if the number goes below zero.

- Take turns to roll the dice. Do what the number on the dice tells you, e.g. you roll 4 so must divide 5000 by 100 (5000 ÷ 100 = 50). The next player rolls a 5 so must multiply 50 by 1000 (50 × 1000 = 50 000).

- Who won?

- Play again by the same rules. Who won this time? Explain if this is a fair game or not.

- Try different starting numbers to make the game fairer. Explain your findings.

Please help your child by reading the instructions and doing the activity together.

Rising Stars Mathematics Year 5 © Rising Stars UK Ltd 2015

12b Mystery number

You need:
- pencil and paper

Osawa started with a mystery number.

He divided it by 100.

Then he multiplied the answer by 10.

After that he subtracted 100 and then multiplied the answer by 1000.

He divided that number by 10, added 1000 and finally divided it by 1000.

The number he ended with was 37.215.

What maths facts and strategies might help you?

- Can you work out Osawa's mystery number?
- Make up your own mystery number puzzle for a friend to solve.

Please help your child by reading the instructions and doing the activity together.

Rising Stars Mathematics Year 5 © Rising Stars UK Ltd 2015 **225**

Population percentages

You need:
- pencil and paper
- Internet access

Here are the populations of some world countries in 2015.

Bermuda	Gibraltar	Monaco	Greenland	Faroe Islands
64 237	30 001	36 950	55 984	48 724

- Find out which percentage represents the greatest number of people. Round your answers to the nearest whole person!

- Find out the population of the UK.

- What percentage of the UK population is approximately equal to the population of Bermuda?

30% of Bermuda's population

45% of Gibraltar's population

50% of Monaco's population

25% of Greenland's population

35% of Faroe Island's population

  Please help your child by reading the instructions and doing the activity together.

Takeaway price increase

You need:
- pencil and paper
- takeaway menu

- Find a takeaway menu in the house (or find one on the Internet).

- Ask each family member to choose a complete meal from the menu.

- Write their choices and the price of each item.

- Find the total cost of each person's meal.

- When you go to collect the food, the restaurant tells you all the prices have been increased by 12%!

- Calculate the new price for each person's meal.

How much more money in total will it cost your family?

Please help your child by reading the instructions and doing the activity together.

13a Prime factor tree

- Start with the number 16. List 1 factor pair for 16, e.g. 2 and 8.

- Take each factor and list 1 of its factor pairs.

- Keep going until all the factors are prime numbers.

- Write a list of them: 2, 2, 2, 2.

- Choose a different factor pair for 16. Repeat the task to find its prime factors. What do you notice?

- Investigate prime factors of 20 and 24 in the same way.

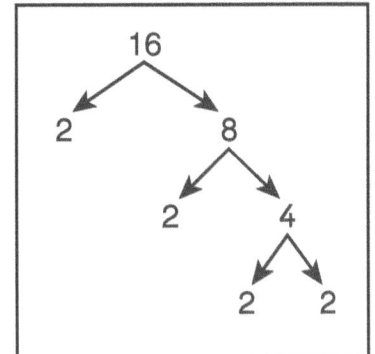

You need:
- pencil and paper

Can you make any general statements?

Please help your child by reading the instructions and doing the activity together.

13a Age factors

- Gather the ages of people in your family and write them in a list in numerical order e.g.:

Granny	76
Daddy	42
Mum	41
Kaylie	17
Mick	8

- For each age, write a list of factors (in pairs if possible).

- Which ages have the greatest number of factors?

- Find out if older people's ages always have more factors.

- Measure and draw a rectangle to represent each person's age and compare them e.g. Mick could have a 2 cm × 4 cm rectangle.

- Do older people always have larger rectangles?

- Can a rectangle be drawn for every person?

- Explain your answers to a grown up.

You need:
- pencil
- paper
- family information

Please help your child by reading the instructions and doing the activity together.

13b Scaling up using multiplication

Miss Percival is putting together goody bags for children to take home at the end of the school trip.

Each bag contains the following items:

1 mask
1 ruler
1 pencil
1 notepad
1 animal picture

You need:

● pencil and paper

- 2 groups of children went on the trip. Using scaling up to calculate the costs of the goody bags. Write the costs in the table.

Price for 1 item	Red group (8 children)	Blue group (6 children)
mask (40p)		
ruler (25p)		
pencil (10p)		
notepad (18p)		
picture (32p)		

- Now find the total cost for each group. Find the total cost for both groups together.

- Look in a catalogue or online to choose items for a goody bag. Scale up the prices to see how much it would cost to give each of your friends a goody bag.

 Please help your child by reading the instructions and doing the activity together.

Rising Stars Mathematics Year 5 © Rising Stars UK Ltd 2015

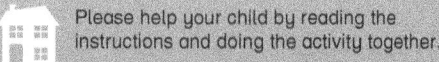

13b Scaling down

- Choose a small item from your bedroom, e.g. a book, a torch or a toy. It should fit onto an A4 sheet of paper.

- Take measurements of the item in centimetres. Take the length, width, height, depth and any others you think are important.

- Make a scale drawing (or scale model) of the item. Your drawing (or model) should be about $\frac{1}{3}$ of the actual size.

- Find an item from the kitchen. It should fit onto an A4 sheet of paper.

- Take some measurements and then make a scale drawing (or scale model). Your drawing (or model) should be about $\frac{3}{4}$ of the actual size.

- Now find something really big from the house or garden. Make a scale drawing (or model) of it which is about $\frac{1}{20}$ of the actual size.

You need:

● pencil and paper
● tape measure or ruler
● items in the house

 Please help your child by reading the instructions and doing the activity together.

Rising Stars Mathematics Year 5 © Rising Stars UK Ltd 2015

13c Using the grid method

- Ranjit is putting together the parts required to make a kit car. The total number of bolts needed is 2365.

- Calculate the number of bolts needed to make 4, 6 and 9 kit cars. Use the grid method to show your working out.

- Is there a quick way to find the number of bolts needed to make 8 kit cars using the answers you have already found?

Using addition only, which other numbers of kit car can you work out the bolts required for?

Please help your child by reading the instructions and doing the activity together.

Rising Stars Mathematics Year 5 © Rising Stars UK Ltd 2015

13c Long multiplication

- Jasmine is on a cycling holiday in Malta. The island is 15 km long and the total shoreline distance around the island is 45 km. It takes her 3240 seconds to cycle the length of the island. How long will it take her, in seconds, to cycle around the whole shoreline?

- By the end of the holiday, Jasmine has cycled around the whole shoreline 24 times. Use a long multiplication method to calculate how much time, in seconds, this has taken her.

- Can you write this time in hours and minutes? You can use a calculator to help you.

- Use the Internet to look up the shoreline distances of other small islands.

- Cycling at the same rate, how long would it take Jasmine to cycle around those islands?

Please help your child by reading the instructions and doing the activity together.

⭐ 13d

Remainders as decimals and fractions

You need:

- pencil and paper
- a partner

- Write down a 2-digit number less than 50, e.g. 24.

- Challenge each other to choose a divisor that will leave a remainder for you to write as a fraction and as a decimal.

- Record your findings like this:

2-digit number	Divisor	Answer	Remainder as fraction	Remainder as decimal	Challenge met?
24	6	4	No remainder	No remainder	x
24	7	3 R 3	$3\frac{3}{7}$	Too hard	x
24	5	4 R 4	$4\frac{4}{5}$	4.8	Yes!

- Take it in turns to choose the 2-digit number. See who can find the 'best' divisor each time.

- Now look at your results chart. Can you see any patterns?

Are all remainders easy to show as fractions? Are some fractions harder to show as decimals?

Please help your child by reading the instructions and doing the activity together.

Rising Stars Mathematics Year 5 © Rising Stars UK Ltd 2015

⭐ 13d

Remainders after division

You need:

- pencil and paper

- Divide each number on the grid by 4. Record any remainders in the matching position on the empty grid.

- Are there any patterns? Can you explain them?

- Investigate patterns when you use a different divisor, e.g. divide each number by 5.

- Can you make any general statements about remainders left after division?

3	6	9	12	15	18	21	24	27	30
4	8	12	16	20	24	28	32	36	40
5	10	15	20	25	30	35	40	45	50
6	12	18	24	30	36	42	48	54	60

⭐ 230

Please help your child by reading the instructions and doing the activity together.

Rising Stars Mathematics Year 5 © Rising Stars UK Ltd 2015

14a Perimeters of rectangles

You need:
- pencil
- ruler
- cm-squared paper

- Draw a set of 8 rectangles on your paper. The rectangles must increase in size by 1 cm length and 1 cm width each time, e.g. rectangle 1 is 1 cm × 3 cm, rectangle 2 is 2 cm × 4 cm, rectangle 3 is 3 cm × 5 cm, and so on.

- Calculate the perimeter of each rectangle. Write them in order from smallest to largest.

- Can you see any patterns?

- By how much does the perimeter increase each time? Can you explain why?

- Investigate with square shapes. Increase the side length by 1 cm each time, e.g. square 1 is 2 × 2 cm, square 2 is 3 × 3 cm, square 3 is 4 × 4 cm, and so on. Is the pattern the same as before?

 Please help your child by reading the instructions and doing the activity together.

Rising Stars Mathematics Year 5 © Rising Stars UK Ltd 2015

14a Finding perimeters

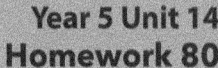

You need:
- pencil and paper
- tape measure
- Internet access or DIY catalogues

- Imagine you are decorating your bedroom. You want to put up a wallpaper border that goes all the way around the room. Set your problem solving out in clear steps.

- Calculate the length of border required. How can you use your knowledge of perimeters to help?

- Look on the Internet or in a catalogue to find a border you like.

- What is the price per metre?

- What will it cost to buy the exact length of border you need?

Don't forget you won't need any wallpaper border where you have doors or windows. So you will have to do some subtracting too.

 Please help your child by reading the instructions and doing the activity together.

14b Areas of rectangles

You need:
- pencil
- ruler
- cm-squared paper

- Draw a set of 8 rectangles on your paper.
  The rectangles must increase in size by 1 cm length and 1 cm width each time, e.g. rectangle 1 is 1 cm × 3 cm, rectangle 2 is 2 cm × 4 cm, rectangle 3 is 3 cm × 5 cm, and so on.

- Calculate the area of each rectangle. Write them in order from smallest to largest.

- Can you see any patterns? By how much does the area increase each time?

- Can you make a general statement and use this to calculate the area of the next 2 rectangles in the sequence?

- Investigate what happens to the areas if the rectangle lengths and widths are doubled, e.g. rectangle A is 1 cm × 3 cm, rectangle B is 2 cm × 6 cm, rectangle C is 4 cm × 12 cm and so on.

- What patterns emerge?

14b Areas and perimeters

You need:
- pencil
- ruler
- cm-squared paper

- Draw a shape with an area of 1 square centimetre.

- There is only 1 shape possible.
  It has an area of 1 cm² and a perimeter of 4 cm.

- Draw a shape with an area of 2 square centimetres.

- How many shapes are possible?
  What are their perimeters?

- Continue to investigate with shapes that have an area of 3 cm², 4 cm² and 5 cm².

- Describe any patterns you notice in:
  - ▸ the number of different shapes that can be drawn (different orientations don't count)
  - ▸ the perimeters of the shapes
  - ▸ the areas of the shapes.

14c Volume patterns

The volume of Box A is
1 cm × 2 cm × 3 cm = 6 cm³ (cubed).

Box B

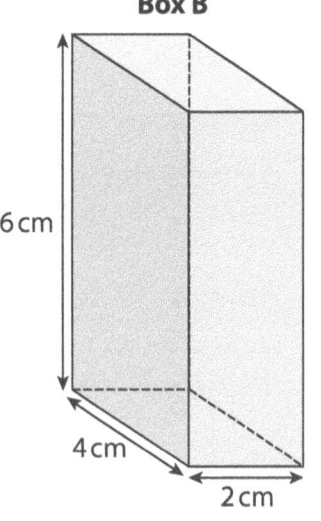

6 cm

4 cm

2 cm

Box A

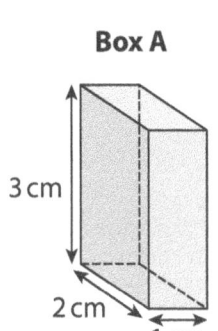

3 cm

2 cm

1 cm

- Box B has all dimensions doubled: 2 cm × 4 cm × 6 cm. Calculate the volume of Box B.

- Box C has all dimensions doubled again. Calculate the volume of Box C.

- Are any patterns emerging?

- Start at the beginning again with Box A. Investigate what happens when the dimensions are tripled instead of doubled. Try to explain any patterns you spot.

14c Investigating volumes

- Picture a cube with a volume of
  2 × 2 × 2 cm (8 cm³ or 8 cm cubed).

- Make it with interlocking bricks if you have some.

- Imagine that you drop the cube into a pot of paint. The bricks on the surface would end up covered in paint but no paint leaks into the cube itself.

PAINT

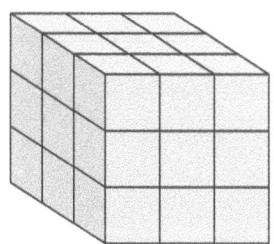

- How many of the individual bricks would have paint on them?

- Repeat this with a cube that has a volume of 3 × 3 × 3 (27 cm³).

- How many of the individual bricks would have paint on them?

- Would only 1 face of all the bricks have paint on?

- Now investigate a cube with a volume of 4 × 4 × 4 cm = 64 cm³ and one with 5 × 5 × 5 = 125 cm³.

- For each cube note the total number of bricks, the number of bricks with paint on and the number of bricks with more than 1 face with paint on.

- Are any patterns emerging?

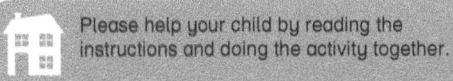

Homework sheets answers

Homework 4
Time conversions
1st = Katy 135 min, 2nd = Fraser 140 min, 3rd = Lucy 150 min, 4th = Alice 156 min, joint 5th = Jon and Kaseem 160 min

Homework 6
Decimal masses
For 100 people: 1200 g, 1.2 kg or $1\frac{2}{10}$ kg butter; 3500 g, 3.5 kg or $3\frac{1}{2}$ kg apples; 2750 g, 2.75 kg or $2\frac{3}{4}$ kg flour; 750 g, 0.75 kg or $\frac{3}{4}$ kg sugar; 1750 ml, 1.75 l or $1\frac{3}{4}$ l milk; 20 eggs

For 500 people: 6000 g or 6 kg butter; 17 500 g, 17.5 kg or $17\frac{1}{2}$ kg apples; 13 750 g, 13.75 kg or $13\frac{3}{4}$ kg flour; 3750 g, 3.75 kg or $3\frac{3}{4}$ kg sugar; 8750 ml, 8.75 l or $8\frac{3}{4}$ l milk; 100 eggs

Homework 8
Capacity
Saturday: park 1 l, town 2 l, garden 1 l; Sunday: park 3 l, town 1 l, garden 2 l. Based on rounding the capacities to the nearest litre, the town had the most rain on Saturday and the park had the most rain on Sunday.

Based on rounding the capacities to the nearest tenth of a litre, the town still had the most rain on Saturday. On Sunday, the park and the garden would have the same amount of rain with 2.5 l.

Homework 10
Population differences
Durham and Stirling

Homework 11
Subtraction reversed
4-digit numbers treated like this always have a difference of 3087.

5-digit numbers have a difference of 41 976.

6-digit numbers have a difference of 530 865.

Homework 12
A new fence
The perimeter is 39.6 m, so 22 panels are needed. 20 panels can be bought at the reduced price and 2 at the full price. Total cost is £689.78.

Homework 13
Square and cube numbers
Last year Jamie was 25. Next year he will be 27. This year he is 26.

When he is 64.

Homework 15
Multiplying by 5 and 20
£358.40 for 1 room, £3584 for 10 rooms, £1792 for 5 rooms, £7168 for 20 rooms

Homework 16
Multiplication facts
There are 9 cards on a full page. Each child has 57 cards. 5P + 12 = 6P + 3 = 4P + 21 (where P = a full page).

Homework 21
Unknown angles
A 90°, B 75°, C 60°, D 62°, E 59°, F 75°

A 70°, B 77°, C 80° (In an isosceles triangle, two angles are the same size.)

Homework 23
Isosceles stretch
As the base lengthens, the angle at the top increases and the side lengths increase too.

Homework 26
Mass comparisons
4265 g + 3.5 kg + 4.6 kg = 12 365 g or 12.365 kg

Homework 28
Temperatures
Max. temp. (July and August) is °C January is -3°C which is 16°C colder. August has a difference of 6°C.

Homework 29
Train timetables
10:00, 11:15, 12:05, 13:10, 14:15, 15:45, 16:20

1 h 55 min, 3 h 40 min, 4 h 15 min

1 h 57 min

Homework 32
Higher and higher
1598 m

421 m + 381 m + 344 m

Homework 33
Subtraction trail

Start	9542	8346	9137	8698
	-8431	-5283	-8993	-3000
Subtotal	1111	3063	144	5698
	-1	-63	-132	-4375
Final answer	1110	3000	12	1323

Homework 34
Record breakers

	100m freestyle	100m butterfly	100m backstroke	100m breast-stroke
Men	41.73	45.27	45.73	52.40
Women	47.8	51.84	52.02	59.15
Difference	6.07	6.57	6.29	6.75

Homework 39
Grams and kilograms
Multiply each ingredient by 20.
margarine: 3000 g = 3 kg = $\frac{3000}{1000}$ of a kg
caster sugar: 3000 g = 3 kg = $\frac{3000}{1000}$ of a kg
self-raising flour: 2200 g = 2.2 kg = $\frac{2200}{1000}$ of a kg
cocoa powder: 800 g = 0.8 kg = $\frac{800}{1000}$ of a kg
vanilla extract: 20 teaspoons
eggs: 60 eggs
icing sugar: 3300 g = 3.3 kg = $\frac{3300}{1000}$ of a kg
butter: 2000 g = 2 kg = $\frac{2000}{1000}$ of a kg
chocolate: 700 g = 0.7 kg = $\frac{700}{1000}$ of a kg

Homework 43
Square areas
They are all square shapes.

1: 225 m², 2: 1225 m², 3: 400 m². Total: 1850 m²

Homework 44
Prime investigation
From prime 7 onwards all answers end in 0 or 8. All answers are multiples of 8. Some pairs of consecutive answers add to produce the next answer. Other patterns may be found.

Homework 46
Which deal is best?
30% of 85 = 25.5, 0.4 of 60 = 24, $\frac{3}{8}$ of 72 = 27. Jack should choose $\frac{3}{8}$ of Jar C.

Homework 47
Growth rate of plants
Ali's

3 cm

They double in height each week.

Ali's = 28 cm, Amy's = 512 cm

Homework 48
Scaling the cost of flowers
Examples: 3 roses + 8 lilies; 6 roses + 6 lilies; 9 roses + 4 lilies; 12 roses + 2 lilies.

Homework 56 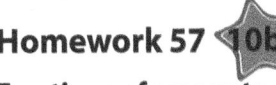 10a
Comparing areas
US, Turkey, UK, Jamaica, Singapore, Monaco, Vatican City

3500 km²

535 757 km²

245 000, 4000, 9 631 000, 781 000

Homework 57 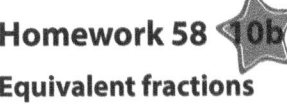 10b
Fractions of amounts
Ben had £100 left.

Homework 58  10b
Equivalent fractions
Numerator increases by 2; denominator increases by 3.

Homework 60  10c
Calculating decimal mass
A = 12.324 kg, B = 4.5 kg, C = 2.762 kg, D = 8.41 kg

Homework 61  11a
Adding and subtracting measurements
3.21 + 1.71 = 4.92

3.21 − 1.71, 2.64 − 1.140

Homework 62 11a
Slush machines
Each machine holds 12 litres in total. This will fill 60 cups.

Milly needs three machines.

Josef needs 28 800 ml of slush and three machines. There will be 7.2 litres (7200 ml) left over.

Homework 63  11b
Fraction puzzle

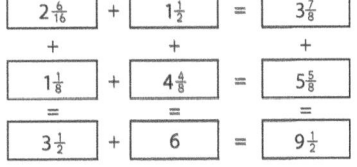

$2\frac{6}{16}$	+	$1\frac{1}{2}$	=	$3\frac{7}{8}$
+		+		+
$1\frac{1}{8}$	+	$4\frac{4}{8}$	=	$5\frac{5}{8}$
=		=		=
$3\frac{1}{2}$	+	6	=	$9\frac{1}{2}$

Homework 65 12a
Fraction of time
$\frac{3}{5}$ hour = 36 min, $\frac{5}{6}$ hour = 50 min, $\frac{2}{3}$ hour = 40 min, $\frac{17}{20}$ hour = 51 min, $\frac{4}{15}$ hour = 16 min, $\frac{10}{12}$ hour = 50 min, $\frac{9}{30}$ hour = 18 min

Homework 66 12b
Weighing and finding fractions
$\frac{6}{8} + \frac{1}{4}$ = 300 g + 100 g = 400 g

$\frac{3}{5} + \frac{4}{10}$ = 240 g + 160 g = 400 g

$\frac{1}{2} + \frac{6}{8}$ = 200 g + 300 g = 500 g

Homework 68 12c
Mystery number
4621.5

Homework 69  12c
Population percentages
19 271, 13 500, 18 475, 13 996, 17 053

Bermuda 64 thousand and UK 64 million, so Bermuda is 0.1% of UK, i.e. 1000 times smaller.

Homework 71 13a
Prime factor tree
Same prime factors 2,2,2,2 result.

Homework 73 13b
Scaling up using multiplication

Price for 1 item	Red group (8 children)	Blue group (6 children)
mask (40p)	£3.20	£2.40
ruler (25p)	£2.00	£1.50
pencil (10p)	80p	60p
notepad (18p)	£1.44	£1.08
picture (32p)	£2.56	£1.92

Homework 75 13c
Using the grid method
9460, 14 190, 21 285

Double the answer for 4 cars = 18 920.

Homework 76  13c
Long multiplication
9720 sec

233 280 sec

3888 minutes = 64 h 48 min

She cycles 15 km in 3240 seconds which is 216 seconds per km. Multiply the shoreline distances in km by 216 seconds to find the time it would take her

Homework 78 13d
Remainders after division

3	2	1	0	3	2	1	0	3	2
0	0	0	0	0	0	0	0	0	0
1	2	3	0	1	2	3	0	1	2
2	0	2	0	2	0	2	0	2	0

3210 pattern repeating in multiples of 3; 1230 pattern repeating in multiples of 5; 2020 pattern repeating in multiples of 6; 0000 in multiples of 4

Homework 79  14a
Perimeters of rectangles
1 = 8 cm, 2 = 12 cm, 3 = 16 cm, 4 = 20 cm, 5 = 24 cm, 6 = 28 cm, 7 = 32 cm, 8 = 36 cm: the pattern is adding 4 cm each time

Add 4 cm each time because there are four side lengths and each side increases by 1 cm each time.

1 = 8 cm, 2 = 12 cm, 3 = 16 cm, 4 = 20 cm, 5 = 24 cm, 6 = 28 cm, 7 = 32 cm, 8 = 36 cm: same pattern

Homework 81  14b
Areas of rectangles
3, 8, 15, 24, 35, 48, 63, 80

Increase each time is 2 cm² more than the previous increase, e.g. +5 cm², +7 cm², +9 cm², +11 cm², etc.

Homework 82 14b
Areas and perimeters
Only one shape is possible: perimeter 6 cm

Homework 83 14c
Volume patterns
48 cm³

4 cm × 8 cm × 12 cm = 384 cm³

Volumes are 2 × 2 × 2 times bigger each time, i.e. 8× bigger each time.

Volumes are 3 × 3 × 3 times bigger each time, i.e. 27× bigger each time.

Homework 84  14c
Investigating volumes
All the bricks have paint on one or more faces, but not on all their faces as some are 'inside' the cube.

Some bricks are now 'buried inside' the cube and will not have paint on any surface.

1, 2, 3

2-dimensional (2-D)
Points in 2-dimensional space lie on a flat surface.

3-dimensional (3-D)
Points in 3-dimensional space occupy a space or a volume.

5, 10, 15… minutes past
Ways of counting minutes on an analogue clock. The minute hand takes five minutes to move between each hour mark on the clock face. See also *analogue clock*.

12-hour time
Counting hours of the day in two blocks of twelve. 12.01-12 noon as a.m. and 12.01-12 midnight as p.m. Often told on a 12-hour clock and known as analogue time.

24-hour time
Counting hours of the day from 0-24. Used on digital clocks. 2 p.m. is written as 14:00.

A

a.m.
From Latin ante-meridian, meaning before midday. See also *12-hour time*.

above/below zero
Temperatures are measured relative to 0°C – the freezing point of water, e.g. 4° below zero is –4°C.

acute angle
An angle between 0° and 90°. See also *obtuse, reflex angle*.

add
A mathematical operation to increase one number (the addend) by another to give the sum.

addend
The number being added in in an addition calculation. See also *augend*.

addition
A mathematical operation combining two or more numbers to find a total. Addend + addend = sum (or total).

addition fact
An addition statement likely to be frequently used, so worth memorising.

algebra
Generalised calculation using symbols (variables) instead of numbers. It can be used to prove statements and show general relationships.

analogue clock
A dial with hands used to show time. The dial shows 12 hours in a full circle. The minute hand moves one complete turn every hour. Times on these clocks are read, e.g. 20 past five or five to four.

angle
The amount of turn between two straight lines that meet at a point. Usually measured in degrees. Symbol: °. See also *acute, obtuse, reflex angle*.

anticlockwise
A rotation or turn in the opposite direction to the movement of the hands on a clock. See also *clockwise*.

approximate, approximately
A number that is not exact, e.g. 2028 is approximately 2000. Symbol: ≈.

arc
Part of the circumference of a circle.

area
The 2-D measure of the size of a surface. Measured in 'square' units: mm², cm², m², km².

array
An arrangement of numbers, shapes or objects in rows of equal size and columns of equal size, used to find out how many altogether.

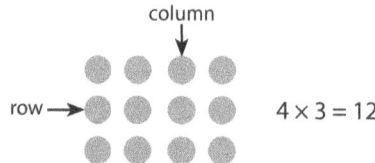

ascending/descending order
Ascending order: rank values from smallest to largest.
Descending order: rank values from largest to smallest.

associative law
A mathematical law or rule where numbers can be grouped in different ways when adding or multiplying, without changing the total, e.g. $(a + b) + c = a + (b + c)$ and $(a \times b) \times c = a \times (b \times c)$.

augend
The number being added to in an addition calculation. See also *addend*.

average
The middle value of a set of numbers. It is found by adding all the numbers together and dividing by how many numbers there are. See also *mean*.

axis, axes
Scale lines, usually vertical and horizontal, used to define positions of points on a grid or graph.

axis of symmetry
An axis of symmetry divides the shape into two identical parts. Also called a mirror line.

B

balance
Things are balanced when both sides have equal value, e.g. 1000 g = 1 kg, 3 + 6 = 10 – 1.

bar chart
A statistical diagram using bars to show the frequency of outcomes.

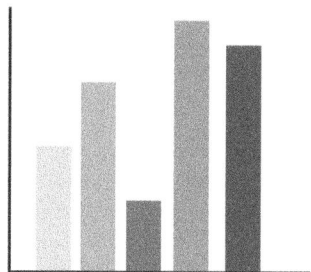

bar line chart
A statistical diagram using lines to show the frequency of discrete outcomes.

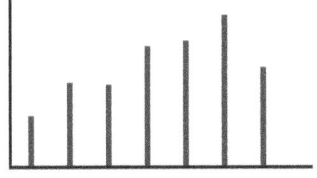

base, square-based
The flat surface underneath a 3-D shape. A square-based pyramid has one square base and four triangular faces.

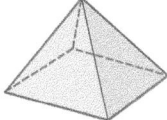

Base 10 system
This is another name for the decimal number system. It increases and decreases by powers of 10. When we multiply a number by, e.g. 10, the digits move one place to the left because the number is made ten times bigger. When we divide by, e.g. 100, the number is 100 times smaller and the digits move two places to the right.

block diagram
A diagram showing statistical information. Each block stands for one object or event.

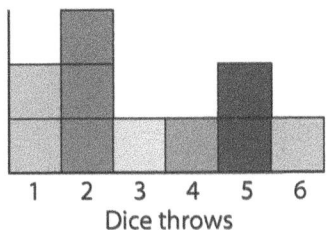

Dice throws

breadth
The same as width.

C

calendar
A list of the days of the year, arranged by month, week and day.

capacity
The amount a container can hold, e.g. the capacity of a 2 l bottle is 2 litres, the capacity of a football stadium is the amount of people it will hold. See also *volume*.

Carroll diagram
A Carroll diagram sorts object according to a criteria and not that criteria. Can be several criteria but always the criteria and not the criteria, e.g. odd numbers/not odd numbers, multiples of 5/not multiples of 5, dogs/not dogs.

category
A group of elements or numbers all with the same property, e.g. dogs, cats, rats are all in the category 'animals'.

Celsius
A scale used to measure temperature. Sometimes called Centigrade. Units are °C.

centilitre
One hundredth of a litre. Symbol: cl. 100 cl = 1 l.

centimetre
A unit of length, $\frac{1}{100}$ of 1 metre. Symbol: cm.

centre
A point at the exact middle of a shape. The centre of a circle is the same distance from all points on its circumference.

century
100 years.

change
The money left over when buying something with a note or coin bigger than the amount needed. The change is given back to the buyer.

chart
A statistical diagram.

circle, circular
A set of points that are all a fixed distance (the radius) from a point (the centre). Like a circle.

circumference
The perimeter of a circle. The set of points a fixed distance from the centre of a circle. See also *arc*.

clock, clock face, hands
A clock is used to show and record time. It can have a circular face with revolving hands to mark hours and minutes, or it can have a digital display.

clockwise
A rotation or turn in the same direction as the movement of the hands on a clock. See also *anticlockwise*.

column
A vertical list of elements or numbers, usually in a table or an array.

combinations
Different combinations made from a selection, e.g. the various different outfits which can be made by choosing one hat and one coat to wear from three hats and four coats.

commutative
Addition and multiplication are commutative. It doesn't matter which way you add or mulitply in, the answer is always the same. Same answer, different calculation, e.g. 3 + 4 = 4 + 3. But subtraction and division are not commutative, e.g. 7 − 2 ≠ 2 − 7.

compound number
A number that is not a prime number.

compound shape
A compound shape consists of two or more simple shapes such as a triangle placed on a square or oblong on top of a square. Also known as a composite shape.

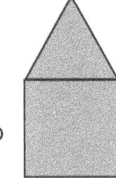

concentric
Circles which share the same centre.

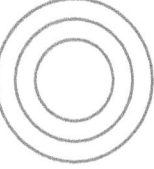

cone
A 3-D shape with a flat, circular face and a curved face. It has one apex directly above the circular base.

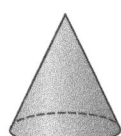

congruent
Shapes are congruent if they are exactly the same shape and size.

consecutive
Numbers that follow each other in a linear pattern, e.g. 3, 4, 5; 60, 70, 80; 17, 19, 21.

Glossary

construct
To draw a shape accurately using a ruler, compasses and a protractor.

coordinate
An ordered pair of (x, y) values that define the position of a point on a Cartesian plane. In 3-D (x, y, z).

corner
A point on a 2-D shape where sides meet. Properly called a vertex (plural, vertices).

cube
A 3-D shape made from six identical squares which all meet at right angles, e.g. a cube of sugar.

cube number, cubed
Formed when a number is multiplied by itself and then by itself again. 2 cubed = $2 \times 2 \times 2 = 8$. The cube numbers are a sequence 1^3, 2^3, 3^3 and so on, which gives the numbers 1, 8, 27, 64, 125 and so on. See also *square number*.

cubic millimetres (mm³), cubic centimetres(cm³), cubic metres (m³), cubic kilometres (km³)
Metric measurements of liquid and solid volume. 1 mm³ is the volume enclosed in a cube of length 1 mm etc.

cuboid
A 3-D shape made from six rectangles. Two or four of the rectangles could be squares, e.g. a cereal box. A cube is a special sort of cuboid.

currency
A money system. In the UK, the currency is pounds sterling (£). In the EU, the currency is the Euro (€).

curved
A line that is not straight, e.g. a circle, or a surface that is not flat, e.g. an egg.

curved surface
A surface of a 3-D shape which is not flat, e.g. the surface of a sphere or cylinder.

cylinder, cylindrical
A 3-D object with circular ends and a uniform cross-section. The top is vertically above the base. Like a cylinder.

D

data
Numbers collected from a questionnaire or survey. Pieces of information usually represented in a special way, e.g. on bar charts and pie charts.

database
A method of storing data, often in large tables on a computer.

date
How we record the passing of time. Usually given as day of the month, month and then year, e.g. 3rd April 2015.

decimal, decimal fraction, decimal point, decimal place, decimal equivalent
Fractions as tenths, hundredths and so on represented as digits after a decimal point, e.g. 0.253 is equivalent to $\frac{2}{10} + \frac{5}{100} + \frac{3}{1000}$ or $\frac{253}{1000}$.

degree
Symbol: °. A unit used to measure the size of an angle. There are 360° in one complete turn. Also a unit of temperature.

denominator
The number underneath the vinculum in a fraction. Also called the divisor.

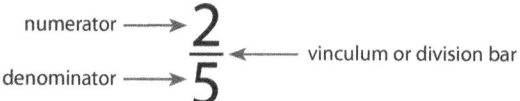

diagonal
A straight line inside a shape that goes from one corner to another (but not an edge).

diagram
A sketch or accurate drawing of a mathematical shape or problem.

diameter
A line passing across a circle, or a sphere, which passes through the centre. See also *radius*.

difference
The result of a subtraction. The difference between 12 and 5 is 7. See also *minuend, subtrahend*.

digit
A symbol from 0-9 in the decimal system. Used to show value. The value of each digit depends on its position, e.g. in 200, the digit 2 represents two hundreds.

digit total/sum
The sum of all the digits in a number, e.g. the digit sum of 435 is $4 + 3 + 5 = 12$. This carries on to $1 + 2 = 3$, so the digit total of 435 is 3.

digital clock, digital time
A system that shows the time as numbers. It can use the 12-hour or the 24-hour clock. 6 o'clock in the evening would show as 06.00 p.m. or 18:00.

discount
A reduction offered on the price of an item for sale.

distance apart ... between ... to ... from
The length of the shortest line joining two points.

distribution
In statistics. The distribution of a set of values.

distributive law
When adding or multiplying, the numbers can be rearranged to support calculating, e.g. $2 \times 13 \times 5 = (2 \times 5) \times 13 = 10 \times 13 = 130$ and $a(b + c) = ab + ac$.

dividend
The number that is divided in a division calculation, e.g. in $12 \div 6 = 2$, 12 is the dividend. See also *denominator, division bracket, divisor, quotient*.

dividing
The process of division.

divisibility
Whether a number can be divided without remainder. All even numbers are divisible by 2.

division
A mathematical operation which groups a number into a given number of parts, e.g. $12 \div 4$ is 12 divided into four parts each of value 3. It is the inverse operation to multiplication.

division bracket
The half box around the dividend in a division. See also *dividend*.

division fact
A division statement likely to be frequently used, so worth memorising.

division (on a scale)
The intervals on a scale, on a ruler or a graph axis.

divisor
The number that is used to divide in a division sum, e.g. in 12 ÷ 6 = 2, 6 is the divisor. See also *denominator, dividend, quotient*.

dodecahedron
A 3-D polyhedron with 12 faces. A regular dodecahedron has pentagonal faces.

double
To multiply by 2.

E

edge
The line made where two faces of a 3-D shape meet.
See also *face, vertex*.

eighths
The fraction of a whole obtained when it is shared into eight equal pieces.

equal sharing
To divide a number or set of items into equal parts.

equals
Symbol: =. Is the same as and equivalent to, e.g. 5 + 3 = 7 + 1.

equation
A mathematical statement showing an equality,
e.g. $10 \times 2 = 4 \times 5$ or $2x + 6 = 16$.

equilateral triangle
A triangle with three equal sides and three equal angles of 60°.

equivalent, equivalent to
Symbol: ≡. Two numbers or expressions that are equal, but which can be in a different form, e.g. £1 ≡ 100p. Two fractions are equivalent if they have the same value, e.g. $\frac{2}{6} = \frac{1}{3}$.

equivalent fractions
Fractions with the same value, e.g. $\frac{1}{4} = \frac{2}{8} = \frac{3}{12}$. These are equivalent fractions.

estimate
An approximate answer, often used to check a complex calculation.

even
A whole number which is divisible by 2. It is a multiple of 2. See also *odd*.

F

face
A flat surface of a 3-D shape. See also *edge* and *vertex*.

factor
Numbers that divide exactly into a number are its factors, e.g. the factors of 12 are 1, 2, 3, 4, 6, 12.

factor pair
Two factors that multiply together to give the number. The factor pairs of 12 are 1×12, 2×6, 3×4.

factorise
To write a number or algebraic expression as a product of two or more factors.

flat
In 2-D and faces of 3-D shapes, not curved.

foot, feet
An imperial unit of length, approximately 30 cm.
12 inches = 1 foot and 3 feet = 1 yard.

formula, formulae
A mathematical sentence using letters or symbols (variables), e.g. area of a rectangle = length × width or $a = l \times w$.

fraction
Part of a whole, written as one number divided by another. In the fraction $\frac{3}{5}$, the numerator 3 is above the vinculum and the denominator 5 is below.

Also known as a fraction, division bar and vinculum.

frequency table
A statistical table listing various outcomes and the frequency that they occur.

G

gallon
An imperial measure of capacity. 1 gallon is approximately 4.5 litres. See also *pint*.

gram
Symbol: g. A unit of mass. There are 1000 grams in a kilogram. See also *kilogram*.

graph
A diagram showing the relationship between two sets of numbers.

greater than
Also called more than. Symbol: >. Used when comparing the size of two quantities or measures. 10 is greater than 7, or 10 > 7. See also *less than*.

greater than or equal to
Symbol: ≥. An inequality showing the lowest value a number can take. $n \geq 7$ means n can have any value from 7 upwards. See also *less than or equal to*.

greatest value, least value
The highest or lowest value that can occur.

grouping
To divide, objects and numbers can be shared or grouped. Grouping is putting objects or numbers into groups of a particular size.

H

half
When a whole is divided into two equal parts.

half past
A measure of time. Half (an hour) past, so half past 5 is the same as 5:30 and 30 minutes past 5. See also *o'clock*.

halfway between
The midpoint between two values, e.g. 15 is halfway between 10 and 20.

heavier than, lighter than
Comparing two masses or weights, e.g. 4 kg is heavier than 3 kg, 3 kg is lighter than 4 kg.

heaviest, lightest
Comparing two or more masses or weights, e.g. of 5 kg, 6 kg and 10 kg, 5 kg is the lightest, 10 kg is the heaviest.

heavy, light
Words used to compare mass or weight.

Glossary

hemisphere
Half of a sphere.

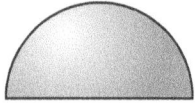

heptagon, heptagonal
A 2-D shape with seven straight sides.

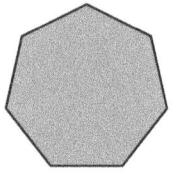 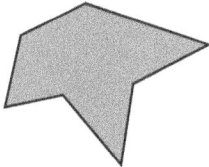

hexagon, hexagonal
A 2-D shape with six straight sides.

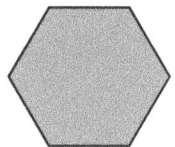 

hollow
Having an outline or surface that curves inwards, e.g. the inside of a hemisphere.

horizontal
Parallel to the horizon. See also *vertical*.

hour
Symbol: h. A measure of time. There are 24 hours in a day and 60 minutes in one hour. See also *minute*, *second*.

hour hand
The hand on a clock that measures the hours. One complete revolution takes 12 hours. See also *minute hand*.

hundred
One hundred, 100, is ten tens or one more than 99.

hundred thousand
100 000.

hundreds
The position in a number where the digit represents hundreds, e.g. in 278 there is a digit 2 in the hundreds place, so there are 2 hundreds.

hundreds boundary
When counting from tens to hundreds, the hundreds boundary is crossed.

hundredths
A fraction $\frac{1}{100}$ or 0.01.

I

imperial unit
A non-metric unit of measure, e.g. inches, yards, miles, pints. Many are still in common use.

in every, for every
A way of expressing proportion (in every) and ratio (for every), e.g. One in every ten pupils has a dog; For every teacher there are 15 students. See also *ratio*.

inch, inches
An imperial unit of length, approximately 2.5 cm. 12 inches = 1 foot.

integer, positive, negative
An integer is a whole number which can be positive or negative, e.g. −4, −2, 4, 100.

intersecting, intersection
Where two lines or curves cross.

inverse
Inverse operations leave the original value unchanged. The inverse of +4 is −4. The inverse of × 4 is ÷ 4 or × $\frac{1}{4}$. The inverse 'undoes' the action.

irregular
Not regular. A shape with sides and angles that are not equal.

isosceles triangle
A triangle with two equal sides and two equal base angles. A right-angled isosceles triangle has one right angle.

K

kilogram
Symbol: kg. A unit of mass. There are 1000 grams in a kilogram. See also *gram*.

kilometre
A metric measure of distance. 1 km = 1000 m.

kite
A quadrilateral with two pairs of equal adjacent sides.

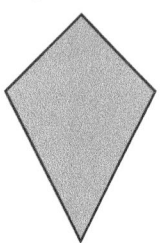

L

least popular, least common
In statistics. The value or outcome that happens least often. See also *most common*.

length, height, width, depth
Words used to describe lengths of lines and shapes, e.g. a cuboid has length 5 cm, width 3 cm and height 6 cm.

less than
Used when comparing the size of two quantities or measures, e.g. 7 is less than 10. See also *more than*.

less than or equal to
Symbol: ≤. An inequality showing the highest value a number can take. $n \le 7$ means n can have any value up to and including 7. See also *greater than or equal to*.

line
A line is straight. It has no thickness and extends in both directions without ending.

line graph
A statistical graph with a continuous line showing the trend or variation in a value.

line segment
Part of a line that has a starting and ending point.

line symmetry
A 2-D object has line symmetry if it can be folded into two identical halves along a mirror line. Each half is a mirror image of the other.

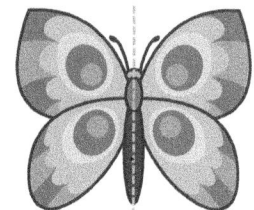

line of symmetry

linear number sequence
A sequence of numbers that increases by a constant difference, e.g. 9, 13, 17, 21, 25 and so on.

litre
Symbol: l. A measure of capacity. 1000 millilitres = 1 litre.

long, longer, longest
A comparison of lengths, e.g. a line is 3 cm, 3 cm is longer than 2 cm. Three lines are 4 cm, 6 cm and 8 cm. The longest length is 8 cm.

M

mass
A metric measure of the amount of matter in an object. Measured in grams (g), kilograms (kg) or tonnes (t). The mass of an object does not change, but its weight alters with any changes in the force of gravity.

maximum/minimum value
The largest/smallest value a number or variable can take.

mean
A measure of average. Mean = total of all data values ÷ number of data points. See also *median, range*.

measure, measurement
The size of a unit, e.g. we can measure area in square metres. Also means the act of measuring something.

measuring cylinder
A graduated cylinder for measuring volume and capacity accurately.

measuring scale
A way of measuring using a line or a dial with equal divisions, like on a ruler.

median
A measure of average. The middle number or value when all the elements of the data set are in ascending (or descending) order. If there is no middle value, then the mean of the two middle values. See also *mean, mode, range*.

mental calculation
Doing a calculation in your head, but perhaps with jottings.

metre
Symbol: m. A unit of length equal to 100 centimetres. 100 centimetres = 1 metre.

metric unit
Any unit used to measure on a metric scale, e.g. kilograms, centimetres, litres. All based on the decimal system.

mile
An imperial measure of distance. Used in the UK and US to measure distances between places. 5 miles is approximately equivalent to 8 kilometres.

millennium
A thousand years (10 centuries).

millilitre
Symbol: ml. A measure of capacity. 1000 millilitres = 1 litre.

millimetre
One thousandth of a metre. 1000 mm = 1 m.

million
1 000 000.

minuend
The starting number in a subtraction calculation, e.g. 10 (the minuend) – 3 (the subtrahend) = 7 (the difference). See also *subtrahend, difference*.

minus
Symbol: – Another word for subtract.

minute
Symbol: min. A measure of time. See also *second, hour*.

minute hand
The hand on a clock face that measures the minutes. One complete revolution takes 60 minutes (one hour). See also *hour hand*.

mixed number
A number with both a whole number part and a fractional part, e.g. $3\frac{1}{2}$.

money
Coins and notes used to buy goods and services.

more than
Also called greater than. Symbol: >. Used when comparing the size of two quantities or measures. 10 is more than 7 or 10 > 7. See also *less than*.

more than or equal to
Symbol: ≥. An inequality showing the lowest value a number can take. $n \geq 7$ means n can have any value from 7 upwards. See also *less than or equal to*.

most common
In statistics. The most frequently occurring outcome. See also *least common*.

multiple, multiple of
A multiple is the product of two numbers, e.g. the multiples of 7 are 7, 14, 21, 28 and so on.

multiplicand
A number to be multiplied, e.g. in $6 \times 3 = 18$, 6 is the multiplicand. See also *multiplier*.

multiplication
A mathematical operation.

multiplication fact
A multiplication statement likely to be frequently used, so worth memorising, e.g. the multiplication table.

multiplication table
A list of multiplication facts for a given multiple, often learned by heart.

multiplier
The multiplying number, e.g. in $6 \times 3 = 18$, 3 is the multiplier. See also *multiplicand*.

multiply
Symbol: ×. A mathematical process equivalent to repeated addition, e.g. $2 \times 4 = 2 + 2 + 2 + 2 = 8$ or repeated grouping.

N

negative numbers
Numbers below zero on the number line. Read as negative 1, negative 2 and so on. See also *integer*.

net (open, closed)
The compound shape resulting from opening out a 3-D shape to show its 2-D faces and how they are connected. A one piece set of connected 2-D shapes which can be folded to make a 3-D shape.

nth term
An algebraic expression that gives the value of any term in a sequence from its position in the sequence. An unknown value.

number
A label given to a quantity, using numerals. There are many different types of number, including counting numbers 0, 1, 2, 3 and so on; fractions; negative numbers; ordinal numbers.

Glossary

number bonds/pairs
Pairs of numbers with a particular total, e.g. the number bonds for 10 are all pairs of whole numbers, like 2 and 8, which add up to 10.

number statement
A mathematical statement using numbers, also called a number sentence, e.g. $4 + 5 - 1 = 8$.

numeral
A symbol used to represent a number. We use arabic numerals 0-9, but there are also Roman numerals and other systems.

numerator
The number above the vinculum in a fraction.

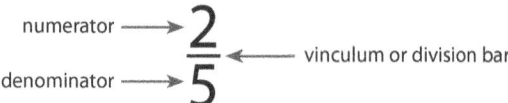

numerator ⟶ $\frac{2}{5}$ ⟵ vinculum or division bar
denominator ⟶

O

oblong
An irregular rectangle. A 2-D shape with two pairs of opposite sides that are equal and the angles are 90°. See also *square*.

obtuse angle
An angle between 90° and 180°. See also *acute, reflex angle*.

octagon, octagonal
A 2-D shape with eight straight sides.

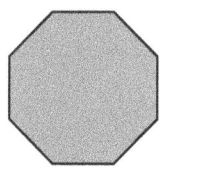

o'clock
A way of describing an exact hour time, e.g. 5 o'clock means the time is 5:00. See also *half past*.

octahedron, octahedral
A 3-D shape with eight triangular faces.

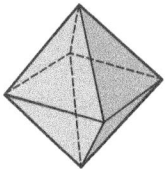
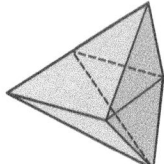

odd
A whole number which has a remainder of 1 when divided by 2. It is not a multiple of 2. See also *even*.

one hundred less/more
A number one hundred whole units more or less than another number. 900 is a hundred less than 1000 and 100 more than 800.

one less
The number one whole before that number on an number line, e.g. 9 is one less than 10.

one more
The number one whole after that number on a number line, e.g. 9 is one more than 8.

one third
A fraction obtained when a whole is divided into three equal parts.

ones
When counting individual items, the next counting number is allocated to the set each time one more is counted. 9 is the largest number of ones. See also *single-digit*.

ones boundary
When counting from a decimal to a whole number, the ones boundary is crossed. See also *tenths boundary*.

ordinal number
A number that tells the order of something, e.g. in a list 1st, 2nd, 3rd and so on.

ounce
An imperial measure of mass. Symbol: oz. 1 ounce is approximately 28 g. 16 oz = 1 pound.

outcome
One of the possible results from a statistical experiment or trial, e.g. when tossing a coin there are two equally-likely outcomes: heads or tails.

P

p.m.
From Latin post-meridian, meaning after midday. 14:00 on the 24-hour clock is 2:00 p.m. See also *12-hour time*.

parallel
Lines that are the same distance apart and never meet.

parallelogram
A 2-D shape with two pairs of opposite sides that are equal and parallel. A rectangle is a special parallelogram, with all the angles 90°.

parts of a whole
A fraction of a whole number or object. If there are five equal parts of a whole then each part is $\frac{1}{5}$.

pattern
A regular arrangement of shapes or numbers that follows a rule.

pentagon, pentagonal
A 2-D shape with five straight sides.

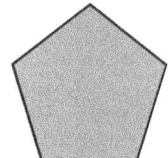

percentage, per cent, %
A fraction or mixed number expressed as hundredth parts, e.g. $\frac{1}{2} = \frac{50}{100} = 50\%$.

perimeter
The total distance measured around the outside of a 2-D shape or area. Calculated by adding the lengths of all the sides.

perpendicular
At right-angles to. Horizontal lines are always perpendicular to vertical lines.

pictogram
A picture to show statistical information. A picture is used to represent one or a number of elements.

pie chart
A statistical diagram that shows proportions of quantities as slices of a circle (a pie).

pint
An imperial measure of capacity. There are 8 pints in 1 gallon. 1 litre is approximately 1.75 pints.

place, place value
Place value has several aspects to it. One is positional, which is where the digit of a number is placed, e.g. in 345, the digit 3 is positioned in the hundreds. Another is multiplicative, which is when we multiply the digit by its position to get its true value. So the 3 in 345 is multiplied by 100 to give 300. A third is additive. This is when all the individual values of the digits are added together to give the whole number, e.g. $300 + 40 + 5 = 345$.

plane
A flat surface.

polygon
The general name for 2-D shapes with three or more straight sides. Includes triangle (three sides), quadrilateral (four sides), pentagon (five sides) and so on.

polyhedron
The general name for 3-D shapes with straight sides. Plural polyhedra. Includes tetrahedron, prisms, pyramids.

pound
An imperial measure of mass. Symbol: lb. 2.2 lb is approximately 1 kg. See also *ounce*.

prime factor
A factor of a number that is also a prime number, e.g. the prime factors of 12 are 2 and 3, since $12 = 2 \times 2 \times 3 = 2^2 \times 3$.

prime number
A number with only two factors, itself and 1. 1 is not a prime number.

prism
A 3-D shape with two identical and parallel ends, joined by rectangular faces. The cross-section of a prism is always the same shape and size as the ends.

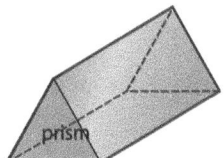

product
The result of multiplying two numbers, e.g. the product of 4 and 3 is $4 \times 3 = 12$.

profit, loss
The money made or lost in a financial transaction. Can be expressed as a money value or as a percentage.

proper/improper fraction
A proper fraction is a fraction that is less that 1, with the numerator less than the denominator, e.g. $\frac{2}{5}$. In an improper fraction, the numerator is larger than the denominator, e.g. $\frac{5}{2}$.

pyramid, square-based
A 3-D shape with a square base and four triangular faces.

Q

quadrant
One of the four regions formed by the x- and y-axes on a Cartesian graph.

quadrilateral
A 2-D shape with four straight sides.

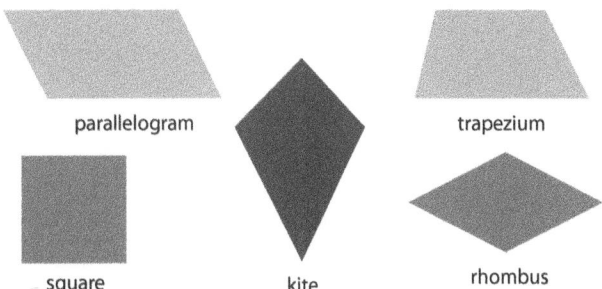

parallelogram   trapezium

square   kite   rhombus

quarter
When a whole is divided into four equal parts.

quarter past, quarter to
15 minutes past the hour or 15 minutes before the hour, e.g. quarter to 12 is 11:45, quarter past 12 is 12:15.

questionnaire
A set of questions given to people to fill in, in order to collect data for analysis. See also *survey, data*.

quotient
The answer to a division calculation, e.g. in $12 \div 6 = 2$, 2 is the quotient. See also *denominator, dividend, divisor*.

R

radius
Any straight line segment from the centre of a circle to the edge (circumference). The radius is half of the diameter. See also *diameter*.

range
A measure of statistical spread. The difference between the highest and lowest values in a set of data. See also *mean, median*.

ratio
A comparison of parts, usually expressed in its simplest form, using a colon, e.g. 12 boys and 15 girls expressed as a ratio is 12:15 or 4:5.

rectangle, rectangular
A four-sided 2-D shape with four right angles and equal opposite sides. A square is a regular rectangle with all four sides equal. An oblong is an irregular rectangle.

rectilinear
A rectangular shape.

reduced to, simplify
To reduce or simplify a fraction or ratio, divide both numbers by the highest common factor, e.g. $\frac{6}{9} = \frac{2}{3}$.

reflect, reflection
To transform an object by reflecting it in a mirror line. The image is the same shape and size as the object.

reflective symmetry

A figure or object has reflective symmetry if there is a line (2-D) or a plane (3-D) which divides the shape into two identical parts.

line of symmetry

Glossary

reflex angle

An angle greater than 180°. See also *acute, obtuse angle*.

regular

A 2-D shape with all the sides equal length and equal angles.

remainder

The number left over after a division sum, e.g. 13 ÷ 3 = 4 remainder 1.

rhombus

A 2-D shape with four equal sides and equal opposite angles.

right angle

A quarter of a full turn. 90°.

right-angled triangle

A triangle with one right angle. Can be isosceles or scalene.

Roman numerals

Numbers used by the Romans. Digits have no place value, e.g. II = 2 , VI = 6, LX = 60.

rotate, rotation

To transform an object by turning it a given direction and angle round a fixed point. The image is the same shape and size as the object.

round up, round down

A method of approximation. 37 rounds up to the nearest 10 so gives an approximation of 40, but 34 rounds down to the nearest 10 so gives an approximation of 30. Digits 4 or less round down and digits 5 or more round up, so 750 to the nearest 100 is 800.

row

A horizontal arrangement of, e.g. objects, shapes or numbers. See also *array*.

rule

An instruction for carrying out a mathematical operation or continuing a pattern. It can be written using symbols or words. See also *sequence*.

S

scalene triangle

A triangle with no equal sides or angles.

scales

A way of measuring using a line with equal divisions, like on a ruler. Also a device for measuring weight.

second

Symbol: s. A measure of time. There are 60 seconds in one minute. See also *minute, hour*.

semi-circle

Half of a circle, made from half of the curved circumference and a diameter.

sequence

A set of numbers made by following a given rule, e.g. the multiples of 3 are 3, 6, 9 and so on.

sevenths

The fraction of a whole obtained when it is cut into seven equal pieces.

shape

A 2-D or 3-D object.

sharing

A model for division, e.g. 10 ÷ 2 = 5 is 10 shared between 2, giving 5 each. Links closely with fractions, e.g. 10 shared between 2 is 5, so 5 is half of 10.

short, shorter, shortest

Words used when comparing lengths or height, e.g. a line is 3 cm, 2 cm is shorter than 3 cm, three lines are 4 cm, 6 cm and 8 cm. The shortest length is 4 cm.

side

A 2-D shape or figure has sides which are line segments. These line segments form the boundary of the shape. See also *corner*.

single-, 2-, 3-digit numbers

The number of digits in a number, e.g. 3 is a single-digit number, 13 is a 2-digit number and 213 is a 3-digit number.

sixths

The fraction of a whole obtained when it is cut into six equal pieces.

sorting

Classifying objects, shapes or numbers into groups according to their properties.

sphere, spherical

A 3-D shape where every point on the surface is the same distance from the centre, like a ball.

square

A regular quadrilateral where all the sides are equal.

square millimetre (mm²), square centimetre (cm²), square metre (m²)

Metric units of measure of area equivalent to a square 1 mm by 1 mm , a square 1 cm by 1 cm or a square 1 m by 1 m. Symbols: mm^2, cm^2 and m^2.

square number, squared

The square numbers are a sequence 1^2, 2^2, 3^2, formed by multiplying each number by itself. This gives the numbers 1, 4, 9, 16, 25 and so on. See also *cube number*.

statement

A number sentence, e.g. 2 + 4 = 6.

statistics

The branch of mathematics which studies the collection, representation and interpretation of data.

subtract

To do a subtraction calculation.

subtraction

A subtraction finds the difference between two numbers. Also called taking away, e.g. 10 (the minuend) – 3 (the subtrahend) = 7 (the difference). See also *minuend*.

subtraction fact

A subtraction statement likely to be frequently used, so worth memorising.

subtrahend

The number that is subtracted from the minuend.

sum

The answer to an addition calculation. The sum of 4 and 5 is 9. See also *total*.

surface

The face or faces of a 3-D shape. They can be flat like the face of a cube or curved like a sphere.

survey

A survey collects data for analysis. See also *questionnaire, data*.

symmetry, symmetrical

A figure has line symmetry if it can be folded along a mirror line into two halves which are mirror images of each other. It has rotational symmetry if it can be rotated to give an identical shape.

line of symmetry

T

table

An arrangement of numbers or objects in rows and columns. See also *array*.

take away

Another name for subtraction. See also *subtraction*.

tall, taller, tallest

A comparison of two or more heights, e.g. Janet is 130 cm tall and John is 128 cm tall. Janet is taller than John, but Sam is the tallest.

tally

A set of marks used for quick and accurate counting. Usually counting in sets of 5 with four downward strokes and the 5th stroke is a diagonal line across the four downward strokes.

tally chart

A table used to collect information using tally counting.

temperature

A measure of hotness. Usually in degrees Celsius or degrees Fahrenheit. Symbol: °C or °F.

ten less

The number ten before that number on a number line, e.g. 40 is ten less than 50.

ten more

The number ten after that number on a number line, e.g. 50 is ten more than 40.

ten thousand

10 000.

tens boundary

When counting from ones to tens, the tens boundary is crossed.

tenths

The fraction of a whole obtained when it is cut into ten equal pieces. The basis for the decimal system of counting.

tenths boundary

When counting from a hundredth to a tenth, the tenths boundary is crossed. See also *ones boundary*.

tetrahedron

A 3-D shape with four triangular faces.

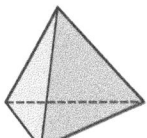

thousand less/more

The number one thousand whole units more or less than another number. 9000 is a thousand less than 10 000 and 11 000 is a thousand more than 10 000.

thousandths

$\frac{1}{1000}$ = 0.001.

three-quarters

A fraction of a whole. Three parts of a whole that has been divided into four equal parts.

$$\frac{3}{4}$$

timetable

A table listing start and finish or arrival and departure times of activities or events, e.g. a school timetable or a public transport timetable.

title

A sentence to describe or explain a chart, graph or diagram.

tonne

A metric measure of mass. 100 kilograms = 1 tonne.

total

The answer to an addition calculation. The total of 4, 3 and 5 is 12. See also *sum*.

translate, translation

To transform an object by moving it a given distance and direction. The image is the same shape and size as the object and in the same orientation.

trapezium

A quadrilateral with one pair of parallel sides. It can also be isosceles.

triangle, triangular

A 2-D shape with three straight sides.

triangular prism

A 3-D shape with two identical and parallel triangular ends, joined by three rectangular faces.

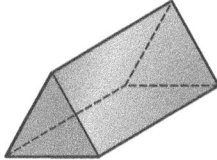

turn (whole turn, half turn, quarter turn, three-quarter turn)

A rotation about a point or line, like a hand around the clock face or a door about the join to the door frame. A whole turn is one complete revolution.

U

units

The standard measures, e.g. the units of length are metres, centimetres.

unknowns

Numbers to be found by solving equations and formulae. Represented by letters or shapes .

V

variable

A quantity that can take a range of different values. Represented by letters.

Venn diagram

A diagram of interlocking circles, used to sort numbers or objects by category.

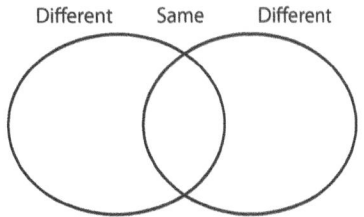

Different   Same   Different

Glossary

vertex, vertices
The point where two sides meet on a 2-D shape and where three or more faces meet on a 3-D shape. See also *face, edge*.

vertical
At right-angles (90°) to the horizontal plane.
See also *perpendicular*.

vinculum
The line that separates the numerator from the denominator.

volume
Liquid volume is the amount of liquid in a container, e.g. 250 ml of water in a 2 l bottle. Measured in cubic ml, litres and so on.

Solid volume is the space a 3-D object takes up, e.g. a fridge in the kitchen. Measured in cubic mm, cm, metres and so on.

See also *capacity*.

W

weight
The force exerted on a mass by gravity. The units are units of force (Newtons). Often confused with mass.

whole-part relationship
How the parts are related to the whole, often illustrated with bars. This can be used when describing relationships between, e.g. addition and subtraction, fractions, percentages and ratio.

written calculation
A mathematical operation using a particular method.

X

x-axis
The horizontal line on a graph or coordinate grid that runs through zero.

Y

y-axis
The vertical line on a graph or coordinate grid that runs through zero.

yard
An imperial unit of length, approximately 90 cm. Symbol: yd. 36 inches = 3 feet = 1 yard. See also *foot, feet, inch, inches*.

Bibliography and further reading

Alexander, R. (2008). *Essays on pedagogy*. Abingdon: Routledge.

Alexander, R. (2012). *Neither national nor a curriculum?* York: Cambridge Primary Review.

Askew, M., Brown, M., Rhodes, V., Johnson, D., and Wiliam, D. (1997). *Effective teachers of numeracy*. London: King's College.

Askew, M., Hodgen, J., Hossain, S. and Bretscher, N. (2010). Theme 10 Textbooks. *Values and variables: mathematics education in high-performing countries*. London: Nuffield Foundation. 34-35.

Barber, M. and Mourshed, M. (2007). *How the world's best-performing school systems come out on top*. McKinsey Education.

Barmby, P., Bilsborough, L., Harries, T. and Higgins, S. (2009). *Primary mathematics: teaching for understanding*. Maidenhead: Open University Press.

Barmby, P., Harries, A.V. and Higgins, S.E. (2010). Teaching for understanding/understanding for teaching. Thompson, I. (Ed.) *Issues in teaching numeracy in primary schools*. Buckingham: Open University Press. 45-57. http://dro.dur.ac.uk/7939/1/7939.pdf

Benton, T. (2014). *A re-evaluation of the link between autonomy, accountability and achievement in PISA 2009*. Cambridge: Cambridge Assessment.

Carpenter, T.P. et al. (1999). *Children's mathematics: cognitively guided instruction*. Portsmouth NH: Heinemann.

DfE. (2011). *The National Strategies 1997-2011: A brief summary of the impact and effectiveness of the National Strategies*. https://www.gov.uk/government/uploads/system/uploads/attachment_data/file/175408/DFE-00032-2011.pdf

DfE. (2014). *National Curriculum in England: mathematics programmes of study*. https://www.gov.uk/government/publications/national-curriculum-in-england-mathematics-programmes-of-study

Drury, H. (2014). *Mastering mathematics: teaching to transform achievement*. Oxford: Oxford University Press.

Fan, L., Zhu, Y., and Miao, Z. (2013). Textbook research in mathematics education: development status and directions. *ZDM: The International Journal on Mathematics Education*, 45: 633-646.

Goldin, G.A. (1998). Representational systems, learning and problem solving in mathematics. *Journal of Mathematical Behavior*, 17(2): 137-65.

Gu, L., Huang, R., and Marton, F. (2004). Teaching with variation: a Chinese way of promoting effective mathematics learning. Lianghuo, F., Ngai-Ying, W., Jinfa, C., and Shiqi, L. (Eds.) *How Chinese learn mathematics: perspectives from insiders*. Singapore: World Scientific Publishing Co. Pte. Ltd. 309-347.

Haggerty, L., and Pepin, B. (2002). An investigation of mathematics textbooks and their use in English, French and German classrooms: who gets an opportunity to learn what? *British Educational Research Journal*, 28(4): 567-590.

Harries, T., and Sutherland, R. (1999). Primary school mathematics textbooks: an international comparison. Thompson, I. (Ed.) *Issues in teaching numeracy in primary schools*. Buckingham: Open University Press. 1-66.

Hiebert, J. and Carpenter, T.P. (1992). Learning and teaching with understanding. Grouws, D.A. (Ed.) *Handbook of Research on Mathematics Teaching and Learning*. New York: Macmillan. 66-97.

Hodgen, J., Brown, M., Coe, R. and Kuchemann, D. (2012). Why have educational standards changed so little over time: the case of school mathematics in England. Paper presented at the *British Educational Research Association* (BERA) annual conference. Institute of Education, University of London.

Howson, G. (2013). The development of mathematics textbooks: historical reflections from a personal perspective. *ZDM: The International Journal on Mathematics Education*, 45(5): 647-658.

Hoyles, C., Morgan, C. and Woodhouse, G. (1999). *Rethinking the maths curriculum*. London: Falmer Press.

Jianhua, L. (2004). Thorough understanding of the textbook: a significant feature of Chinese teacher manuals. Lianghuo, F., Ngai-Ying, W., Jinfa, C., and Shiqi, L. (Eds.) *How Chinese learn mathematics: perspectives from insiders*. Singapore: World Scientific Publishing Co. Pte. Ltd. 262-280.

Lai, M.Y. and Murray, S. (2012). Teaching with procedural variation: a Chinese way of promoting deep understanding of mathematics. *International Journal for Mathematics Teaching and Learning*. Retrieved on 12th May 2015 from http://www.cimt.plymouth.ac.uk/journal/default.htm

Lo, M.L., and Marton, F. (2012). Towards a science of the art of teaching: using variation theory as a guiding principle of pedagogical design. *International Journal of Lesson and Learning Studies*, 1(1): 7-22.

Macintyre, T. and Hamilton, S. (2010). Mathematics learners and mathematics textbooks: a question of identity? Whose curriculum? Whose mathematics? *Curriculum Journal*, 21(1): 3-23.

Maclellan, E. (1997). The role of concrete materials in constructing mathematical meaning. *Education 3-13*, 25(3): 31-35.

Mason, J. and Johnston-Wilder, S. (Eds.) (2004). Learners powers. *Fundamental constructs in Mathematics Education*. London: Routledge Falmer. 115-142.

McCulloch, J. (2011). *Subject to change: should primary schools structure learning around subjects or themes?* London: Pearson Centre for Policy and Learning.

Merttens, R. (2012). The "concrete-pictorial-abstract" heuristic. *Mathematics Teaching*, 228: 33-38.

Morris, P. and Adamson, B. (2010). *Curriculum, schooling and society in Hong Kong*. Hong Kong: Hong Kong University Press.

Morris, P. and Auld, E. (2013). Comparative education, the 'new paradigm' and policy borrowing: constructing knowledge for educational reform. *Comparative Education*, 13th August 2013.

National Centre for Excellence in the Teaching of Mathematics. (2010). Developing mathematics in primary schools. Headteachers talk about creating and sustaining excellence in the teaching of mathematics. *National Centre for Excellence in the Teaching of Mathematics*, 24.

National Centre for Excellence in the Teaching of Mathematics. (2014). *Mastery approaches to mathematics and the new National Curriculum*. https://www.ncetm.org.uk/public/files/19990433/Developing_mastery_in_mathematics_october_2014.pdf

National Centre for Excellence in the Teaching of Mathematics. (2015). *NCETM Mathematics Textbook Guidance*. https://www.ncetm.org.uk/files/21383193/NCETM+Textbook+Guidance.pdf

Nisbet, I. (2013). Is there a place for China's wise laoshi? *TES*, 14th June 2013.

Nuñes, T., Bryant, P. and Watson, A. (2009). *Key understandings in mathematics learning*. London: The Nuffield Foundation.

Oates, T. (2010). *Could do better: using international comparisons to refine the National Curriculum in England*. Cambridge: Cambridge Assessment.

Oates, T. (2014). *Why textbooks count: a policy paper*. Cambridge: Cambridge Assessment.

OECD. (2010). *Strong performers and successful reformers in education: lessons from PISA for the United States*. Paris: Organisation for Economic Co-operation and Development.

Ofsted (Office for Standards in Education). (2011). *Good practice in primary mathematics: evidence from successful schools*. London: Ofsted. https://www.gov.uk/government/publications/good-practice-in-primary-mathematics-evidence-from-successful-schools

Ofsted (Office for Standards in Education). (2008). *Mathematics: understanding the score*. London: Ofsted. https://www.gov.uk/government/publications/mathematics-made-to-measure

Ofsted (Office for Standards in Education). (2012). *Mathematics: made to measure*. London: Ofsted. https://www.gov.uk/government/publications/mathematics-made-to-measure

Rabel, S. and Wooldridge, I. (2013). Exploratory talk in mathematics: what are the benefits? *Education 3-13*, 41(1): 15-22.

Raiker, A. (2002). Spoken language and mathematics. *Cambridge Journal of Education*, 32(1): 45-60.

Reynolds, D. and Farrell, S. (1996). *Worlds apart? A review of international studies of educational achievement involving England*. London: HMSO for OFSTED.

Rowland, T., Huckstep, P. and Thwaites, A. (2003). The knowledge quartet. *Proceedings of the British Society for Research into Learning Mathematics*, 23(3): 97-103.

Shulman, L.S. (1986). Those who understand: knowledge growth in teaching. *Educational Researcher*, 15(2): 4-14.

Sierpinska, A. (1994). *Understanding in mathematics*. London: Falmer Press.

Sowell, E.J. (1989). Effects of manipulative materials in mathematics education. *Journal for Research in Mathematics Education*, 20(5): 498-505.

Sun, X. (2011). "Variation problems" and their roles in the topic of fraction division in Chinese mathematics textbook examples. *Educational Studies in Mathematics*, 76: 65-85.

White, R. and Gunston, R. (1992). *Probing understanding*. London: Falmer Press.

Williams, P. (2008). Independent review of mathematics teaching in Early Years settings and primary schools. *Department for Children, Schools and Families*, 90.

Xu, B. (2013). The development of school mathematics textbooks in China since 1950. *ZDM: The International Journal on Mathematics Education*, 45(5): 725-736.

Yan, Z. and Lianghuo, F. (2006). Focus on the representation of problem types in intended curriculum: a comparison of selected mathematics textbooks from mainland China and the United States. *International Journal of Science and Mathematics Education*, 4(4): 609-626.

Yang, D.C. and Huang, F.Y. (2004). Relationships among computational performance, pictorial representation, symbolic representation and number sense of sixth-grade students in Taiwan. *Educational Studies*, 30(4): 373-389.